Studies in
Political Morality

JEREMIAH NEWMAN
Professor of Sociology
at St. Patrick's College,
Maynooth, Ireland

SCEPTER
DUBLIN
LONDON

First published 1962

172 ✓
(i)
15

This book is set in 11 pt. on 12 pt. Old Style Type.

© *Scepter Publishers Ltd., Dublin* 1962

PRINTED AND BOUND IN THE REPUBLIC OF IRELAND BY O'GORMAN LTD. GALWAY. NIHIL OBSTAT : HERBERT J. MCKERNAN. IMPRIMI POTEST ✠ JOANNES CAROLUS, ARCHIEP. DUBLINEN., HIBERNIAE PRIMAS. DUBLINI DIE 29 JUNII, 1962.

CONTENTS

CONTENTS

FOREWORD

IN this age any work on political morality is welcome, so unfashionable is it to regard political theory and practice as field in any way for moral directives. When the work is from the scholarly and wide-ranging Professor of Catholic Sociology in Maynooth it is all the more welcome. We have the guarantee that the abstract and the concrete, principle and practice both, will receive their due consideration. What *is* in politics—as in so many other departments of life—is seldom that which *should be;* but, on the other hand, we must know what can and does happen in order to prescribe what is most desirable.

Politics has been described as the art of the possible. But this does not mean that it should eschew all principle. Not all that is possible for us human beings is morally permissible. Those in politics, those who man the machinery of Party or State, are human beings like the. rest of us. Admittedly the machinery has a strength of its own and is geared to work in a way of its own. In ultimate analysis, however, it is man-made and man-manageable; if it is too unresponsive, it can be discarded and new machinery forged in its place. Admittedly too, political decisions, especially in democratic countries, are seldom personal decisions, in the sense that any one individual person is wholly responsible for them. They are committee or assembly decisions; and the natural tendency is for the individual person to feel little or no responsibility at all for that for which he is just one of the assenting majority. Yet some real responsibility he certainly has. And where there is responsibility, there is need for guiding principle to exercise it.

The actions of the man of politics seeking office and when in office, then, are legitimate material for ethical questioning and assessment. Indeed never more so than in this age when the State has newly assumed so much power in so many depart-

I

ments of human life and in consequence of which the exercise of this power by its ministers and officials affects all in the community far more intimately than State power did its subjects in the past.

More fundamental even than the problems of the scope and forms of the State's dealings with its citizens are the problems of the origin of political authority; national autonomy; rebellion; Church and State relations; inter-State relations; just war, etc . . . Is it to be a matter of 'they shall take who have the power; and they shall keep who can'? Or are there more ultimate guiding principles? The fact that 'power politics' is the order of the day is no good proof that it is best or indeed in any way right at all that it should be so. Again the fact that the principle and spirit of nationality have been such a force in shaping modern political theory and practice is no proof that it will, or should, continue so. Nationality divides as truly as it unites. Now that peoples are brought so close to each other by trade, travel and the means of communication generally, perhaps it should recede somewhat into the background. Indeed, perhaps the whole notion of State sovereignty or, rather, of one-hundred-per-cent-sovereign States is an anomaly in the light of modern tendencies and conditions.

A great danger in the world today is that the good men in it may become despondent. So many of those who claim to be independent thinkers are in fact hidden propagandists! And there is so little anyway that the individual can do! While those who hold the world's power seem so little open to moral suasion! It would be the greatest mistake, however, to think that morals has had its day in the world. The inescapable fact is that bad as human nature is, it is not wholly bad. No man and no age but will feel the force of the right and the true when brought face to face with them. For that reason, if for no other, the struggle for the mind of man, and in this case for the mind of the man or the masses with political power, must go on. It is precisely because of the 'treason of the clerks', because the men of ideas have propagated so many false ideas, that the modern world is so unashamedly materialistic, un-idealistic and irresponsible. It devolves on a new generation of 'clerks' to restore truth and justice to their pedestal. Indeed the world may well welcome their message, so general is the feeling of disillusionment and fear.

We in Ireland have special reasons for being interested in the basic problems of political morality. Though we are a small nation, we have an influence altogether out of proportion to our numbers in international affairs. How are we using that influence? How should we use it? We are known the world over as a Catholic people. What are the distinguishing marks, if any, of a Catholic people in the political order? Finally we have our own many unsolved problems. We are a divided nation; we are a dwindling people; we are a country neither altogether in Europe nor yet altogether outside it. What has the future for us? Have we any plan for shaping our destiny? One thing is certain; we cannot expect the men of politics among us to find the right answers to these questions, if left to themsleves or to the amoralists. They have to be informed in the best sense of the word. Indeed it is of the very essence of our democratic system in theory that those who rule welcome — and require — our criticisms and opinions in all that concerns government. Even if the philosophers seldom make good rulers themselves, it is no less true that without their guidance there can be no good government.

Dr. Newman does not deal with the whole field of political morality. But what he does cover, he deals with authoritatively and fairly. His conculsions and his exposition—particularly on the home front—may not please everybody. But they are reasoned and balanced. If we choose to disagree with them, we must be no less reasonable and balanced. As for myself I cannot but admire both his courage and his argumentation.

✠ CORNELIUS LUCEY

AUTHOR'S PREFACE

THE present volume has been in the making—intermittently —for nearly eight years. During this period its general plan has undergone far-reaching changes while its content has been modified in the light of helpful criticism which I was fortunate to secure from a variety of sources.

It would be impossible for me to enumerate here the very many friends to whom I am indebted for suggestions concerning the book. I must offer special thanks, however, to the Reverend James Kavanagh of University College, Dublin, Mr. Vincent Grogan, M.A., B.L. and Mr. Seamus Grace, M.A., who were kind enough to read through the script in its entirety. My thanks are also due to a number of people who read individual chapters—Professor Alfred Cobban of London University; Dr. M. B. Crowe, Dr. John Watt and Mr. Brian Farrell of University College, Dublin; Mr. Maurice Gaffney, B.L.; and my colleagues Dr. Enda McDonagh and Father Tomas O'Fiaich, M.A., Lic. Hist. Sc., of Maynooth College. While I have incorporated many of the points to which they drew my attention, it should be understood that they do not necessarily share the views which I have expressed.

I am particularly grateful to his Lordship Most Reverend Dr. Cornelius Lucey, Bishop of Cork, my former Professor of Ethics in Maynooth, for his kindness in contributing a Foreword to the book.

I have the temerity to hope that my treatment of the political questions dealt with herein may be of practical use in Ireland and elsewhere.

JEREMIAH NEWMAN

Maynooth College,
1st May, 1962.

INTRODUCTION

POLITICAL SCIENCE has an important moral aspect. Side by side with purely technical questions regarding forms of government, methods of election, the separation of powers etc., politics is also concerned with wider and more philosophical issues. These include the problem of the origin of political authority, the nature of the right of a political community to determine its independent destiny, the extent to which war and conquest may be resorted to in the pursuit of this, the right of the citizens to revolt against their government in certain circumstances and the proper relations between the Church and the State.

At the present time each of these problems has a new interest. Questions are raised the world over which cannot be answered without an intelligent grasp of the fundamentals of political philosophy. Is the Chiang-Kai-Shek regime the legitimate government of mainland China? If not, how did it lose its authority, in the sense of a moral claim to rule its subjects? On the other hand, if it is still regarded as the legitimate government, does this mean that the regime which displaced it by force can never be anything else than a usurper? If so, would the Chinese people have a right to revolt against it? Had the Hungarian people a right to revolt when they did? Or again, what of the Algerian rebels? Did these have a right to fight for self-determination and political separation from France? And speaking of self-determination, what are the limits to which it may be claimed? The effort of Katanga to secede from the Congo has raised this question again with a new and practical relevance.

The whole problem of the use of armed force is in the melting pot. Can warfare between sovereign states be any longer regarded as moral, now that any war, however small, creates the terrible danger that a greater war—with disastrous consequences —may follow? Should we accept the position of the growing

7

number of contemporary pacifists by whom war, in all circumstances, is outlawed? Or if we do decide that war can sometimes
still be justified, what are the circumstances, in the modern
world, in which this is so? The Suez affair and the Indian invasion
of Goa have created a new interest in the rights and wrongs of
even non-nuclear war.

A problem of peace engages attention today also: To what
extent can democratic values be respected in practice? In particular, how can order and self-protection be maintained by a
State while preserving intact a democratic framework of civil
liberties? This is one of America's premier problems of the
moment. Added to it is that of the place of religion in the democratic State. And, more especially, the place of Catholicism in
a democracy. What if American Catholics should come to constitute an overall majority? Would the separation of Church and
State continue to exist in such radically altered conditions, or
would it be replaced by Church establishment of some sort? And
if so, would non-Catholics suffer intolerance of a kind that is incompatible with the principles of democracy?

All of these are important and difficult questions towards
the solution of which any guidance would be welcome. It is not
without significance that they also represent the most central
problems in Catholic political philosophy. Not that Catholic
writers are in unanimous agreement in their approach to them.
Indeed on many points there are considerable differences of
opinion as well as many untangled difficulties and latent ob-
scurities. By and large, however, it is true to say that Catholic
political philosophy provides a reliable guide to the elucidation
of these problems and a new exposition of what it has to say
about them may be worth while.

It is difficult to treat of such questions *in abstracto;* I have
already mentioned some examples from different countries.
In fact, however, one need not look further than the situation
arising from the partition of Ireland, so much so that a study
of these questions is at once an exercise in political philosophy
and a source of practical guidance in regard to the concrete
problems of a divided Ireland.

It is now nearly forty years since the partition of Ireland
was established. Looked on by many at the beginning as but a

temporary arrangement, partition today, or rather the question of its abolition, has become a burning topic both North and South of the border.

What is hoped for, however, is one thing; what is proposed with a view to realising hopes is another. On the question of ways and means of ending partition there is a chorus of discordant voices. For over thirty years what might be called the orthodox policy has been consistently pursued by Southern statesmen. It has found its foremost exponent in President Eamon de Valera, whose concept of one nation in one island under one government is too well known to need further elaboration. In so far as it includes any concrete measures for the solution of partition, they would seem to consist mainly in the use of propaganda, in the hope that in the end the pressure of international public opinion will inevitably bring about the unity of Ireland.

Mr. Lemass appears to have introduced certain modifications into this approach. In an interview given to the *Belfast Telegraph* in 1959, he outlined his views on the subject. On the surface they appear to be the same as those of his predecessor. 'It is a fundamental right of the people of a single country that they should be governed on a basis of political unity'. Variation is introduced with a suggestion for economic co-operation between North and South. But it would be a misinterpretation, I think, to regard this as a new programme that has been designed specifically for the eventual undoing of partition. That Mr. Lemass may hope it will contribute to this is very possible, but it is probable that his proposals, in themselves, are designed for immediate economic rather than political ends.[1]

[1] 'I have no illusions about the strength of the barriers of prejudice and suspicion which now divide the people, but, given good will, nothing is impossible. Meanwhile, better relations can be fostered by practical co-operation for mutual benefit in the economic sphere . . . Even at present, and without reference to any wider issue, we would be prepared to consider and to discuss proposals as to how policy might be directed so as to ensure that the economic progress of both parts of the country will be impeded as little as possible by the existing political division'— *Irish Independent*, 10 July 1959.

It is only to be expected that people desirous of quick results should be impatient with what they regard as the slow progress of the orthodox policy. The emergence of the new movement of Sinn Fein was part of this. Its basic policy was that of physical force.[1] There can be little doubt that had Sinn Fein secured a majority in the Dail and come to power in the Republic of Ireland, the logical entailment of its principles would have been war to secure the ending of partition.[2]

A second effort at a new departure—along very different lines—has been gaining wide support throughout the entire country for the past few years. By way of reaction, perhaps, to the excesses of the appeal to arms, this second approach would rely on persuasion rather than on coercion. It rejects equally both the bomb and bullet of the extremists and what it regards as the empty propaganda and vain hopes of the orthodox policy. Co-operation is the keynote of its alternative, co-operation in a climate of charity and tolerance, between the Republic and the Six Counties as corporate entities and between Northern Nationalists and Unionists as individuals. Waiving altogether the rights and wrongs of partition as a historical fact,

---

[1] Before an election in 1957 for a seat in Dublin, Sinn Fein issued a manifesto to electors, part of which read as follows: 'You are tired of politics and politicians. So are we and for the same reasons. Sinn Fein is not a political party but a National Movement and we desire that our ideals should permeate throughout the people . . . We proclaim as essential principles the necessity:

   1. To convene the Elected Representatives of All-Ireland as the National Assembly of the Independent Irish Republic.

   2. To proceed to legislate for All-Ireland.

   3. To use every means in our power to overcome opposition to the Republic.

   4. To repudiate all Treaties, Pacts and Laws that in any way curtail the Nation's independence'—*The United Irishman*, November 1957.

[2] 'The British Conquest must be ended. This land of ours must be returned to its true owners, the Irish people . . . That is the order of the day. Every Irish citizen must think out this conclusion to its logical end. The time for foolishness is long past. The time for action is upon us.' *Loc. cit.*

even leaving aside the question as to whether Ireland is inhabited by people of only one or of two nationalities, a plea is made for a spirit of friendliness and practical understanding between the pro- and anti-partitionists wherever they may be.[1]

Many prominent men on both sides of the border—Protestant as well as Catholic, Unionist as well as Nationalist—are presently disposed towards such friendly co-operation. This policy has in addition received considerable publicity through the efforts of an independent intellectual group, *Tuairim*, which has produced two important pamphlets on the subject. The first of these is by Mr. Donal Barrington, one of the founders of *Tuairim*. The second, by Mr. Norman Gibson, is a Northern Protestant viewpoint on the matter.

Mr. Barrington's appeal is to the South. He is very emphatic about his rejection of coercionist policies against the North. 'The time has come', he says, 'for us to abandon the coercionist policies we have been following hitherto, and to replace them with policies designed to reduce tension and to create an atmosphere in which a unity of wills can grow'.[2] He urges that, as Southern Irishmen are the people who most believe in the creation of a united Ireland, it lies with them to make the first move in that direction. To this end they must make it clear that they unilaterally renounce all use of force against the North and thus prove, by respecting the wishes of Northern Protestants while outside a United Ireland, that they would equally be respected inside it. Mr. Barrington adds that the North in turn should give effective guarantees to protect Northern Nationalists against unjust discrimination. Indeed if these were forthcoming, he would recommend that the Southern government should 'recognise the Government of Northern Ireland as

---

[1] Much attention was attracted to these views in 1957 by the Social Study Conference at Garron Tower, Co. Antrim. During a week's discussion, in which both Nationalists and Unionists participated, the whole question was subjected to frank examination. Particular notice was given to papers by Miss Mary McNeill and Mr. G. B. Newe in which the role of Catholics in Northern Ireland was critically analysed from both the Protestant and Catholic points of view.

[2] Donal Barrington, *Uniting Ireland*, Dublin 1958, p 17.

an Irish Government entitled to respect not only from the people
of the Six Counties but from all Irishmen. Such an argument
would be the foundation on which the new policy designed to
create a unity of wills would rest'.[1]

The suggestion that the South might give formal recognition
to the government of Northern Ireland raises the question as to
what kind of recognition is accorded to it at present. It is clear
that the Republic does not give *de jure* recognition to Stormont,
but what the position is, in positive terms, is not agreed upon.
Thus, within the space of six months, we find Mr. Lemass being
asked in an interview with the *Belfast Telegraph* whether, if the
government of the Irish Republic declines to give *de jure* recognition to the Constitution of Northern Ireland, any other means
might be devised to better relations between North and South;
while Lord Pakenham, at a Press Conference in Belfast, was
asked whether he thought the Dublin government should give
de facto recognition to Stormont? No matter how one looks at
it, this is very confusing. On the supposition that both inter-
viewers asked meaningful questions, the position must be, either
that *de facto* recognition has been given but cannot be discerned,
or else that the attitude of the Southern government to the
Northern represents a *tertium quid* that is quite unknown to the
textbooks of political philosophy. Mr. Barrington's proposal has
at least the merit that it would introduce clarification.

He hastens to add that this should merely be a beginning.
It should be followed up by co-operation in many fields—
athletic, educational, economic. What we need is a new form
of nationalism 'broad enough to meet the needs of a society of
men of different origins and different religions . . . The new
Irish nationalism will have to be tolerant and non-exclusive'.[2]

It is on the question of toleration and the possibility of the
co-existence of different religions in a United Ireland that
Northern Protestants have the greatest doubts. They are given
frank expression by Mr. Norman Gibson in his *Tuairim* pamphlet.[3] As Mr. Gibson puts it: 'The cleavage at the heart of North-

[1] Barrington, *loc. cit.* p 18.
[2] *Loc. cit.* pp 21-22.
[3] Norman Gibson, *Partition Today: A Northern Viewpoint*, Dublin
1959.

ern Ireland, and indeed Irish society as a whole, is a religious-philosophic difference which unfortunately manifests itself in Northern Ireland in opposed political affiliations. Basically the Partitionist fears the exclusiveness of Roman Catholicism, its claims to absolute truth and the consequences that seem to follow from this position . . . As I understand it the Roman Catholic Church believes herself to be both the guardian of the faith and the protector of the faithful. In practice this appears to mean that in order to obtain conformity within a community to her moral and social teaching, she will as far as possible augment her own authority with the authority and power of the State'. Hence it is, Mr. Gibson goes on to add, that the Partitionist is inclined 'to ask what guarantee he would have that his religious freedom would be secure in a predominantly Catholic society. After all from the point of view of the Catholic or his Church the beliefs and practices of the Protestant are heretical and erroneous and must constitute a threat to the peace of mind and perhaps the loyalty of the faithful'.[1]

Such fear is extensive and deep-rooted amongst many otherwise well-disposed Northern Protestants. And it will be a difficult task for Catholics to dispel it. We find Mr. Brian Faulkner, Unionist Chief Whip, maintaining that the promises of tolerance made by individual Catholics should not be overestimated and that too much attention should not be paid to Catholic moves towards co-operation unless they have the official backing of their Church.[2] There was no evidence, said Mr. Faulkner, that 'the Roman Catholic Church held the view that there should be acceptance of Ulster's consititutional position by its adherents'.[3] Mr. Faulkner may or may not have been making political capital, but the view which he expressed would find reflection amongst many Northern Protestants.

Early in March, 1957, His Eminence John Cardinal D'Alton put forward some suggestions for the reunification of Ireland. Prefacing his remarks by saying that he was speaking, not as a Churchman but personally and as a citizen, His Eminence said

[1] *Loc. cit.* pp 6-7.
[2] Speech at Ballinamallard, 12 August 1958.
[3] Speech at Raffrey, 23 August 1958.

that he was convinced that a solution to partition could be found if both sides were prepared to make concessions in a spirit of good will and with a sympathetic understanding of the other's point of view. Pointing to the fact that a number of European countries, including Germany and France, have shown that they are willing to forego something of their old conception of sovereignty in order to live in friendly co-operation with their neighbours to their mutual advantage, he indicated how a similar spirit might help to end the deplorable condition of things caused by the partition of Ireland.

Continuing, the Cardinal said:

'If the Northern Government agreed to unite with the South as a federal unit, then I think that Ireland should associate itself with the Commonwealth as an independent Republic on the same basis as India. That would guarantee the North its link with the Commonwealth and should also help to safeguard its economy . . .'

'It seems clear that in present world conditions under which the very existence of our European civilisation is being threatened, no country in the West can afford to live in complete isolation. Even a proud country like Spain has reverted a long-standing policy, and allowed bases to be erected on her territory. I would suggest that a re-united Ireland should offer bases to N.A.T.O. Naturally England and America, the most prominent members of that organisation, would be the ones most immediately concerned'.[1]

These suggestions, which have come to be known as the 'D'Alton Plan' received far too little attention at the time. Nobody seemed to ask the question whether there might be any ethical obligation on statesmen to investigate whether they should be implemented. It is a question that is particularly relevant to membership of N.A.T.O. Apart from adequately ensuring its own defence, has a nation any duty to participate in the collective defence of a community of nations? Is self-determination so sacrosanct that it is never to be sacrificed?

Amid the volume of opinion on the problem of partition,

[1] Cf *Irish Independent*, 4 March 1957.

it is surprising to find almost a total lack of ethical discussion, at least at any scientific level. There have been many investigations of the historical and political aspects of the question;[1] the economic issues at stake have also been weighed.[2] Yet apart from one or two conferences and some brief magazine articles,[3] there has been no analysis of the moral aspects of the many knotty problems which partition and the question of its dissolution have raised. While the present book does not intend to provide cut and dried answers to these problems, it will, it is hoped,— by attempting to elucidate a number of central questions in Catholic political philosophy — supply the moral principles on which a solution must be based.

[1] E.g. Frank Gallagher, *The Indivisible Island*, London 1957; Denis Gwynn, *History of Partition*, Dublin 1950; Benedict Kiely, *Counties of Contention*, Cork 1945.

[2] Labhras O'Nuallain, *Ireland: Finances of Partition*, Dublin 1952.

[3] Cf Dr. A. O'Rahilly, in *Hibernia*, January, February and March 1957.

CHAPTER ONE

THE ORIGIN OF POLITICAL AUTHORITY

THE distinction between legitimate and illegitimate political
authority, between *de jure* and *de facto* government, has sometimes been denied altogether. During World War I, Baron von
der Lancken, head of the Political Department of the German
occupying government in Belgium, made a particularly striking
statement to this effect. 'A division of legislative power is
impossible and therefore what is *de facto* is also *de jure*. What,
after all, really matters is merely the exercise of legislative
authority and its docile acceptance by the population.'[1]

In other words, every effective government is a *de jure* one.
This view was vigorously rejected by Cardinal Mercier, in accordance with traditional Christian moral teaching which insists on the distinction. But traditional teaching is also insistent
that a *de facto* government *can become* a *de jure* one in certain
circumstances. It can acquire the genuine authority that it did
not have originally. How this happens is a further and more
fundamental question regarding the source or sources of political
authority.

TWO THEORIES

On this subject there are two main theories, known respectively as the Translation Theory and the Designation Theory.

[1] This attitude received philosophical elaboration in the works of
non-Catholic writers such as Gumplowicz and Jellinek. It is sometimes
termed the doctrine of 'consummated facts', i.e. that all completed

Each of these recognises that the ultimate source of political authority is God himself, but as to how it derives proximately to this or that government they are at variance. In general, according to the Translation Theory, political authority does not come directly to any government, but is always channelled, as it were, through the consent of the people. It comes first to and resides in the people, who then choose the form of government and ruler or rulers under whom they wish to live and— explicitly or implicitly—transfer authority to them. This theory has had many supporters through the centuries. They include the Scholastic Contractualists, such as Bellarmine and Suarez and, with individual differences, Cajetan, Vittoria and Soto.[1]

political events contain a title to right in themselves. Hence the phrase *jus facti completi* (*das Recht der vollandeten Thatsache*) and *possessio jure belli* (*Eroberungsrecht*). This view is scathingly criticised by Balmes in his *Protestantism compared with Catholicity*, English trans. London 1849, pp 276-281. It was condemned by Pope Pius IX in the *Syllabus of Errors* under the form of the following proposition: "The successful and lucky injustice of an accomplished fact (such as revolution, a war of conquest, the capture of a city, the overthrow of a dynasty, etc.) is not in anyway an infraction of the sacredness of rights"— Proposition no. 61.

[1] Bellarmine, *De Laicis*, Bk. III, c. 6; Suarez, *De Legibus*, Bk. III, c. 3; *Defensio Fidei Cath.*, Bk. III, c. 2.

Some members of the Protestant school of Natural Law developed a version of their own of the contractualist theory. They include such notable figures as Puffendorf and Burlamaqui. There is quite a difference between them and their Scholastic counterparts. Whereas the former regard the contract as something that is assented to singly by each citizen, and therefore not obligatory on dissenters, the Scholastics look on it as issuing from the community as an organised whole and as binding on all its members. It is not in itself the source of this obligation, but rather the *conditio sine qua non*, which, when posited, induces an obligation flowing from natural law. Because of this, J. Donat says that Scholastic contractualism lays more emphasis than that of Puffendorf on the natural necessity of civil authority. See his *Ethica Specialis*, Innsbruck 1921, p 111.

Modern defenders of Scholastic contractualism include:

J. Balmes, *Protestantism compared with Catholicity*, Engl. trans. London 1849; J. Gredt, *Elementa Philosophiae Aristotelico-Thomisticae*,

Amongst modern Irish writers it has received backing from Dr. Peter Coffey,[1] Dr. Alfred O'Rahilly[2] and Fr. Gabriel Bowe O.P.[3]

According to the Designation Theory, on the other hand, authority comes immediately from God to a government which has been designated in any of a number of possible ways. The consent of the people is one such way, but it does not entail any actual transfer of power from the people and, in addition, is only one of many ways in which the designation can be effected. In brief, there are many sources of political authority, any of which confers a title to legitimate rule. In fact anything which, while not violating existing rights, effectively sets a ruler over the people, constitutes him their *de jure* government. This theory has been held, amongst others, by Taparelli, Liberatore, Castelein, Cathrein, Schiffini and Meyer.[4] In Ireland it has been defended by Drs. Patrick Murray and Walter McDonald of Maynooth and by Dr. Michael Cronin of University College, Dublin.[5]

vol. II, 8th Ed., Barcelona, 1946; C. Macksey, *De ethica naturali*, Rome 1914; G. Moral, *Philosophia Moralis*, Santander 1948.

[1] P. Coffey, The Conscription Menace in Ireland and Some Issues Raised by It, in *The Irish Ecclesiastical Record*, Fifth Series, vol. X (1918).

[2] A. O'Rahilly, The Catholic Origins of Democracy, in *Studies*, vol. VIII (1919); Some Theology about Tyranny, in *The Irish Theological Quarterly*, vol. XV, (1920); The Sovereignty of the People, in *Studies*, vol. X (1921).

[3] Gabriel Bowe O.P., *The Origin of Political Authority*, Dublin 1955.

[4] L. Taparelli, *Saggio Teoretico di Dritto Naturale*, Livorno 1840; M. Liberatore, *Institutiones Philosophicae*, vol. 3, Naples 1871; Castelein, *Institutiones Philosophiae Moralis*. 1899; V. Cathrein, *Cursus Philosophicus*, Part VI, Friburg 1905; S. Schiffini, *Disputationes Philosophiae Moralis*, vol. 2, Turin 1891; T. Meyer, *Institutiones Iuris Naturalis*, Part II, Friburg 1900.

This theory is also held by: A. Vermeersch, *Philosophia Moralis;* S. Reinstadler, *Elementa Philosophiae Scholasticae*, vol. II, Friburg 1933; J. Ricaby, *Moral Philosophy*, London 1892.

[5] P. Murray, The Right to Resistance to the Supreme Civil Power, in *Essays, Chiefly Theological*, vol. III, Dublin 1853; W. McDonald, *Some Ethical Questions of Peace and War*, London 1919; M. Cronin, *The Science of Ethics*, 4th imp. Dublin 1939, vol. II.

The Designation Theory has been strongly opposed by Dr. Alfred O'Rahilly, notably in a famous article on the 'Theology of Tyranny', which he published in the *Irish Theological Quarterly* in 1920 and for which he was arrested by the British administration.[1] That he still continues to hold the same views is evidenced by more recent articles.[2] As Dr. O'Rahilly sees it, the Designation Theory is not traditional. It is, in fact, the fruit of 19th century Catholic reaction to the excessive claims that were then being made in the name of democracy and the sovereignty of the people. The theory, he says, appears to have been first put forward by Taparelli in 1840-41; earlier than that it is not to be found. Traditional teaching is solidly behind the idea that political authority has its source in the consent of the people. This is said to represent the continuous and practically unanimous opinion of writers ever since the 13th century.[3] In his 1920 article Dr. O'Rahilly claimed that he had found fifty-two writers, between the 13th century and the time of Suarez, who defend the necessity of consent, and eighty-seven more between Suarez and the 19th century.[4]

There is no denying that he has made an impressive case. Yet I am doubtful whether it has been established beyond question. It is probably true that the 19th century vogue of the Designation Theory was due to a reaction to the then prevailing spirit of extreme democracy. In face of this, Catholic philosophers sought to defend monarchical authority. On the other hand, it is equally true that the Translation Theory received its full elaboration during an earlier age of Catholic reaction to absolute monarchy. In addition, it should be remembered that the Designation Theory does not deny that the consent of the people is a just title to political authority; what it insists on is that there are other titles as well. It should be

---

[1] A. O'Rahilly, Some Theology about Tyranny, in *The Irish Theological Quarterly*, 1920.

[2] Cf *Hibernia*, Jan., Feb., March 1957.

[3] Cf O'Rahilly, The Sovereignty of the People, in *Studies*, vol. x (1921).

[4] In his article The Sovereignty of the People, Dr. O'Rahilly gives a full list of these writers.

remembered too that the Translation Theory does not necessarily mean that the only form of legitimate government is a
democratic one. It allows the people freedom to choose any form
that suits them, including monarchy, aristocracy and dictatorship. Nor is the historical argument in favour of the Translation
Theory exactly watertight. It is by no means clear that it was
unequivocally held by each and every author with whom it has
come to be associated. There are considerable difficulties in both
Cajetan and Vittoria that would take a lot of explaining on the
part of those who claim these writers on the side of the Translation Theory.

Even the great upholder of the theory, Suarez, has to admit
that, in certain circumstances, the people can be *deprived* of
political authority by the will 'of another who possesses a just
title to it.'[1] By 'just title' here he means victory in a just war,
or prescription consequent on victory even in an unjust war.
He realises how often such factors have been operative in the
past and, to be realistic, is forced to take account of them.
'It happens through a just war that the people are really deprived of the power which they had, and the ruler who has
conquered them has acquired a real right and authority in that
kingdom, because if the justice of the war be supposed, then
this would be a just penalty . . . However, it chances often that
a kingdom is occupied through an unjust war—in this way
nearly all the more renowned empires were extended—in which
cases neither supreme authority nor any true power is acquired
at the beginning, since all just title is wanting, but in the
course of time it happens either that the people give their consent or that the supreme power is got by the successors through
bona fide prescription.'[2]

It will be noticed that, in order to harmonise the acquisition
of legitimate authority through just war with his defence of the
Translation Theory, Suarez has to fall back on the idea of
quasi-contract—submission to the exigencies of just punishment taking the place of the normal contract. There is question

[1] Suarez, *Def. Fidei*, Bk. iii, c. 2.
[2] Suarez, *loc. cit.*

of a consent that is *due* rather than actually given. This in itself is a rather weak explanation and, in any case, fails to account for the acquisition of authority through prescription.[1]

But the greatest difficulty in the way of the Translation Theory is created by the teaching of Pope Leo XIII and Pope Pius X. In the Encyclical *Diuturnum illud* the former writes: 'The choice (of the people) determines the person of the sovereign; it does not confer on him the rights of sovereignty. It is not authority that is constituted in him; it is decided merely by whom it ought to be exercised.' And in his letter on the *Sillon* Pope Pius X condemned the main idea of this movement, namely, that authority 'resides primordially in the people and emanates from them by way of election or, better still, selection, yet not so as to leave the people or become independent of them.' Pope Leo XIII, he says, 'formally condemned that doctrine.'

Fr. Gabriel Bowe O.P., in his book *The Origin of Political Authority*, interprets these statements to mean that what the Popes were opposed to was the idea—which originated with Rousseau and the rationalists of the 18th century—that civil power derives *exclusively* from the people.[2] It is true that Pope Leo XIII made explicit mention of these and aimed his criticism at them rather than at the Catholic defenders of the Translation Theory. But Pope Pius X seems to have rejected the doctrine —irrespective of paternity—that authority comes solely by way of the consent of the people. Fr. Bowe is inclined to doubt this on the grounds that, according to Pope Leo XIII, 'the

---

[1] Dr. O'Rahilly has to admit that the difficulty is embarrassing and that it is only by a quibble that Suarez subsumes enforced consent under free consent. At best, he says, Suarez is linking consent with conquest by way of the *jus gentium*, which is based on world consent. Cf The Sovereignty of the People, in *Studies*, vol. x (1921), pp 50 and 51, note 1. But it is only conquest in just war that is based on the *jus gentium* whereas Suarez speaks of a title to rule that can follow even unjust conquest. Besides, the consent that is accorded to the *jus gentium* is of an entirely different kind from that which is in question here.

[2] Bowe, *op. cit.* pp 16-24.

people have a role to play.'[1] In support of his interpretation he quotes the Pope to the effect that 'the power to rule of itself is not necessarily bound up with any particular form of government; it can rightly assume this or that form provided it is really effective for the common welfare and utility.'[2] What this proves is hard to see. More reliance might be placed on the following passage: 'There is no reason why the Church should not approve of the common welfare. Consequently, within the limits of justice, the people are not forbidden to choose the form of government that is more in keeping with their natural character, and with the customs and manners of their forefathers.'[3]

But this does not establish the *necessity* of consent. All it says is that it is *allowable* for the people to choose their government. It does not say that the only legitimate government is one that rests on consent and certainly not that such consent involves a translation of authority. Indeed the Pope adds: 'It is important to observe here that those who rule the State may in certain cases be chosen by the will and judgment of the people, and that herein Catholic doctrine offers neither dissent nor opposition; but that choice marks out the person who shall govern; it does not delegate power, it designates the person by whom it shall be borne.'[4] While it is true that the Pope was not concerned here with giving a full exposition of the Catholic philosophy and theology of political authority, it would be hard to find a statement more suggestive of the Designation Theory.

For these reasons the eminent Louvain Professor, Jacques Leclercq, says that it must be admitted that these Popes 'expressed a preference' for the Designation Theory. He maintains, however, that they did not wish to bind Catholic thinkers in this respect.[5] He sums up the position by saying that 'the thesis of mediate collation cannot claim for itself the privilege

---

[1] Bowe, *op. cit.* p 20.

[2] *Immortale Dei.*

[3] *Diut. Illud.*

[4] *Diut. Illud.*

[5] Cf Jacques Leclercq, *Leçons de Droit Naturel*, vol. II: *L'État ou la politique*, Louvain 1947, p 162.

of orthodoxy, but neither has the thesis of immediate collation received this privilege.'[1] It is Leclercq's view that, while the dispute is not just a purely theoretical one, because of the effect on practical politics which one's views on it can entail, it need never have arisen in the first instance. It grew gradually out of the medieval struggle between Empire and Papacy, which occasioned a certain confusion between the orders of revelation and nature as far as the origin of political authority is concerned. Biblical references to divine intervention in the constitution of kings, the direct institution of the Church by God and its reception of power immediately from Him—all this tended to cloud the minds of theologically disposed men to the fact that political authority is normally a natural institution and, as such, comes from God in the course of nature.

The question, therefore, whether political authority comes to human rulers directly from God, or whether it is translated to them from Him mediately, is not the bone of contention.[2] In general the important difference between the Translation Theory and the Designation Theory is the place which each assigns to the consent of the people. According to the former, consent is essential in order that a government be legitimate; according to the latter, it is only one of a plurality of ways in which a legitimate government can be designated. Whether authority comes mediately or immediately from God is an altogether separate question. Indeed, even some of the supporters of the Designation Theory, while insisting that there is no transfer of authority from the people, hold that the only legitimate mode of designation is the consent—explicit or implicit—of the community. Amongst these are Zigliara, Schwalm and Billot.[3] But it is a consent that *designates* who is to hold power rather than one that actually *transfers* the power itself.

Hence, in order to get rid of the confusing overtones relating to this matter of the mediate or immediate derivation of political

[1] Leclercq. *op. cit.* vol. II, p 162.
[2] Cf Th. Meyer, *op. cit.* vol II, p 350.
[3] Card. Zigliara, *Summa Philosophica*, vol. III, Paris 1891; P. Schwalm, *Leçons de Philosophie Sociale*, vol. II, Paris 1910; Card. Billot, *De Ecclesia Christi*, vol. I, Rome ed. 5, 1927.

authority, I think it will be better to confine ourselves simply to the question as to whether the consent of the people is essential to its acquisition. As is already clear, there is a difference of opinion about this. According to one view, the source of political authority is confined to consent; according to the other it can derive also from certain other titles which come into play in the interests of the common good. I shall call the former of these views 'The Consent Theory' and the latter, for want of a better term, 'The Common Good Theory'. It will be recognised, of course, that consent plays a limited role in the Common Good Theory, while the Consent Theory is not incompatible with the common good. I might add that, although he does not always make this quite clear, what Dr. O'Rahilly defends is really the Consent Theory of political authority rather than the Translation Theory as such.

BY WAY OF HISTORY

One can easily be attracted to the Consent Theory and appreciate the considerations which give rise to it. Yet I wonder if it is not inspired by an exaggerated consciousness of democratic values, which have by no means been respected by all peoples at all times. Without doubt democratic political systems have a much longer history than is commonly thought. It would be the height of folly to think that they appeared for the first time with the French Revolution. Sir Erskine May produced two large volumes on *Democracy in Europe*,[1] which traced them back to early Greece. Sociologists report that they exist even amongst primitive peoples, for example, the North American Indian tribes.[2] But such evidence does not constitute apodeictic proof that legitimate political authority emerges only through the consent of the people. It is necessary to make some sort of survey of the views of philosophers—particularly scho-

[1] London 1877.
[2] Cf E. A. Hoebel, *Man in the Primitive World*, New York 1958, ch 28.

lastic—if we are to establish the age and respectability of the Consent Theory.

In an article on 'The Catholic origins of democracy' Dr. O'Rahilly has named the scholastic writers who, he maintains, 'upheld the ideal of popular rights and government by consent.'[1] As well as Suarez and Bellarmine, his list includes St. Thomas Aquinas and Nicholas of Cusa, Nicholas d'Oresme, Antoninus of Florence and Vittoria, Castro, Covarruvias, Molina and Banez, some lesser known names such as Almain and Driedo, the Scotsman John Major and others. It should be noted that all these writers, with the exception of St. Thomas Aquinas and Nicholas d'Oresme, lived and wrote after the year 1400. Indeed, apart from St. Thomas, the majority of the writers adduced by Dr. O'Rahilly in support of the Consent Theory pertain to the period of the Conciliar Movement. He himself is aware of this restriction. He seeks to get over it by saying that his enumeration is due to the fact that it was from these Conciliar writers that the later founders of modern democracy drew their inspiration. While this may well be true, it is quite another matter to regard their views as representative of the earlier scholastic tradition. I find it hard to see how Dr. O'Rahilly can say that Nicholas of Cusa's view that 'all government, whether by written law or a prince, is based on the consent of the subject'[2] is 'practically a medieval commonplace' if by this he means that the Consent Theory of the origin of political authority was widely held in medieval times.

Nicholas of Cusa's position was really a product of the Conciliar period. First mooted by John of Paris (d. 1306) in his defence of Philip the Fair against the Papacy, passed on by Marsilius (d. 1342) and Occam (d. 1349) in furtherance of a similar task for Louis of Bavaria, the theory that the faithful can depose a Pope, if necessary, came to be looked upon as the key to a settlement of the Great Western Schism. Proposed for this purpose by Conrad of Gelnhausen in 1378, it was given ever more radical expression—as the Schism continued—by

[1] A. O'Rahilly, The Catholic Origins of Democracy, in *Studies*, vol. VIII (1919).

[2] *De Concordantia Catholica*, II, 14, in *Opera*, Basel 1565, p. 730.

Cardinal Zabarella, Peter d'Ailly and Gerson.[1] Nicholas of Cusa's *De Concordantia Catholica* (1434) reflects these ideas which, in themselves, are not at all a medieval commonplace but the intellectual apparatus of a particular and controversial problem.

The crucial question is whether there were earlier medieval writers from whom the Consent Theory, as such, could have been drawn. Specific and unequivocal evidence is necessary. There is little use, for example, in pointing to the fact that the later English Convenanters, in seeking for principles with which to combat the Divine Right of Kings, found inspiration and support in Bracton and Fortescue and the forgotten schoolmen of the 12th and 13th centuries. Everybody knows that these were champions of natural rights and were vehement in maintaining that the community is not bound by a tyrranical oppressor, whose commands are not law but its violation. Emphasis on the rights of the community in this sense—while it could undoubtedly be used against exaggerated claims of Divine Right—in no way proves a belief in the Consent Theory of political authority.

The ideas of the Conciliarists assume importance as reflective of general medieval opinion only if it can be shown that they are not unprecedented novelties invented in the course of controversy. Yet, strange to say, not until recently was any systematic effort made to do this. It is true that they had been traced to the early 14th and even the 13th centuries. In 1903 the German scholar, K. Hirsch, had pointed out that the first Conciliarists, Conrad of Gelnhausen and his colleague Henry of Langenstein, had been anticipated half a century previously by Marsilius of Padua and William of Occam.[2] Shortly afterwards H.-X. Arquillière had pushed their origin back further, to the 13th century work of John of Paris 'On royal and papal power'.[3] Even at that they remained very much the product

---

[1] Cf Walter Ullmann, *The Origins of the Great Schism*, London 1948, pp 176 *et seq.*

[2] K. Hirsch, *Die Ausbildung der konzilaren Theorie*, Vienna 1903.

[3] H. X. Arquillière, L'origine des théories conciliaires, in *Séances et Travaux de l'Académie des Sciences et Politiques*, CLXXV (1911). See also V. Martin, Comment s'est formée la doctrine de la superiorité du concile sur le pape, in *Revue des Sciences Religieuses*, XVII (1937).

of controversy; their Conciliar background had merely yielded place to that of the Investiture Conflict. In 1955, however, Brian Tierney's *Foundations of the Conciliar Theory* showed that they had older roots which gave them greater claim to objectivity. Tierney has marshalled plenty of evidence to prove that 12th and 13th century canonists held the view that, even in the Church, authority did not come to the ruler entirely without the consent of the people. The commentary on Gratian of Joannes Teutonicus, the writings of Pope Innocent IV and Hostiensis, and many other sources are produced to support this. What the canonists wanted to emphasise was that, even though ecclesiastical power is hierarchical, it is conferred for the good of the Church as a whole rather than for the personal glory of any prelate or prelates. It was for this reason that they urged that the clergy should be ministers rather than masters, a moral principle which their juridical treatment quickly built into a legal doctrine of the prelate as manager or proctor of his church viewed as corporation.

To this extent it must be admitted that the Conciliarist theories of popular sovereignty had precursors in the writings of the canonists of the 12th and the first half of the 13th centuries. Here too, however, it needs to be realised that in this the canonists were influenced by the revival, for polemical purposes, of certain concepts of Roman Law. This aspect of the matter has been dwelt on by Fr. Joseph Lecler[1] and is important for evaluating the 'Consent Theory' of the canonists and for situating it in the mainstream of medieval thought. The concepts in question began to appear in the 11th century, during the struggle between Pope Gregory VII and Henry IV, in the course of which the King's supporters made use of the famous *Lex Regia* of Roman Law to the effect that it was the Roman people that had conferred his political power on the emperor.[2] Once granted, this power was regarded as absolute and the

---

[1] In *Etudes* (1935) pp 5-6.

[2] Cf Ulpian, *Dig.* Bk. II, tit. 4, *De Constit. Princ.:* 'Quod principi placuit, legis habet vigorem, upote cum lege regia, quae de imperio eius late est, populus ei in eum omne suum imperium et potestatem conferat'.

people could not relieve the emperor of his crown. The papal defenders in turn did not lack the ability to see how this consent idea could be turned into an ally. It was invaluable to them in so far as it assigned a human origin to political authority, for this *ipso facto* brought it into subordination to the Church as guardian and expositor of things divine. We are not surprised therefore to find Manegold of Lautenbach, in defence of Gregory VII, placing the origin of political power in the people. He was careful not to regard the transference as absolute; authority could be recalled by the people or by the Pope in the event of its not being properly exercised.[1] By the 12th and 13th centuries the idea of a transference of power from people to ruler had become very current not only among the romanist lawyers of Bologna but also amongst the ecclesiastical lawyers. The fact that they were divided as to whether the transference was absolute or revocable shows the strategic use to which the consent idea was put by opposing parties.

It was precisely the same strategy that led Honorius Augustodunensis to elaborate the very different idea that secular government had been instituted by God through the mediation of the Church. For Honorius the fact that kings are consecrated as ministers of God meant that in some sense they must be officers of the Church.[2] At least he was ready to argue thus in furthering the interests of the Papacy. What I am suggesting is that the Investiture Conflict, no less than Conciliarism, was a fruitful source of 'party' political theories. The theory of popular sovereignty, even as held by the canonists, was one such. It had an intensely pragmatic import and cannot be regarded as general medieval teaching unless support for it can be found amongst uncommitted philosophical minds.[3]

[1] Cf *Ad Gebehardum Liber*, ed. K. Francke, in MGH, *Libelli de Lite*, vol. I, p 365. For extract from same in English see E. Lewis, *Medieval Political Ideas*, London 1954, vol. I, p 165.

[2] Cf Lewis, *op. cit.* p 145.

[3] Carlyle speaks of the 'harsh' and 'abnormal' terms in which Manegold of Lautenbach expresses his views: vol. III, p 184 and vol. V, p 472. Gerhoh of Reichersberg indicated that Manegold's position was an ex-

The authority of Gierke is frequently cited on the side of the view that the Consent Theory had this support. Indeed it is Gierke's view that the very idea of community (*Genossenschaft*) is typically medieval, as is also, by implication, the idea of a unifying force by which the community is held together and acts. This is all quite true as far as it goes. The trouble is that—despite his great learning—Gierke's interpretation is vitiated at its root by reason of his advocacy of the 'organic theory' of the State. In support of this Gierke saw 'community' everywhere, 'community' in the sense of a fully formed, moral personality endowed with some kind of psychological reality. His only complaint was that the medievals, although they stressed the idea of community, did not realise that it possessed a real group personality. As he saw it, they 'confused the single act whereby a community unifies itself with a mere obligatory contract made among individuals.'[1] For him communities all grow; they are not made. He was not at all happy in having to record that 'the Medieval Doctrine brings the hypothetical act of political union under the category of a Contract of Part-

treme one that was not generally approved. Cf Epistola ad Innocentium Papam, in MGH, *Libelli de Lite*, vol. III, p 232. The point is sometimes made that the intellectual respectability of the Consent Theory during these times is strengthened by the fact that there is not a trace of any rival or even alternative theory. This is by no means accurate. The theory of the immediate divine appointment of kings is defended in the work *De Modus Uniendi Ecclesiam* (c. 1410); also by Petrus de Marca, in *Concord. Sacerd. et Imp*. Bk. II, c. 2; and by Victor, *Relect. de Pot. Civ*. n 8. Cf Hergenrother, *Katholische Kirche und Christlicher Staat* (1872). English trans. London 1876, vol. II, p 238, note 2. Admittedly too much store should not be placed on this, as some of the defenders were unorthodox, themselves committed to the cause of Louis of Bavaria. All the literature of the Boniface VIII—Philip the Fair struggle is classed by Carlyle as 'controversial', while E. F. Jacob speaks of the 'opportunism' of Nicholas of Cusa's writing. Cf E. F. Jacob, *Nicholas of Cusa*, in F. J. C. Hearnshaw, ed., *The Social and Political Ideas of Some Great Thinkers of the Renaissance and the Reformation*, London 1925, p 34.

[1] O. Gierke, *Political Theories of the Middle Age*, Trans. by F. W Maitland, Cambridge 1900, p 89.

nership or "Social Compact".'[1] But he was quite sure that what
we have called the Consent Theory of authority was a primary
characteristic of medieval political theory in general.

The validity of Gierke's interpretation has been questioned
on very many scores. His corporate personality ideas, in particular, have been criticised. The historian of law, J. W. Jones,
has written that the jurists of the school of Gierke 'who have
attempted to explain the nature of the *real group will* . . . as
an entity formed by *kneading* or *crystallising* or *distilling* the
wills of individuals . . . have been more concerned to bolster
up legal theories with some show of amateur psychological
speculation than to inquire seriously into what lies behind the
term *group mind*.'[2] Gierke's attribution of a real personality
to every community has been attacked from diverse angles.[3]
Gurvitch's criticism of it from the point of view of Sociology
of Law is especially relevant to us. It is directed at Gierke's
tendency to see 'community' where, at best, there exists only
a loose form of association. 'Unfortunately, Gierke, despite his
reference to mixed cases, does not distinguish between "forms
of sociality" and "real collective units", and consequently his
jural typology of groups is far too simplistic and summary.'[4]
Equally open to criticism is his belief that medieval corporation
ideas in any way resembled those of the contractualist philosophers of the 17th and 18th centuries.

E. F. Jacob has suggested three medieval elements of association from which the Conciliarist idea of popular sovereignty may have taken shape. It may have been derived, he
says, 'partly from the peculiarly Germanic idea of the Fellowship (*Genossenschaftsidee*) which, to quote Gierke . . . is based
on the 'aboriginal and active Right of the group taken as a

[1] *Ibid.*

[2] J. W. Jones, *Historical Introduction to the Theory of Law*, Oxford
1940, p 189.

[3] E.g. by M. de Wulf, L'Individu et le groupe dans la scolastique du
XIIIe siècle, in *Revue Néo-Scolastique de Philosophie*, XXII (1920) and E.
Lewis, Organic Tendencies in Medieval Political Thought, in *American
Political Science Review*, vol. XXXII (1938).

[4] Georges Gurvitch, *Sociology of Law*, London 1947, p 74.

Whole'; partly from an interpretation of the *Lex Regia* by the Glossators, who found in the *Corpus Juris* the express indication that the will of the people was the source of rulership; and partly from the contractual element in feudalism with its inherent notions of compact and consent as the condition of the tenure of office or power.'[1] We have already referred to the revival of the *Lex Regia* and have argued that its implications were more closely relevant to contemporary polemic than to the general political philosophy of the Middle Ages. In any case it would have been impossible to transpose its Roman connotation entirely unchanged into the medieval world. The idea of a community of equal and autonomous citizens was unknown to the medieval mind. We have Tellenbach's word for it that 'the medieval state grew from essentially different roots. The notion of equality of rights and the transference of authority were in origin foreign to medieval thought, which took a far simpler view of the grounds of political obligation.'[2]

What were the roots from which the medieval State did grow? The answer to this provides us with *the* explanation as to why associationist concepts loom so large in medieval political writing of even early vintage. In particular, it shows that the contractual element in feudalism wove a pattern of ideas somewhat analogous to those of the Consent Theory. The key concept is the notion of kinship. Vinogradoff has pointed out that kinship was the warp and woof of the early Germanic clan or tribal system.[3] Concerted social action was to be found only amongst family relations and political obedience forthcoming only to a leader who was also a relative. So important was kinship that, where it was lacking, efforts were made to substitute for it by way of adoption, artificial brotherhood and the like. Only in this way could a family strengthen itself in the world. But it was also capable of being used to create a defensive

[1] *loc. cit.*

[2] G. Tellenbach, *Church, State and Christian Society*, Oxford 1940, p 13.

[3] P. Vinogradoff, Foundations of Society (Origins of Feudalism), in *The Cambridge Medieval History*, vol. ii, p. 631. Also Marc Bloch, *Feudal Society*, London 1961, ch. ix.

alliance between a number of strong men who, through it, became a joint civil power.[1] It is easy to see in this the forerunner of vassalage, or contract of service, for which medieval times are famous.[2] As a contract it involved mutual obligations. In return for protection by his lord the vassal pledged him certain duties, which varied according to the circumstances. The protection afforded by the overlord could also vary; each vassal had his own peculiar rights and customs which his lord was expected to respect and protect. A good example of the relations between a feudal overlord and his vassals is to be found in the coronation formula of the kings of Aragon: 'We (the Cortes) who are as good as you, swear to you, who are no better than we, to accept you as our King and sovereign Lord, provided you accept all our liberties and laws; but, if not, we do not.'

It is immediately clear that feudalism introduced a system of private law in place of the public law of Roman times. So much so that the very being of the State tended to become but an idea, an abstract notion with almost no basis in reality.[3] What existed was a system of relationships between man and man, a complex network of *ad hoc* adjustments whereby protection was secured for some and strength and influence assured to others. At the top of the scale stood the king, the very apex of the hierarchical feudal structure. Through vassalage and through vassalage alone could he succeed in extending his dominion and prestige. The bond of his society was personal attachment (enfeoffment), or what in Merovingian times was known as *trustis*. As time wore on it became increasingly difficult for the king to regard his more powerful vassals as subjects. The Aragon formula speaks for itself in this connection. In England the barons' revolt, the Wars of the Roses etc. sprang from a group of knights who regarded themselves the equals as well as the subjects of the king.[4] Not only was sovereignty

---

[1] Cf Vinogradoff, *loc. cit.* p 635.

[2] Cf Vinogradoff, Feudalism, in *The Cambridge Medieval History*, vol. III, p 460-1.

[3] Cf J. Calmette, *Le monde feodal*, Paris, p 167; F. L. Ganshof, *Feudalism*, London 1952, p 53.

[4] Cf Vinogradoff, *loc. cit.* p 466.

disrupted by the substitution of private law for centralised jurisdiction, but even the personal rule of the king came to depend very largely on the consent of his greater vassals. In theory a baron, being a sovereign in his own right, could be subjected to no will but his own. The result was that any arrangement by which he was to be bound had to be effected after the manner of modern international agreements.

In this way the notion of 'consent' entered the picture. In Touraine-Anjou it was expressed as follows: 'The baron has all manner of justice in his territory, and the king cannot proclaim his command in the land of the baron without the latter's consent; nor can the baron proclaim his command in the land of his tenant without the consent of the tenant'.[1] Inextricably connected with this idea of consent was that of custom. The consensual relations between lord and subject were defined by custom, in that the former could demand and the latter would afford only the tax or service that had consent or precedent behind it. It was in this sense that the idea was forged that taxation is lawful only to the extent that citizens consent to its imposition. It was also the sense of the idea of law as the custom of the community, for which cause new legislation, or adaptation of custom, needed the consent of the community in order to be valid.[2] But it took a very long time before this became

[1] Cited in Vinogradoff, *loc. cit.* p 471.
[2] Cf A. J. Carlyle, *Medieval Political Theory in the West*, vol. 1, Edinburgh 1927, ch 19. An interesting example of the idea that English law in Ireland was binding only because 'received' is to be found in a 1320 declaration of a Parliament in Dublin which ordained 'that the Statutes of Westminster . . . and the other statutes made in England by the King and his council be read and examined before the King's council . . . and that the points which are applicable to the people and the peace of the land of Ireland be from thenceforth confirmed and held, saving always the good customs and usages of the land'—*Statute Rolls of the Parliament of Ireland*, H. F. Berry ed., Dublin 1910, vol. 1, pp 281-283. It was in encroachments by the English Parliament upon that of Ireland that the rebellions of 1641 and after had their constitutional roots. The same principle lay behind the Americans' stand on the point that they should be subject to no legislation or taxation by a body on which they were not represented. Cf C. H. McIlwain, *The American*

explicit, especially in a theory of the role of the community as such. Up to the 13th century the consent of the barons was essentially an individual consent, each one binding himself in a personal way, even though he might do so at an assembly of his peers. There was nothing at all like community action by way of majority vote; opinions were weighed in terms of the strength of those who expressed them rather than counted in any 'democratic' way.[1]

It may be objected that, whatever about the rest of Europe, medieval Germany had a highly developed notion of communal consent as the basis of political authority. There can be no gainsaying the fact that, among the Teutonic tribes in general, the consent of the people played an important part in kingship. A. J. Carlyle has devoted an entire chapter in the first volume of his great work to what he calls the 'elective character of the monarchy of the ninth century'.[2] He has provided illustrations of the idea in the case of Charlemagne's successors right up to the end of the century. The promises made by the ruler to observe the customary law remind Carlyle of 'something like a compact between the ruler about to be elected and his subjects'. At times the very word *pactum* itself occurs in the documents which describe the obligations of the king.[3] It is doubtful, however, whether one is entitled to regard such evidence as conclusive proof of belief in the consensual origin of political

Revolution: A Constitutional Interpretation, New York 1923, pp 148-185. It was for this reason too that, during the American War of Independence, the Irish regarded the American cause as their own. Members of the Irish House of Commons argued that, if Great Britain subdued the American colonies, "the next step would be to tax Ireland in the British parliament"—*Proceedings of the House of Commons in Ireland* (1776).

[1] Vinogradoff insists, however, that these feudal assemblies of barons are important as necessary precursors of later constitutional developments in that they expressed the idea of a convention in a definite manner. He also says that the distinction between greater and lesser barons was the germ of the subsequent Houses of Lords and Commons. —*Loc. cit.* pp 471-2.

[2] *Op. cit.* ch 20.

[3] MGH, *Leg.*, sect. II, vol. II, n 262. *Cap ad Francos* (856 A.D.).

authority. Speaking of the Merovingian period, the historian of feudalism, Calmette, is particularly emphatic on this point. Many jurists, he says, and especially German jurists, often make the mistake of considering the Frankish monarchy as resting on well-established principles endowed with the force of public law. This, he maintains, is a great mistake. The truth is that the 5th and 6th century monarchies of the West were built entirely on 'purely empirical foundations'.[1] As I have already put it, they were the result of *ad hoc* arrangements by which relatively unified political power came to be exercised. Much the same thing would seem to hold as late as the 9th century. Even Carlyle will not say that the elective element in the Carolingian monarchy was the fruit of philosophical conviction about the origin of authority. Whereas, he says, it was a fundamental principle of the Roman jurists that the source of all political authority was the Roman people, 'there was this far-reaching difference between the Roman legal theory and the principles of the Teutonic societies, that the Roman theory was a theory of origins, while the Teutonic principles were those of actually existing conditions'.[2] One wonders whether he really means that the Germanic system, while it did indeed involve the consent of the people in some peculiar way, did not at all involve the Consent Theory of political authority.

The evidence seems to point in this direction. That the people played a part cannot be questioned; what can be questioned is the precise part they played. For it is equally certain that at this same period European monarchies were regarded as resting on divine appointment and hereditary succession. Against this background the part of the people recedes from genuine election and appears rather as some kind of ratification of the monarch by way of the explicit assumption that he will respect the customary law and the implicit assumption that, if he will not, he can be deposed. Not every one was agreed on this

[1] *Op. cit.* p 156. Calmette's views cut across those of Dr. O'Rahilly that a social contract lay at the base of Gothic rule in Spain, as well as of the Merovingian and Carolingian monarchies: The Sovereignty of the People, p. 41, n 1.

[2] *Op. cit.* vol. III, p 11.

latter possibility, due to an exaggerated respect for the idea that the king is appointed by God. We find Hincmar of Rheims satisfied that the deposition of Louis the Pious (833) was in order, while Rabanus Maurus took the opposite view. But even in the case of those who assigned to the people the most far-reaching role, one cannot say simply that they stood for an elective monarchy. Carlyle is so keenly aware of this that, when he uses the word 'election' in connection with the role of the people, he qualifies it by adding the phrase 'or at least recognition'.[1] One is reminded of John of Paris's contention that the powers of a bishop are derived at once from God and the people: *a Deo . . . immediate, et a populo eligente vel consentiente.*[2] It did not necessarily mean that authority stemmed from the consent of the people, but that lawful authority was accompanied by their consent.

That the consent of the community could not have been the sole origin of political authority is better realised if it is remembered that feudal times had no clear-cut concept of community. At a time when vassals owed simultaneous obedience to several lords, when areas of jurisdiction were dotted profusely with immunities, a geographical concept of community was entirely impossible. A political community could have been delineated only in terms of the totality of individuals who owed allegiance to a particular overlord. Its unity depended on the ability of the overlord to retain their allegiance and it usually tended to have a 'shifting population'.[3] Only with difficulty can it at all be called a State, if anything like the modern State is meant.[4] In such a context it is only natural that democratically consititued political communities took longer to develop than might otherwise be the case. Representative assemblies,

---

[1] Carlyle, *op. cit.* vol. I, pp 250-1.

[2] Citied in Tierney, *op. cit.*, p 243.

[3] See E. Lewis, *op. cit.* vol. I, pp 194-5. Also Bloch, *op. cit.*, ch. xv: The Man of Several Masters.

[4] See L. Hartmann, *The Early Medieval State*, English trans. London 1949, *passim.* Cf also S. Z. Ehler, On applying the modern term 'State' to the Middle Ages, *Medieval Studies Presented to Aubrey Gwynn, S.J.* Dublin 1961.

capable of embodying the consent of a whole community, were the final term of a protracted evolution.

While it is likely that Spain and Italy were the pioneers of representative practice,[1] the English pattern of its growth is fairly typical. Its earliest form, the Anglo-Saxon *Witan*, was merely a body of royal advisers, without definite rights and largely dependent on the royal pleasure. Before the Norman Conquest it had been replaced by the local councils of shire and hundred, but these too had no mandate from the people whom they represented, nor is it at all certain that their members were elected. Then came the national council, or *Magnum Concilium*, which was made up of representatives of the shires and boroughs. But even by the 13th century this was still no more than an occasional expedient to be used solely at the discretion of the king.[2] All these bodies functioned mainly in a judicial capacity. Seeing that medieval administration required an intimate knowledge of the customs of the community, one judge was not enough to arrive at decisions. Representative members of each district were pressed into service to enable the king to observe the law which he had promised to respect and also, and significantly, to provide agreement to measures of taxation when the need arose. They did not have to be and usually were not elected representatives; election does not seem to have entered the picture until the middle of the 13th century.[3] These courts were therefore in no way democratic institu-

[1] Cf G. Post, Roman Laws and early Representation in Spain and Italy, in *Speculum*, 1943; also C. W. Previté-Orton, The Italian Cities till c. 1200, in *The Cambridge Medieval History*, vol. v.

[2] Cf A. Hattersley, *A Short History of Democracy*, Cambridge 1930, pp 79-80.

[3] According to E. Lewis, 'the idea of representation was not necessarily connected in medieval thought with the idea of election. An hereditary King could represent the entire realm, certain magnates with a customary right or duty of attendance could represent the entire estate of nobles, and their representation was conceived to be no less complete than if they had been elected. No one elected the electors of the Holy Roman Empire. As time went on, the opinion grew that election was the best way of filling representative offices. The act of election was felt to be the formal means by which the power of the com-

tions. In fact the extent of a king's ability to compel local representatives to act was also the measure of his strength in imposing his rule. The shadow of things to come, but no more than that, may be seen in the fact that the courts could decide not only on what obligations were owed to a lord by his vassals, but also whether the lord himself had kept faith with these.[1]

Magna Charta simply gave a formal structure to the tissue of rights and duties which already existed. And in so doing it hastened the day when the representatives of the realm would govern themselves. We are still a long way from this, however, in 1215. Previté-Orton has noted that the assent given to the Great Charter itself 'is still several rather than joint'.[2] Nevertheless the day is over when the feudal barons would rest content with individual pressure on the king to maintain feudal privilege and law. Constitutional government is being gradually elaborated, not through the assertion of abstract principles of government but through the vindication of concrete rights. The rapid development of representative practice which succeeded Magna Charta is made clear by the summons of Edward I in 1295 to the delegates to the Model Parliament. Whereas, in 1213, John had requested each county to send 'four discreet men . . . to talk with us concerning the affairs of our kingdom', King Edward requested representatives from shires, towns and boroughs, bringing 'sufficient power from their communities' so that 'the business in hand may not be held up through lack of such power'.[3] The representative—and democratic—aspect is coming more to the fore, but even yet the convening of parlia-

munity was properly conveyed to its representatives; but hereditary authority could be made compatible with this conception through the assumption that the community had originally elected a family and set the terms on which its representative right was transmitted from son to son. Accordingly, the development of the idea of representation did not mean the democratisation of medieval political thought'.—*Op. cit.* vol I, p 264.

[1] Cf A. J. Carlyle, *op. cit.* vol. III, ch 4.

[2] C. W. Previté Orton, The Medieval Estates, in *The Cambridge Medieval History*, vol. VII, p 673.

[3] Cf J. Morrall, *Political Thought in Medieval Times*, London 1958, pp 62-63.

ments is very much at the discretion of the king. Only in the smaller States—which were to inspire the democratic thought of Marsilius of Padua—was representation looked on as a permanently essential part of government. It was not until the 14th and 15th centuries that the large territorial States moved in this direction.[1]

The importance of parliament grew concurrently with the emergence of the 'estates'—the clergy, the baronage and the commons.[2] The development of these was slow. In parliament each spoke only for itself; it was a collective unit which acted for the class which elected it but not for the community as a whole. The estates were summoned to thrash out in public the problems posed by the king, and their answers were generally different. It was for the king to effect some kind of composition which would satisfy the interests of the greatest number. Then too not until the 14th century did English practice demand the participation of the estates in the promulgation of statutes. And not until the 15th century did it come to be realised that the representatives of the estates in parliament were not merely assisting at an authoritative finding of law but were themselves a legislative body.

All in all the interpretation of what evidence there is suggests that the kind of representative practice that is needed to give historical backing to the Consent Theory is not commonly found until the 14th century. Sir Ernest Barker has attempted to show the contrary by arguing that, long before this, political practice had been influenced by the practice of the Church in such a way as to have incorporated consent.[3] There had been concrete instances of popular sovereignty in certain Church councils, in cathedral and collegiate chapters, the constitutional framework of the older Military Orders (e.g., the Hospitallers, whose rule was confirmed in 1120) and the system of representative government which was adopted by the Dominicans. While this is true, its effects should not be exaggerated. As far as

[1] Cf Morrall, *op. cit.* p. 124.
[2] Cf E. Miller, *The Origins of Parliament*, London 1960.
[3] E. Barker, *The Dominican Order and Convocation*.

England is concerned, it has been pointed out that the thesis is greatly weakened by the fact that there were no Dominicans in that country before 1221 and it is to their influence that Barker mainly attributes the introduction of secular institutions of representation. No matter how one views the scene, one is brought close to the 14th century before one can be at all sure of a widespread recognition in practice of the idea that political authority stems from the consent of the community.

The same is true in the domain of theory. Prior to the adoption of Aristotelianism, the dominant political theory was that of the school generally known as the Augustinian. It has been noted repeatedly that the Augustinians were not interested to any extent in the theoretical problem of the origin of political authority. Their problem was primarily a practical one—how to combat the anarchical tendencies which followed the barbarian invasions and to get the authority of rulers respected. They were not interested much in whether these were established by consent or by force or were directly instituted by God himself. What they emphasised was that human authority was the inevitable complement of a fallen race; its purpose was to restore order and justice and what really mattered was that men should respect it. They concentrated on teaching that it was derived ultimately from God and that obedience to it was a Christian duty.[1] St. Augustine himself had pointed to this sacred character of secular government; it was developed further by St. Gregory the Great. The latter in fact built it up into a kind of theory of divine right, the ruler being regarded as the vicar of God, irremovable by the people. These views were repeated by many writers during the 9th and 10th centuries and provided a direct counter to any ideas on the popular origin of political authority.[2]

Walter Ullmann has summed up the whole story in his *Principles of Government and Politics in the Middle Ages* (London, 1961) by saying that the period was characterised not by any one conception of the origin of political authority but by both

[1] Cf Lewis, *op. cit.* vol. I, pp 142 seq.; Hattersley, *op. cit.* pp 95-96; Carlyle, *op. cit.* vol. I, ch. 13.
[2] Cf Carlyle, *op. cit.* vol. III, ch 4.

an 'ascending' and a 'descending' conception.[1] According to the former government and law were ascribed to the community or *populus;* according to the latter they were regarded as descending from God himself through human rulers. Corresponding to the one was what Ullmann calls a populist notion of kingship and to the other what he calls a theocentric notion of royalty. Related to them too, in the domain of law, was the distinction between *Volksrechte* and *Königsrecht.*

The theocratic conception—evidenced by the linking of the phrase 'Dei gratia' with the acquisition of authority—goes back as far as the Byzantine emperors of the 5th century. By the 8th century it was commonly used of Frankish bishops and secular rulers and had come to symbolise an idea of the origin of authority that was to dominate European thought until the 14th century. The extent of its aversion to any role on the part of the community in the conferring of authority is made clear by the fact that it insisted that, during an interregnum, political power reverted to Christ by escheat. Ullmann provides an account of how feudalism tempered this understanding of authority and represents a kind of stepping stone between the theocratic and populist conceptions. For feudalism meant that the king was not outside and above the community but a member of it, and bound to act in accordance with feudal contract. Not that the contractual element in feudal kingship was at all the same as the populist idea of sovereignty. In no way did it imply that the king had no standing other than that which the people as the repository of authority had conferred on him. Yet within feudalism both king and subject had a share in law-making and were involved in a sort of mutual compact. Ullmann has advanced the interesting view that to the extent that feudalism prevailed over theocratic rule, modern democracy was made possible of speedier introduction. It is in differences of evolution in this connection that he sees the fundamental explanation of the divergent political histories of England and France. Whereas in the former feudal kingship was early accentuated at the expense of theocratic, in France it did not become a reality of govern-

[1] For similar themes in later period see O. Gierke *Natural Law and the Theory of Society*, Cambridge 1934.

ment with the result that it took a revolution there to oust it.

Throughout the medieval period, despite the currency of the theocratic conception of authority, there persevered what Ullmann calls 'atavistic remains of the ascending theme in the less articulate strata' of society. They provided a living bridge between the primitive European period and the modern era and were made progressively easier of full expression by the growth of feudalism. Struggling to the forefront after a thousand years of dominance by the descending thesis, these various versions of the ascending theme had come, by the late Middle Ages, to represent the birth-pangs of a new and democratic Europe. They found institutional expression in guilds, town and village communities and in free associations and were given some theoretical development by certain heretical sects from the 12th century. It is most significant, however, that Ullmann has no hesitation in declaring that they received little treatment at the hands of the learned writers, the glossators, commentators, summists and so on: 'The doctrinal expression of the theocratic theme was entirely in the hands of the learned writers'. There is nothing here to justify the idea that the Consent Theory of political authority found philosophical support during the high medieval period.

THE THOMISTIC VIEW

The authority of St. Thomas has been regularly claimed for both theories but it is admitted by all that he wrote no *ex professo* treatment of the origin of political authority. The most one can find on this are certain *obiter dicta*, scattered here and there throughout his works. Fr. Bowe has based an argument for the Consent Theory on one of these,[1] to the effect that what is called 'dominion' (authority) derives from the law of nations.[2] The argument turns on what St. Thomas understood by the latter. This law, while natural to man in that it is arrived at by way of conclusions from the principles of natural law, goes

---

[1] Cf Bowe, *op. cit.* p 85 *seq.*

[2] *2a 2ae*, Q. 12 art. 2.

beyond these and may be considered to be positive human law in so far as it needs the decision of men to elaborate it. But because of their natural foundations, such conclusions, says St. Thomas, find ready acceptance amongst men.[1] In other words, the law of nations is intermediary between natural law and positive; it consists of conclusions from the law of nature that are established by the intellectual effort and consent of men. Private property and authority in the concrete are two institutions that are said to rest on this foundation. 'It follows, therefore', says Fr. Bowe, 'that, for St. Thomas, authority is legitimately in this or that ruler only as the result of the operation of the rational powers and the consent of men.'[2]

This could easily mislead. All that St. Thomas says, in effect, is that the institutions of authority rest ultimately on the law of nations and, as such, derive from the consent of men. In saying this, he is not treating at all of the question as to whether a government, in order to be *de jure*, needs a title that is derived immediately from the consent of the citizens. The kind of consent that is given to authority as an institution of the *jus gentium* is a very different consent from what is entailed by the Consent Theory. It is a radical consent on the part of men in general, whereas what the Consent Theory requires is a proximate consent on the part of the citizens, qua citizens, to a given government. In adopting the *jus gentium* men simply consent to the institution of authority; the possibility is not ruled out that the titles to its legitimate exercise may include factors other than the consent of the citizens.

Fr. Bowe admits that St. Thomas does not hold that the consent of the community is an exclusive title to authority.[3] It is the fundamental one, he says, and must always be present, but there are also proximate titles which do not demand *express* consent. Such, for example, is heredity, which can be a legitimate source of authority without explicit election if the long-standing custom of a community makes this permissible. But then it still remains true that this custom itself 'implies the

[1] 2a 2ae, Q. 95 art. 4 ad 1.
[2] *Op. cit.* p. 87.
[3] *Op. cit.* p. 90.

consent of the governed'. For the same reason Fr. Bowe declares that, according to Thomistic teaching, even 'a ruler who has taken over a country by unlawful means may become the legitimate ruler if and when the people give their consent to his rule'. But only, apparently, if and when they give this at least implicitly.

In an article in *Studies* for March 1920, Dr. O'Rahilly has dealt at greater length with this subject. While admitting that one cannot find the Consent Theory in Aquinas in the same detail as it is developed by 17th century writers, he defends the view that St. Thomas held it. Some of his arguments to prove this need not detain us. There is not much point in saying, for example, that St. Thomas 'is democratic' in that 'he takes no account of the inclusive imperial conception which the world was destined to outgrow'. The fact is that he was not involved in the controversies between Pope and Emperor. He spent most of his life in France under King St. Louis, whose regime was in complete harmony with the Papacy, and he wrote no treatise in defence of any particular political theory. For this reason, if for no other, Professor Leclercq has cautioned that St. Thomas can only be appealed to with moderation on the the question of the origin of political authority.[1]

It is true that St. Thomas, in common with many writers of his time, insisted that a tyrannical government is not just, for it is not worked for the common good, and that to disturb such a government is not equivalent to sedition.[2] It is true too that, in his *De Regimine Principum*, he made suggestions as to how such tyranny might be avoided.[3] And it is true to say, as does Dr. O'Rahilly, that the kind of thing St. Thomas wrote in this respect could have been penned only by one who was an enemy to all autocracy whether regal or parliamentary. But does this mean that he held that all legitimate government is contractual? Surely not. What it means is that under any system of government, democratic or monarchical, a people never slavishly alienates all its rights and must be governed justly if

[1] Cf J. Leclercq, *op. cit.* vol. II, p 155.
[2] *2a 2ae*, Q. 42, art. 2, ad 3.
[3] *De Regimine Principum*, Bk. I, c. 6.

its ruler would retain his title to govern legitimately. This is a
far cry from upholding the theory that his legitimate title to
rule can only be the consent of the people. That he rule for the
common good is what St. Thomas wants to inculcate, thereby
stressing that failure to do so entails the loss of his title. The
question of what the title itself consists in is not treated.

Purcell's *Life of Manning* tells us that the Cardinal claimed
that he learned from St. Thomas that 'God gives sovereignty
immediately to society and mediately *(mediante societate)* to
the prince, president or consul, one or more, whom society may
legitimately designate'.[1] Dr. O'Rahilly confesses that he himself
has not been able to find any quotation in St. Thomas to this
effect. The text of which most is made runs as follows: 'To
order anything for the common good is the function either of
the whole people or of someone taking the place of the people
(vicem gerentis). Therefore law-making pertains either to the
whole people or to the public person who has charge of the
whole people. For, as in everything else, to order for an end is
the function of the being whose end it is'.[2] Dr. O'Rahilly claims
that he has examined thirty commentators on this text and
has found that they are unanimous in holding that it means
that political authority resides primarily in the community, and
secondarily in one to whom the community has transferred the
power and who is therefore the people's vicegerent. Undoubtedly Cajetan held this view and regarded it as evidence for the
Consent Theory—and indeed the Translation Theory.[3] Unquestionably too there have been others of a like opinion. But
this, in itself, does not prove that St. Thomas held the Consent
Theory. It has frequently been pointed out concerning the text
in question that St. Thomas is here dealing with law in general
—religious as well as secular. If he were speaking of secular
law alone, then without doubt the *vicem gerens* could mean the
representative of the people, whose powers derive from them
by way of his appointment. In the case of ecclesiastical law,

[1] Vol. II, p 630.

[2] 1a 2ae, Q. 90, art. 3.

[3] Cf Cajetan, *Opera S. Thomae*, Leonine Ed., VII, p 151; also his
commentary on 2a 2ae, Q. 50, art. 1; *loc. cit.* VIII, p. 375.

however, it is difficult to attribute to St. Thomas the idea that the Pope as legislator is only the delegate of the community of the faithful. After the Great Schism, at the time of the Conciliar Theory, such views might have been held, but in the 13th century they could have only been an anachronism. The *vicem gerens* of St. Thomas's text must be understood in the wide sense of 'taking care of the people'.[1] 'It is not possible therefore', says Fr. Joseph Lecler S.J., 'to utilise this celebrated text so as to attribute to St. Thomas the thesis of political philosophy which makes the social body, taken in its totality, the premier titulary of sovereignty.'[2] Indeed that he did not hold this is positively suggested by the passage in his *Commentary on the Sentences* in which he states that authority is held *vel per consensum subditorum vel per auctoritatem superioris.*[3]

Dr. O'Rahilly argues further, however, that the view that authority cannot be exercised over a people without their consent is a logical consequence of St. Thomas's defence of the idea of equal natural rights (*2a 2ae*, Q. 104 art. 5) and his rejection of that of any natural superiority (In 2 *Sent.*, D. 369 Q. 1 art. 4, ad 5). He certainly rejected the Aristotelian idea that some men are superior in their essential nature, in virtue of which they should rule over others.[4] For which reason Dr. O'Rahilly remarks that it is ironical that a theory of quasinatural designation, which is practically equivalent to this discredited Aristotelianism, is to be found in many, if not most, contemporary expositions of Scholasticism. But is the Common

---

[1] Cf J. Lecler, Les théories démocratiques au moyen âge, in *Etudes*, 1935. Also Th. Meyer, *op. cit.* Part II, p 388, note 1 and J. Donat, *op. cit.* p 111. Meyer points out that this was also Cajetan's interpretation of the text, despite the fact that this admission was inimical to his own support for the Consent Theory. Indeed Suarez himself, as Cathrein has noted (*op. cit.* p 381), was forced to adopt the same interpretation. Cf also in addition Taparelli, *op. cit.* vol. 1: '*S. Tommaso non giustifica la sovranita del popolo*', pp 339-340.

[2] *Art. cit.* p 192.

[3] *In 2 Sent.*, D. 44, Q. 2 art. 2.

[4] Cf *Politics*, III, 17, 1288a, 15.

Good Theory, with its acceptance of methods of designation other than consent, fairly described as 'practically equivalent' to what Aristotle held? To me it seems clear that it is not. The kind of designation which it would accept as marking off an individual as suitable to rule, and vesting legitimate ruling power in him, is not the 'natural superiority' in which Aristotle believed, but something that derives from the fact of accidental disparity amongst men who are otherwise equal as persons and in essential nature. There was nothing to stop St. Thomas from holding a theory that implied only this. And, in point of fact, he does write that those who are suited for the active life should be directed by those who excel in mental faculties.[1] 'Homines intellectu vigentes sunt naturaliter aliorum rectores et domini.'[2]

All we can be certain of is this: that St. Thomas held that some form of democracy is always a desirable aspect of government. Different polities, he says, are expedient according to men's different conditions.[3] A democratic regime is unsuitable to a corrupt and unenlightened people. But it is a necessary aspect of the best political regime, which he describes as follows: 'One man is according to merit set at the head to preside over all, and under him are other rulers according to merit. Yet such a regime is the concern of all, because the rulers are not only elected from all but also are elected by all. Such is every good polity, combining monarchy, in as much as one is at the head, aristocracy inasmuch as there are many rulers (elected) according to merit, and democracy, i.e. the power of the people, inasmuch as the rulers can be elected by the masses and the election of rulers is the business of the people'.[4] In other words, an element of popular government is desirable. In this sense, but in this sense only, does St. Thomas advocate what is called the Consent Theory of political authority. On the contrary,

[1] S. Contra Gentiles, III, 78, 3; also ibid., 81.

[2] Proleg. in Metaph.; Cf also In Pol., III, 8.

[3] 1a 2ae, Q. 105, art. 1.

[4] De Regimine Principum, I, c. 4.; Note also: 'All should have some part in government, for thus the peace of the people is preserved and all love and observe such a regime'—1a 2ae, Q. 105 art. 1.

the evidence is against his holding this. For while he undoubtedly preferred a democratic system, as being more stable, he also
admitted the normality of pure forms of government. As for
reducing the origin of political authority in any of these to
delegation from the people, with a transmission of power—
whether absolute or conditional—'he does not', says Fr. Lecler,
'even seem to have dreamed of it'. All that R. Lane Poole[1] is
prepared to say is that he approaches nearer to the (democratic)
political opinions of the modern period than most people at his
time. Carlyle too simply describes his theory as the best example in medieval times of a defence of 'a limited and constitutional method of government.'[2]

We can agree entirely with this description. St. Thomas, in
common with the general tendency of medieval writers, was
quite prepared to give the people a role in law-making. But it
is equally clear that he regarded the ruler as the normal source
of positive law. For him even custom, or popular legislation,
depended for its validity on the assumed consent of the ruler.[3]
In so far as the medievals, including Aquinas, gave a political
role to the people, it was with a view to securing protection
for individual rights. They refused to regard the State as having
an end or purpose that was different from that of its individual
components. The 12th century civilist Irnerius expounds their
attitude on this rather well: 'The corporate whole, that is the
people, has this function, namely, to care for the common interests of individual men as its members'.[4] Aquinas expressed the
same idea when he wrote that 'the end of the human multitude

[1] R. Lane Poole, *Illustrations of the History of Medieval Thought
and Learning*, London 1884, p 245.

[2] *Op. cit.* vol. v, p 472. It is certainly false to say, as did Ernest
Barker in an early essay, that 'St. Thomas—like the clerical thinkers of
the Middle Ages in general—is a Whig; he believes in popular sovereignty, popular institution of monarchy, a pact between King and
people, and the general tenets of Locke'—Medieval Political Thought,
in Hearnshaw ed., *The Social and Political Ideas of Some Great Medieval
Thinkers*, London 1923, pp 21-22.

[3] *De Reg. Principum*, Bk. III, ch 29.

[4] *De Aequitate*, ch 2. Cited in Lewis, *op. cit.* p 209.

must be the same as the end of any one man'.[1] It was this that caused him to develop a more positive view of the function of the State than had the Augustinians, declaring that it had the duty to foster the living of the virtuous life—something much more than providing a remedy for sin. It was this too that lay at the root of John of Salisbury's[2] insistence that it behoves the ruler to serve justice and righteousness. In like manner Bracton and a host of others saw the king's duty to consist in the service of right.[3]

As I have already said, it was in so far as justice was embodied in the customary law that the people were given a role in its discovery. It is interesting to note how this Common Law drifted away from popular formulation as the Aristotelian concept of natural law became better defined and its content worked out by clerks and scholarly laymen appointed to hear the complaints of the kingdom. Slowly but surely justice done in the king's name by men like Glanvil became justice *par excellence*, surpassing local custom.[4] Centuries later Locke was to dissolve this natural law into a naked system of individual rights.[5] Deprived of divine basis and no longer linked to a ruler expected to do justice, such rights could rely only on the influence of the community for protection. Locke was at least logical in assigning a foremost place to Parliament and in developing a Consent Theory which would provide a basis for revolution if it were necessary. But how wrong it is to regard this as an elaboration of a theory of consent that was present from medieval times. Speaking of the social contract, Carlyle says that 'in the popular mind this conception is supposed to belong to the seventeenth and eighteenth centuries, but the real truth is that it is a medieval conception'.[6] The real truth is that there

[1] *De Reg. Princ.*, Bk. I, ch 4.

[2] Lewis, *op. cit.* pp 276-8.

[3] Lewis, *op. cit.* pp 279-284.

[4] Cf Richard O'Sullivan, Natural Law and the Common Law, in *Natural Law Institute Proceedings*, vol III, Notre Dame 1950.

[5] Cf Ed. S. Corwin, Natural Law and Constitutional Law, in *Natural Law Institute Proceedings*, vol. III.

[6] *Op. cit.* vol. III, p 12.

is a very wide gulf between medieval ideas of consent and those of Locke. And not only in that the former were ensconced in a framework of conviction that authority and law came from God. The medieval ideas knew nothing of self-sufficient individuals who freely agreed to certain 'natural' rights. Nor had they any room for a political authority that rested solely on the free consent of men. They did not even have room for the kind of Consent Theory of Suarez and Bellarmine. 'Medieval thinkers saw no reason why the existence of a common human end should be paralleled by an equality of men in political rights. They saw no reason why the organisation that existed to serve all its members should be governed by all its members. Their concern for the moral freedom and responsibility of men did not carry them to the modern democratic conclusion that man can be free only in subjection to an authority in which he himself actively participates . . . The medieval applications of the theory of consent were little more than the rationalisation of a hierarchic construction of power and some check against its abuse; its revolutionary effect had to wait for a later era in which the structure was itself undermined by the profounder revolutions of social and economic change'.[1]

Hence, while it is probably true to say that neither the Romanist theory of popular government nor the Aristotelian ideas of Aquinas won a total victory in medieval thought, it cannot be said that the Consent Theory of political authority was the normal tradition of the Middle Ages. J. N. Figgis hits the mark when he observes that the late medieval Conciliarists raised the constitutionalism of the past three centuries to a higher power and expressed it in a more universal form. It is a pity that he should have added that 'this is why it seems truer to regard the movement as medieval rather than modern in spirit.'[2]

GOVERNMENT BY CONSENT

If we turn to the writers, from Bellarmine and Suarez on, who indisputably championed the Consent Theory, we are again

[1] Lewis, *op. cit.* vol. i, pp 221-222.
[2] J. N. Figgis, *From Gerson to Grotius*, London 1916, p 47.

struck by the fact that many of them were controversialists, who sought a means of countering the then nascent monarchical absolutism and the theory of the Divine Right of Kings. Prior to the 16th century, European monarchy was constitutional in the sense that it generally recognised that there were just limits to its rule. Although strongly consolidated, following the decline of the feudal lords, it had a democratic aspect that was none the less real because of the fact that it was not guaranteed by political institutions. The people were safeguarded by the Rule of Law, which was above the king and of which he was but the administrator.[1] The advent of Protestantism changed all this, the power of the monarch becoming exalted to such a degree that he would not be human if he did not tend towards despotism.[2] It was this, I am certain, that led Bellarmine to develop the doctrine that the power of the king is derived from the people, with the implication that he is beholden to them for the use which he makes of it. For here indeed was a powerful check to the abuse of authority. So powerful in fact that James I of England felt called upon to reply personally to 'the great and famous writer of Controversies, the late un-Jesuited Cardinal Bellarmine (who) must adde his talent to this good worke, by blowing the Bellowes of Sedition, and sharpening the Spurre to Rebellion.'[3] And was it not to support his brother in religion that Suarez addressed his defence of government by consent to 'the most serene James, King of England'?

The debate was clouded from the beginning by the preoccupations of the respective contestants, the King seeking to repel any idea that would seem to curb royal power, the Jesuits

[1] Cf J. Newman, *Foundations of Justice*, Cork 1954.

[2] I do not mean that the theory of the Divine Right of Kings was Protestant in origin. Something very much resembling it had been put forward by Louis of Bavaria in the 14th century and it was also defended, after the Reformation, by Catholic Gallican and Spanish regalists. But it was Protestant in tendency in that it made for a whittling down of the power of the Papacy.

[3] *Apology for the Oath of Allegiance*. Cf. also A Remonstrance for the Right of Kings, in *The Political Works of James I*, C. H. McIlwain ed., Cambridge Mass. 1918.

striving to establish, in the manner most likely to convince, that royal power is limited. It seems to me that this was the kernel of the dispute and that the theories for and against rule by popular consent were made to subserve it. In truth, it should not have mattered a whole lot in practice which of these theories was valid. A Christian ruler should regard his authority as severely delimited, whether or not it derived from the consent of the people.[1] In the circumstances, however, civil rulers, who were anxious to place their power on a level with that of the Papacy, were tempted to propound the doctrine that they received their power from God in the same immediate manner as Popes.[2] It was to this end that King James told his Parliament 'that God had appointed him absolute master and that all privileges which co-legislative bodies enjoyed were pure concessions proceeding from the bounty of kings'. Thus was the Theory of the Divine Right of Kings, and what it implied, irrevocably intermixed with the theory of the immediate, as against the mediate or consensual, derivation of authority.

For this reason, when one finds 17th and 18th century writers denying that authority can come directly from God to a civil ruler, it is not always easy to be sure whether they are bent on defending the Consent Theory or rather on attacking the Divine Right of Kings. The issue seems to have been bedevilled by this confusion right down to the 19th century. It was only when revolutions and popular agitation began to undermine the political framework of Europe that writers commenced to re-examine the Consent Theory. They were less disposed now than before to favour a view which, through its connection with the idea of a transference of power from community to ruler, could so easily be aligned with and further the designs of Rousseau's *Contrat Social*. The majority, as we know, preferred to adopt the Common Good Theory to the effect that political authority derives immediately from God to the ruler, who can be designated in more ways than by the consent of the people.

[1] Balmes has pointed out this very ably in his *Protestantism compared with Catholicity*, London 1849, p 254 *seq.*

[2] Cf Balmes, *op. cit.* p 257.

I have said earlier that the notion of 'transference' is not necessarily entailed by the Consent Theory. But, in fact, it continued to be associated with consent by many writers.[1] This is why so many Catholic writers of the 19th century would have nothing to do with the Consent Theory. In the same way, during the previous period, opposition to the Divine Right of Kings had led Catholic writers to champion nothing but consent. Only when both 'transference' and 'divine right' have been isolated from the discussion, is it possible to see its terms in their true light.[2]

The same might be said for the terms 'immediate' and 'mediate'. For, strictly speaking, even the Common Good Theory does not mean that a ruler, in the ordinary course of nature, is ever designated by God immediately to possess authority. Rather is he designated by various contingent facts.[3] Contrariewise, it would also admit that, in a wide sense of the word, all such authority must be said to derive mediately from God, in that it comes to man through the accidents of the natural historical process.[4] Its use of the term 'immediate' is solely by way of opposition to the use of 'mediate' that was— unfortunately—adopted by the Consent Theory. In truth the field of discussion needs to be cleared of many obstacles before one can see one's way through it with success.

The fact is that, in my opinion, the respective merits of the Consent Theory and the Common Good Theory in themselves have never had a chance to be evaluated objectively until the present. There was always some ulterior purpose or distortion of vision which prevented the true position from being grasped. Full recognition of all its factors has come slowly; understanding has deepened *pari passu* with the challenge of error. Just as some aspects of the Church have received scientific development only after the appearance of heresy, so Catholic teaching

---

[1] Cf Balmes, who wrote in the middle of the century, *op. cit.* p 254.

[2] Note that Meyer protests that his thesis in no way involves this theory of Divine Right, *op. cit.* part 2, pp 400-402.

[3] Cf Cathrein, *op. cit.* pp 380-381.

[4] Cf Meyer, *op. cit.* pp 358-360 and 399-400.

on the origin of political authority has taken time in growing to adult stature.

I may be reproached with devoting too much attention to history and with neglecting the actual arguments in favour of these two theories themselves. It is well to remember that the 'argument from tradition' has been one of the main weapons in the arsenal of the consent theorists. Suarez himself placed considerable store by it,[1] even though, in his day, it was not as impressive as it is now. Dr. O'Rahilly too has placed very great reliance on it. The other arguments for both theories almost cancel each other out, so powerful and numerous have been the salvoes from the rival camps. Not all the arguments are equally good; both sides have made points that can be discounted. For example, when, in reply to their opponents' contention that a situation can arise when an outstanding individual will have the right to rule even without the backing of the community, the consent theorists maintain that he can only have the right to receive this backing, they are asserting something rather than proving it. Or again, when they reject the historical argument that seemingly legitimate rulers have at times lacked such backing, on the flimsy grounds that they must have had it implicitly.[2] Their opponents likewise fire dummy shells. There is little point in rejecting the Consent Theory merely because it sails close to the wind of Rousseauism. Nor can a mortal blow be delivered to it by emphasising the difficulties confronting a 'transference' of power, seeing that such transference is not necessarily an aspect of the theory.[3]

The consent theorists are on their best ground when they press home the argument that society itself is the primary natural subject of authority by reason of the fact that care for the common good pertains to authority only in so far as it represents the community and that society itself, by its nature, gives no indication that any particular individual is more fitted

[1] Cf *Def. Fidei Cath.*, Bk. III, c. 2, nn 10-12.

[2] For a list of such objections and replies see Gonzalez Moral, *op. cit.* pp 552-554.

[3] Cf Meyer, *op. cit.* pp 366-376.

than any other to exercise such authority.[1] Bellarmine[2] and Suarez[3] were careful to stress this consideration. It cannot be denied that authority is an attribute of society; it is a moral fact consequent on the existence of a community. Its only purpose is the good of the community; the community has an exigency for it; without the community it could not exist.

Critics of the Consent Theory, on the other hand, cannot get themselves to forget that the consent of the people to the authority that ruled them is not always conspicuous—to put it mildly—in the pages of history. Their main argument is that the causes which determine the subject of political authority are analogous to those which materially constitute the body social.[4] What they mean by this is that, historically, the formation of States has been due to multiple and diverse situations.[5] It is an organic process in which many factors play their part, some freely chosen, others not. To demand consent as essential to authority would be incongruous, for example, in the case of the kingdoms founded from patriarchal families in the course of sacred history.[6] The same holds for the emergence of rulers among the Romans and barbarians through the transformation into political power of the *auctoritas patrisfamilialis*.[7] It is true too in the case of the political societies which resulted when a number of families came to be ruled by the owner of the lands on which they had settled.[8] And what of the situation in which a community has no alternative to the rule of an outstanding individual or of him who has conquered in a just war?[9] In all such contingencies consent plays no part.[10]

[1] Cf Balmez, *op. cit.* p 242.

[2] Cf Bellarmine, *De Laicis*, c. 6.

[3] Cf Suarez, *Def. Fidei Cath.*, Bk. III, cc. 2-3; *De Legibus*, Bk. III, cc. 3-4.

[4] Cf Meyer, *op. cit.* p 390 *seq*.

[5] Cf Donat, *op. cit.* pp 108-109.

[6] Cathrein, *op. cit.* p 377.

[7] Liberatore, *Ethica et Jus Naturae*, pp 243-245.

[8] Taparelli, *op. cit.* vol. I, c. 9.

[9] Donat, *op. cit.* pp 112-113.

[10] That acceptance of their position by such people is different from

GOVERNMENT FOR THE COMMON   GOOD

In any case, this is not a matter which can be decided merely
by appealing to theorists or even by considering the political
systems that have appeared in Europe.[1] Realism demands that
the net be cast over a much wider area. In this, as in so many
other matters, the mind of the ethician is adequately informed
only if it takes account of the factual findings of anthropology,
particularly relating to primitive peoples. I am not saying that
ethical principles are moulded solely by facts. What I am saying
is that there have been historical periods and peoples which
knew nothing of even the elements of democracy and which
in no way associated legitimate rule with the consent—even
implicit—of the people; that throughout the course of history
there are to be found political regimes that were established,
and continued, on some other basis and which it would be folly
to regard as illegitimate just because of this. Reason demands,
not that each and every government be regarded as legitimate,
but that some other source, or sources, of political authority
be recognised in addition to the consent of the people. The

the 'pact' which the Consent Theory entails is emphasised by Cathrein,
op. cit. p 380.

   [1] I cannot agree that 'science and prudence' demand that discussion
of this question be confined to 'the verifiable history of civilised peoples
—the Republic and Empire of Rome, the Jewish Kingdom, the Frankish
Monarchy, the Holy Roman Empire—in whose constitutional theories
consent and election were included'—O'Rahilly, The Sovereignty of the
People (Studies, March 1921, p 53). It seems to me that no limit should
be placed to the fund of factual knowledge by which the question may
be illuminated. It may be objected that, fundamentally, the problem
is moral and juridical, not historical at all (O'Rahilly, loc. cit. p 53), that
philosophical decision about the origin of political authority has nothing
to do with what did or did not happen in time. The big trouble with this
attitude is that it may be leaving open the possibility that, over a large,
if not the greater, part of human history, political regimes were not
ethically valid because they lacked consent. Some philosophers may be
happy to accept this position; the majority of men will require a more
realistic approach.

Common Good Theory claims to provide just this.

Of course it admits that popular election is a genuine source, as is also even the tacit and reluctant consent of the people. But, as well as these, it says that, in certain circumstances, the fact of possession alone can constitute a ruler in legitimate power. This occurs, for example, if he is exercising control over the community, in some capacity other than political, when the State first comes into being. In this way the patriarchs of old got their authority, quite independently of all consent of the people. They were designated, as it were, by nature to rule. The same holds for those that have exclusive ability to govern. Finally, the Common Good Theory maintains that legitimate political authority can sometimes be acquired by conquest. It has no doubt that this can happen after just conquest, without the consent and even despite the opposition of the people. It maintains too that, under certain circumstances, it can also happen after unjust conquest. Let us examine the way in which it arrives at all this.

The Common Good Theory agrees that, even after a just war, the victor has no right, merely because of his victory, to become the ruler of the vanquished people. But it does declare that he can do this if it is the only way in which just compensation can be extracted. So also if it is required in order to secure the necessities of life for the conquering State and the conquered has superfluity of resources. Or for military reasons of defence, which may entail the annexation of some or all of the former enemy's territory. Sometimes a sufficient cause is also found in the higher civilisation of the conqueror.

Victory in an unjust war can lead to the acquisition of a similar right. It is true that an unlawful act cannot, of itself, ever give rise to rights. The undisturbed enjoyment of his spoils by a thief cannot change him from being an unjust possessor. But an unlawful act can sometimes give rise to facts and circumstances which are not themselves unlawful and out of which rights can arise.[1] For example, in Canon Law the widespread violation of a purely human law can create a contrary custom

[1] Cronin, *The Science of Ethics*, Dublin 1939, vol. II, p 522.

which, in time, can nullify the obligation of the ordinance and even give rise to an opposed one. The original violation is certainly wrong and is never, in itself, the justification for the later change. But it can lead to the gradual appearance of a situation in which the law is honoured more in the breach than in the practice and in which it is no longer an injustice to ignore it. In somewhat the same way, what was originally merely a *de facto* government can in time become legitimate or *de jure*. This does not at all derive formally from the original unjust act which set it up. Rather is it made necessary by contingent facts of which I shall now go on to treat.

A grasp of the nature of this process is vitally important. Failure to understand it would lead one to think that the argument seeks to justify all regimes. The Spanish writer Balmes seems to have been under this misapprehension, for he reasoned in support of the Consent Theory as follows: 'If Napoleon had succeeded in establishing his power amongst us, the Spanish nation would still have maintained the right on account of which it revolted in 1808; victory could not have rendered usurpation legitimate . . . The simple fact does not create a right either in private or in public affairs; and so soon as such a principle is acknowledged, every idea of reason and justice disappears from the world . . . What will be safe here below if we admit the principle that success ensures justice and that the conqueror is always the rightful ruler'?[1] The truth, of course, is that the emergence of a legitimate government after unjust conquest is not simply due to success in the war, but to success *plus* one or another of two important circumstances.

These are 'prescription' and 'consent', each of which has been treated of at length by the theologian Lessius. Prescription never confers a natural title to unjustly acquired property, although natural law urges that the civil law make it a legal title. But it does confer a natural title to political authority, granted the presence of certain conditions. The reason for this, according to the Common Good Theory,[2] is that society

[1] Balmes, *op. cit.*
[2] Cronin, *op. cit.* p 524.

needs a ruler of some kind, unlike material goods which do not necessarily have to be owned. The condition of a people caught between two competing governments is a very difficult one. They are in the unhappy position of being torn by conflicting loyalties. Such is the case after unjust conquest. Now in comparison with the need of the people for sure and stable rule, the claims of competing governments are only of secondary importance. The essential thing is that the welfare of the people be looked after. Hence, the theory goes, if sufficient time has elapsed, an effective *de facto* government that is working for that welfare becomes *de jure*.

This is said to hold even if the usurping government does not find favour with the people and even, in fact, in face of their opposition. It is in their own interests that it should be recognised as legitimate, for it provides them with a definite ruler, something that is badly needed. In addition, there is the fact that, after a certain period of its rule, it is usually harder on the community to lose this government than to retain it. For it will have performed many acts that would be difficult to undo. These include all or some of the following: the building up of a party or body of support in the community, the creation of vested interests, the settlement of property, mercantile transactions, alliances with foreign States involving perhaps financial obligations. There will also be innumerable private contracts that have been made by the citizens on the faith of the government. All these cannot easily be ignored if a change would mean that the obligations entailed by them would be neglected. The natural law tends to give permanence to the system that ensures respect for the rights thus acquired.[1]

The difficulty is to decide how much time must elapse before prescription can operate so as to legitimate a *de facto* government. Writers on the Common Good Theory say that distinctions must be made here. A lot depends on whether the usurped government has lost all or only part of its territory and, in the former case, whether it is still in existence or has disappeared. A longer period is obviously required in the case in which the

[1] Cronin, *op. cit.* pp 528-9.

usurped government continues to exist and hopes to regain
what was seized. It is said too that legitimation of a usurping
government cannot be effected during the lifetime of the original claimants. This applied particularly in the days of widespread monarchy, when the theory received extensive elaboration. But in regard to any government—whether monarchical
or not—the theory holds that legitimation of the usurper is
brought about by prescription once the possibilities of restoring
the usurped government have completely disappeared and the
machinery of its rule has entirely passed away. This is regarded
as never happening for at least two generations. Finally, even
if the pretending government continues to exist and has some
hope of a come-back, it loses its claims after four or five generations. The reason for this is that, after so great a length of time,
the overthrow of the usurper would inflict greater evil than
good on the people.[1]

Consent is also recognised by the Common Good Theory as
a method whereby a *de facto* government can be legitimated.
The consent, that is, either of the people in the usurped territory
or of the usurped government itself. But, as in the case of prescription, it is held that this can happen only in certain conditions. Some say that the consent of the people is sufficient
in any circumstances. The majority, however, say that this is
not so. It would not hold, they maintain, in the case of a
monarchy, while the usurped king is still alive and has hopes
of returning. But they are quick to add that, even in this case,
if his cause is lost and the people are in need of a definite ruler,
their consent can legitimate the *de facto* government. The people
are said to become a kind of residuary legatee of the dethroned
monarch.[2] In a democracy, of course, their consent is clearly
effective at any time.

This consent can be given formally, by fair plebiscite of the

---

[1] Meyer expresses the situation by saying that the usurped government loses its title either when it becomes *physically* impossible to restore its rule or *morally* impossible to do so in view of the disturbance
of order in the community which this would involve. *Op. cit.* p 502.

[2] Cronin, *op. cit.*

people, or by acts which, though not expressive of consent, imply it. The implication in question can in turn be made negatively, i.e. by the people's not protesting when they could and should have done so, or positively, i.e. by their performing acts which tend to consolidate the usurper in power. Examples of such acts would be a general recognition on the part of the people that army and civil service posts could be accepted by them, their taking shares in government loans etc., and their acceptance of the system of local government under the central authority.[1]

A VIA MEDIA

It would seem then that there is a lot to be said in favour of the Common Good Theory of the origin of political authority. On the other hand, there is considerable historical backing for the Consent Theory and it is probably true to say that it is inspired by the general principles of traditional Christian morality, which re-erected the ancient Roman idea, that political power comes from the people, on a new philosophical and theological respect for man. In the Christian tradition, while political power has always been regarded as a necessity, there has also been an unswerving insistence on the fundamental liberty and equality of men.[2] Because of this, we find the idea reiterated that no man has a right to impose his will upon others, unless this is necessary and allowable in the circumstances. Because of this too, many Christian writers, as far back as St. Augustine, speak of a pact between ruler and ruled as being at the origin of civil society and civil authority.[3] From Patristic times until the

---

[1] Cronin, *op. cit.*

[2] E.g. St. Augustine, *De. Civ. Dei.*, xix, 15: 'Rationalem factum ad imaginem suam voluit (Deus hominem) nisi irrationabilibus dominari non hominem homini, sed hominem pecori . . . Prima ergo servitutis causa peccatum est, ut homo homini conditionis vinculo subjiceretur'. Also *De Doctrina Christi*, i; St. Gregory the Great, *Regul. Pastor.*, Part ii, c. 6, i. 21; St. John Chrysostom, *In Rom.*, hom. 23, n 1.

[3] E.g. St. Augustine, *Confess.*, iii, 8: 'Generale quippe pactum est societatis humanae obedire regibus'.

extreme assertion of it in Rousseau's *Social Contract*, the notion of such a pact was a common one.[1] And, though it would be erroneous to think that their duty was regarded as resting exclusively on this, it played an important part in ensuring that rulers would not be tyrannous.

The democratic ideas of the Consent Theory are therefore highly respectable. In one sense too they are practical and realistic. Historians and philosophers throughout the ages have recognised the importance of favourable public opinion for effective rule. 'Sovereigns do not command in an effective and durable way', says de Maistre, 'except in the domain of things approved by opinion, and it is not they that determine this domain'.[2] It was a realisation of this that prompted J. H. Laski, in more modern times, to maintain that absolute sovereignty is only an idea that is not and cannot be realised in practice; the most absolute of rulers are limited by the people in many ways.[3] Even the great absolutist of the past, Machiavelli, had to admit the importance of popular support for effective rule.[4]

For all these reasons, it seems necessary to assign a special place to the consent of the people in connection with the origin of legitimate political authority. An effort to do this has been made by Professor Leclercq. His solution is that, as long as a choice of means is possible and appointment by way of consent is open, this is the only source of legitimate civil power. He assumes further that this is the normal state of affairs and that the circumstances are exceptional which—of necessity—lead to the setting up of a ruler in some other way. In other words, the consent of the people is the 'habitual' or 'normal' title to legitimacy. Any government which ignores this and, without

[1] The difference between the Roussellian and Christian notions of the pact is that whereas for the latter authority derives to the ruler in virtue of divine and natural law, for the former however it stems from a purely voluntary arrangement and is transferred in virtue of an entirely arbitrary human convention. *Non est opus naturae sed artis.* Cf Cathrein, *op. cit.* pp 373-374; Meyer, *op. cit.* pp 361-362.

[2] J. de Maistre, *Soirées de Saint-Petersbourg*, 7.

[3] Cf Harold Laski, *A Grammar of Politics*, London 1934.

[4] Machiavelli, *The Prince*, ch xx.

necessity, imposes itself on a people against their will, is not legitimate, even if it governs well. And it remains so as long as it is possible to substitute a government in its place that is in conformity with popular desires.[1] But he adds that governments that conduct affairs in a way that is detrimental to the common good cannot be legitimated, no matter how great their popularity.

The cases of necessity, which suspend consent, are of interest to us. Leclercq has provided an example. If, by reason of the circumstances, it should happen that there is, in a country, only one man who is capable of exercising civil authority in the way which the common good demands, such a man has the right to exercise it and the people have the duty to acknowledge him. If they refuse to do so, he has the right—and indeed the duty —to impose his rule upon them by force. His title springs from the circumstances rather than from his own will, for the community needs to be governed competently.[2]

It is Leclercq's view that, in virtue of this, the assumption of power by Napoleon might be justified. We might recall too the case of the patriarchs to whom I have already referred. In modern times a very interesting example of a claim to rule on this basis was that put forward by General de Gaulle during World War II. In the first volume of his memoirs, *A Call to Honour*, he describes how, after his escape to England following the fall of France in 1940, he refused to acknowledge defeat or to recognise the Petain regime, which he regarded as merely a puppet government, and which sentenced him to death as a traitor for proclaiming himself to be the incarnation of France, 'the inflexible champion of the nation', who sought to build up a Free Fighting France and to rally all Frenchmen everywhere around him.[3] In the second instalment, *Unity: War Memoirs*,[4] he gives the reasons for which he believed in these actions, which, as the war drew to a close, tended to exasperate the

---

[1] Leclercq, *op. cit.* vol. II, pp 176-177.

[2] Leclercq, *op. cit.* vol. II, p 174.

[3] Charles de Gaulle, *A Call to Honour*, London 1955.

[4] Charles de Gaulle, *Unity: War Memoirs*, London 1959.

Allies, because of the claims, in the name of France, which they led him to make. If he had not taken the course which he did, he says, France 'would pass into a permanent coma; from a slavery imposed by her enemies she would decline into a subordination enforced by her allies . . . (The) future could be safeguarded on condition that France, at the end of the drama, was a belligerent re-united by a commitment to a single authority . . . Against the enemy, despite the Allies, regardless of terrible dissentions, I would have to centre round myself the unity of lacerated France.'[1] France became for him 'de Gaulle-France'.

He was not thinking of philosophic justification. He saw himself as France's 'Man of Destiny'. When, in 1942, Churchill, infuriated by his mysticism, shouted at him: 'You claim to be France! You are not France! I do not recognise you as France! France! Where is France now?' his attitude was, as later, when he replied to Churchill: 'I can understand your fears. But you will easily overcome them if your conscience is clear'. 'My conscience', growled Churchill, 'is a good girl. I can always come to terms with her'. One reviewer of the memoirs remarked that it might be speculated whether de Gaulle's infallibility left room for a conscience. Be this as it may, as de Gaulle saw things: 'A call to honour from the depths of history, as well as the instinct of the nation itself, had led me to bear responsibility for the treasure in default of heirs: to assume French sovereignty. It was I who held the legitimate power. It was in its name that I could call the nation to war and to unity, impose order, law and justice, demand from the world respect for the rights of France'.[2] Philosophical justification for this action—along the lines indicated by Professor Leclercq—was offered later by Leon Blum.[3]

History provides us with other examples of similar actions; France is by no means alone in providing de Gaulles. Realism forces us to recognise the fact that political power must some-

[1] *Op. cit.* pp 7-8.

[2] *Op. cit.* p 322.

[3] Leon Blum, *Discours aux secretaires generaux du parti Socialiste*, May 1945.

times be exercised under conditions in which popular support for it is impossible. After legitimate conquest, in particular, this is frequently the case. In short, while the Christian tradition will have us assert that the *normal* source of legitimate political authority is the consent of the people, cases of necessity can and do arise in which—in the interests of the common good—a legitimate title is otherwise forthcoming. The trouble with the defenders of the Common Good Theory, Leclercq points out, is that they give the impression of regarding such cases of necessity—caused by violence etc.—as of quite frequent occurrence, whereas in fact they will always remain exceptional. Still, we must be grateful to them for their realism in recognising the possibility of such circumstances and for providing a theory of the origin of political authority that takes account of them.

The dominating consideration is the welfare of the community. Perhaps the weakest link in the Consent Theory is its inability to show that the welfare of the State necessarily and universally demands that authority be derived from the consent of the people. Vice versa the strength of the Common Good Theory—whence its name—consists in showing that this welfare demands the recognition of other sources. And whenever welfare depends upon a consensual basis of authority, the Common Good Theory gives it practical recognition. Thus, in a sense, the truth lies with neither theory in isolation but with both taken together and subject to qualification.

An example of their interconnection that is relevant to contemporary politics is provided by the acquisition and loss of authority by colonial governments. It would be senseless to maintain that a savage or semi-savage people should have the right to prevent a civilised power from ruling over them legitimately by not according it their consent to do so. In such circumstances the welfare of the people would be hindered rather than promoted by attempts to govern themselves. But under the just rule of another it is only to be expected that the people will eventually develop a mature political consciousness and acquire sufficient capacity to govern themselves with some competence. When this happens and the people wish to exercise it, their right to do so must be regarded as prevailing. The welfare of the people will again be at stake. For even when the alien rule is capable of giving a more efficient government, as far as the technique of legislation and administration goes, this advantage will usually be more than neutralised by reason of the unrest which results from lack of popular consent and co-operation. In such a case, a technically less efficient government that has the backing of the people may well be more efficient in terms of human welfare. For this reason it might be said that a politically conscious and moderately capable community has always the right to make its consent a necessary condition of political rule—provided it be added that it is in a position to do so.[1]

The difficult question is to decide exactly when a people is fit to choose its government so that its consent is a condition of legitimate authority over it. It has rightly been said that there exists a wide 'twilight zone' in which it is difficult, if not impossible, to decide.[2] We can agree with the suggestion that, if a people has already had some experience of self-government, this will create a strong presumption in its favour. We can agree too that it should be given the benefit of the doubt where doubt exists. Even when already ruled by an efficient government of its own choosing, such a people is entitled to change it later if it so wishes. It used to be maintained that the people had no such right, that if ruled adequately by a monarchy, for example, it could not depose this merely in the interests of having a republic.[3] The principle of 'the welfare of the State', however, suggests that it can—provided, of course, that there is question of the true and genuine welfare of the State.[4] For the question boils down to retaining a good government with which the people have become dissatisfied or introducing a better one which will have their support. If the majority of the people want this and are seriously determined in their wishes, nothing but

[1] Ryan and Boland, *Catholic Principles of Politics*, New York 1941, p 89.

[2] Ryan and Boland, *op. cit.* p. 90.

[3] Cronin, *op. cit.* vol. I, p 533. This view was defended by Bellarmine (*Disputationes*, I, 229), Suarez (*De Legibus*, III, ch. 4) and Molina (*De Jure et Justitia*, D. 22, nn. 8-10).

[4] Ryan and Boland, *op. cit.* p 92.

ill to the State can come of denying them the right to have it. It is silly to think that all future generations must be bound by the action of the first generation that sets up a hereditary monarchy. In this respect Suarez was mistaken in thinking that when the people have once conferred authority they cannot recall it unless it is being positively abused.[1] Whenever the welfare of the State comes to depend substantially on popular acceptance of the government, then, in order to be legitimate, a government needs to have this consent if the circumstances are such that it can be freely given. For which reason a people can change from a monarchy to a republic when it wishes, whether or not the monarchy was originally established with its consent. Governing authority is fiduciary, not proprietary; it should be manipulated according to the exigencies of the common good.

But what *can* be done in practice is an entirely different story and frequently changes the situation very radically. After conquest, for example, whether just or unjust, the consent of the people usually cannot be had. In such circumstances nothing short of successful revolt can replace the usurping government with one of the people's own choice. When this is the case it would in turn be silly to demand consent as a necessary prerequisite for legitimate government. Rather must the welfare of the State be consulted. If the usurper has been in long possession and is ruling justly then, as we have earlier explained, the common good is often better served by allowing him to remain than by revolting against him.[2]

Our position then as regards the age-old problem of the origin of political authority is a kind of *via media* between the traditional theories. While it refuses to base this authority exclusively on the consent of the people, it is keenly conscious that the purpose of authority is the people's welfare. It is Maritain who has drawn attention to the overtones in St.

[1] *Def. Fid. Cath.*, III, 3, 3.
[2] Concerning the Consent Theory our position resembles that of Hergenrother who writes: "The theory fails, however, when it is carried too far. It must not be used as a universal rule to be applied always and in all cases"—*op. cit.*, p 244.

Thomas's reference to the ruler as the 'vicar of the multitude'.[1] It means that his authority is the very authority of the people themselves, participated in to a known extent and within certain limits. For although authority does not inhere in the community as its proper subject, it pertains to the community in that it is something that is required for social stability. It is therefore an authority which must be exercised in the true interests of the people, even if doing this incurs their displeasure. In so far as possible, of course, it should fulfil its obligations in communion with the people, united with rather than separated from them. There are times, however, when a rift is unavoidable and when the real welfare of the people demands that their ruler follow a course that may be highly unpopular.

He does not lose his authority merely by reason of becoming unpopular. He may continue to hold it even by force if his rule is just and necessary in the circumstances. For it is not an authority which derives to him from the people as from a source of authority, even secondary under God. For the same reason, in certain circumstances, a ruler can acquire authority in the first instance by ways and means that are other than the consent of the community.

[1] J. Maritain, *Man and the State*, London 1954, pp 121-125.

CHAPTER TWO

MODERN WAR AND PACIFISM

THE Catholic teaching on war has received its most recent statement from the Archbishops and Bishops of Ireland. In January,
1956 they issued a letter on the subject, the opening paragraphs
of which ran as follows:

'Catholic moral teaching lays down precise conditions in
order that war be at all lawful. War is the cause of very great
evils, physical, moral and social. It is not lawful unless it be
declared and waged by the supreme authority of the State. No
private citizen has the right to bear arms or to use them against
another state, its soldiers or its citizens. Just as no private
citizen has the right to inflict capital punishment, so he has not
the right to wage war. Sacred Scripture gives the right to bear
the sword and to use it against evil-doers to the supreme authority and to it alone. If individuals could arrogate to themselves
the right to use military force there would be disorder and chaos
leading inevitably to tyranny and oppression.

'The second condition for a lawful war is that there be a
just cause. It must be certain that all peaceful means have been
tried and found unavailing, that the matter at issue far outweighs the havoc that war brings and that it is reasonably
certain that war will not make things worse. No private individual has authority to judge these issues, or to involve the
people from whom he has received no mandate in the serious
losses inevitable in hostilities'.[1]

Strictly speaking, by 'war' is understood the attempt by

[1] Cf *Catholic Documentation*, vol. I (1956), n 4, p 46.

one sovereign State to impose its will upon another sovereign State by using armed force. Commonly, however, the term is also used to cover armed attacks on a State by outside groups, armed violence between party political interests in the same State and armed insurrection or revolt against an established government. In other words, it covers the total range of the use of armed force for political purposes. Any such act is an act of war.

WAR IN TRADITIONAL TEACHING

The Irish bishops have stated the traditional conditions which must be fulfilled before war can be lawful. Although they have dealt with the matter succinctly in two paragraphs, their exposition includes no fewer than five conditions, which are normally treated separately by theologians. In addition to the conditions that war be declared by lawful authority and for a just cause, these are that all possible peaceful means must first have been tried, that there be due proportion between the good hoped for and the evil that will ensue, and that there be a reasonable hope of success. It is usual for theologians to add two further conditions, viz. that the war be waged with a right intention and that only lawful methods be employed in its prosecution. A little reflection shows, however, that these are unnecessary. The latter refers to the conduct of the war rather than to the morality of its inception, while the former relates to subjective rather than to objective morality.

In his treatment of the subject, just prior to World War II, Fr. Gerald Vann sought to link the condition regarding intention with the objective morality of war. In his view a right intention meant that war should be undertaken only to 'promote good and avoid evil for the world as a whole'.[1] It is hard to see how this is saying anything more than that there should be due proportion between the evil which war entails and the good which it hopes to achieve. The famous French writer on the morality of war, A. Vanderpol, has offered a different inter-

---

[1] Gerald Vann O.P., *Morality and War*, London 1939, p 35.

pretation of the meaning of 'right intention'.[1] It is that war be not undertaken if satisfaction for injury is otherwise forthcoming and if there is no adequate reason why it should not be accepted. Here again, however, one is forced to think that no more is being said than has already been covered by the condition that war should be a last resort. M. Vanderpol adds as further explanation of intention the idea that war should not be pursued for its own sake. But again we are no further informed by this than we already are by the condition which demands a just cause. There seems no adequate reason, therefore, why the conditions for an objectively lawful war should necessarily include reference to a right intention.

The Catholic teaching on war—at least in its general outlines—can be traced as far back as St. Augustine. It was further developed by St. Thomas, Vittoria and Suarez and represents a consistent if evolving tradition.

The first condition is that, in order to be moral, war must be waged by the decision of lawfully constituted authority. In the past this has normally been the government of the country immediately concerned either with initiating hostilities or repelling attack. Throughout history, however, there has been a continuous search for a supra-national authority that could be called upon to establish justice in international disputes. Time was when the Papacy was arbiter in the matter, Pope Leo XIII acting in this capacity less than a century ago in the dispute between Germany and Spain over the Caroline Islands.[2] After World War I the League of Nations sought to arrogate to itself the right of deciding when war might legitimately be waged. In 1931 a Theological Conventus at Fribourg was of the opinion that the League had already reached such a stage of development that war on private State authority was no longer lawful.[3]

[1] A. Vanderpol, *La Guerre devant le christianisme*, Paris 1911, p 117.
[2] Cf P. Sauvage, *L'Église est-elle pour ou contre la guerre?* Paris 1936, pp 26-33; J. Eppstein, *The Catholic Tradition of the Law of Nations*, London 1935, pp 463-474.
[3] 'Although international society does not yet enjoy the full authority which it might well possess, both from the very nature of things and from the consent of men, yet it is clear that it has now been devel-

We know of the failure of the League to live up to these expectations and by 1938 at least one theologian had expressed the
opinion that it was doubtful whether the contractual obligations arising from membership of the League still bound those
nations who remained members.[1] The suggestion was that, in
defect of an efficient instrument of international justice, the
right to make war on its own exclusive authority had reverted
to the supreme authority in the individual State.

The question has primary relevance to the initiation of
hostilities rather than to resistance by a State if actually attacked. For even the presence of an effective international authority does not annul the right of any State to defend itself as
best it can against aggression. Nothing can take away its right
of defending itself against unjust attack. The initiation of war
—for whatsoever reason—is a different matter altogether, particularly granted the existence of adequate international organisation. In this respect the United Nations has sought to take up
where the League abandoned the problem of a world authority.
Its Charter has gone so far as to ban the term 'war' from political vocabulary, all 'war' or 'threat or use of force' being prohibited. Only United Nations 'enforcement action' is allowed
in the settlement of international disputes, as well as individual
or collective defence against armed aggression that has actually
been launched on a State or its allies.[2] Still, at its present stage
of development, one must have certain reservations about the
ability of the United Nations Organisation to dispose exclusively of armed force in imposing international justice. The

oped into a form of positive law in such a way that it is consolidated by
many juridical and political instruments, which are designated to establish human order and peace. Because of this a war declared by a state
on its own authority without previous recourse to the international
institutions which exist cannot be a lawful social process'.—Eppstein,
op. cit. p 140.

[1] Jeremiah O'Sullivan, *The Theology of Modern War*, Dissertation
presented to the Faculty of Theology, St. Patrick's College, Maynooth
1941.

[2] Cf James Hogan, The New Dimensions of War and Peace, in
Philosophical Studies, vol. x (1960), p 165.

politically effective organisations are still primarily the nation States and there is no functional political body that can claim with reason to have reached that degree of independent supranationality that would warrant its being accorded an exclusive right in the matter of using armed force in international disputes. The United Nations, as yet, is certainly limited in this respect. The Secretary General in his report to the 1958 Assembly gave clear expression to the fact that it could serve only as a permanent framework for multilateral diplomacy.[1] Despite recent events, it does not seem that it can yet lay claim to being the only legitimate source of decision as regards the use of force in international disputes.

Indeed it is very difficult to deprive the individual State altogether of the right to decide for itself whether to use force in support of its claims. One cannot disregard the possibility that a State might reasonably refuse to abide by the arbitration of even the highest international authority. What is certain is that, until the definitive emergence of a competent world authority, the individual State cannot be totally deprived of the right to go to war. Even today the teaching of Suarez on the point has force: 'Just as lawful authority for punishing crimes is necessary in order that peace may be preserved inside a State, so also in order that several States may live in peace, it is necessary that there be in the world an authority to punish the injuries done by one to another. This power does not reside in a superior, since the several States have none . . . Therefore it must reside in the supreme ruler of the injured State, to whom the other ruler becomes subject by reason of his crime. Hence a war of this sort takes the place of a just vindicative judgment'.[2] But Suarez clearly implies that the advent of an effective international authority would limit the right of the State in this respect.

The undertaking of war is not a matter for private individuals or groups within the State as long as legitimate authority is available to make the decision. As we shall see later, such

[1] Cf Wm. H. Robert, The International Political Common Good, in *World Justice*, vol. II (1960), n 2.

[2] Suarez, De Bello, in *Opera*, vol. XII, Paris 1868, disp. XIII.

private elements have no right to object to a lawful war; they have even less right to engage in war on their own authority. And this holds, it is important to remember, even if they have the majority of the people behind them. The reason for this is that it is the government that is given the special right and duty of catering for the political common good.

Writers in political philosophy sometimes discuss the question of whether the government should consult its citizens before going to war. It was a practical issue in the United States before Pearl Harbour.[1] It is generally agreed that this should not be done.[2] It is felt that the people might sometimes rush rashly into war, yielding to emotion and without sufficient knowledge of military matters. Then too, if this were to be done, why should the people not be consulted on all important questions of foreign policy? In any case, such a procedure would rob government of all real power. No—the lawful government alone must have the right of deciding—in default of other authority—when a State shall or shall not engage in war.[3]

[1] Cf Raymond de Martini, *The Right of Nations to Expand by Conquest*, Washington 1955.

[2] The idea of consulting the people has been championed by John K. Ryan, *Modern War and Basic Ethics*, Milwaukee 1940, pp 56-57. He regards this as implied in the Pastoral Letter of the American Hierarchy in 1919, which suggested that 'the calm and deliberate judgment of the people, rather than the aims of the ambitious few, shall decide whether, in case of international disagreement, war be the only solution. Knowing that the burdens of war will fall most heavily on them, the people will be slower in taking aggressive measures . . . '. Fr. John Courtney Murray takes the stronger view that 'as a moral problem in the use of force, war is not simply, or even primarily ,a problem for the generals, the state department, the technologists, the international lawyers. Here, if anywhere, 'the People shall judge'. This is their responsibility . . . My impression is that this duty in social morality is being badly neglected in America at the moment'—Theology and Modern War, in Wm. J. Nagle, *Morality and Modern Warfare*, Baltimore 1960, p 76, n 5.

[3] The mistaken nature of the following argumentation should be clear from what has been said on the question of who can lawfully decide to engage in war: On the supposition that British rule in Northern Ireland is unjustified, 'all Irishmen must, in pursuance of the virtue and

The second condition for a lawful war is that it be declared for a clearly just cause. The 'cause' in question can be reduced to 'defence against injury'; a war of pure aggression can never be lawful. This is the teaching of, amongst others, Vittoria and Grotius[1] and it was accepted earlier by St. Thomas Aquinas without comment.[2] St. Augustine taught that there were three instances of the just cause: defence, indemnity and punishment. The first of these means defence against 'injury threatening', the second and third defence in relation to 'injury sustained', i.e. the effort to make it good.

Defence against injury threatening the State is justified, says Grotius, in the same way as is self-defence by the individual.[3] A State can attack another in order to prevent it. The danger in question must, however, be immediate and there must at least be moral certainty of its presence. Despite a contrary opinion held by some writers during the 17th century, probabilism cannot be employed in this connection. As will readily be realised, the ascertaining of the immediacy of such danger is made singularly difficult at the present day owing to the rapidity with which modern striking power can be mobilised. It is a problem which troubles the greater nations of the world, or at least those that have not lost all moral sensibility.

As in the case of the individual, it is also lawful for the State to defend itself by seeking to undo injury already suffered. This includes the repulsing of an unjust attack, for this is indeed a very grave injury. It includes too the effort to right past wrongs by seeking to regain, for example, territory that is unjustly held by another state.

duty of patriotism, strive to overthrow British rule in Ireland. It is the Dublin Government's bounden duty under the moral law to conduct and lead the struggle: if they refuse or neglect to do so, they lose their governmental authority because they have defaulted in the primary function of government, i.e. the protection of the national territory from outside aggression'—Ciaran Mac an Fhaili, Partition and Force: A Republican Viewpoint, in *Hibernia*, March 1957.

[1] Vittoria, *De Jure Belli*, n 424; Grotius, *De Jure Belli ac Pacis*, Bk. 2, ch I, sec. 3.

[2] *2a 2ae*, Q. 40 art. 1.

[3] Grotius, *loc. cit.*

Since World War II a growing number of moralists has tended to deny altogether the liceity of the use of armed force as a means of settling international disagreements. Earlier ages, of course, also had their pacifists, but they were few in number and, by and large, rather isolated. Among them were Erasmus and the Anabaptists. It was to the Anabaptists that Bellarmine made his famous reply: 'We however, teach what the whole Church has always taught by word and example, that war is not by its very nature unlawful for Christians, as long as the conditions . . . are fulfilled'.[1]

PACIFISM IN THE CHRISTIAN TRADITION

Not all pacifists adopt precisely the same attitude.[2] Some are opposed to war of every kind, on the grounds that the Gospel and early Christian tradition have outlawed the use of armed force. Theirs is essentially the position of the *simpliste*, who fixes his attention on one aspect only of a problem and treats it as if it were the whole. The pacifist who concentrates on Christ's command to Peter to put up his sword (*Matt.* 26, 52) is quite forgetful that it was Christ who also commanded that he who has no sword should sell his coat to buy one (*Luke* 22, 36). The extreme pacifist is just as exaggerated in his interpretation of the Christian tradition as is the warmonger who says it is enough for him that St. Augustine held that war is justified, ignoring the fact that what was war for St. Augustine is not necessarily war for men today.[3] The truth is that the Christian teaching on war is very *nuancé;* while retaining always its con-

---

[1] Bellarmine, *De Laicis*, Bk. 3, ch 14.

[2] For an exposition and examination of the different varieties of pacifism see Max Scheler, *L'idée de paix et le pacifisme*, Paris 1953; also J. Folliet, A Dissection of Pacifism, in *World Justice*, vol. II (1960), n 2.

[3] The romantic notion that 'war is divine because it is a law of the world' is frequently attributed to Joseph de Maistre, *Soirées de Saint Petersbourg*, VII. A. Vanderpol, however, says that this is a mistake. The idea occurs in the seventh section of the *Soirées*, in which it is not de Maistre who speaks but somebody who is referred to as 'the Senator'. De Maistre was usually called 'the Count' in the *Soirées*. Cf Vanderpol, *op. cit.*

sistency, it shows a delicacy of appreciation of fact that causes it to modify periodically its statement of principle.

Too much should not be made of the fact that the very early Christians were opposed to military service and war.[1] Although the Jews, as a people, were not pacifist, they were nationalist and anti-Roman and the majority of Christians in the first century were Jews. As such they would be unlikely to serve in the army. In the second century, of course, Christians were more widespread in the Empire, yet we still find a notable absence of Christian soldiers. But this in itself can scarcely serve as a basis for argument. At this period we have little positive evidence either for the existence of Christian artisans or doctors. Then too by now Christianity had become centred in the cities, which would help to explain why so few Christians appear to have entered the army, as the legions were largely recruited in the frontier territories where they were usually based. The most important reason for the reluctance of Christians to join the army, however, was undoubtedly its practice of Emperor worship. Officers were compelled to offer sacrifice to the Emperor, while ordinary ranks had to assist at the ceremony. These provisions were not always carried out and at the end of the second century there is evidence that there were many Christian soldiers.[2] They could justify their action—if justification were necessary—by appeal to the writings of the earliest Fathers. Clement of Rome[3] and Ignatius of Antioch[4] had spoken highly of the soldier's calling. And during the defensive period of the Empire, from 170 to 260 A.D., Christians flocked to the standards of Rome.

It was during this period that a form of doctrinal pacifism first emerged. Around 202 A.D. Tertullian in his *De Idololatria* left no doubt about his condemnation of military service.[5]

---

[1] Cf Edward A. Ryan, The Rejection of Military Service by the Early Christians, in *Theological Studies*, vol. xii (1952), pp 1-32.

[2] Cf Letter of Marcus Aurelius appended to the first *Apologia* of St. Justin Martyr, in Migne, *Pat. Graec.*, vol. 6, cc. 435-440.

[3] *Epist. I ad Corinthios*, c. 37. Funk, *Patres Apostolici*, vol. i, p 147.

[4] *Epist. ad Polycarpum*, VI, 2. Funk, *op. cit.* p 293.

[5] *De Idololatria*, c. 19. C.S.E.L., xx, 53.

Origen in his Commentary on I Corinthians[1] did likewise, as also did the *Apostolic Tradition* of Hippolytus.[2] But on closer scrutiny it becomes clear that what these were opposing was not the profession of arms in itself so much as the danger of idolatry to which service in the army exposed the contemporary Christian. The very title of Tertullian's work is indicative of this; his later reaffirmation of the same views in his *De Corona*[3] was coloured by the Puritanism and rigorism of the Montanist heresy which by then he had come to adopt. In his early writings, such as the *Apologeticum*,[4] he had shown an attachment to the Empire and an acceptance of the army as an institution. For Origen it is clearly the danger of idolatry that is in mind, for 'idolatry is the sin of the army.'[5] In his *Contra Celsum*, written in old age, he is more disposed to tackle the problem of military service as a specific question relating to the moral use of armed force. For the first time he introduces here the distinction between just and unjust war, saying that 'it is lawful to fight in a just cause' and that Christians should pray for its success.[6] There were some Fathers who never had doubts about the legitimate nature of the soldier's profession. Amongst these, as well as those already mentioned, was Clement of Alexandria.[7]

If there was widespread pacifism in the early Church, leading to trouble with the State, it was due to the influence of the writings of people like Tertullian and Origen.[8] And it was lar-

---

[1] For the commentary on *I Corinthians* see *Journal of Theological Studies*, vol. IX (1907-8), pp 366-99.

[2] Cf *Constitutiones Eccl. Aegyptiacae*. Trans. in *C.S.E.L.*, XI. Text in Funk, *Didaschalia et Constitutiones Apostolorum*, Paderborn 1905, vol. II, pp 97-119.

[3] *De Corona*, II, in *Corpus Christianorum, Series Latina, Tertulliani Opera*, vol. II, pp 1041-2.

[4] *Apologeticum*, 30. Funk, *Didaschalia*, vol. I, pp 141-142.

[5] Origen, *loc. cit.*

[6] *Contra Celsum*, VIII, 73. Migne, *Pat. Graec.*, vol. II, cc. 1626-7.

[7] Cited by Eppstein, *op. cit.* p 40.

[8] These writers were opposed also in principle to *Christians* taking part in bloodshed, but not seemingly to warfare on the part of non-Christians.

gely a matter of protecting the Christian soldier's faith rather than a conviction about the immorality of the use of armed force. I find it hard to agree that 'Christian thought for a time hovered in a half-way house, possible only in a non-Christian State of which Christians formed but a small part and for whose public conduct they seemed to have no responsibility.'[1] On the whole they regarded war as justifiable; their apparent strictures on it were directed primarily at other factors. After the conversion of Constantine there was no longer need for fear on this score and we find the Church for the first time, at the Council of Arles (314 A.D.), giving positive approbation to military service. The excommunication of deserters shows that she regarded the just war as an enterprise which citizens can have a duty to further. In the light of this it is scarcely true to say that the early Christian tradition regarded a Gandhian-type of non-violence as an ideal.[2] Nor is it true to say that 'we must voluntarily, as a *counsel* . . . renounce all violence in the spirit of martyrdom.'[3]

CONTEMPORARY PACIFISM

Contemporary pacifism in general is of a different calibre. It has no difficulty in admitting the traditional teaching on the conditions for a just war, but insists that they can no longer be fulfilled in the modern world. It has been elaborating its position and seeking authoritative backing for over forty years. Early after World War I, Cardinal Faulhaber of Munich spoke on the need for new thinking on the subject of war. Soon after was founded the *Friedensbund Deutscher Katholiken*, a Catholic peace association for the promotion of pacifist views. Then, in 1929, the German Dominican, Fr. Stratmann, declared that war is something to be morally outlawed.[4] These views seemed

[1] Eppstein, *op. cit.* p 31.

[2] Cf Dom Bede Griffiths O.S.B., The Ideal of Non-Violence, in *Morals and Missiles*, London 1959, pp 69-76.

[3] C. Mac an Fhaili, From Arrows to Atoms: the Morality of War, in *Doctrine and Life*, vol. 9 (1959), p 82.

[4] F. Stratmann, *The Church and War*, London 1928.

to be supported by Cardinal Ottaviani in the third edition of his authoritative textbook of Public Ecclesiastical Law, published in Rome in 1947. Paragraph 86 in volume I of Ottaviani's work is headed 'War is to be altogether forbidden'. The reason given is that the conditions for its liceity are never fully verified at the present day.[1] The 'total character' of modern war prevents them from being realised in practice; a 'limited war' seems to be regarded only as a theoretical possibility.

The pacifists derived courage from this and became more and more emphatic about the immorality of modern war. The traditional conditions, they explained, had been hammered out to meet the problem of the use of armed force in general; they dealt specifically with war only in the wide sense of the word and cannot at all be used to justify war as it is known today. They are all agreed that nuclear war, in any form, is immoral; non-nuclear but total conventional war is similarly classified. In practice the attitude adopted by pacifists is that all war what-soever is unlawful. Because of the danger today of 'chain re-action' and 'push-button warfare', to engage even in limited war is regarded as courting nuclear disaster. For practical pur-poses therefore, irrespective of theoretical distinctions, pacifism tends logically towards complete non-violence at least in the sphere of international relations. To distinguish in practice be-tween the different kinds of pacifism is to be guilty of loose thinking rather than its opposite.

The frankest of the pacifists themselves have no hesitation in proclaiming that war of any kind is morally unlawful. This was the thesis of a book by a French Jesuit, which appeared

---

[1] 'The conditions which theoretically make it (war) justified and permissible are never present . . . There is no reason so weighty as to be commensurate with so many evils, so much slaughter and destruction, such denial of religious and moral values . . . In practice, therefore, it is no longer permissible to declare war; not even a defensive war is to be waged unless the lawful authority responsible for the decision is sure of victory, and even more certain that the good accruing to the nation from a defensive war outweighs the monstrous evils which will result both for this nation and for the world'—Card. Ottaviani, *Institutiones Juris Publici Ecclesiastici*, vol. I, 3rd ed., Rome 1947.

in 1948,[1] while in 1956 *Actualité Religieuse dans le Monde* carried a comprehensive account of a similar contention made at a symposium on non-violence at the Institut Catholique by the French section of the Pax Christi movement. In addition, due to the dependence of modern war on universal military conscription, conscientious objection has come to be defended as a moral right. This aspect of the matter has been taken up particularly by the American newspaper *The Catholic Worker*, under the influence of Peter Maurin and Dorothy Day. In Europe the most effective exponent of the pacifist position is Fr. Stratmann whose thought on the subject has become progressively hardened. Throughout his lifetime successive technical developments at the service of war have convinced him of its inhuman and unchristian character. If in 1918 he was writing that 'the whole character of war is changed since the advent of the machine gun', so that a just war was 'almost an impossibility',[2] it is only to be expected that he should rule it out altogether now that 'a new difficulty presents itself in that the modern form of defence is atomic'.[3] Faced with this fact there is room only for pacifism.

It is Fr. Stratmann's contention that a review of Christian teaching on the subject of war over the course of history shows a progressive accommodation to its employment.[4] Assuming that the early Church held for a 'clear rejection of war', he opines that international violence first became baptised, as it were, when the sword was used at the service of faith during the Crusades. Since the 16th century a further decline is evident, war coming to be permitted in the pursuit of national claims even where the moral guilt of the attacked was entirely absent. There has, in fact, been a 'steadily descending curve' in moral teaching; 'the point has been reached where it must rise again' through the rejection of war by the Christian conscience. In his

---

[1] Pierre Lorson S.J., *La symphonie pacifique*, Strasbourg 1948. Cf also Daniel Parker, *Refus de la guerre*.

[2] F. Stratmann, *The Church and War*, p 38.

[3] F. Stratmann, War and Christian Conscience, in *Morals and Missiles*, p 34.

[4] *Loc. cit.* p 29.

most recent book, *War and Christianity Today*,[1] Fr. Stratmann took it that the pacifist position was invulnerable, due particularly to what he regarded as the testimony of Cardinal Ottaviani. Referring back to the early pacifist moves between the wars, he declared that the mentality which they represented was the right one. 'Against wide contrary publicity, and despite the aloofness of many, even Catholics, we of the German Catholic Peace Association were saying in words and in writing what today finally appears as correct'. He went on to insist on the Church's duty to work for peace and almost went so far as to say that the Pope himself should authoritatively condemn war utterly.[2]

The pacifist renunciation of war is understandable once its modern context is fully appreciated. There can be no doubt that, for the past fifty years, war has tended—almost of its very nature—to overstep the bounds of morality. The condition of proportionality has been all but lost amid the chaos wrought by modern weapons of destruction. The principle that non-combatants and their property should not be direct objects of attack was early abandoned during World War I. Long-range bombardment, aerial bombing and undersea warfare came to be employed with an alarming neglect of discrimination. So much so indeed that it is true to say that, in the 20th century, to fight means to fight with means that are intrinsically dis-

---

[1] London 1956.

[2] 'What can the Pope do himself in practice? We known how he continuously applies his great diplomatic skill to ease threatening political tensions, how he contends with God and the devil and humanity to exorcise the apocalyptic catastrophe of a third World War. Can't he do still more? 'War is to be altogether forbidden', says Cardinal Ottaviani, the canonist who is in high respect at the Vatican. Who is to forbid war he does not say. As is well known, numerous people, Catholic and non-Catholic, are of the opinion that in a certain situation and considering the urgency threatening mankind, the Pope could declare against total war, that overthrows everything. Several international peace organisations have sent petitions along this line to Pope Pius XII'. Stratmann, *War and Christianity Today*, p 18.

proportionate by the standards of previous centuries.[1] Nor has international agreement to aught else been forthcoming. There has been no serious effort and certainly no successful one to regulate the means to be used in war. On the contrary, international statesmen have come to accept the proposition that non-combatants can no longer be inviolable.

In face of this it is also understandable that the question should be asked whether Christians might not change their attitude to war. It is only natural that a process of heart-searching should take place to see whether the traditional principles are adequate any longer. Hence the appeal to history by Fr. Stratmann in an effort to show that the teaching on war needs revision. His interpretation leaves much to be desired. While it is true that, during the course of history, the teaching on war underwent change, this was always of a progressive nature in accordance with the changing pattern of war and is such as will allow us today, when confronted with a further new situation, to introduce additional qualification into the moral principles involved. We have already dealt with the attitude to war of the early Church and have seen it to be something quite other than a 'clear rejection'. Nor is it true to say that full acceptance of it came only with the Crusades. St. Augustine has a well-rounded body of teaching on the just war, to the basic elements of which we have already referred. It was taken up and developed by writers like Isidore of Seville, Gratian and Yves de Chartres.[2]

---

[1] Wm. V. O'Brien, Nuclear Warfare and the Law of Nations, in Nagle, *op. cit.* p 137.

[2] Cf Yves de la Brière, *Les étapes de la tradition théologique concernant le droit de juste guerre*, in *Revue Générale de Droit International Public*, March-April 1937; also A. Vanderpol, *Le droit de guerre d'après les théologiens et les canonistes du moyen âge*, Paris 1911, reissued in 1919, together with Vanderpol's other work mentioned in note 3, under the title of *La doctrine scolastique du droit de guerre*. Cf also John K. Ryan, *op. cit.* The first systematic treatise on the morality of war seems to have been that of Johannes de Lignano, *Tractatus de Bello* (1365). Next came Johannes Lupus, *De Bello et bellatoribus* (1496) and later Franciscus Arias, *De Bello et eius iustitia* (1533), Martinus Gariatus, *De Bello*,

The most interesting feature of this development is how the
principles gradually evolved from a simple to a complex fabric.
They did so as the pattern of war itself changed. For St. Augustine there was only one item of importance, viz. that war be
defensive.[1] For a long time there is no reference even to legitimate authority to engage in war, the reason probably being
that for centuries such authority was hard to find amid the
entanglements of personal feudal loyalties. By the time of St.
Thomas three conditions are ennumerated—legitimate authority, just cause and a right intention.[2] A right intention is
described by Aquinas as being present when 'good is to be promoted and evil avoided'. From which it is clear that he meant
it to cover what later came to be known as a 'due proportion'
between the good achieved and the evil entailed by war. This
helps us to understand both the absence of reference to proportion in his treatment of war and the reason why there is no
need today to include intention among conditions for war that
already specify proportion.

I have already mentioned that St. Thomas accepted without comment the idea that the only just cause for war is the
need for defence. Vittoria later drew out the implications of this,
saying that 'the sole and unique just cause of war is the violation of right'.[3] Granted justice on one's side, however, it seems
that Vittoria was prepared to allow what today would be called
'total war'. His writing on this could only be regarded as brutal
were it not that at his time the engines of war were limited
both in efficiency and extent of destruction. For this reason
Vittoria may be condoned when he writes that 'whatever is
necessary for the defence of the commonwealth is permitted in
war'.[4] Vittoria's teaching was repeated by Banez and Molina,
who amplified it in certain respects. Molina, for example,

Paride de Puteo, *De Re Militari*, (15th and 16th centuries) and Balthazar
Ayala, *De Jure et Officiis bellicis* (1581). Vittoria's great treatise *De Jure
Belli* was written in 1539.

[1] *Ep.* 138, *ad Marcellinum, C.S.E.L.*, XLIV, 139.

[2] *2a 2ae*, Q. 40 art. 1.

[3] Vittoria, *De Jure Belli*, c. 10.

[4] *Op. cit.* n 15.

broached something new when he said that the adversary in a
just war need not be culpable. Earlier writers had tacitly assumed that he should; they had all regarded war as something
punitive.[1] Molina urged that it may sometimes be difficult if
not impossible to know who is culpable, in which case there is
need of conciliation. He also argued that material injustice,
involving no culpability, constitutes a sufficient just cause for
engaging in war. Even more that this, he envisaged the situation in which—due to invincible ignorance about who is right
—war can be just on both sides at the same time.[2] For the same
reason Suarez also supported the view that war can be objectively just on both sides.

The teaching of these writers may seem lax and even retro-
grade until one balances the aspects of it that I have outlined
with others. With Vittoria and Suarez the teaching on war
receives important development in the introduction of the condition relating to proportion. Vittoria's championing of 'total
war' is therefore tempered; while anything may be permitted
in war that is necessary for the just defence of the State, this in
turn is lawful only for ends that are not only just but proportionate and known with certainty. As war became more destructive this new condition of proportionality assumed an ever
more important role in moral teaching. It is interesting to note
that its introduction was immediately accompanied by the dropping of explicit mention of a right intention. This is the case,
for example, with Suarez.[3] It is made up for, however, not only
by the inclusion of proportionality, but by a special condition
regarding the means to be used in the waging of war. The growing destructivity of war is reflected in this—the exclusion of acts
that directly injure innocent people.[4]

By the 16th century we are left with three conditions for a
lawful war—legitimate authority, a just cause and due proportion. These conditions proved quite adequate for deciding on
the morality of war from then until the end of the 18th century.

[1] Molina, *De Justitia et Jure*, Cologne 1733, vol. I, tract 2, disp. 101.
[2] *Op. cit.* vol. I, tract 2, disp. 102, 2.
[3] Suarez, *loc. cit.* section 4.
[4] Suarez, *loc. cit.* section 7.

They are repeated without elaboration by Tanner and Busem-
baum, Lacroix and St. Alphonsus Ligouri. With the 19th century and Napoleon came a change. From being private disputes
between monarchs, with their professional armies, wars became
the concern of nations as a whole. The German writer, von
Clausewitz, is the greatest exponent of the changed character
of modern war.[1] 'War had suddenly become an affair of the
people . . . every one of whom regarded himself as a citizen of
the State . . . By this participation of the people in war, instead
of a cabinet and an army, a whole nation with its natural weight
came into the scale. Henceforward, the means available—the
efforts which might be called forth—had no longer any definite
limits; the energy with which war itself might be conducted had
no longer any counterpoise, and consequently the danger for
the adversary had risen to the extreme'. Von Clausewitz's conclusion is peculiar: 'Therefore, since the time of Bonaparte, war
. . . has assumed quite a new nature, or rather it has approached
much nearer to its real nature, its absolute perfection'. There
is no intrinsic limit to modern war except 'the energy and enthusiasm of the Government and its subjects'.

Don Luigi Sturzo has described a further characteristic of
modern war.[2] In addition to being national, conscriptive and
quite unlimited, responsibility for it has become so diffused as
to be hard to pin down. Whereas formerly the responsibility
for war was left almost exclusively to kings, with the advent of
democracy the reasons for undertaking it became a matter for
parliaments. The result was that, in place of a presumption of
validity in favour of the king's reason for waging war, a new
presumption in favour of the nation was introduced. 'Every
national claim is just and justifies war' became a cardinal principle of the 19th century. Even moralists seemed to oppose war
in practice only for the reason that the majority of them disapproved of the Liberal regimes that waged it.

[1] K. von Clausewitz, *Vom Kriege*, Berlin 1832.

[2] Luigi Sturzo, *Nationalism and Internationalism*, ch 6. This essay
is also contained in Sturzo's *Les guerres modernes et la pensée catholique*,
Montreal 1942.

During this period there is little doubt that there was a considerable decline in the quality of the Christian attitude to war. By 1867 such an impasse had been reached that a Scotsman, David Urquhart, was prompted to pen his *Appeal of a Protestant to the Pope for the Restoration of the Law of Nations*. It was followed by many similar petitions from England and France, while forty bishops formulated a series of 'postulates' on the question for presentation to the Vatican Council. They had unfortunately not been attended to before the Council was suspended and the outbreak of the Franco-Prussian war seemed to mark the disappearance of the idea of a Christian morality in international affairs. Any value it had was purely esoteric, a matter for textbooks and scholars. It is Sturzo's contention that even Catholics came to give unquestioning support to any wars that were waged by their respective countries. 'Political motives and religious preconceptions took preference over a sound ethical criterion'.[1]

THE MODERN PREDICAMENT

It is true that the traditional teaching continued to be repeated, as by Pope Leo XIII in a letter to the First Hague Conference. But in practice a coach and four was all too easily driven through it, as was instanced in 1911 by the Italian conquest of Libya on the pretext of finding an outlet for emigration and of spreading the faith. The outbreak of World War I saw both the French and German hierarchies each justifying its own country's position. The anomaly occasioned a renewed debate regarding the objective criteria of a just war, but the issue at the time was so confused that not even Pope Benedict XV would venture a declaration on the rights and wrongs of the struggle. The same attitude re-emerged during the Abyssinian war and the seizure of Austria and Czechoslovakia by Germany. Many Catholics tended to support the aggression of Italy and Germany against the efforts of the League of Nations to assert its authority.[2] The same was true after the commencement of hostilities

[1] *Nationalism and Internationalism*, p. 187.
[2] Cf Sturzo, *op. cit.*

in 1939, although the German bishops refused to sanction the invasion of Poland. It is not surprising, of course, that in total-itarian countries the edge of moral opinion should have been blunted. It could be formulated at all only with difficulty and had little hope of being effective with government. But in the democracies the same decay set in. The policy of 'unconditional surrender' adopted by the Allies during World War II is a classic example of inattention to the factor of proportionality. Yet it has been noted that no sustained criticism was made of the policy by Catholic spokesmen.[1] A certain apathy prevailed that did little to stem the tide that was eventually to result in Hiroshima and Nagasaki.

It is not difficult to find oneself in sympathy with those whose reaction to this is an extreme pacifism which would by-pass the construction of a doctrine on war that would be ade-quate to the needs of our time. There are many, in fact, who feel that such a doctrine is no longer useful. 'I think', writes Fr. John Courtney Murray, 'that the tendency to query the uses of the Catholic doctrine on war initially rises from the fact that it has for so long not been used, even by Catholics. That is, it has not been made the basis for a sound critique of public policies, and as a means for the formation of a right public opinion . . . I think it is true to say that the traditional doctrine was irrelevant during World War II'.[2] Fr. Murray wisely re-marks, however, that this is no argument against the traditional doctrine itself. The Ten Commandments do not lose their rele-vance simply because they are not obeyed. On the contrary it is pacifism that is unrealistic. From the historical and techno-

---

[1] Cf John Courtney Murray S.J. Theology and Modern War, *loc. cit.* p 83. A notable exception, described by Canon J. McCarthy as 'a fine courageous' article was J. C. Ford's The Morality of Obliteration Bomb-ing, in *Theological Studies*, vol. v (1944), pp 261-309. Fr. Courtney Mur-ray describes it as 'the most significant wartime study of a particular problem': Remarks on the Morality of War, in *Theological Studies*, vol. xx (1959), p 61, n 44. This latter article is reproduced without the footnotes in Nagle, *op. cit.* and also in Fr. Murray's book *We Hold These Truths*. New York 1960.

[2] *Ibid.*

logical viewpoints it is abundantly clear that it is impossible to call a halt to the progress of military invention or to place a complete ban on the employment of any weapons. A lesson was learned by the second Council of the Lateran in 1139, which declared the use of the crossbow in warfare between Christians to be immoral. In our time the question of banning gas warfare has been widely discussed, but again with no success, at least at the legal level. It is the official view of the United States that there is no binding prohibition in international law against the use of gas. In common with the other major powers, the U.S. has not neglected the production of a wide range of chemical and bacteriological weapons.[1] In the same way there is little prospect of imposing a total ban on the employment of nuclear devices. The position is likely to remain in the future as at present stated in the U.S. Army's Field Manual: 'The use of explosive 'atomic weapons', whether by air, sea or land forces, cannot as such be regarded as violative of international law in the absence of any customary rule of international law or international convention restricting their employment'.[2]

It is impossible therefore for pacifists to accomplish anything in practice by taking a theoretical stand against war in every form. It is quite useless to lay down flat prohibitions and bans which have no hope of being widely respected. We have here the factor that continues to bedevil efforts at disarmament and that would make unilateral disarmament suicidal. Professor James Hogan has pointed out that, for reasons deep in their nature, the Communist States cannot be expected to co-operate in any system of international positive law. To expect them to do this would in fact be to expect that they should change their very nature and aims.[3] In such circumstances to expect the West to disarm itself unilaterally would be to ask it to deliver itself—and its Christian heritage—to the mercy of a militant atheism.[4]

[1] Cf Wm. V. O'Brien, Nuclear Warfare and the Law of Nations, in Nagle, *op. cit.* p 133.
[2] Cited in O'Brien, *loc. cit.* p 139.
[3] Cf Hogan, *loc. cit.* pp 142-143.
[4] The suggestion that the West should do this has been made by

It may be urged, of course, that realism—or human wisdom —is one thing, morality something entirely distinct. The pacifist may well argue that, even if his stand is suicidal, it is the more Christian attitude, indeed the only attitude of moral integrity. The argument at best is specious. It is impossible to contemplate with equanimity the enormities that would result if the course of injustice were to be entirely unchecked. One is forced to the conclusion that their prevention, even at terrible cost, is frequently sufficient compensation for the hardships involved in war. In any case, fortitude is a natural virtue which urges men to the defence of what they prize. The fact that war today is more terrible by far than heretofore does not vitiate the main substance of what I am driving at. It would be absurd to maintain that just because an aggressor today is equipped with terrible weapons, it is *ipso facto* immoral to oppose him. There is not much to the point that modern war almost inevitably involves attacks on non-combatants and the killing of the innocent. To conclude from this to a general condemnation of war would be 'as illogical as it would be for the Scholastics to condemn all war in their day because of the excesses, such as looting and killing of the innocent, by the soldiers of the time'.[1] Fr. Stratmann himself would not deny that war in the service of justice is, as such, impregnable against theoretical pacifism. His difficulty is that in our time such a war can no longer be waged; it should not therefore be considered when discussing war.[2] Here is a matter on which views will sharply differ. While

Prof. Herbert Butterfield in his *International Conflict in the Twentieth Century*, London 1960. It is critically examined by Prof. James Hogan in the article already cited, *Philosophical Studies*, Maynooth 1960.

[1] Cf O'Sullivan, *op. cit.*

[2] 'The fact that war is a destroyer bringing much suffering in its wake would not be sufficient cause to forbid it. When war is waged in the name of outraged justice, then is its work of upheaval holier than any consideration of property or life apart from justice. The purely abstract consideration is theoretically unassailable; but we ask ourselves where, in the concrete world of man and nature, war can really be waged in this high and holy way as the servant of Justice and as the protector of the moral ordering of the world'—F. Stratmann, *The Church and War*, p 38.

recognising the moral certainty of mixed motives for war, the majority view continues to be that war can still serve the interests of justice and in certain circumstances even be a duty for men of principle. One should not surrender one's principles without at least some resistance; the only question is how much resistance is in order. At this stage the traditional teaching on war reasserts itself, authorising the use of all means which bear a reasonable proportion to the end defended.

AN ETHIC REAPPLIED

There is no question then of the West being faced with the impossible dilemma of either compromising Christian principles and arming itself for possible war or else preserving its principles and morality intact by 'going it alone' in unilateral disarmament. The fundamental question is 'what kind of' or 'how much' force can be used so that both morality and realism are preserved. Let us first treat of non-nuclear warfare. It is divisible into 'limited' and 'total' war according as to whether limits to the employment of the weapons used are or are not admitted. The chief characteristic of modern 'total' non-nuclear warfare is the saturation (or obliteration) bombing of open cities. The pulverisation of the enemy's cities came to be accepted policy in World War II. The reason for it was its effects on civilian morale and the destruction of the will to fight. It must be said at once that such total war is immoral. There is little use in defending the opposite under cover of the principle of double effect. Modern cities are not the small, compact, fortress-like units of the past which were impossible to reduce without suffering to the civil population. The residential areas of modern cities are so extensive, defined and discernible that attack on them cannot normally be the indirect result of the destruction of military targets.[1] It has been well said that it is impossible to justify as incidental the use of a sledge hammer to swat a fly on a man's head.[2] It is psychologically and honestly im-

[1] Cf Ryan, *op. cit.* p 105.
[2] Cf John C. Ford, The Hydrogen Bombing of Cities, in Nagle, *op. cit.* p 27.

possible to avoid the direct intent of killing the man. Indeed this seems to be actually implicit in the choice of the sledge hammer in the circumstances. There is no use in attempting to justify saturation bombing on moral principles; it is terror bombing intended to weaken resistance by killing non-combatants.

Total war then, even of the non-nuclear kind, must be firmly condemned by moralists. What is to be thought of limited war? As far as bombing goes, this would replace saturation bombing by strategic bombing, using weapons aimed at destroying only military targets. I should hasten to say that such warfare has by no means ceased to be a practical proposition. During the past fifteen years—the first fifteen of the nuclear age—we have witnessed a succession of wars in which nuclear warfare, or even total conventional warfare, would have made little sense. Not only political but military considerations ruled this out.[1] The recent emphasis by the U.S. on improved conventional weapons argues strongly to the conclusion that there is still room for limited conventional war.

Turning to nuclear warfare it is immediately clear that there can be question of its morality only to the extent that it measures up to the principle of limitation. Total nuclear warfare is even more reprehensible than total conventional warfare because of a greater lack of proportionality of means. And this even if its destructive effects were controllable in the sense that its indirect result would not be a menace to mankind entire. In truth, in the context of nuclear warfare, the very concept of 'control' becomes relative. The atomic bomb that was dropped on Hiroshima killed something around 100,000 people. An American scientist tells us that the hydrogen bomb has a destructive capacity equal to one thousand times that of the bomb dropped on Hiroshima.[2] Even if warfare using such bombs

---

[1] Cf James E. Dougherty, The Political Context, in Nagle, *op. cit.* p 27.

[2] L. Pauling, *No More War*, London 1958. For a scientific commentary on modern warfare see Just War, *Sword of the Spirit* Pamphlet 1959. The view of Admiral Arleigh Burke, U.S. Chief of Naval Operations, as reported in the Dublin *Evening Press* of 20 May 1961, is indefensible

can be regarded as controlled, it is certain that their indiscriminate use is morally wrong no matter what the exigencies of the
military situation. This does not mean that the West cannot
morally seek to buttress its defence with the threat of total
nuclear war if attacked. 'Massive retaliation', as it is called, has
its uses as an instrument of strategy in the cold war. Up to the
present the nuclear stalemate has been in large measure responsible for the maintenance of world peace.

Limited warfare—even nuclear—is a very different matter
and, given the usual conditions for a just war, it can be lawful.
It is also much to the fore in current military thinking. The
fear of total nuclear retaliation serves as a powerful deterrent
against any power engaging in its prior use. There is also the
fact that the victor after a total nuclear war would find little
left to gratify his greed.[1] For these reasons limited nuclear warfare is the only variety of nuclear warfare that is thinkable.
Small atomic weapons are commonly classed in the stockpile
of 'conventional' weapons. It is certain that, should war break
out, they would be conventional. The NATO defences are solidly
built on a basis of tactical atomic weapons, while the Polaris
submarines, the Strategic Air Command and ICBMs are sufficient indication of American intentions in the matter. The important thing to note is that these are rapidly becoming an
adequate deterrent in their own right, whose actual employment could be morally justifiable.[2] Striking at economic

from the moral point of view. The Admiral was reported as declaring
to a Congressional Committee that 'if cities must be attacked as a matter
of national survival, they are going to be wiped out, and then it had
better be done in the most efficient manner'. He is said to have replied,
when Senator Symington asked: 'Do you mean the populations wiped
out'?—'Yes, if the only way we can survive is by wiping them out'.

[1] 'The destruction caused by one thermonuclear bomb landing on
a large city is so out of proportion to the advantage gained from destroying even a large portion of another nation that a national decision to
begin such a war is highly improbable'—John K. Moriarty, Technology,
Strategy and National Military Policy, in Nagle, op. cit. p 41.

[2] Further backing for this significant thesis can be found in the
article of Thomas E. Murray, of the U.S. Atomic Energy Commission,
Rational Nuclear Armament, in Life, 6 May, 1957 (Reprinted in The

targets in industrial cities is not the way in which a war of the future will be won.[1] It is more important to eliminate the rocket potential of the enemy and this is becoming increasingly dispersed and even mobile. The threat of tactical nuclear missiles, delivered in a variety of ways, constitutes a sufficient deterrent against enemy aggression.

There is no doubt that the use of tactical atomic weapons is morally excluded if directed at targets that are virtually incapable of isolation from areas of high density civilian population. Much of Western Europe and parts of America and Asia fall immediately into this category. But the danger of their being employed against such areas does not in itself constitute a valid objection against limited nuclear warfare. Neither does the danger that this may spark off total nuclear warfare, a contingency that is, in any case, rather remote. The really valuable aspect of the idea of limited nuclear warfare is that it brings both the Western and Communist blocs into the same universe of military discourse, even if for reasons that are not coincidental.[2] As a moral concept limited warfare is unknown to the Communist countries. Were it not that today it is also a

---

Catholic Mind, Sept.-Oct., 1957). Cf. also T. E. Murray. *Nuclear Policy for War and Peace*, New York, 1960.

[1] 'The United States needs a real deterrent; one which will constitute a tangible threat to the Soviet Union and yet which would be a sound, credible and morally justifiable course of action if it actually had to be put into effect. For such a deterrent, long-range bombers and submarines, coupled with missiles and small nuclear weapons, will undoubtedly be required. But we do not need nuclear weapons of megaton size, with their tremendous blast-areas and fallout that is world-wide. We do not need to think in terms of targets which are primarily civilian in nature or which contribute to the ability of the Soviet Union to fight a long war. If the purpose is to deter, then the United States could announce beforehand that it will destroy with precise nuclear weapons, from secure retaliatory locations, certain targets of as great value as possible to the Soviet Union, but with a minimum impact on the civilian population'—Moriarty, *loc. cit.* p 53.

[2] It is interesting also to note that it is a significant point of contact between Catholic and Protestant ethics, at least in America. Cf Paul Ramsey, *War and the Christian Conscience*, Duke University, 1961.

realistic military concept, the West would find itself confronted with the impossible dilemma of sacrificing either morality or military effectiveness. It would seem, in fact, to be exactly what is needed today both to satisfy conscience and ensure adequate defence.[1]

We should therefore cease to speak about the morality of war in the abstract and, in particular, about the morality of nuclear war as such. It is certainly a mistake to insist that in general it is *malum in se*. A contemporary expert on international law and polity assures us that 'it should be evident to those that have kept abreast of technological and military developments that there is, properly speaking, no such thing as "nuclear warfare" in the abstract'.[2] There are many varieties of nuclear warfare and many situations in which it could be waged. It is impossible to encompass all these variables in one judgment; each variety must be appraised in its own context before its morality can be decided with any certainty. This is true in fact of all kinds of modern war. When any moralist says that war is to be altogether forbidden, one usually finds that he is speaking only of total war. This is certainly the case with Cardinal Ottaviani, whose paragraph on the subject explicitly refers to 'the atrocious massacres of our times, with their total ruin of the warring nations.' He expressly allows limited defensive war against unjustified military aggression.

In the light of the foregoing it can be seen that the pacifist

---

[1] 'The idea of keeping war limited for moral and humanitarian reasons, and of using no greater force in war than is necessary to accomplish a rational political objective, is deep-rooted in Western culture. The revival of this notion in the nuclear age represents a commendable effort to resolve the dichotomy of modern strategic thought, polarized as it is between the extremes of absolute pacifism and the militarism of total war. Both the pacifists and the militarists have managed with equal effectiveness to drive a wedge between military strategy and ethics, the former by contending that the employment of force to defend the moral order is never justified, and the latter by refusing to place any moral boundaries on the use or force. The advocates of limited war are sincerely trying to end the schism which rends the modern Western mind . . . '—Dougherty, *loc. cit.* pp 22-23.

[2] Cf O'Brien, *loc. cit.* p 142.

position has little to recommend it either from the point of view of realism or that of morality. One would not be surprised, in fact, to find a papal statement which rejected it. The defence of the West is so important and the influence of pacifism so insinuating that one might reasonably expect a papal statement on the conditions under which war can be lawfully waged. Even in the thirties it could be said that 'the history of the Papacy will be searched in vain for any major pronouncement upon the justification of war'.[1] Since the Christmas Broadcast of Pope Pius XII for 1956 it is no longer possible to maintain this thesis. The Pope expressed himself clearly on the subject of war and in a way that was quite contrary to the pacifist extreme. While desirous of peace and resolutely against the horrors of war, he sharply stopped the trend towards pacifism among Catholics. He reiterated the traditional teaching that war can still be justified in the interests of defence and for this purpose can be declared by legitimate authority when peaceful means have been expended in vain. He added the important consequence that, when this is the case, conscientious objection to war is not lawful.[2] Coming as it did soon after the Hungarian uprising, the papal broadcast was held by many to have had this in mind. Some saw in it even wider issues involving almost the idea of a crusade against Communism. What is quite certain is that the Pope envisaged the possibility of circumstances in which—even in modern times—the conditions for a just war can still be verified.

[1] John Eppstein, *Must War Come?* London 1935, p 17.

[2] 'It is clear that in the present circumstances there can be verified in a nation the situation wherein, every effort to avoid war being expended in vain, war—for effective self-defence and with the hope of a favourable outcome against unjust attack—could not be considered unlawful. If, therefore, a body representative of the people and a Government—both having been chosen by free elections—in a moment of extreme danger, decide by legitimate instruments of internal and external policy, on defensive precautions, and carry out the plans which they consider necessary, they do not act immorally; so that a Catholic citizen cannot invoke his own conscience in order to refuse to serve and fulfil those duties the law imposes'.

There is one aspect of the Pope's thought which is difficult
to interpret and which has given rise to a difference of opinion.
It is where he declared that 'every war of aggression . . . is a
sin, a crime, an outrage against the majesty of God'.[1] 'It is a
duty', he said, 'binding upon all . . . to do everything possible
to proscribe and banish the war of aggression once and for all
as a legitimate solution of international disputes and as an
instrument of national aspirations'. He spoke emphatically of
the need to put an end to 'the crime of a modern war which is
not demanded by the absolute necessity of self-defence'.[2] From
this it is concluded that, although the Pope did not state it
categorically, he implicitly ruled out war—undertaken on a
nation's own authority—as a means of settling international
disputes.[3] Fr. Courtney Murray interprets him as seeming 'to
deny to individual states, in this historical moment, the *jus
belli* (*compétence de guerre*) of the modern era of the unlimited
sovereign state . . . The use of force if not now a moral means
for the redress of violated legal rights. The justness of the cause
is irrelevant; there simply is no longer a right of self-redress;
no individual state may presume to take even the cause of
justice into its own hands'.[4]

Fr. Murray comments that the Pope gives no real definition
of aggression, indeed that 'he seems relatively unconcerned to
give an exact definition' of it.[5] He is concerned, Fr. Murray
suggests, more with the concept of 'injustice' than with that
of 'aggression', injustice of all kinds being the inevitable complement of allowing States to decide for themselves whether
they should pursue their national aspirations by going to war.
I feel somehow that this conclusion is rather hasty. I submit
that a good deal of light can be thrown on the question by an
examination of what is usually meant by a war of aggression.
The Malines *Code of International Ethics* (1937) by no means

[1] Christmas Message 1948. *A.A.S.*, xli, p 13.
[2] Allocution of 3 October 1953. *A.A.S.*, xlv, p 730.
[3] Cf L. Mcreavy, The Debate on the Morality of Future War, in
The Clergy Review, New Series, vol. xlv (1960), p 84.
[4] Murray, *loc. cit.* pp 75-76.
[5] Murray, *loc. cit.* p 76, n 5.

ruled out all *offensive* war. War, it says, 'is offensive from the point of view of the State which begins hostilities; it is defensive from that of the State which has recourse to armed force in order to repel attack . . . Reason justifies a defensive war by which a State endeavours to repel an unjust aggressor, an offensive war by which it seeks the restitution of an essential right, and a war of intervention by which an allied or friendly power gives armed assistance to a belligerent in similar circumstances'.[1] It is extremely doubtful whether the Pope wished to exclude all offensive war in the sense intended by the Malines Social Union. The distinction between 'offensive' and 'defensive' is not always an easy one to maintain in practice. There are occasions when a country may be driven to attack if it is to survive. On other occasions attack may be closely related to defence by being aimed at recovering a right as against preventing its violation. It is quite a different thing from a punitive expedition.

It is more likely that by 'aggressive' war the Pope understood an offensive war that is launched without submitting the dispute to the arbitration of international authority. Offensive moves in themselves do not necessarily constitute aggression in this narrow and more specialised meaning. In this connection some remarks of the American Professor J. T. Shotwell in 1930 are interesting examples of what has changed and what still remains in international theory and practice concerning aggression.[2] 'The mere crossing of a nation's geographic frontiers', says Prof. Shotwell, 'is no sure test of aggression'. The example which he gave is very relevant in view of events since then. It would not be aggression, he suggested, for Britain to go to war for the maintenance of the Suez canal, 'the most vital single link in Imperial defence'. Any attack on it should be resisted by the British Empire 'as an act of self-evident defence . . . Legitimate defence is not confined to repelling invasion within a country's borders'. For Prof. Shotwell 'the aggressor is the power which in going to war violates its already given pledge to

---

[1] *Code of International Ethics*, English trans., Oxford 1937, pp 69-70.
[2] J. T. Shotwell, *War as an Instrument of National Policy and its Renunciation*, pp 206-209.

settle its disputes peacefully'. It is essentially a violation of a juristic frontier rather than a geographic one and it is this juristic frontier which alone furnishes an adequate test of aggression and legitimate defence.

According to this conception the initiation of hostilities in itself is not necessarily to be regarded as aggression. On the other hand, going to war without submitting the dispute to international arbitration is very definitely to be regarded as aggression. From this point of view the Anglo-French attack on Suez in 1956 would have to be classified as aggression before the bar of international law. Whether morality would go thus far is debatable. I have argued earlier that the findings of an international court may not be acceptable to the parties to a dispute, in which case, in the present state of international organisation, it would be difficult to deny to the aggrieved party the right to go to war on its own authority. It should be remembered that what the Fribourg Conventus, already referred to, forbade was a war declared by a State on its own authority without previous recourse to the international institutions which exist'. It is proper to note that the Conventus remarked that it could at that time 'be reasonably foreseen that the case of lawful defence will become less frequent in international life the more true security has been attained by the co-ordinated protection of all States in common and the institution of arbitration'.[1]

I suggest that it is at least possible that it was aggression in the sense just outlined that Pope Pius XII intended to exclude as immoral. It may be objected that war of this kind was always unlawful by reason of being declared without having explored all possible means of peaceful solution. This is not the case in the context of the sovereign State, which did not regard itself as bound to seek any aid beyond its frontiers in the settlement of international disputes. I suggest that it is precisely this that the Pope is questioning and that he is imposing a new outlook in international affairs in the name of morality. In short he is canonizing, as it were, the teaching on

[1] Cf Eppstein, op. cit. p 141.

war that had been privately urged in the thirties by the Fribourg group. There is no conflict here with the traditional teaching on war, but only a development, in view of contemporary realities, that is quite in line with the kind of evolution that has been undergone by the traditional teaching during the course of history.

POPE PIUS XII AND UNILATERAL DISARMAMENT

As regards nuclear warfare, in an address to the International Congress for the Documentation of Military Medicine (19 October 1953. *A.A.S.*, vol. XLV) the Pope declared that the question of its morality is solved by the application of the same principles as hold for the legitimacy of war in general. He added immediately that the condition relating to a proportionately grave cause is of special importance where there is question of ABC—atomic, bacteriological and chemical—warfare. But he left the door open to the possibility that such warfare could sometimes be moral. In 1954 he made a further clarification. It was that if the setting in motion of ABC warfare meant loosing destructive power that was uncontrollable, it would be immoral even if used in the cause of just defence. It has been suggested that, in envisaging uncontrollable warfare, the Pope was going beyond present scientific capabilities.[1] Whatever of this, it is clear that not all nuclear warfare is unlimited and, that in the Pope's view, it is capable of lawful employment. It is a mistake to approach the question of the morality of such warfare—even the use of the hydrogen bomb—on the assumption that it must necessarily mean total war or at least neces-

---

[1] 'Around this time (1954) there was a lot of loose and uninformed talk about weapons that really would go beyond human control, for instance, of the so-called 'cobalt bomb' and its 'unlimited' powers of radioactive contamination. It is impossible to know what were the sources of the pope's scientific information . . . (Even high-megaton weapons) do not 'escape from the control of man'. Their blast and fire effects, and their atmosphere contamination effects, have been fairly exactly measured—J. C. Murray, *loc. cit.* p 81, n 7.

sarily entail the annihilation of cities.[1]

Hence Pope Pius XII did not condemn the organising of armies for just defence, or their arming with what he called 'the indispensable means of effective action'.[2] This is important in view of the hostile attitude that had just previously been manifested by some German Catholics towards the equipping of the new West German army with atomic armaments.[3] The same hostility—again for moral reasons—had also been expressed by the General Synod of the Evangelical Church in Germany.[4] The Pope's statement has changed the situation considerably and views similar to his have been expressed in a Collective Manifesto by seven of Germany's leading Catholic theologians.[5]

One cannot conclude without adding that the Pope urged the banning of ABC warfare by international agreement, involving the renunciation of tests, the renunciation of use and the general control of atomic weapons.[6] In fact he declared that there was an obligation on statesmen to work towards the adoption of these provisions. For this purpose he wished for nothing better in the international sphere than to see the authority of the United Nations Organisation strengthened.[7]

It should be carefully noted, however, that the Pope called for the 'sum total of these three precautions as an object of international agreement' in order that 'equal security be

---

[1] E.g. J. McCarthy, The Morality of the Hydrogen Bomb as a War Weapon, in *Problems in Theology*, vol. II, pp 180-185. Contrast P. Zamayon, Moralidad de la guerra en nuestros dias y en el porvenir, in *Salmanticensis*, (1955) pp 42-79; also John R. Connery, Morality of Nuclear Armament, in Nagle, *op. cit.* pp 92-97.

[2] Address to Spiritual Assistants to the Italian Armed Forces, 21 May 1958. *Documentation Catholique*, n 1279.

[3] Cf Declaration of fifty-one Catholic personalities on the subject, in *Katholische Nachrichten-Agentur*, 17 May 1958.

[4] Cf *Service oecumenique de presse et d'information*, 9 May 1958.

[5] Cf *Katholische Nachrichten-Agentur*, 5 May 1958; also *Documentation Catholique*, n 1279.

[6] Christmas Message 1955. *A.A.S.*, XLVIII, p 26 *seq.*

[7] Christmas Message 1956. *A.A.S.*, XLIX, p 5 *seq.* For a summary of the papal teaching see the booklet *Just War* already mentioned.

established for all'. Indeed the 'reason they are morally binding is also that equal security be established for all'. Thus unilateral nuclear disarmament finds no support at all in the Papal teaching which urges the banning of nuclear weapons.

For this reason one is surprised to find a number of Catholic writers maintaining that unilateralism is perfectly in accordance with Catholic teaching. The year 1961 saw the publication of quite a few books and articles in which their position was explained and defended. The best known of these in the English language is *Nuclear Weapons and Christian Conscience*, edited by Walter Stein.[1] In all of them the debate has been somewhat clouded by some confusion between the morality of the present intentions of the great powers should war break out and the morality of modern war *in the abstract*.[2] Let us be quite clear that no Catholic moralist could rightly suggest that, even in lawful defence, unlimited warfare can be moral or cannot be legitimately objected to by the conscience of the individual. So that if the policy of the NATO powers, for example, were based on deterrence by way of actual massive nuclear retaliation against non-military targets such as cities, it would be quite immoral and nobody could lawfully co-operate in its execution. But the crucial question with which the above-mentioned book and its like are really dealing is whether modern war, as such, is immoral and so repugnant to the Christian conscience that Christians have a right if not a duty to work for nuclear disarmament—even unilateral.

---

[1] *Nuclear Weapons and Christian Conscience*. Walter Stein, ed., London, 1961; cf. also *Kann der Atomare Verteidigungskrieg ein Gerechter Krieg sein?* Various authors. Munchen 1960; *Atomare Kampfmittel und christliche Ethik, Diskussionsbeitrage deutscher Katholiken*, Munchen 1960; for expository article on the German discussions see A. Janssen, *Les armes atomiques et la morale chrétienne*, in *Ephemerides Theologicae Lovaniensis*, vol. XXXVII (1961), pp. 98-105.

[2] Cf L. L. McReavy, Morality and the Bomb, in *The Christian Democrat*, vol. II (1960), n. 12 and M. P. Fogarty, Morality and the Bomb—A Reply, in *The Christian Democrat*, vol. XII (1961), n 2. Cf also controversy in *The Tablet*, October (all issues) 1961.

Nuclear Weapons and Christian Conscience was the subject of a critical review in the *Tablet* by the Bishop of Salford, Most Rev. Dr. Beck.[1] Dr. Beck's treatment of the subject is interesting and instructive. While agreeing that the morality of nuclear war 'is one which must be left to the individual conscience' and that the individual citizen is quite entitled to 'urge a policy of unilateral disarmament on his government', he added a number of qualifications which are of pre-eminent importance.

There can be no doubt that one should always follow one's conscience. Even if it urges the doing of something that is objectively immoral, a man is bound to follow the dictates of his conscience if he is genuinely unable to see the error of his convictions. Hence, says the Bishop, 'the individual must try seriously and prayerfully to form his own conscience —but to form it by taking into consideration the *magisterium* of the Church'. And he immediately added: 'I do not think that they (i.e., the authors of the book referred to) have adequately established in the light of Papal teaching the duty to refuse to undertake military service'.

The Bishop was being charitable in understatement. It was precisely because of similar inattention to Papal teaching, particularly the Christmas broadcast of 1956, that Cardinal Wendel, Archbishop of Munich, and Archbishop Seiterich of Freiburg found it necessary to rebuke certain German Catholic pacifists for their failure to take adequate account of the Papal message. The 1956 message leaves no room for doubt that it is Papal teaching that a just war is still a practical possibility, even in our nuclear age, and that conscientious objection in such circumstances is out of order. It is well to remember the words with which the Pope introduced his teaching. 'Present-day conditions, which find no counterpart in the past, should be clear to everyone . . . when . . . the threat

[1] Rt. Rev. G. A. Beck, The Christian Conscience and Nuclear Weapons, in *The Tablet*, 7 October, 1961. Cf also Mgr. Guerry, Archbishop of Cambrai, La conscience chrétienne en face de la bombe atomique française, in *La Documentation Catholique*, n 1321 (February, 1960).

is made of using atomic weapons to gain certain demands, be they justified or not'. It was *immediately* after this that the Pope went on to say that even in these circumstances the traditional conditions for just war can be *verified*. 'Verified' was the word he used, verified, that is, in the concrete and in an atomic context. There is no escaping the conclusion that it was the teaching of Pope Pius XII that the use of nuclear weapons in a just war is a practical possibility.

There is no suggestion here that could provide any kind of support for a programme of unilateral nuclear disarmament. It is true, of course, as Bishop Beck noted, that the individual citizen has the right to urge such a policy on his government. But that is not the end of the story. Whether he should exercise his right or should be followed by the government are distinct questions. As the Bishop put it: 'Has that government, in the light of all its responsibilities, the duty or even the right, to take such a decision?' And he answered the question by producing two quotations from Pope Pius XII:

'The community of nations must reckon with unprincipled criminals who, in order to realise their ambitious plans, are not afraid to unleash total war. This is the reason why other countries, if they wish to preserve their existence and their most precious possessions and unless they are prepared to accord free action to international criminals, have no alternative but to get ready for the day when they must defend themselves. This right to be prepared for self-defence cannot be denied, even in these days, to any State' (3 October 1953).

'This is the reason why no nation which wishes to provide, as is its right and imprescriptible duty, for the security of its frontiers, can do without an army proportionate to its needs, lacking nothing which is indispensible for bold action" (21 May 1958).

The 'somewhat selective' treatment in the pacifist volume to which we have referred, said the Bishop of Salford, 'seems to have overlooked these and some other similar Papal pronouncements'. These pronouncements imply the possibility of just war even today and make it quite clear that there is still a duty of defence against unjust aggression, even if atomic weapons and their use are required for it. This being so, there is little room for unilateralism. For whatever may be the right of the individual to try to form policy taken in itself, he is certainly not entitled to do or say anything that would undoubtedly conduce to the failure of his government to do its duty.

And here we have the kernel of the whole thing. Nations may use every necessary and legitimate means of self-defence against unjust aggression. In the present world context such means include, as a last resort, nuclear weapons, provided they are controllable, as at least some of them are, and are used against lawful targets, i.e., military targets. These conditions can in fact be fulfilled. And conscientious citizens and statesmen must try to ensure that, if it is ever necessary to invoke these weapons, they will be used only under such conditions. That these weapons may never have to be used is the earnest wish of all of us. And Catholics who work for that multilateral disarmament which will effectively guarantee world peace and national security are to be highly commended. On the other hand advocating unilateral nuclear disarmament today amounts to advocating self-surrender and a dereliction of duty for which no genuine statesman could accept responsibility.

There is no point in objecting that the argument of the last paragraph is over simplified, that, in particular, it takes no account of the fact that, in order to be just, even defensive war must have reasonable hope of success and entail good effects that are at least proportionate to its evil consequences. 'There are certain values of such importance to humanity', declared Pope Pius XII, 'that their defence against unjust aggression is without any doubt fully justified' (Christmas 1948). And as regards success who can say with certainty that all defensive war today must be unsuccessful? A great deal depends on what is meant.

We can be confident therefore that there is no formal Papal teaching which would justify the position of the pacifists. The most that these can fall back upon—and the argument is unscientific—are the reiterated Papal appeals for peace. Mr. Khruschev himself has been known to do this—after the Radio Address of 10 September, 1961, by Pope John XXIII, in which a further insistent call for peace was made to the nations. The Soviet Premier saw the Pope's call as one for disarmament by

the West, or what the Christian pacifists call unilateral disarmament. As reported in *Pravda* he commented on it as follows: 'I read
the speech of the Pope of Rome and I must say I read it with interest. In our time we must listen to every public figure who raises
a voice of protest against the dangerous playing with fire sparked
by the aggressive forces in the West . . . Will such adherents of
the Catholic faith as John Kennedy and Konrad Adenauer and
others heed the sacred warning of the Pope of Rome?'

The sharp retort of *L'Osservatore Romano* is significant.
'Doctrinally and objectively', it wrote, 'the peace message of
Pope John XXIII was addressed to everyone, governments and
people. It purposely refrained from any reference to or judgment
of particular situations, . . . It cannot be supposed, nor is it
justifiable, that such a message could be forced into a single interpretation'. Pacifism can certainly find no support in it. There
are aspects of the problem of modern war on which discussion is
still free and is to be encouraged. There is also a wide field open
to Catholics in working for true peace among nations. But the
question of the morality of pacifism—whether 'absolute' or
'relative' has been authoritatively decided for Catholics.

The question is sometimes raised whether what is called
'vocational' or 'prophetic' pacifism is also to be regarded as excluded. By this is meant a pacifism which is upheld in the interests of an *ideal* of non-violence. The ideal in question is not confined to Christians and is certainly very praiseworthy in itself.
The situation is different, however, if it is pursued to such an
extent that one refuses to serve even if commanded to do so by
lawful authority. The Church, which claims immunity from
military service for her clergy, instructs them to obey should
their civil governments seek to enlist them. And Catholic moralists go so far as to say that, even if there is doubt about the
morality of its action, lawful authority must always be given
the benefit of it.[1] Vocational pacifism can find no support here.[2]

---

[1] Cf Mgr Charrière, Bishop of Lausanne, Geneva and Fribourg,
Devoir militaire et conscience chrétienne, in *La Documentation Catholique*, n 1232 (August, 1956).

[2] Cf Ducattillon, *op. cit.*, p. 106. *Patriotisme et Colonisation*, Tournai
1957, p 106.

Pacifism of all kinds is therefore out of harmony with Catholic teaching. So much so indeed that the American pacifist Gordon Zahn, writing in the periodical *America*, said that the Papal broadcast of Christmas 1956 seemed to involve 'an apparent departure from the traditional recognition of the inviolability of the individual conscience, even an erroneous conscience formed in invincible ignorance', so definite was it that conscientious objection is unlawful for Catholics, given the conditions for a just war which it regarded as verifiable today.[1]

THE DIRECTIVES OF THE CHURCH

In view of this, the continuing pacifist issue raises a problem concerning the nature and extent of the Church's authority that more frequently arose in the past out of the very different situation in which armed force was used contrary to the directives of the Church. The Hierarchy, said the militarists, may know the theological principles governing warfare, but their application is something entirely different. It involves a full knowledge and appreciation of many facts, which, it is presumed, the Hierarchy lacks.

Strange to say—or is it strange?—precisely the same attitude has been adopted by many to the statement of the late Pope which censured pacifism. An article in *The Catholic Worker* for January 1957 distinguishes between the teaching authority of the Pope or Bishops and their private opinions[2] in dogmatic and moral matters. It grants immediately that in regard to the hard core of moral and dogmatic teaching 'which must be followed because it is true, because it has upon it the seal of the Holy Spirit', the teaching of the Church's Hierarchy must be categorically obeyed by every Catholic as a condition of his very membership of the Church. In addition to this, there is another area of authority, which is concerned less with doctrine as such than with the implementation of the Church's teaching in the

---

[1] Gordon C. Zahn, German Pacifists, in *America*, 18 May, 1956.
[2] Edmund J. Egan, Freedom and Authority in the Church, in *The Catholic Worker*, January 1957.

concrete. Such authority is binding 'not because of the truth of
its decisions, but because of that hierarchical, authoritative
structure of the Church which is necessary if she is to exert a
general influence from day to day in the care of souls'.

This authority, the article continues, is concerned with what
is essentially a *social* matter, in which the superior's command
and the subject's obedience dovetail. They collaborate, as two
aspects of the same task, that of securing the common good of
the Church, in whole or in part. But precisely because of that,
this authority, though possessing a certain genuine binding
power, cannot directly command *individual* consciences. All
binding power is not absolutely binding. In other words, while
authority binds the faithful—even apart from the rectitude of
its direction—it must needs be distinguished from absolute
authority and, though the presumption is always in its favour,
the individual conscience can defy its command if it has strong
certitude and grave reason for doing so.

The chosen example of this authority is Pope Pius XII's
command to Italian citizens to vote in elections as a major
moral duty. 'In such a matter Catholics would generally be
bound under obedience to comply, but given the case, for example, of a sincerely convinced Christian Anarchist, who would
regard voting as proximate co-operation in a seriously immoral
enterprise, an exception would obtain to the binding power of
the command'. In other words, authority of this kind is binding,
but not unequivocally binding. It is of quite a different nature
from that attaching to a papal decision which authoritatively
settles an existing theological opinion—say in the matter of
artificial birth control. The latter is really a directive issued in
the context of making a moral definition and, as such, is not
just legislation alone but the official and irrefutable teaching of
the Church. The conscience of the individual must necessarily
be brought into harmony with it.

The statement of the Pope on conscientious objection is then
examined in the light of these distinctions. It is first observed
that no new interpretation of Catholic faith or morals has been
made by it. The Pope simply restated the ordinary conditions
for a just war, thus confirming these principles in the moral
teaching of the Church. But then the article continues: 'It must

be realised, however, that this statement of principle is seriously circumscribed by what was *not* treated by His Holiness, and that the *very issues which Christian pacifists have found most germane to the problem of war are the issues absent from the Pope's message'*. The whole question of means, especially regarding nuclear weapons, is said to have been scarcely touched upon. So also is any serious consideration of the question of proportionality.

For this reason, it is argued that when the Pope concludes that conscientious objection to a just war is morally unlawful, he is assuming what remains to be proved, namely, that such a war is in fact a real possibility. The same applies to his endorsement of conscription. And so the article goes on: 'The personal ethical evaluations of the man who is Pope, as well as his political, economic and cultural critiques, are basically to be evaluated on their intellectually accessible merits, as are the opinions of other men. If, as it would appear in the Christmas Message, the Holy Father assumes the probability of just means in modern war, and assumes the *fact* that certain moral principles are verified in present circumstances [such as the very debatable notion that "every effort to avoid war (has been or is being) expended in vain"], we ought to regard these positions as what they are, perfectly fallible analyses of a difficult situation. And of course a papal statement as to what constitutes right action is likewise in the area of opinion if the statement relies upon, as well as moral principle, data which is not certain, and not itself in the realm of faith or morals. *It must be remembered that a political situation entails a dynamic complex of variables, which cannot be treated as a fixed condition in the application of moral principle'.*

Hence, owing to the fact that the pacifist thesis involves an appreciation of the concrete political situation, it is concluded that the teaching of the Pope's 1956 Christmas broadcast has little bearing, as authority, on it. 'It is very likely, of course, that the *effects* of the message will do harm to pacifism conceived as a cause desirous of increasing its following and its acceptability; but such "harm" is at most a very accidental thing to pacifism conceived as a movement . . directed to maintaining a perceived moral truth with a certain purity and intransigence'.

Similar thinking is frequently applied to the episcopal magis-

terium. In the United States, for example, we find it in relation
to the directives of bishops regarding the attendance of Catholics at certain film shows. We are told that the authoritative
pronouncements of bishops never define Christian teaching in
any binding fashion, such as would command assent, but are
rather directives of action. When a bishop commands the obedience of his people in any matter concerned with faith or
morals, he does so not with absolute authority but with that
which binds generally. The individual's conscience has always a
certain latitude provided it has sufficiently good certitude to
consider itself exempt. And there is always the addendum that
episcopal authority binds at all only within its prescribed area
and when its commands are not conditional on factual data
etc., which—despite the opinion of a bishop—may be open to
debate.

For instance, it is readily agreed that in the case of a film
like 'The French Line', an order such as that of Archbishop
Ritter of St. Louis, forbidding Catholics to see it, is binding on
all, save perhaps those—e.g. film critics—who may have serious
reasons for doing so. On the other hand, if a bishop were to
forbid his flock to see a film which, though objectionable in
certain respects, represented a serious artistic achievement, any
individual with genuine aesthetic appreciation would be free
to disobey the directive. By these means a way is found, in
practice, to ignore the directives of bishops on many concrete
issues.

It is impossible here to give an adequate account of the
nature and extent of the Church's teaching authority. I have
dealt elsewhere with certain aspects of it.[1] Some brief points
of clarification must suffice. In the first place, it should be noted
that the authority of the teaching Church is not restricted to
infallible pronouncements regarding revealed truths. It extends
to official teaching of every kind. Encyclical letters are a good
example of the kind of medium in which this can be found. It
must not be thought, says Pope Pius XII in *Humani Generis*,
'that what is contained in Encyclical letters does not of itself
(*per se*) demand assent, on the pretext that the Popes do not

---

[1] J. Newman, *What is Catholic Action?* Dublin 1958, pp. 95-101.

exercise in them the supreme power of their ordinary *magisterium*, of which it is true to say: "He who hears you, hears Me"; and very often, what is proposed and inculcated in Encyclicals already pertains to Catholic doctrine for other reasons. Hence if the Supreme Pontiffs in their acts (*data opera*) pass judgment on a matter hitherto debated, it is evident to all that, according to the mind and will of the same Pontiffs, these questions may no longer be a subject of free discussion among theologians'.[1]

It is clear from this that a firm, interior, intellectual assent to the teachings of the Papal Encyclicals is required of all the faithful, in regard to matters on which the Popes take a definite stand in these documents. These represent the Catholic position; they leave no room for argumentation on any others.[2] But it should be carefully noted that it is only when the Popes *clearly* single out an opinion for endorsement that such an assent is demanded. Very frequently what is provided by the Encyclicals is simply a framework for lawful discussion. We should add that these same considerations hold in the case of Papal Allocutions and Decrees of the Roman Congregations when they are addressed directly or indirectly to the whole Christian world.[3]

On the teaching authority of bishops, we receive some guidance from the Code of Canon Law. 'Individual bishops', says canon 1326, 'or even groups of bishops in particular councils, are not infallible in teaching, yet they are, under the authority of the Pope, true teachers of doctrine for those under their charge'. By divine right they are the authoritative teachers of faith and morals, each for his own diocese and people. 'Besides the Roman Pontiff for the universal Church, and bishops for the faithful entrusted to their care, there are no other teachers for the faithful divinely constituted in the Church of Christ'.[4]

[1] Cf A. J. Walsh, The Extent of the Church's Authority, in *The American Ecclesiastical Review*, June 1959, pp 399-411.

[2] *Ibid.* p 406.

[3] Cf W. O'Connor, *Catholic Social Teaching*, Westminster 1956, p 53 seq.

[4] Pope Pius XII, *Address to Cardinals and Bishops*, Rome, 31 May 1954.

The difficulty is in determining the extent of the domain of morals. An American bishop has put the position well: 'It happens that the sphere of morals is less well defined than the sphere of faith. This is not to say that the Church is uncertain about what is moral or immoral. It is merely to point out that the problem of morality is inextricably interwoven with all human relations. It is bound up with government, with politics, with economics, with sociology, with art, with literature, with applied science and even with entertainment. It involves the application of the virtues of justice, prudence, temperance and fortitude to all these manifold and highly intricate relations. Where the distinction between right and wrong is clearly defined, the Church has not hesitated to speak out . . . But she has not pronounced, and she could not reasonably be expected to pronounce, on every item . . . throughout the free world. Especially is this true in areas in which debate is still justified. All such issues are by no means solidly black and white. It is not always clear whether they are injurious to human rights or are actually beneficial to them. In such areas she prudently prefers to abide the clarification of the points under debate. In other words, the Church is not a sort of universal umpire ready at all times to jump into every discussion with a cut-and-dried answer. In many instances individual theologians and even individual bishops may feel that the issues are sufficiently clear to warrant their pronouncement upon them. The Church, save in notorious cases of imprudent action on obviously faulty thinking, does not forbid this'.[1]

But the bishops reserve the right and the duty to speak out on the moral aspects of any issue that calls for their intervention. When they do so, their teaching is authoritative and must be obeyed by their subjects quite independently of its intellectual cogency. We cannot do better than reproduce Pope Pius XII's exposition of the exact position: 'There are some noticable attitudes and tendencies of mind which presume to check and set limits to the power of bishops (the Roman Pontiff not excepted), as being strictly the shepherds of the flock entrusted

[1] Most Rev. Robert J. Dwyer, Bishop of Reno, in *Catholic Documentation*, Sydney, June 1956. Article : Who Speaks for the Church?

to them. They fix their authority, office and watchfulness within
certain bounds, which concern strictly religious matters, the
statement of the truths of the faith, the regulation of devotional
practices, administration of the Sacraments of the Church and
the carrying out of liturgical ceremonies. They wish to restrain
the Church from all undertakings and business which concern
life as it is really conducted—the 'realities of life', as they say.
In short, this way of thinking in the official statements of some
lay Catholics, even those in high positions, is sometimes shown
when they say: "We are perfectly willing to see, to listen to and
to approach bishops and priests in their churches, and regarding
matters within their authority; but in places of official and
public business, where matters of this life are dealt with and
decided, we have no wish to see them or to listen to what they
say. For there, it is we laymen, and not the clergy—no matter
of what rank or qualification—who are the legitimate judges".

'We must take an open and firm stand against errors of this
kind. The power of the Church is not bounded by the limits of
"matters strictly religious", as they say, but the whole matter
of the natural law, its foundation, its interpretation, its application, so far as their moral aspects extend, are within the
Church's power . . . Therefore, when it is a question of instruc-
tions and propositions which the properly constituted shepherds
(i.e., the Roman Pontiffs for the whole Church and the bishops
for the faithful entrusted to them) publish on matters within
the natural law, the faithful must not invoke that saying (which
is wont to be employed with respect to opinions of individuals):
The strength of the authority is no more than the strength of
the arguments'.[1]

It is important to arrive at a correct understanding of the
place of conscience in Catholic moral teaching. Pope Pius XII's
statement on pacifism, of which we have been treating, has
caused an old charge to be resuscitated to the effect that the
moral teaching of the Catholic Church is authoritative to the
extent of being anti-individualistic. It depends exclusively on
obedience, not to conscience and God, but to the authority of

[1] Pope Pius XII, *Address to Cardinals, Archbishops and Bishops,*
Rome, 2 November 1954.

the Church, so that it is nothing more than an exterior conformity in a society. This charge about the subordination of
the individual was very common in the last century, particularly on the part of German Protestant theologians. The idea
of duty in Catholicism, said O. Pfleiderer, is conceived 'as the
sum total of temporal and ecclesiastical legislation.'[1] In contrast with the Protestant view of the inwardness of duty as
dictated by conscience, in Catholic morality, it was said,
'ethical obligation is found in an extraneous law; it is somehow imposed upon man from without'.[2]

The German Catholic theologian, Joseph Mausbach, devoted one of his major works to a rebuttal of this serious charge.[3]
He discoursed learnedly and convincingly on the point that the
Catholic conception of Christian morality has nothing at all in
common with the heteronomy spoken of by Kant. He went to
pains to show that for Catholics morality is by no means merely
a collection of rules laid down by the Church. The Church is
bound to reflect the law of Christ in her teaching and her directives; she simply declares to the individual the content and
implications of the faith in which he believes. Hence Mausbach
maintained that, once the Catholic standpoint has been properly understood, it is possible to connect it with the idea of
legislation from without only if it is permissible to speak of
God Himself as something entirely external to man. Since it is
in God that we live and move and have our being, and since
we recognise Him as the source of our intellectual powers, He
is the innermost foundation and support of all our moral
actions.[4]

The problem still remains of explaining the dilemma which
arises when the Church's teaching conflicts with what the
conscience of an individual tells him. In virtue of the impor-

---

[1] O. Pfleiderer, *Grundriss der christl. Glaubens und Sittenlehre*, p 256.

[2] Stange, *Einleitung in die Ethik*, 1901, vol. II, p 95.

[3] J. Mausbach, *Catholic Moral Teaching and its Antagonists*, New
York 1914. See especially Part II, ch 1, *The Law of God and Conscience;*
ch 3, *Law and Freedom: Probabilism*, and ch 9, *The Authority of the
Church and the Liberty of the Individual.*

[4] Cf Mausbach, *op. cit.* p 139.

tance of the subject it is rather surprising that more has not
been written on it.[1] Fundamental to the whole problem is the
fact that every free and moral act is an act of obedience to a
judgment of reason. Scholastic philosophy provides elaborate
proof of the thesis that the freedom of the will consists in being
obedient to reason. It also shows that moral action consists of
an acceptance of the order of reason and what it demands.
By the light of reason itself, says St. Thomas, 'we discover what
we have to do. Any human action that is in keeping with this
light is good; whatever is contrary to it is unnatural to man
and evil'.[2] In virtue of this he can say that man 'is his own
lawgiver, since he instructs himself and urges himself on to that
which is good'.[3] From which it follows that moral action is a
manifestation of spiritual freedom; it is man's deliberate obedience to a law of conduct imposed by reason.

The question before us is whether the intrusion of authority
by way of the imposition of duties on man represents an alien
force which destroys the inner freedom of the individual and
consitutes an objectionable heteronomy. The clue to the answer
depends on a full understanding of what is meant by reason.
The reason of the individual man is very prone to error; only
too well do we know how subject it is to false judgment. All
too easily does it follow evil under the guise of good, leading man
to use his freedom at the service of sin, for he retains his freedom—as obedience to reason—even when the latter fails him
and directs him along the path of error. As a result it is clear
that morality—and true inner freedom—cannot consist in a
blind following of individual reason but of reason as such which,
when the individual reason conforms to it, is called 'right'

[1] For a bibliography on the question see however E. von Kuehnelt-
Leddihn, *Liberty or Equality*, London 1952, p 339. For a general dis-
cussion of conscience see Georges Leclercq, *La conscience du chrétien*,
Paris 1946 and Eric D'Arcy, *Conscience and its Right to Freedom*,
London, 1960, *passim*. An excellent examination of our problem has
been conducted by Fr. John Courtney Murray S.J. in *Theological
Studies*, vol. VI (1945), pp. 244-262.

[2] *In II Sent.*, D. 42, Q. 1 art. 4, ad 3.

[3] *In Ep. ad Rom.* c. 2.

reason. It is reason in this wide sense that is the source of natural law—ultimately the reason of God the creator and proximately that of the individual man.[1] 'The human will', says St.
Thomas, 'is subject to a twofold rule: the first is a proximate,
homogeneous rule, viz., human reason; the other is . . . the
eternal law, which is, as it were, the divine Reason itself'.[2]

St. Alphonsus Ligouri begins his *Moral Theology* with a like
statement: 'There is a twofold rule governing human action,
one remote and the other proximate. The remote or material
rule is the law of God; the proximate or formal rule is conscience'.[3] We know, however, that this is not the end of the
story; what of the vast provinces of divine positive and human
law? It is with human law—that of the Church—that we are
concerned here, its binding force, irrespective of its arguments.
The directives of human law are also the expression of the demands of reason concerning the requirements of the social life
of man. In this sphere it is abundantly clear that 'right' reason
must get preference over the arbitrary and often anarchical
dictates of purely individual reason. The law of the State is
compelled to reject that political individualism which would
erect the freedom of choice of the individual into a supreme
value. In the interests of realism as well as of reason it has to
refuse to regard its function as merely the protection of the
conflicting freedoms of individuals. It has no option but to enforce the moral law that is relevant to social life by enshrining
right reason in its laws and ordinances. The achievement of
this, without overstepping the mark and deteriorating into

[1] This close connection of the Natural Law with the divine as well
as with human reason is not always retained in expositions of Natural
Law, e.g. D. O'Donoghue, The Thomist Concept of Natural Law, in *The
Irish Theological Quarterly*, vol. XXII (1955), n 2. To whittle down the
connection means to sail close to Grotius's idea of Natural Law as
the law of human reason, which would be 'the same even if God never
existed'. It was this concept of Natural Law, however unintentionally,
that opened the door to relativism in men's conception of what is moral
—and ultimately ended in a positivist concept of human law.

[2] 1a 2ae, Q. 71, art. 6, c. o.

[3] *Theol. moral*, I, I.

totalitarianism, is a perennial problem for the rulers of States.

The role of Church law *vis-a-vis* the conscience of the individual bears a close analogy to that of the State *vis-a-vis* its citizens. To allow the moral law to be left solely to the intelligence and determination of the individual conscience would produce not only moral chaos but ecclesial anarchy. The idea that it should so be left has in recent years been built into the doctrine that is commonly known as 'Situation Ethics'. According to this, every man's conscience is something closed up within itself, the absolute master of its own decision. There is no such thing as 'right' reason in the sense of the immutable principles of a universal law; reason and morality is what the conscience of the individual decides in the unique situation which constitutes the background to every moral decision.

Situation ethics was criticised by Pope Pius XII on a number of occasions[1] and was finally condemned by a decree of the Holy Office in 1956.[2] Its main error is to conceive the function of conscience as creating the law of human conduct. For it is the practical reason of the Creator that makes the moral law; human reason merely issues what it discovers of it. Morality is given to men in general by God; it is given to the individual man by way of the operation of his conscience. In this consists the dignity and autonomy of man, that he imposes a heteronomous law upon himself. But it is also the ground of the truth that it is a debasement of the dignity of conscience to demand as its right the ignoring of the reason of the ultimate Lawgiver.

It is a basic obligation of conscience, then, to seek to educate itself in the sense that it strive to be 'right' in the decisions which it makes.[3] It needs the illumination of what moral science is likely to be helpful to its decisions, as well as a sufficient formation in the discipline of the moral virtues and adequate cultivation of the virtue of prudence. Some important conse-

---

[1] Cf *A.A.S.*, vol. xxxxiv, p 274 and pp 413-319.

[2] Cf *A.A.S.*, vol. xxxxviii, pp 144-145. For a good discussion see A. M. Carr, The Morality of Situation Ethics, in *Proceedings of the Twelfth Annual Convention of the Catholic Theological Society of America,* 1957, pp 75-100.

[3] Cf J. C. Murray, *loc. cit.* pp 256-262.

quences follow from this. While it must be granted as a general principle that one must always follow one's conscience, it is essential to add a number of limiting qualifications. First of all, in the case of a dubious conscience, it is clear that this is no adequate rule of moral action and that it cannot be followed without sinful indifference to the law of God. It calls for formation in some way of a kind that will produce the certainty that is required for genuine moral choice and action. The case of the erroneous conscience is more difficult to settle, for here there is certainty though in error. This is the case with the Catholic pacifists, which has led to our treatment of conscience in these pages. As they see it they are entitled to follow their lights; neither Pope nor bishop can impose the duty on them of doing otherwise.

It will be realised, on reflection, that the ignorance of the moral law on which an erroneous conscience is necessarily based can and does vary in nature and degree. At times a person with an erroneous conscience will have a suspicion that it is in ignorance, as a result of which its decision is not to be trusted. Such a man can dispel his ignorance by seeking knowledge from the proper quarters; his ignorance is what the theologians call 'vincible'. There can be no doubt that he has an obligation to seek to inform himself adequately; should he fail so to seek, his acting on his conscience is based on a certainty that is only of a surface kind and not far removed from bad faith. In the case of invincible ignorance, on the other hand, a man is in an entirely different position; he can do nothing about it because he does not at all suspect its presence. It is necessary to add that, once Pope or bishop has taught something that is at variance with the opinion of the individual conscience, it is difficult to hold that the latter's ignorance is not vincible? Likewise is it not reasonable that—in the interests of society—an erroneous conscience should have no rights against social authority as far as action in the external forum is concerned?

All this should be remembered if one is to understand the position of Pope Pius XII when he declared that a Catholic citizen 'cannot invoke his own conscience in order to refuse to serve' when his country needs his help for its just defence.

CHAPTER THREE

THE ETHICS OF CONQUEST

CONQUEST may be defined as a coercive act whereby territory is acquired by a State through the use of armed force. Ethicians divide it into 'conquest per se' and 'conquest per accidens'. Conquest per se is conquest simply for the purpose of expansion; conquest per accidens is based primarily on some other reason.

It is only too true that, throughout the course of history, conquest per se has been very much in evidence. Indeed it may be regarded as the main fount of empires. Lord Moreley, speaking of the occupation of Chitral in North India in 1895, gave a frank description of the British mode of practising it. There are five stages, he said, on the road to high conquest:

'First, you push your territories where you have no business to be, and where you had promised not to go; secondly, your intrusion provokes resentment, and in these wild countries resentment means resistance; thirdly, you instantly cry out that the peoples are rebellious and that their act is rebellion (this in spite of your assurance that you have no intention of setting up a permanent sovereignty over them); fourthly, you send a force to stamp out the rebellion; and fifthly, having spread bloodshed, confusion and anarchy, you declare with uplifted hands that moral reasons force you to stay, for if you were to leave, this territory would be left in a condition which no civilised power could contemplate with equanimity or composure'.[1]

Conquest of this kind—motivated by greed for wealth and

[1] Cited in Raymond de Martini, *The Right of Nations to Expand by Conquest*, Washington 1955.

power—has been condemned by Christian teaching from the beginning. St. Augustine unhesitatingly rejected it, despite the great contributions to civilisation and opportunities for the spread of the Church which the Pax Romana had brought to the world. The reason is that such conquest is, by its definition, a matter of pure aggression and, therefore, can never be lawful. It is a direct infringement of the natural rights of a just possessor. Indeed it is unlawful whether or not the possessor has a legitimate title, because the attacker does not ask himself this question. He is motivated solely by expediency which can never of itself be a source of right.

THE PRINCIPLES

Conquest per accidens is a very different matter. Here there is question of expansion that is not motivated merely by aggrandisement. Rather is the position that some other good is sought, which can only result from an effective war of conquest. It is Christian teaching that such conquest can be just if prosecuted because of some extremely grave and pressing necessity. Theologians hold that there is question of just conquest whenever a State, which is in extreme need through no fault of its own, employs belligerent means, after all peaceful means have failed, in order to acquire territory or its equivalent from another State which has superfluity of goods.

It will be noticed at once that the principle is hedged round by certain conditions. These have been developed by moralists over the course of centuries, for it was by a process of trial and error that the Christian conscience became properly informed on the question. Four writers, in particular, contributed to this —the Spanish Catholic Francisco Vittoria and the Protestant thinkers Grotius, Puffendorf and Vattel.

Vittoria (1480-1546) is regarded as the founder of International Law. He lived during the hey-day of the Spanish conquests in the New World and was personally confronted with the problems to which they gave rise. At a time when some of his countrymen were in doubt about even the humanity of the

American Indians,[1] it is not to be wondered at that these were not always treated with justice. Vittoria was particularly uneasy about the conduct of the conquest of Mexico, which led him to draw up some principles governing lawful colonisation. He was forced to admit that the matter was brimful of difficulties. Nevertheless, he listed a number of what he regarded as legitimate titles to conquest, as well as a number of titles which he termed 'not adequate'.

The latter include such claims as that the Spanish Emperor is lord of the earth and can subjugate anyone at will; that the Pope can grant territory to a ruler anywhere he wishes; that the fact of 'discovery' in itself constitutes a sufficient reason for the exploring power to assume rulership over primitive peoples; that refusal to accept the Christian religion, or the existence of immorality against nature, can cause a people to forfeit the right to self-government and, finally, that the Spanish nation has a right to conquest in virtue of a special grant from God.

On the other hand, Vittoria regarded as legitimate titles to conquest in the Americas violation of the Spaniards' right to travel there; refusal to allow Christian missionaries to preach the Gospel; the forceful prosleytism of native Christians by the Indians; the need to have a Christian government for converted natives and, in general, the need to stamp out tyranny and introduce progressive government. Vittoria approached the subject in the concrete rather than in the abstract. Nevertheless, the general idea emerged that the only just conquest is conquest because of some necessity.[2]

Grotius, Puffendorf and Vattel effected further develop-

[1] Cf Lewis Hanke, *Aristotle and the American Indians*, London 1959, *passim*.

[2] Cf. deMartini, *op. cit. passim*. Vittoria's treatment of the titles to conquest is found in his *De Indis* (1539), English edition in James Brown Scott, *F. Vitoria and His Law of Nations*, Washington, 1917. The right of emigration and immigration is included in a modernised version of Vittoria—J. M. de Aguilar, O.P., The Law of Nations and the Salamanca School of Theology, in *The Thomist*, vol. IX (1946), p 220.

ments. These included the extension of the just titles to cover conquest demanded by the interests of defence and a recognition that the need to find adequate living space is something for which a people can lawfully cater by taking extreme measures. The importance of this, in the eyes of these authors, is interesting as, at that time, Europe was nowhere overcrowded, its population being little more than fifty millions. It was for this reason, perhaps, that Vittoria had not mentioned 'living space' as a title to conquest except by way of one or two vague references. Grotius too did not envisage so much expansion due to overcrowding as the needs of travellers, merchants, preachers and refugees. Puffendorf and Vattel explicitly allowed the need to find an outlet for ordinary migration as constituting a legitimate title to conquest.

They insisted, however, that, before this title can be pressed in practice, three important conditions must be fulfilled. These are, firstly, that the need be extreme; secondly, that the territory to be conquered be not reduced to a like need as a result of the conquest; and thirdly, that all peaceful means of solution have previously been exploited in vain.

Since the days of these early theorists the ethics of conquest have been further clarified, but the basic principle remains unchanged. Just conquest means conquest because of necessity, which in turn can relate to two different kinds of need. On the one hand, it can cover the need to conquer in the interests of defence against armed aggression and, on the other hand, the need to conquer in the interests of defence against famine or poverty by providing for one's people at the expense of the goods of another State.

The need in question has got to be extreme. 'Common need', such as is widely experienced, is not sufficient. Neither is what the moralists call 'grave need', which obtains when a very notable shortage of external goods prevails or is imminent, or when there is probable danger of a notable loss of such goods. Extreme need exists only when there is a lack of things that are essential to life, or its equivalent, or when there is certain danger of losing these permanently. If such goods, which nature intended to be common to all men, cannot be acquired without the assistance of another State, the nation which requires them is said to be suffering from extreme need. To this category belongs also what is called 'quasi-extreme need', i.e., when a nation is on the verge of extreme need. In short, in the present context, what is called 'extreme need' means actual or imminent danger to the existence or well-being of a State, arising from lack of living space, food, natural resources or trade, which cannot be removed without going outside the State for aid. It should be unnecessary to add that this must be an unavoidable and not an induced need.

Every State has the duty of providing its citizens with the means of normal development. If it becomes impossible to do so, the State is in extreme need. This is not at all to be confused with a situation in which poverty exists for a minority of the people. But it does obtain if, in general, the citizens cannot enjoy living conditions comparable to the average found in other States, without gaining access to new territory, or when they are definitely on the verge of being in this position. Thus in 1921 Pope Benedict XV said that Austria had a natural right not merely to exist but to live, i.e., to enjoy average prosperity. Other States have a duty towards the individual State in such need and if they fail to come to the rescue it can lawfully resort to conquest provided certain other important conditions are fulfilled.

The State attacked must have superfluity of resources. The reason for this is that nobody is required to give what he has to another if by doing so he reduces himself to a situation of similar need. In such circumstances he cannot be legitimately deprived of his goods. The same holds when the possessor is a State. In addition, the superfluity must relate to the things of nature—to natural resources or living space. The fact that these are not being used here and now is not enough to make them superfluous; the possessor may have some need of them in the immediate future. But any territory that is abandoned, un-cultivated or sparsely inhabited, and which is not necessary in the foreseeable future for the maintenance of the State's pro-sperity, can certainly be regarded as superfluous.

The existence of superfluous territory can usually be estab-

lished by inquiring whether the needs of the population have
been adequately supplied for several decades by other areas.
For, if this be so, it is very unlikely that it will need the unde-
veloped areas in the immediate future. And the present *actual*
need of another State that is in extreme want is more important
than any *possible* future need of a State with present adequacy.
Needless to say, too, it must be certain that, in the areas to be
conquered, there is sufficient to meet the needs of the country
in want.

It is all too easy for a nation in need to turn its eyes on
the resources of its nearest neighbour. Ideally, superfluity
should be established by a body of experts—preferably international in composition. If it is found to exist, then the State
that enjoys it has a duty to help the State in need—by giving
it direct aid or by granting it rights in the matter of tapping
resources, of migration or even of actual territory. If it refuses
to do so, it is in the position of being an unjust aggressor and
can lawfully be forced to yield up its superflua.

Finally, conquest can only be resorted to when all peaceful
means of relieving extreme need have failed. These include
appeal to the Society of States, offer of purchase, tenancy,
migration etc. Some moralists would say that the nation in
need has the right of choice of peaceful solutions, although they
are not prepared to say that this right can be enforced by
hostilities. But all agree that, if all peaceful methods have been
tried in vain, just resort can be had to conquest for the purpose
of migration and plantation or, at a minimum, of exploiting the
raw materials of another State.

The question as to whether restitution must be made by the
conqueror is disputed. Grotius and Puffendorf thought that it
should. The more probable opinion is that this is not necessary
as the conquest is effected at the expense of an unjust possessor.
It is insisted though that, in itself, just conquest does not allow
the annexation of the territory or the setting up of a planters'
government in it. This can be done only if the planters would
otherwise have to demean themselves, by submitting to the
rule of a less civilised people, or because, by reason of different
ideologies, integration into the existing order is impossible.

An example of conquest in the past that is relevant to contemporary politics is to be found in the case of Northern Ireland. It is seldom—if ever—that its ethical aspect is brought into discussion of the problem of partition. To date this question has been discussed on somewhat different grounds. The usual approach is that adopted, for example, by Dr. Alfred O'Rahilly when he supposes that the basic ethical problem of partition is whether the people of Ireland can, *here and now*, be regarded as constituting a *natural* political unit, in such a way that only the entire population of the country as a whole has the right to decide on how the whole is to be governed.[1] He assumes this, but admits that it is difficult to prove. In common with Dr. Walter McDonald[2]—famous Maynooth Professor at the beginning of the century—he affirms that it is hard to see how Ireland in the past, not to speak of the present, was ever a unified political community. 'We rely', he says, 'on *a priori* instincts, though historically this island never had a unified native Government'. He does not, however, prove this point, while Dr. McDonald's proof is confined to ancient and medieval times.

A CONCRETE EXAMPLE: IRELAND

The question whether the people of Ireland can be said to constitute one *nation* is not the crucial one in relation to the moral problem posed by partition. The important thing is whether they constitute one *natural political community*. Granted such unity, it is urged that only the people of the island as a whole can legitimately decide on how Ireland should be governed.

One can readily agree that the question of nationality is a secondary one. History provides us with many examples of the same nation spread over a number of States while, conversely, we find unified and justly constituted States whose populations are heterogeneous from the point of view of nationality. Undoubtedly if it could be proved clearly that the people of Ire-

---

[1] A. O'Rahilly, Articles in *Hibernia*, January, February and March 1957.

[2] Walter McDonald, *Some Ethical Questions of Peace and War*, London 1919.

land make up one nation, this would strongly suggest—though not necessarily—that they also constitute a natural political community. But it would be a mistake to think that the latter can have no other basis, or that, granted such unity, the Stormont government is immediately deprived of ethical support. As I see things, from the point of view of ethics, the question is threefold: firstly, whether, prior to partition, the people of Ireland ever did possess such unity; secondly, whether, on the principles which govern just conquest, there was sufficient reason for the separation of the Six Counties from the rest of the country; thirdly, whether the present Stormont government is legitimate—with or without the consent of the people of all Ireland. My reasons for this tripartite approach are centred on the contention that I regard partition as deriving fundamentally from what was English conquest in Ireland, that the ethics of conquest attach no special importance to the consent of the conquered in order to effect a just annexation of territory and, lastly, that the consent of the people is not the only source of legitimate government.

Whether or not Ireland constituted one political community in ancient or medieval times, there is no doubt that it came to do so well before the modern period. Note well that there is question of geographical political unity rather than of national unity as such. In my view, no matter what the position may have been in earlier ages and apart altogether from the question of national unity, all Ireland was constituted into one political community after the defeat of the Gaelic chieftains at Kinsale. In other words, at the beginning of the Stuart period Ireland cannot but be regarded as one State. The whole country was actually as well as theoretically under one government, that of the Irish Parliament. True, this only met rather infrequently and was but an instrument for the implementation of English policy. Nevertheless the country was a unified, if merely a satellite, State.[1]

[1] Irish interpretation of the constitutional position was always on the side of the legislative independence of Ireland. Thus in 1641—on the eve of the rebellion—the Irish House of Commons declared that 'the subjects of this His Majesty's Kingdom of Ireland are a free People,

To my mind, the moral root of the present 'Ulster' problem is whether the Stuart Plantation in the North (1608)—and the later influx there of Scots and English—was morally lawful on the principles of just conquest. For it is this settlement, and others like it, that have given rise to partition. In other words, the first question is whether the conquest of 'Ulster' was originally justified by necessity on the part of the colonisers, the predecessors of the present-day Northern Unionists?

and to be governed only according to the Common Law of England, and Statutes made and established by Parliament in this Kingdom of Ireland'. This argument was developed by Patrick Darcy, a member of the House, in his *An Argument Delivered by Patrick Darcy, Esquire, by the Expresse Order of the House of Commons in the Parliament of Ireland*, Waterford 1643. It was repeated in 1644 in a pamphlet entitled *A Declaration setting forth How, and by what Means, the Laws and Statutes of England from Time to Time came to be in force in Ireland*. This has been attributed both to Patrick Darcy and to Richard Bolton, the Chancellor of Ireland. Again, in 1698, the same argument reappeared in Wm. Molyneux's *The Case of Ireland's Being Bound by Acts of Parliament in England Stated*. Once more it was used from 1747 on by Charles Lucas in his *Addresses* and still later, just before the Union, by Grattan (Cf *Speeches*, London 1822, vol. I, p 38 *seq.*). English writers, from the very outset, sought to rebut it. Mayart's answer to the *Declaration* of 1644 laid down the lines which they were to follow: 'Ireland is a part and member of England, both being governed by the Laws thereof, and subject to the Laws made by the Parliament there . . . The liberties, lives and estates of those in Ireland should be bound by statutes made in England, because they are members of that Commonwealth . . . If the King of England should conquer any territories beyond the sea, and give them the laws of England, I think none will say that the distance of place will shake off the Power of the Government of England . . . So it is in this case of Ireland . . . Ireland is under the jurisdiction of the Parliament of England and subject thereto'—in W. Harris, *Hibernica*, part II, pp 160-193, 196-197. Cf. also 14 and 15 Charles II: "Almightie God hath given your Majestie, by and through your said English and Protestant subjects, absolute victorie and conquest over the said Irish and Popish rebels so as they, their lives, liberties and estates are now utterly at your Majestie's disposition. "—in *Irish Statutes Revised* 1310-1800, ch II, 1662, London, 1885. Charles Howard McIlwain, after an examination of the question, says that the evidence tends 'to incline the balance of

Let me reply at once to the charge that this is an over-simplification. I am well aware that the occupation of the territory in question was not accomplished all at once. Antrim and Down, the two counties in which Unionism is strongest today, did not at all come under the plantation of James I. In fact the counties then planted have and always had a Nationalist majority. Some of them are part of the Republic. Still, in one way or another, the Unionist bloc in the Six Counties as a whole traces its origin to successful confiscation and plantation. Prior to the Stuart plantation, during Elizabethan times, there were plantations in counties Antrim, Down and Monaghan. In some instances land was parcelled out to small-holders; in others very large tracts were given to noble families. Into these latter estates, at the beginning of the 17th century, a great number of Scottish and English immigrants was introduced. In this way the lands in County Down of Sir James Hamilton and Sir Hugh Montgomery were repeopled. In the same way, in County Antrim, the McDonnells introduced Scotsmen into formerly Irish-owned lands that had at one time or another been either seized by the English Crown or inveigled from the Irish chiefs. In all this can be traced the ultimate cause of the present separate government in the North East.

It is essential to discern the import of the argument. There is no questioning the moral as well as the legal title to their possessions of the present-day descendants of these settlers. It may be true that the dispossessed Irish families have long memories, that you will still find homes on the mountain slopes of Derry, Tyrone and Antrim, whose members continue to identify with accuracy the lands on the plains that once were theirs. Despite this, the view of the moralists would be that they had forfeited all just claim to these properties. For while it is certain that mere possession cannot give a morally just title to robbed property, many other considerations have to be taken into account. There is more than the fact of possession to be thought about. The passing of three centuries has involved

probability decidedly towards the Irish view of Parliament's powers'— *The American Revolution: A Constitutional Interpretation*, New York 1923, p 78.

so many changes that a reversion to former ownership is unthinkable, even where the original families can, in general, be
established. Ownership has, in many cases, passed through
many hands and the original families, even when known, have
become fragmented.

It is with the confiscations and settlements themselves that
we are concerned. There is no reason why it should not be
possible to decide on their morality by applying the ordinary
ethical principles governing conquest. Indeed there is every
reason why this should be done. After all it was precisely during
the period when the confiscations were taking place in Ireland
that the ethics of conquest were being worked out in relation
to the seizure of the lands of the American Indians. And even
a cursory consideration of these principles in relation to the
confiscations in Ireland raises the suspicion that these were
entirely unjustified.

Take first the Elizabethan confiscations. Even granting for
the moment that, during the Elizabethan wars, the country
did not constitute a political unity and that opposition to the
English was entirely on the part of a federation of petty States,
the defeat of these, in itself, would not justify the confiscation
of territory in any of them. On what moral grounds could the
conquest of any of these States be advanced? In what way was
it imperative to the self-defence of England? There is no escaping the suspicion that the Elizabethan conquest in Ireland was
but an implementation of the greedy plans for expansion and
imperial hegemony that marked the reign of this Tudor Queen.

The case of the plantation of Ulster under James I (1608)
is even clearer, for this time the official reason for it has come
down to us—the philosophical reason, as it were, to give countenance to the seizure of territory. 'No man's private worth',
wrote King James to his Lord Deputy, 'is able to counter-
balance the safety of a kingdom, which this plantation, being
well accomplished, will procure'.[1] If the suggestion here was
that the plantation was necessary to ensure the safety of England against Irish aggression, it would be hard to think of a
more ill-founded claim. Perhaps then there was question of

[1] *Concise View of the Irish Society* (1832), Appendix, pp 183-184.

safety in a wider sense, through securing needed living space for the population of the neighbouring island? Here again the plantation could have no basis. Not only was the population in question itself small at the time, but there was no superfluity of territory in Ireland. The Earls, it is true, had fled the country, but the common people remained on their lands. Nevertheless, on the plea that 'if the empty veins of Ulster were once filled with good British blood the whole body of this commonwealth would quickly recover perfection of health',[1] the plantations were effected with assumed righteousness.

THE PLANTATION OF ULSTER

But let us investigate the matter more closely. By the plantation of 1608 nearly four million acres of Ulster territory were distributed amongst English and Scottish undertakers and ex-servicemen. We may pass over the less basic question of the propriety of the plantation before the bar of the civil code of the English realm. Whatever may have caused the flight of the Irish Earls—and the matter is obscure—they were denounced as outlaws and their lands declared escheated[2] to the crown in virtue of a recognised mode for the transference of property in English law.[3] Not indeed that this procedure cannot be ques-

[1] *Ibid.*

[2] Cf 'Collection of such Orders and Conditions as are to be Observed by the Undertakers upon the Distribution and Plantation of the Escheated Lands in Ulster', in Hill, *The Plantation of Ulster*, Belfast 1877, p 78 *seq.*

[3] In Sir Francis Bacon's *The Use of the Law* we get the basis of the Crown's claim to this. 'Upon attainder of treason the King is to have the land, although he be not the lord of whom it is held, because it is a royal escheat . . . The Conqueror got by right of conquest all the land of the realm into his own hands in demensne, taking from every man all estate, tenure, property, and liberty of the same. . . . and as he gave any of it out of his own hand, he reserved some retribution of rents, or services, or both, to him and to his heirs, which reservation is that which is called the tenure of land . . . Now concerning what attainders shall give in escheat to the lord, it is to be noted that it must either be by judgment

tioned even on its own ground and within the legal framework on which it was based. In particular, it ignored the Brehon law, according to which land belonged to the whole clan, and which, when it suited their purposes, had been appealed to by English jurists to prove that Irish chiefs owned only the land in the immediate vicinity of their residences. Even English law itself —having abolished the Irish law of gavelkind (1605)—could legitimately have regarded the crown, after the flight of the Earls, as entitled only to the demesne lands which they possessed.[1]

It is more profitable to examine the plantation in the light of the principles of international law and the moral criteria on which this is ultimately based. Of course it would be foolish to think that everybody involved in promoting the plantation was concerned that these principles should be respected. The English servitors, civilians and soldiers, who had taken part in the Seven Years' War, were interested only in receiving a reward for their loyalty. When, for a while, it appeared that O'Neill might be left in possession after his defeat, there were many ready to re-echo Sir John Harrington's Pauline litany of the trials—'eating horse flesh in Munster' etc.—which he had endured in suppressing the Irish rebel.[2]

After the Earls had fled, these came out into the open. In 1607 we find Sir Geoffrey Fenton reminding Salisbury of the opportunities for plantation that had presented themselves in Ireland.[3] Later in the same year Sir Arthur Chichester, the Lord

of death given in some court of record against the felon found guilty by verdict, or confession of the felony, or it must be by outlawry of him . . . '—*The Works of Lord Bacon*, London 1841, pp 577-580.

[1] Cf 'Gavelkind', Appendix v to Charles Dickson, *Revolt in the North*, Dublin 1960, pp 213-214. Cf also Sir Henry Maine, *Early History of Institutions*, London 1905, pp 185-186.

[2] 'How I did labour after that knave's destruction. I adventured perils of sea and land, was near starving, eat horse flesh in Munster, and all to quell that man who now smileth in peace at those who did hazard their lives to destroy him'—in Hill, *op. cit.* p 57.

[3] 'What a door is opened to the king, not only to pull down for ever these two proud houses of O'Neill and O'Donel, but also to bring in Colonies of the English and to plant both counties, to a great increase

Deputy, added his own voice to the gathering chorus.[1] And lest the King might be tempted to let out the Irish lands directly to a few tenants, we find Sir John Davies, the Attorney-General, urging that 'the disposition whereof (of the six counties) by plantation of colonies is a matter of great consideration'. Pointing to the fact that certain other plantations in the past had been 'in part rooted out by the Irish', he warned that the new plantation must be such that this could not happen again.[2] On no account must the suggestion of Sir Oliver St. John be followed to the effect that the Northern lands should be 'let out to natives of the country', even 'at high and dear rates'.[3]

Sir John Davies had no need to be disquited. In England the Lord Chancellor, Sir Francis Bacon, had taken it on himself to advise his lord and master on the subject. His *Considerations touching the Plantation in Ireland*, presented to James I in 1606, is of primary importance in discovering the philosophical reasons for the measure. Its interest permits quotation at some length.[4]

'It seemeth God hath reserved to your Majesty's times two works, which amongst the works of kings have the supreme

in His Majesty's revenues and to settle the countries perpetually in the Crown, besides that many well deserving servitors may be recompensed in the distribution without charge to His Majesty'. Letter to Salisbury, 9 September 1607, cited in Dickson, *op. cit.* p 28.

[1] 'They (in London) should observe, that this great territory is with great felicity escheated to His Majesty, who is now sole proprietor of the most part of it, as the native lords thereof were formerly accounted and known to be. His Majesty may retain and keep the same by a firm establishment in his crown forever, for his honour and increase of his revenues, which, once perfected, will reduce the whole kingdom to more civility and obedience'. Letter to Salisbury, 14 October, 1608, cited in Hill, *op. cit.* pp 68-69.

[2] 'The same will happen to this plantation within a few years if the number of civil persons to be planted do not exceed the number of the natives, who will quickly overgrow them as weeds overgrow the good corn'. Letter to Salisbury, 5 August 1608, cited in Hill, *op. cit.* pp 69-70.

[3] Letter to Salisbury, 9 October 1607, cited in Hill, *op. cit.* p 68, note 3.

[4] *The Works of Lord Bacon*, vol. I, pp 470-471.

pre-eminence; the union, and the plantation of kingdoms . . .
It hath pleased the Divine Prudence, in singular favour of your
Majesty, to put both these kinds of foundations or regenerations
into your hand: the one, in the union of the island of Britain;
the other, in the plantation of great and noble parts of the
island of Ireland . . . (Touching this matter of plantation) I will
speak somewhat of the excellency of the work . . . .

'For the excellency of the work, I will divide it into four
noble and worthy consequences that will follow thereupon. The
first of the four is honour . . . When people of barbarous manners are brought to give over and discontinue their customs of
revenge and blood, and of dissolute life, and of theft, and of
rapine; and to give ear to the wisdom of laws and governments;
whereupon immediately followeth the calling of stones for building and habitation; and of trees for the seats of houses, orchards,
enclosures, and the like. This work therefore, (is) of all the most
memorable and honourable your Majesty hath now in hand;
especially, if your Majesty join the harp of David, in casting
out the evil spirit of superstition, with the harp of Orpheus, in
casting out desolation and barbarism'.

'The second consequence of this enterprise is the avoiding
of an inconvenience, which commonly attendeth upon happy
times . . . An effect of peace in fruitful kingdoms, where the
stock of people, receiving no consumption nor diminution by
war, doth continually multiply and increase, must in the end be
a surcharge or overflow of people more than the territories can
well maintain; which many times, insinuating a general necessity and want of means into all estates, doth turn external peace
into internal troubles and seditions. Now what an excellent
diversion of this inconvenience is ministered, by God's providence, to your Majesty, in this plantation of Ireland wherein
so many families may receive sustentation and fortunes; and
the discharge of them also out of England and Scotland may
prevent many seeds of future perturbations . . . So shall your
Majesty in this work have a double commodity, in the avoidance of people here and in making use of them there.

'The third consequence is the great safety that is like to
grow to your Majesty's estate in general by this act; in discom-
fiting all hostile attempts by foreigners, which the weakness of

that kingdom hath heretofore invited; . . . the indisposition of that kingdom hath been a continual attractive of troubles and infestations upon this estate . . . .

'The fourth and last consequence is the great profit and strength which is like to redound to your crown, by the working upon this unpolished part thereof: whereby your Majesty, being in the strength of your years, are like, by the good pleasure of Almighty God, to receive more than the first-fruits; and your posterity a growing and springing vein of riches and power. For this island being another Britain, as Britain was said to be another world, is endowed with so many dowries of nature, considering the fruitfulness of the soil, the ports, the rivers, the fishings, the quarries, the woods, and other materials; and especially the race and generation of men, valiant, hard and active, as it is not easy, no not upon the continent, to find such confluence of commodities, if the hand of man did join with the hand of nature. So then for the excellence of the work, in point of honour, policy, safety and utility, here I cease.

That Sir John Davies was quick to learn from and even improve on this emerges from a letter to the Earl of Salsibury in 1610. It specifically concerned 'the state of Ireland' and particularly the recently completed plantation of Ulster. Having first dismissed the Brehon laws as constituting no obstacle to the plantation, Sir John continues: 'The only scruple which remains consists in this point—whether the King may, in conscience, or honour, remove the ancient tenants, and bring in strangers among them. Truly his Majesty may not only take this course lawfully, but is bound in conscience to do so.

'For . . . his Majesty is bound in conscience to use all lawful and just courses to reduce his people from barbarism to civility . . . Now civility cannot possibly be planted among them but by this mixed plantation of civil men, which likewise could not be without removal and transplantation of some of the natives . . . Again, his Majesty may take this course in conscience, because it tendeth to the good of the inhabitants many ways . . . for when the undertakers are planted among them (there being place and scope enough both for them and for the natives) . . . all the land shall be fully stocked and manured, 500 acres will be better value than 5,000 are now . . . Again, his Majesty's conscience may be satisfied in that his Majesty seeks not his own profit, but doth suffer loss by this plantation, as well in expense of his treasure as in the diminution of his revenue: for the entertainment of commissions here and in England, and the extraordinary charge of the army for the guard of the Lord Deputy and Council . . . hath drawn no small sum of money out of his Majesty's coffers . . . Lastly, this transplantation of the natives is made by his Majesty rather like a father than like a lord or monarch . . . as his Majesty doth in this imitate the skilful husbandman, who doth remove his fruit trees, not with a purpose to extirpate and destroy them, but that they may bring better and sweeter fruit after the transplantation'.[1]

In truth the ideas of Milord Bacon had found a glossator. It appears, however, that at least some of the reasons for which Bacon urged the plantation correspond to the just causes for conquest that were later enumerated by the Natural Rights school of international law. The needs of defence and an outlet for population figure amongst them. Not that Bacon himself is likely to have been interested in providing a genuine moral backing for the plan. It was the same Bacon who wrote in his *Essays Civil and Moral* that 'above all, for empire and greatness, it importeth most that a nation do profess arms as their principal honour, study and occupation'.[2] If ever it were preached, we have here a eulogy of conquest *per se*. And, in the case of the Irish plantation, what Bacon did was to develop considerations of expediency under the specious guise of the doctrine of necessity. The most notable practitioner of this art was Machiavelli.

In his *Letters as Secretary of State of Florence*[3] and his *Art*

---

[1] Letter to Salisbury, 8 November 1610, in Sir John Davies, *Historical Tracts*, Dublin 1787.

[2] Cf *Works*, vol. I, p 286. Contrast Vattel: '(The) true glory (of a nation) consists in the favourable opinion of men of wisdom and discernment: it is acquired by virtue, or the qualities of the mind and the affections and by the great actions that are the fruit of these virtues', *Le Droit des gens ou principes de la loi naturelle*, London 1758. English trans. London 1783, p 83.

[3] N. Machiavelli, *Works*, English trans., London 1775, vol. IV.

of War,[1] the latter developed one of the earliest statements on
national sovereignty and the extent to which it can be defended.
One hundered and fifteen years before Grotius and working
from entirely different premises, he arrived at conclusions that
are sometimes startlingly similar to those of the natural law
philosopher. Though unscruplous in the extreme, he showed
that realistic opportunism may sometimes lead in the same
direction as the most conscientious approach. Indeed when the
appearance of justice and fair dealing suited the purpose of the
statesman, Machiavelli recommended that it should be assumed
even by him who had it not.[2] Expediency was his cardinal
principle. It should be remembered, though, that Machiavelli
did not claim to be a moralist or a legal philosopher, nor did
he ever set out to write an abstract treatise on government.
He was concerned simply with what operated to the benefit of
his city. Bacon, in contrast, sought to invest expediency in the
cloak of justice.[3]

The legal philosophers of Bacon's England are wide open

---

[1] *Ibid.*

[2] Cf Burleigh Cushing Rodick, *The Doctrine of Necessity in International Law*, New York 1928, pp 7-10.

[3] In a New Year's message to James I (1611) Bacon wrote as follows: 'I many times do revolve in my mind the great happiness which
God hath accumulated on you. Your people military and obedient; fit
for war, used to peace. Your Church enlightened with good preachers,
as heaven with stars. Your judges learned and learning from you; just
and just by your example. Your nobility in a right distance between
Crown and People; no oppressors of the People, no overshadowers of the
Crown. Your servants in awe of your wisdom, in hope of your goodness'
—*Works*, vol. VI, pp 56-57. G. P. Gooch's comment is that 'what the
great Chancellor saw was seen by nobody else'—*Political Thought in
England from Bacon to Halifax*, London 1927, p 57. Gooch's summing
up of Bacon is interesting: 'There was a strain of recklessness in Bacon's
thought which was restrained neither by moral principles nor by consideration for the enduring interests of his country . . . A nationalist of
the exclusive school, Bacon was totally lacking in the sense that statesmen and rulers owe allegiance to European civilisation and to humanity
at large'—*op. cit.* pp 27-28.

to censure in that they erected expediency into a body of international law.

SIXTEENTH CENTURY ENGLISH LEGAL PHILOSOPHY

It is not surprising to find that the recognised founder
of what is known as the Historical School of international
law[1] was an Oxford professor of Bacon's time. Albericus
Gentilis (1552-1608), Italian immigrant and Regius Professor
of Law, produced a corpus of literature well-suited to the English climate.[2] It relied little on the kind of natural law concepts
that are so evident in Vittoria and in the later writings of
Grotius and Puffendorf. Instead it tended to build international
law on the presentation of a series of facts which had been
instrumental in shaping the course of international relations in

[1] Burleigh Cushing Rodick, *op. cit.* p 21.

[2] Appointed to his Chair in 1587, from 1590 on Gentilis resided in
London and employed a deputy to lecture at Oxford in his stead. His
influence is very noticable in John Selden (1584-1654), who matriculated
at Oxford in 1600. In 1609 Grotius published his *Mare Liberum*, which
maintained that, according to international law, the seas were open to
the ships of all nations. This ran counter to the prevailing English attitude and, some time later, after the English had confiscated some Dutch
vessels for fishing in Greenland waters without the King's licence, Selden
was commissioned by James I to compose an essay in support of the
English claim to dominion of the seas. Though not published until 1635,
for fear of alienating the King of Denmark, Selden's resulting *Mare
Clausum* is in the tradition of Gentilis. Even the *Dictionary of National
Biography* is forced to comment that, despite its learning, its 'propositions in support of which that learning is used are so directly at variance
with the most elementary rights of men, that the learning was wasted'.
The main thesis of Selden's work was that 'the King of Great Britain
is lord of the sea flowing about, as an inseparable and perpetual appen-
dant of the British Empire'.

As early as 1613 William Welwood, Professor of Civil Law at the
University of Aberdeen, had made a similar claim in his *Abridgement of
all the Sea-Lawes*. He repeated it in his *De Dominio Maris* in 1615. Cf
Grotius, *The Freedom of the Seas*, New York 1916; translated by R. van

the past.[1] Again and again, as with Machiavelli, we find Gentilis
weighing equities in such a way that greater needs should pre-

Deman Magoffin and edited with introduction by James Brown Scott.
It is interesting to contrast the English views with those of the Spanish
writer Vasquez de Menchaca, who maintained that the freedom of the
seas to the Indies was not a Spanish prerogative—*Controversias Ilustres*,
Ed. Valladolid, 1931. On the other hand, the Portuguese writer Freitas
thought it lawful for a country to seek to monopolise the freedom of
the seas—*De Justo Imperio Lusitanorum*. Cf. H. Munoz O.P., The
International Community according to Francis de Vitoria, in *The
Thomist*, vol. X (1947), n 1. Through his deputy, John Budden, Gentilis
also influenced Sir Arthur Duck (1580-1648) and Sir Richard Zouch
(1590-1661). The impact of his ideas would also have been felt at Cambridge, due to the mixing of jurists from both univerities in the College
of Advocates for London practice. Is it possible that Sir Robert Filmer,
who matriculated from Cambridge in 1604, had not read or heard of
the great Gentilis? There is a material if not a formal connection between Gentilis's views and the absolutism of Filmer's *Patriarcha*. Gentilis was frequently consulted by the government on the legality of
international measures. His *De Legationibus Libri Tres* (London 1585)
was a fruit of this. Dedicated to Sir Philip Sidney, it may have earned
Gentilis his Chair at Oxford.

[1] Cf *De Iure Belli Tres Commentationes*, London 1589; *Hispanicae
Advocationis Libri Duo* (published originally in 1612 after Gentilis's
death), 2 vols. Introduction, text and translation by Frank Abott, New
York 1921 (*Classics of International Law*, edited by James Brown Scott).
According to Abott, Gentilis 'broke away from ecclesiastical tradition.
Most of his predecessors, men like Covarruvias, Suarez, Molina and Soto,
who were Catholic theologians, carried over into their discussions of
international law the principle of the canon law and the method of a
priori reasoning. Gentili was a jurist by profession; his adherence to
Protestantism released him from ecclesiastical preconceptions, and the
bent of his own mind seems to have led him to the practice of examining
concrete cases of his own time and of drawing practical rules from them.
He may therefore with propriety be called the founder of the modern
historical school of international law'—p 19a. He adds that Gentilis
cited Roman law only 'by way of confirming or illustrating rules derived
from contemporary usage'—p 20a. T. E. Holland has sought to defend
Gentilis by saying that he was never content with a *nuda historiarum
recitatio*. What he sought was not to construct law on a pure basis of
fact but to examine facts in the light of the law of nations—Early

vail over lesser. Again and again too we find that the results of his debates closely resemble what is arrived at from different principles by the writers on natural law.

Albericus Gentilis deserves a more prominent place in English history than has been given to him heretofore by historians. I can find no reference to him, for example, in J. R. Black's *The Reign of Elizabeth*[1]. There is a chapter of this book devoted to literature, art and thought, but it lacks any account of the legal developments of Elizabethan England. Yet, as far as I can see, these developments were highly significant, particularly in the domain of international law. They represent a positivist interlude that would be hard to improve upon. In so far as English writers mention Gentilis at all, they deny this. *The Dictionary of National Biography* suggests that a considerable portion of the work of Grotius was inspired by and based on that of Gentilis.[2] J. N. Figgis sees him as the link between Vasquez, Suarez and Grotius. He says that Gentilis appealed continually to principles of equity and that he was careful to

Literature on the Law of Nations, in *Studies in International Law*, Oxford 1898, ch 2. It cannot be denied, however, that Gentilis viciously attacked the canon law as the fruit of the Dark Ages and that he had no time for the opinions of the theologians. J. L. Brierly says that he 'was perhaps the first to make a definite separation of international law from theology and ethics and to treat it as a branch of jurisprudence. 'Let theologians hold their peace', he writes, 'in work that belongs to others than they' '—*The Law of Nations*, Oxford 2nd ed. 1936.

[1] Oxford 1936.

[2] 'Gentilis combines for the first time the practical discussion of the Catholic theologians with the theory of natural law which had been mainly worked out by Protestants . . . The three books of the *De Jure Belli* supply the framework and much of the materials of the first and third books of the *De Jure Belli ac Pacis of Grotius*'. It would be hard to find a better example of wishful thinking than is exemplified by this passage. It chooses to forget altogether the natural law thinking of Vittoria, to whom Grotius himself referred, in the first draft of his famous work, as the author of the specific and unimpeachable axiom of the law of nations. It was this draft that was later published under the title of *Mare Liberum* and which drew from Gentilis's pupil the typically Gentilian positivist reply *Mare Clausum*.

accept the prescriptive guidance of Roman Law only when it was suitable from the point of view of a higher morality.[1] Having examined Gentilis, I find no basis for these assertions. But it will be more convincing to give Grotius's view of the matter. In the Prologue to his *De jure Belli ac Pacis* he tells us that Gentilis adopts too narrow an approach in supposing the Roman Law to be the Law of Nations, that he leans too heavily on the authority of doubtful sources, which arrived at decisions not so much to settle truth as 'to flatter those who consulted them', and that he leaves 'many very notable questions totally untouched'.[2]

[1] Cf J. N. Figgis, *Studies of Political Thought from Gerson to Grotius, 1414-1625*, Cambridge 1923, p 186. According to Holland: 'In point of fact, the general scheme of the immortal work of Grotius is taken from that of his predecessor (Gentilis), and both works rest upon the same conception of natural law'—*loc. cit.* p 2. It is clear, however, that Gentilis knew nothing of natural law literature beyond the treatise on war of Joannes de Lignano (written in 1365 and first published in 1477). And in his will he ordered his books to be burnt because of their imperfections. It is impossible not to agree with the interpretation by which Gentilis is considered as 'the *chef de l'école* of modern positivism'—A. H. Dantas de Brito, *La philosophie du droit des gens*, Washington 1944, p 37.

[2] Grotius, *De Jure Belli ac Pacis Libri Tres* (1625). Trans. by F. W Kelsey, 3 vols. Oxford 1925, Prolegomena, n 38. Grotius says that whereas Vittoria, Joannes de Lignano and others lacked 'the illumination of history', this has been supplied by Gentilis. He continues: 'Knowing that others can derive profit from Gentilis's painstaking, as I acknowledge that I have, I leave it to his readers to pass judgment on the shortcomings of his work as regards method of exposition, arrangement of matter, delimitation of inquiries and distinctions between the various kinds of law. This only shall I say, that in treating controversial questions it is his frequent practice to base his conclusions on a few examples, which are not in all cases worthy of approval, or even to follow the opinions of modern jurists, formulated in arguments of which not a few were accomodated to the special interests of clients, not to the nature of that which is equitable and upright'—pp 22-23.

Grotius was particularly critical of Gentilis's doctrine on war. The following passages refer explicitly to this: 'Quite untenable is the position, which has been maintained by some, that according to the law of nations it is right to take up arms in order to weaken a growing power

In the matter of the liceity of war and conquest there are outstanding differences between Gentilis and the Natural Law school. In his *De jure Belli*[1] Gentilis speaks of three principal causes for which war may legitimately be undertaken. They are the *causa necessaria, causa utilis* and *causa honesta*. Of these the *causa necessaria* seems to correspond with what the Natural Law writers also called a necessary cause. The *causa utilis*, however, is unknown to these. It means a reason for war against another State simply because it is growing in power and may one day constitute a danger. Lastly, the *causa honesta* means an excuse for war under the pretext of helping a friendly State. The remarks of Grotius on this teaching are pretty scathing. Referring explicitly to Gentilis, he utterly rejects the *causa utilis* and also qualifies the extent to which use can be made of the *causa honesta*.[2] Indeed the Natural Law writers made a point of observing that justice and utility are not the same and were wont to insist that a war of utility is lawful according to the law of nations only if and when it is permitted by natural law.[3] Such moral clarity is missing from Gentilis.

In view of this, need it be surprising if English international practice at this time be found to cut a poor figure from the point of view of morality? Ward's *Enquiry into the Foundations*

which, if it become too great, may be a source of danger. That this consideration does enter into deliberations regarding war, I admit, but only on grounds of expediency, not of justice'—pp 184-5. Again: 'Not less unacceptable is the doctrine of those who hold that defence is justifiable on the part of those who have deserved that war be made upon them'. And again: Those writers 'err in this also (who) think that a war undertaken for the defence of one's person or property does not require a declaration'—p 639.

[1] Book I.

[2] 'Every consideration of equity condemns the idea that one has the right to use force just because there is some danger that one could suffer violence. Indeed it is a natural consequence of human affairs that complete security can never be attained. In the face of uncertain evils, safety is to be looked for from divine providence and from unobjectionable measures, but not from violence'—*op. cit.* p 185.

[3] E. g. J. Burlamaqui, *Natural and Political Law*, English trans. Dublin 1791, vol. I, pp 184-185 and 166-167.

of the Law of Nations in Europe to the Age of Grotius (Dublin,
1795) is very critical of many aspects of it. Referring to Elizabeth, it notes how she stood behind the piratical Drake, on
the flimsy grounds that he was engaged in legitimate commerce
with the Americas, which the Spaniards had no authority to
forbid as 'contrary to the Law of Nations', their title to America
being but the 'Bishop of Rome's donation' which she did not
acknowledge.[1] Ward's commentary on such sophistry is eloquent testimony to the low state of international law at the
time. 'It is not perhaps altogether impossible to account for
this backwardness of the Law of Nations in comparison with
other improvements. Mankind in fact, had not yet thrown off
the trammels in which almost all knowledge had hitherto been
held, and if we consider the manner in which public men, even
the best-intentioned, endeavoured to account for their public
duties, we shall not be much surprised at their want of perfection in these particulars . . . The Law of Nations about this
period, was a vague and indeterminate phrase in everybody's
mouth, but with few precise ideas annexed to it. It consisted . . .
of a string of undigested precedents, the facts even of which
were but little understood, so that they might be made to bend
almost every way that suited the purpose of those statesmen
who affected to take them for their guide'.[2]

It needs no imagination to link Gentilis with the arbitrary
rule of Elizabeth and James I in Ireland. In seeking justification for the plantation of Ulster, it would be a serious omission
to fail to remember that it took place at the time when the
Divine Right of Kings was defended in England. James I himself penned some extreme statements of this, claiming to be
above and outside the ambit of all human law.[3] Albericus
Gentilis too produced a treatise on the subject[4] which he dedicated to the king and which, if anything, is even more extreme

[1] Ward, vol. II, p 283.

[2] Vol. II, pp 363-365-366-367.

[3] 'Kings are not only God's lieutenants upon earth and sit upon
God's throne, but even by God Himself they are called Gods'—*The
Political Works of James I*, Cambridge, Mass. 1918, p 307.

[4] *De Potestate Regis Absoluta*, London 1605.

than the work of the Frenchman Jean Bodin, who is most commonly associated with the origins of such absolutism. 'Quod principi placuit', agrees Gentilis, 'legis habet vigorem'; ('Principes) supremi sunt, quibus est nulla supra'; 'Lex est quodcumque placuit principi'; '(Rex) est arbitrii plenitudo, nulli vel necessitati, vel iuris publici regulis subiecta'; in short, 'Princeps est Deus in terris'.

Not that the era of unblushing positivism had as yet arrived. Gentilis affirms that the king must respect the natural law and the law of nations.[1] But philosophy of law has commenced a

---

[1] God is described by Gentilis as *simpliciter absolutus*, the King as *secundum quid absolutus*. He did not deny that the King should respect the law of God. There was little safeguard in this, however, as long as it was also held that the King alone is the judge of what the law of God enjoins. In his *True Law of Free Monarchies* James I gave expression to the substance and consequence of the royal claims: 'Kings are justly called gods, for they exercise a manner of resemblance of Divine power upon earth. For if you will consider the attributes of God, you shall see how they agree in the power of a King. God hath power to create or destroy, make or unmake at His pleasure, to give life or send death, to judge all and to be accountable to none. And the like power have kings. They make and unmake their subjects; they have power of raising up and casting down; of life and death; judges over all their subjects and in all cases, yet accountable to none but God. They have power to exalt low things and abase high things and to make of their subjects like men at chess'. We are told that when Ralph Brownrigg, Fellow of Pembroke, invited some friends to his rooms and asked 'May the King, for breaking fundamental laws be opposed?' he was suspended from all his degrees. Cf G. P. Gooch, *English Democratic Ideas in the Seventeenth Century*, New York 1959, p. 59, n 4. Contrast the encouragement of criticism by their subjects which was extended at the time by Spanish monarchs—Cf. L. Hanke, Free Speech in Sixteenth Century Spanish America, in *Hispanic American Historical Review*, vol. xxvi (1946), pp. 135-49; Also Balmes, Freedom of Speech under the Spanish Monarchy, *op. cit.*, ch 52.

The famous incident in the Star Chamber (1616) is worth another reporting. In the course of a speech James I said: 'It is atheism and blasphemy to dispute what God can do . . . So also it is presumption . . . in a subject to dispute what a King can do or say, that a King cannot do

slow and inevitable downward slide once the decision of the ruler himself has become accepted as the only proximate criterion of the justice of his own measures. The natural law is open to being interpreted as suits the policies of the ruler and only time is necessary before reference to it will be quietly dropped altogether.

It remains for us to plumb the influence of Gentilis and to show his connection with the Irish scene. Are we to suppose that the ideas of their master had no effect whatever upon Oxford undergraduates of the time? And are we to suppose that they had no effect in the sphere of practical politics in which these young men were later to participate? As far as academic matters go, it is certain that the views of Gentilis were to continue to be maintained for a considerable time to come. His successor, Sir Richard Zouch,[1] was also a supporter of the

this or that: but rest in that which is the King's Will'.

Coke: 'Your Majesty, the law is the golden measure to try the causes of his subjects . . . The King cannot take any case out of his courts and give judgment upon it himself. The Judgments are always *per curiam* and the Judges are sworn to execute justice according to the laws and customs of England'.

James I : 'This means that I shall be under the law which it is treason to affirm'.

Coke: 'Sire, Bracton saith that the King ought to be . . . under God and the Law'.

Whereupon His Majesty 'fell into that high indignation as the like was never known in him, looking and speaking fiercely with bended fist, offering to strike him; which the Lord Coke perceaving fell flat on all fower'. Cited in Richard O'Sullivan, *The Common Law of England*, London 1948, p 17, n 7.

Cf *Select Statutes and other Constitutional Documents illustrative of the Reigns of Elizabeth and James I*, Ed. G. W. Prothero, Oxford 1894; *The Political Works of James I*, with introduction and notes by C. H. McIlwain, Cambridge, Mass. 1918; J. W. Allen, *English Political Thought*, 1603-60, London 1938; W. L. McElwee, *The Wisest Fool in Christendom; the Reign of King James I*, London 1958.

[1] A pupil of Gentilis's deputy, John Budden, Zouch became Scholar of New College in 1607 and Fellow in 1609. In 1620 he succeeded Budden as Regius Professor of Civil Law at Oxford. Faithful to Gentilis, Zouch found favour with Bishop Sanderson of Lincon, who contributed the

historical approach to international law. The very title of his work indicates this;[1] a swift perusal of the contents confirms it. Again and again we find the same ideas as in Gentilis.[2] At the level of concrete practice they persisted still more palpably. In Ireland particularly—at that time almost the only English colony— their outlook on conquest was given application by the very many English noblemen who, as Lytton Falkiner has noted, were associated with the country at this period. Are we surprised to find that Sir John Davies, the driving force behind the Ulster plantation, was a law student during the Gentilis period at Oxford?[3]

Indeed with every step the 'plot' gets thicker. Thomas Hobbes too was an Oxford undergraduate at the time of Gentilis. It was during his second year at the University that the latter published his treatise on the absolute power of the ruler. Did it have no influence on Hobbes's later *Leviathan*, the most

preface to Archbishop Ussher's rather absolutist treatise *The Power Communicated by God and the Reverence and Obedience required by the Subject* (1640). In 1647 he took the side of the King and, together with Dr. Sanderson, drafted the 'Reasons' of the University of Oxford for disagreeing with the Solemn League and Covenant. There is no disputing his substantial contribution to the growth of the historical school of international law. His use of the phrase *jus inter gentes* was later to inspire Bentham to coin the term 'international law'.

[1] *Juris et Judicii Fecialis, sive Juris inter Gentes et quaestionum de eodem explicatio qua Quae ad Pacem et Bellum inter diversos Principes et Populis spectant, ex praecipuis Historico-Jure-peritis, exhibetur*, Oxford 1650. New edition by T. E. Holland, translated by J. L. Brierly, Washington (Carnegie Institute) 1911.

[2] Thus in discussing 'whether Elizabeth . . . justly assumed the protection of the Netherlands against the King of Spain', Zouch declares that 'fearing . . . lest the power of the Spaniard might spread more dangerously than ever in territories which were almost contiguous to her own realm and conveniently situated for effecting an invasion of England, she resolved . . . to take thought for the safety of the people committed to her care by frustrating the machinations of her enemies' —*Juris et Judicii Fecialis*.

[3] Cf The Life of Sir John Davies, in Davies, *Historical Tracts*, Dublin 1797.

thorough-going statement of State absolutism to come out of England? Did Gentilis too have no influence on the thought of Hobbes's *Elements of Law*[1] or on his *De Cive*, which contains an excursus into international problems? 'Every independent Commonwealth', says Hobbes, 'has a right to do what it pleases to other Commonwealths'.[2] For 'it is a proverbial saying that *inter arma silent leges*. There is little to be said concerning the laws that men are to observe one towards another in time of war, wherein every man's being and well-being is the rule of his actions'.[3]

This was before the appearance of the work of Grotius, when expediency ruled the roost in international affairs. Hobbes does not even regard as necessary the elaborate efforts of Gentilis to erect arguments from history and prescription into an international code. He was honest enough to realise that such procedure lent itself all too easily to being twisted as desired. It is not hard to find his mentor in this matter. Speaking of international law before Grotius, Ward remarks that it used to be said that 'Bacon was the first who perceived the imperfection of the science of the Law of Nations', so much so, indeed, that he could justify almost any measure in practice. We can well imagine the young Hobbes, when serving as personal secretary to Bacon, having the practical possibilities of what he had learned at Oxford pointed out to him by one wiser in the ways of the world than the bookish student. We can see them together, thinker and amanuensis, during Bacon's philosophical peregrinations. For 'His Lordship . . . was wont to contemplate in his delicious walkes at Gorambery . . . (and) His Lordship would often say that he better liked Mr. Hobbe's taking his thoughts than any of the others, because he understood what he wrote'.[4]

---

[1] Second Treatise in Hobbes's *Tripos;* its title is *De Corpore Politico*. Cf *Tripos*, 3rd ed. London 1684.

[2] *De Cive*, c 2; ed S. Lamprecht, New York 1949.

[3] *De Corpore Politico*.

[4] John Aubrey, *Brief Lives*, ed. Clark, vol. 1 (1898). Of Hobbes himself Aubrey relates that 'he walked much and he had in the head of his

Bacon was a better master of the art of duplicity than the honest and forthright Hobbes. He could wrap up his designs for expansion in Ireland under the heads of 'honour, policy, safety and utility'. But from what we know of him and his time, we are not startled to find that there was no excuse, in justice, for the plantation of Ulster. In particular, there was no basis for claiming that the causes for conquest recognised by the Natural Law school were present in relation to Ireland. The idea of overpopulation in Jacobean England is simply ridiculous. In fact, in the case of the plantation of Derry, it was necessary to tempt the planters to come. It was for this purpose that a memorandum was prepared entitled *Motives and Reasons to induce the City of London to undertake plantation in the North of Ireland*.[1] The profits to be reaped from land and river were meticulously outlined therein. The country was said to supply 'such an abundance of provisions as may not only sustain the plantation, but may furnish provisions yearly to the city of London . . . It affords fells of red deer, foxes, sheep and lambs, cony, martens, squirrels etc.' Which 'confluence of commodities' was eagerly exploited by the Londoners, as records of their selfish destructiveness and the setting of their lands to the natives at exorbitant rents attest. Small wonder that Hill should find it necessary to say that they 'had gone into this colonising transaction only with the one real object of self-aggrandisement'.[2] But 'the age of hypocritical cant had then unmistakenly set in, and many people had learned to conceal their predatory designs on Ireland and the Irish by assuming the mask of patriotism or religion'.[3]

Superfluity of resources was not to be found in fact in Ireland. A document of 1609 envisaged that 'restraint' would have to be used to secure the quitting of the confiscated territories

staffe a pen and ink-horne, carried always a note-book in his pocket, and as soon as a thought darted, he presently entered it into his booke . . . thus that booke was made'.

[1] Cf Hill, *op. cit.* pp 360 *seq.*

[2] Hill, *op. cit.* p 419.

[3] Hill, *op. cit.* p 363.

by their former owners.[1] That 'restraint' is a very mild word to describe the measures actually employed cannot be hidden even by the pious humbug of Chichester's letters.[2] Hill has given us an insight into the ensuing misery of the dispossessed.[3] It is not difficult to appreciate his picture of those of the Irish gentry, who had been children in 1610, as old men, wearing freize coats in 1670, farming the miserable scraps of land that had been left to their fathers.

Such is the 'inside' story of the plantation of Ulster, related in terms of the history of ideas, particularly in the domain of the philosophy of law. The 'consent' of the Irish Parliament did not change its character. The confiscation was essentially a forced one, about which the Parliament, even if it wished, could do nothing. Let us recall again our description of Ireland at the time as a satellite State and introduce an analogy with Hungary after the abortive revolution of 1956. Who would regard as justified then a 'peaceful' confiscation by Russia of areas in Hungary, on the grounds that it was necessary to ensure the continued existence of the country as a satellite and buffer State, of vital importance to the self-defence of the Soviet Union? And this even with the consent of the Hungarian govern-

---

[1] 'The natives yet dwell dispersedly over all the counties, who are to be drawn into certain limits before the undertakers can begin any plantation; which restraint must be effected by the countenance and power of the Lord Deputy'. Cited in Hill, op. cit. p 134.

[2] 'I intend by God's permission to be at the Cavan on St. James's Day, the 20th instant, there to begin that great work on the day of that blessed saint in heaven and great monarch (James I) on earth; to which he prays God to give good and prosperous success, for they shall find many stubborn and stiff-necked people to oppose themselves against and to hinder the free passage thereof, the work of removing and transplanting being to the natives as welcome as the sentence of death'. Letter to Salisbury 1610; cited in Hill, op. cit. pp 221-222.

Even after the plantation had been completed, Chichester was doubtful as to whether it could be successful without the maintenance of force, 'for to displant the natives, who are a warlike people, out of the greatest part of six whole counties, is not a work for private men'—Hill, p 446.

[3] Cf Hill, op. cit. p 349.

ment and without any renewed resort to the use of arms. The actual use of arms is not always necessary in order to make a conquest forcible.

It should be evident by now that the English interpretation of international law in the 16th century was such as to leave much to be desired. Its defenders can only fall back on the argument that at least it was no worse than that generally received at the time. They tend to be particularly critical of the Spanish interpretation, which they frequently charge with ignoring the principles of justice.[1]

No bigger mistake of judgement could be made. So much so indeed that a contemporary American writer has devoted a large volume to proving that 'the Spanish conquest of America has been, much more than a politico-military event, one of the greatest attempts ever made in history to have Christian principles prevail in international relations'. Neither before nor since, says Lewis Hanke, has the world seen such an effort in the cause of justice.[2] From the first protest by the Dominican Antonio de Montesinos in 1511 to the promulgation of the basic law on the Indians in 1573, the struggle for the principles of just conquest raged in Spain. It involved a long succession of books and debates and Royal Commissions. The first Commission to investigate the question issued regulations in 1512 by which the conquistadors were subjected to numerous and detailed obligations as regards the natives. During the same year Matias de Paz brought out one of the first treatises on the ethics of conquest, dealing with the power of the Spanish Emperor over the Indians.[3] Another Commission of theolo-

[1] Cf J. H. Parry, *The Spanish Theory of Empire in the Sixteenth Century*, Cambridge 1940.

[2] L. Hanke, *Colonisation et conscience chrétien au XVIe siècle.* Translated from American edition, Paris 1957, p. 311.

[3] *De Dominio Regum Hispaniae super Indos* (1512). Ed. Rome 1933. Cf. also Palacios Rubios, *Libellus de Insulis Oceanis quas vulgus Indiam appelat* (1512. Unpublished MS in the Bibl. Nacional, Madrid). Both of these writers, however, defend the validity of the title conferred on Spain in 1493 by Pope Alexander VI. In doing so they were only following the more commonly received opinion since the early

gians was set up in 1513 with the task of reviewing the whole question of conquest.

Contemporaneously with this intellectual probing into the principles on the matter, a series of humane experiments in conquest was made by the Spaniards. From 1517 to 1533, inspired by the great Dominican Bartholomew de Las Casas, attempt after attempt was made to find whether the Indians could govern themselves in liberty while respecting the interests of the Spaniards in their territories. It was to this end, during 1518-'20, that unsuccessful experiments were launched to see whether the Spaniards could settle peacefully in Venezuela. It was to the same end, from 1537-'56, that purely peaceful methods of evangelisation were tried in vain in Guatemala. Similarly in 1542 the encomienda system was abolished, whereby the Spanish settlers had a right to requisition Indian manual labour.

The most spectacular evidence of the 16th century Spanish interest in securing international justice is supplied by the famous controversy of Valladolid (1550-'51). It provides abundant proof, in the person of Gines Sepulveda, that by no means all Spaniards thought correctly on the matter at the time. Sepulveda has become notorious for his urging that the Indians should be treated ruthlessly in view of the gravity of their idolatry, their sins against nature, their rudeness of character and the need to evangelise them.[1] From 1547 on he had been maintaining this position in face of opposition from Las Casas

Middle Ages, which made much of the idea that such a title could stem from the *altum dominium* of the vicar of Christ. It had been defended in the 13th century by Hostiensis and in later centuries by St. Antoninus, Sylvester and Joannes Kupus. Vittoria was the first to denounce it as valueless, on the ground that the papal Bull conferred not a title to conquest as such but to the evangelisation of the Indians exclusively by the Spaniards.

[1] Sepulveda expressed his views in a manuscript entitled *Democrates alter, sive de justis belli causis apud Indos* (1547). This was reproved by the Council of the Indies and refused permission to be printed by a Commission of Professors of Alcala and Salamanca. Sepulveda defended it in a second work, *Apologia pro libro de justis belli causis* (1550).

and others. Which led the Council of the Indies to advise the
King that the dangers to his conscience involved by the conquest of America were so great that no further expedition should
be licensed without investigation as to whether the laws which
had been previously issued governing conquest were likely to be
observed by the colonisers. It was as a result of this that a
theological debate was staged at Valladolid in an endeavour to
decide as between Sepulveda and Las Casas. 'Probably never
before or since', remarks Lewis Hanke, who has written a second
book on the Valladolid debate, 'has a mighty emperor . . .
ordered his conquests to cease until it was decided if they were
just'.[1] Although the official decision was inconclusive, the debate won many supporters to Las Casas. The most notable of
these was Vasquez de Menchaca, whose writings on conquest
took the side of the Indians.[2]

Lewis Hanke's verdict on the whole episode is important.
'Today it is becoming increasingly recognised that no other
nation made so continuous or so passionate an attempt to discover what was the just treatment for the native peoples under
its jurisdiction than the Spaniards'.[3] Criticism of the Spanish
philosophy of conquest is certainly out of place on the part of
English writers. It was an Englishman, William Cunningham,
who in 1559 described the Indians as 'comparable to brute
beasts'.[4] Hanke records some resolutions of the New England
colonists: 'The earth is the Lord's and the fulness thereof.
Voted. The Lord may give the earth or any part of it to his
chosen people. Voted. We are his chosen people. Voted'.[5] A
more likely ground for English conquest, which Hanke has not
noted, was expressed in Richard Hakluyt's tract on the arguments in favour of colonisation as a public policy, which was
written in 1584. In this, entitled *A Particular Discourse con-*

[1] L. Hanke, *Aristotle and the American Indians*, London 1959, p 37.

[2] *Controversiarum Illustrium*, Ed. Valladolid 1931.

[3] *Op. cit.*, p. 107.

[4] *The Cosmographical Glasse*, London 1559. Cited in Hanke, *op.
cit.*, p. 99.

[5] *Op. cit.*, p. 100.

cerning Western Discoveries,[1] Hakluyt sought to justify Raleigh's colony on Roanoke Island in accordance with the prevailing principles of mercantilist economics. The central theme was
the quest for 'treasure'—so as to free England from the need
for purchasing from foreigners, as well as increase her shipping
and naval strength. We find the same ideas repeated in the
1630's in Thomas Mun's *England's Treasure by Forraign Trade*.[2]
Nowhere was anything like a counterpart produced to
Vittoria's famous *De Indis*.

Today, four centuries after the great era of conquest, the
whole subject presents itself in a different setting. Whether
original conquests themselves were just or unjust is a secondary
question to the exigencies of the present. In many colonies the
original settler stock has intermarried with and become almost
indistinguishable from the native peoples. In others colonial
governments, however illegitimate they may have been at the
beginning, have acquired just titles by way of consent or prescription.

It is probably true to say that, as the present day, the only
problem which still presses is that of deciding when a colonial
government should cede its powers to a native administration.
In other words, when it should relinquish the right to tutelage
in virtue of which it was originally established. It is well to
note that the first introduction of reference to this right was
made by modern writers rather than by those of the 16th
century.[3] It was the conscience solvent of the 19th and 20th
century colonial powers who, if they could not fall back on the
Vittoria type excusing causes for conquest, sought to justify this
on the grounds that their government was needed in the countries colonised if peace and civilisation were to prosper. Cardinal

---

[1] First published in 1877 in volume II of *The Collections of the
Maine Historical Society*, Second Series. Cf J. A. Williamson, Richard
Hakluyt, in *Richard Hakluyt and his Successors*, Ed. E. Lynam, London
1946. Cf. also D. B. Quinn, The Failure of Raleigh's American Colonies,
in *Essays on British and Irish History in honour of J. E. Todd*, London
1949.

[2] Ed. W. J. Ashley, London, 1903, p 7.

[3] J. V. Ducattillon, *Patriotisme et Colonisation*, Tournai 1957.

Mercier, drawing a distinction on this basis between colonisation and colonialism, declared the former to be an act of collective charity.

It is interesting to note that Vittoria, although aware of the possibility of this approach, refused to commit himself to it. He neither affirmed its legitimacy nor yet condemned it. What he did say was that the title of tutelage would be legitimate if there were question of a people who could not otherwise behave themselves better than infants or lunatics. He was not prepared, however, to number the Indians amongst such and seemed ready to grant that they should be allowed to freely choose who should govern them: 'Each State can choose its ruler, and for this a unanimous consent is not indispensable; it seems that the consent of the majority of the members suffices'.

Vittoria made much of the freedom and equality of all peoples. But, as R. P. Delos has noted, it is important that his understanding of this freedom should not be taken in too subjective a sense.[1] The most that can be said is that every people have the right to try to provide the best concrete political measures for themselves. They have no right to stand outside the general law of progress. Which means that there is still room, even in the world of today, for the exercise of political tutelage. Indeed some have argued that there is more need of this today than ever before in the interests of education towards a responsible world society.[2] The question is intimately related to those of the right to national self-determination and the right to revolt which we go on to treat of immediately in a separate chapter.

In doing so let us carry with us some thoughts from Balmes: 'In some instances a consummated fact, in spite of all its injustice . . . acquires such an ascendancy that by not accepting it, or by being determined to destroy it, we should let loose a train of troubles and commotions, and perhaps without effect. . . . In such a case, we should not commit an injustice by not attacking the illegal interests, or by not endeavouring to obtain

[1] Cf. *Semaine Sociale de Marseilles*, 1930, p 126.
[2] Ducattillon, *op. cit.*, p 56.

redress; the government in such a case, may be compared to a man who, beholding robbers loaded with the fruit of their theft, is without the means of forcing them to make restitution . . . Observe, also, that this remark applies not only to a physical impossibility, but also to a moral one. Whenever the government possesses the material means of obtaining reparation, a moral impossibility will be constituted when the employing of these means would cause serious difficulties to the State, endanger the public peace, or sow the seeds of future insurrection. Order and public interest require their preference, for these are the primary objects of all government. Consequently that which cannot be accomplished without endangering them ought to be considered as impossible. The application of these doctrines will always be a question of prudence, that cannot be subjected to any general rule. Depending as it *does* upon a thousand circumstances, it cannot be decided upon principles, but by the condition of existing facts, duly appreciated and considered by political tact. Such is the case of the respect due to consummated facts; the injustice of these facts is apparent, but we must not overlook their force. Not to attack them is not necessarily to sanction them'.[1]

[1] Balmes, *op. cit.*, pp 280-281.

CHAPTER FOUR

REVOLT AND SELF-DETERMINATION

SOME ethicians define 'rebellion' very narrowly as meaning exclusively insurrection against 'just' rule.[1] Thus defined, it is clearly never lawful. It is better to understand by 'rebellion' both insurrection against lawful rule and against tyranny. The same holds for the terms 'resistance' and 'revolt'.

It is usual to distinguish two kinds of tyranny. 'A nation is held tyrannically', says Cajetan, 'either (a) in sovereignty, as happens in the case of those who forcibly constitute themselves sovereigns, whether immediately or through the forced consent of the subjects; or (b) in the effects and mode of government, as happens in the case of those who, though they are the true sovereigns, do not seek the public good but their own'.[2] In other words, a government can be tyrannical in that its title to rule is not well founded, or because of the fact that, though legitimate, it rules unjustly. In the former case, tyranny is identical with usurpation; in the latter it is the same thing as oppression.

---

[1] For an example of the narrow approach cf Meyer, *Institutiones Iuris Naturalis*, Friburg, vol. II, p 509. Also M. Cronin, *The Science of Ethics*, Dublin 1917, vol. II, p 540: 'In rebellion . . . it is the citizens who take the offensive against the government, making an unprovoked attack on it, in order to effect its overthrow'. 'Resistance' is the term used by Cronin to describe lawful defence against tyranny. *Op. cit.* vol. II, p 541.

[2] *Summula*, ed. 1627, p 623.

THE MEANING OF TYRANNY

That revolt against tyranny can be lawful, as organised self-
defence against unjust aggression, is traditional Christian and
Catholic teaching. It has been the almost universal view of
moralists and Scripture scholars.[1] It is true that the early
Christians up to the time of St. Augustine were against it, as
is evidenced by passages from Tertullian, St. Cyprian, Lactantius and St. Ambrose.[2] Passive resistance alone was then allowed. Various reasons have been put forward in explanation
of this;[3] we must refrain from going into the question in detail.
Certainly from the 4th century the right to armed revolt has
been recognised by the majority of Christian theologians.[4] There
are certain notable exceptions and some disputed cases,[5] but by
and large the teaching has been constant.[6]

[1] Some exceptions can be found among 17th century theologians,
influenced by the legitimist theories of Gallicans, Febronians and regalists in general. In the 19th century Carriere seems to have held that
rebellion is unlawful in any circumstances. See his *De Justitia et Jure*,
Paris 1839, vol. II, p 408. Taparelli taught that it was *illicita per se*. See
his *Saggio teoretico di dritto naturale*, vol. II, ch 3.

[2] Cf H. Clavier, *The Duty and the Right of Resistance*, Strasbourg
1956, pp 60-65.

[3] Cf Meyer, *op. cit.* vol. II, pp 530-531. Bellarmine took the unlikely
view that the early Christian attitude to the use of force against a per-
secuting empire was due entirely to the fact that the Christians lacked
adequate strength to stage a successful revolt. Balmes thought that they
were also uncertain about how a legitimate government could, in the
circumstances of the time, be established.

[4] For the views of Luther, Calvin and the French Huguenots, see
Clavier, *op. cit. passim*. For those of the early Anglican divines, particularly Hooker, see F. J. Shirley, *Richard Hooker and Contemporary Political Ideas*, London 1949, pp 183-198.

[5] For example, the exact position of Bellarmine is not clear. Cf J.
Broderick, *Blessed Robert Bellarmine*, London 1928, vol. I, p 229.

[6] For the early Jesuit teaching on the right to revolt see Guenter
Lewy, *Constitutionalism and Statecraft during the Golden Age of Spain:
A Study of the Political Philosophy of Juan de Mariana*, Geneva 1960.

Seeming statements to the contrary, by Popes Gregory XVI and Leo XIII, were aimed rather against the arbitrary over-throwing of all established government that was accepted as normal in an age of revolution.[1] The same holds for the views of some 19th century theologians. That the liceity of rebellion is the official teaching of the Church was made clear by Pope Pius XI's Encyclical *Firmissimam Constantiam* on the situation in Mexico (1937) and the New Year Pastoral for 1936 of the Archbishop of Valladolid. The most recent treatise on the sub-ject of lawful revolt is that of the German moralist, Max Pribilla.[2]

It can sometimes be a very difficult question to decide whether a government has become tyrannical by reason of op-pression. According to some, for example Fr. Joseph Ricaby, S.J., it must have become 'substantially and habitually tyran-nical, that is, when it has lost sight of the common good, and pursues its own selfish objects to the manifest detriment of the subjects especially where their religious interests are con-cerned'.[3] Balmes wrote that this is so when the 'supreme power makes a scandalous abuse of its faculties, extends them beyond their due limits, tramples on the fundamental laws, persecutes religion, corrupts morality, outrages public decorum, attacks the honour of citizens, exacts illegal and disproportionate con-tributions, violates the right of property, alienates the patri-mony of the nation, dismembers provinces, inflicts ignominy and death on the people'.[4] And Pope Pius XI described tyranny as being present when 'the constituted authorities rise up

---

[1] Gregory XVI, Encycl. *Mirari Vos;* Pius IX, *Syllabus*, prop. 63; Leo XIII, Encyclical *Quod Apostolici*. Cf. Luigi Sturzo, The Right to Rebel, in *Politics and Morality*, London 1938, pp 195-199; also O'Ra-hilly, Some Theology about Tyranny, in *The Irish Theological Quarterly*, vol. xv (1920), pp 8-9.

[2] Max Pribilla, *The Right to Resist*, Oxford 1952.

[3] J. Ricaby, in *Moral Philosophy*, London 1892, p 341. This teaching has been reproduced by M. Cronin, *The Science of Ethics*, vol. ii, p 540.

[4] Balmes, *Protestantism compared with Catholicity*, London 1849, p. 283.

against justice and truth to the point of destroying the very foundation of authority'.[1]

It should be clear from this that not any and every grievance justifies rebellion in the name of oppression. Ordinary injustice should be remedied by constitutional means as far as possible. This can usually be done in modern democracies, or at least in those in which democracy is not just a word. St. Thomas declares that only 'excessive tyranny', a despotism so great as to be insupportable, allows armed revolt.[2] Faced with moderate tyranny a people should show restraint and endurance; their condition will not last forever and revolt may only occasion greater evils. Even Pribilla, the most ardent modern defender of the right to resist, says that, for armed rebellion to be lawful, 'there must be an extraordinary misuse of political power'. And he adds: 'Such misuse betrays itself especially in the trampling on all freedom and the supplanting of justice by might and of the common good by Party interests'.[3] This is the common teaching of ethicians. But it is also admitted that the oppression that is necessary to constitute tyranny need not go so far as to be 'cruel'. It is sufficient that a government be ruling merely in its own interest 'or in that of a section of the people only'.[4]

Turning to 'tyranny' in the sense of a government's lack of a legitimate title to rule, it would seem that it is on this ground that most 'nationalist' revolutions are based. The moralists of the past have devoted very little attention to this. They were concerned more with the question of revolt against monarchs who were guilty of tyranny by oppressing their own people.[5] There may be treatises on revolt of the other kind prior to the

---

[1] Encycl. *Firmissimam Constantiam*, 28 March, 1937.

[2] *De Regimine Principum*, Bk. I, ch 6; 1a 2ae, Q. 96 art. 4, ad. 3.

[3] Pribilla, *op. cit.* p 21.

[4] Cronin, *op. cit.* vol. II, p 541.

[5] In so far as the Scholastics did acknowledge the case of two nations under a common monarch, they were concerned only with insisting that they should be governed for the equal benefit of both, because 'a kingdom is a kind of whole and not a part'—Martinez, *Comm. in 1a 2ae*, Q. 90 art. 2, dub. I.

19th century, but I do not know of any. I suppose the two peoples most likely to have produced them were the Poles and the Irish. I cannot say whether the Poles ever did so; the Irish certainly did not. I have, however, come across a number of modern contributions on the subject.

The first is a little-known essay by the 19th century Maynooth Professor Dr. Patrick Murray.[1] Dr. Murray notes that he himself knew of no Catholic exposition of the right to revolt in the English language apart from a translation of the work of the Spanish theologian Balmes. In fact one gets the impression from Murray that, at his time, theological literature on revolt of any kind was sparse. He himself, with the perspicacity of which his *Essays* give much evidence, is careful to distinguish between what he calls '*tyrannus administrationis*', based on abuse of lawful authority, and '*tyrannus usurpationis*', based on a lack of a legitimate title to govern. But what he has to say on the subject seems to indicate that he did not at all envisage the case of revolt for *nationalistic* reasons against a usurper who has succeeded in firmly establishing his rule. This is surprising on account of his well-known leanings towards the Young Ireland Movement. Because of its interest, I will quote the relevant passage in full.

'As to the usurper, we consider him either as engaged in the struggle for mastery, not yet possessed of it; or we consider him as successful, and actually in possession of the supreme power. In the former case, not only is it not a duty to obey him, but it is a strict duty not to acknowledge him as the sovereign; a duty which springs from, or rather is identical with, the obligation of allegiance to the rightful sovereign. In the second case, if the contest be over and there be no further reasonable and certain hope of reinstating the lawful ruler, then, though we are not bound to obey the usurper in virtue of any allegiance we owe him or of any claim he has (as a legitimate ruler would have) to our obedience; yet we are bound to obey him on the principle of expediency. For it is evident that, in this case, continued resistance would be injurious to the public weal, would perpe-

---

[1] P. Murray, The Right of Resistance to the Supreme Power, in *Theological Essays*, Dublin 1853, pp 379-407.

tuate strife and anarchy, without hope of attaining a compen-
sating good: it would be doing an act whence nothing but pure
evil would follow—for, by the supposition of the case there is
no hope of success.'[1]

The second part of this passage is not satisfying, due to its
assumption that the kind of revolt in question cannot be
successful. Revolt of any kind is not legitimate under such
conditions. Later, Dr. Murray admits the possibility of lawful
revolt—granted reasonable hope of success—against 'an established and legitimate government which abuses its power'.
But what of revolt against an established but illegitimate
government that is not abusing its authority? That is the
question which we want answered. In virtue of his belief in the
possibility of acquiring political authority through prescription,
we know that Dr. Murray would hold that such a government
can, in time, become legitimate. But what of the intervening
period? Can a lawful revolt be raised against it during this time?
It seems to me, from the passage which I have quoted, that Dr.
Murray's answer would be in the negative, on the grounds that,
once the usurper is physically established, successful revolt—
and therefore lawful revolt—is out of the question. He either
did not envisage, or was not prepared to face up to, the question
of whether, granted reasonable hope of success, revolt for purely
nationalistic reasons could be lawful.

Dr. Murray's avoidance of this question may have been
motivated—consciously or unconsciously—by the political condition of Ireland in his day. A revived nationalism was beginning to manifest itself amongst the people, some of whom were
prepared to revolt in its name. The year 1848 had just seen an
abortive attempt to do so. In any event, Dr. Murray's treatment
of the subject leaves one unsatisfied regarding the question of
the liceity of revolt in the name of nationalism.

Curiously enough, for different reasons, the same is true of
a more recent Irish discussion on the subject. I refer to Dr.
O'Rahilly's article 'Some Theology about Tyranny'. Written
against the background of an actual revolt that gave real hope

---

[1] Murray, *loc. cit.* pp 391-392.

of being successful, Dr. O'Rahilly's article was an apologia for resurgent nationalism. Drawing his evidence from all possible traditional theological and philosophical sources, its author built up what was really a case for the liceity of the then Sinn Fein rebellion. The argument in brief is as follows. Any government that is not based on the consent of the people is tyrannous. Lawful revolt against tyranny is possible. Hence—although the writer, for obvious reasons, did not actually point this conclusion—the current revolution in Ireland might be lawful, since the people had withdrawn consent to British rule.

My difficulty with this is that it rests entirely on Dr. O'Rahilly's thesis—already examined—that political authority has its exclusive origin in the consent of the people. Granted the view that consent is not the only source of political authority, one cannot conclude that a government becomes *ipso facto* tyrannous immediately the people withdraw their acquiescence to its rule. If this is so, we are at once deprived of the most obvious basis on which to rest a case for the liceity of 'nationalist' revolution.

This question is made particularly difficult because of the fact that the ethics of revolt has been discussed mainly by supporters of the Consent Theory of political authority. What they have to say on the subject is of very little use to us. I have, however, found at least one supporter of the Common Good Theory who—even prior to the 19th century—came close to admitting a right to revolt for what would later be regarded as nationalistic reasons. 'It is to be noted', says Lessius, 'that a tyrant may be so by usurpation of power (such as he who, without any right, has invaded a country and holds it in bondage); while another is so by use of power, being true sovereign otherwise and having legitimate authority. Here we contemplate one who is a tyrant by usurpation and now rules in peace; the country no longer resisting him for lack of means'.[1] The case envisaged is the one which Dr. Murray failed to face. Lessius does not hesitate to do so, declaring that revolt, if it can be mounted, is lawful.

[1] Lessius, *De Justitia et Jure*, Bk. II, c. 29, dub. 9.

To this should be added a final consideration that does not appear to have been thought of until the 20th century. It is that a government that has been justly constituted by the acquisition of a legitimate title, can subsequently become tyrannical through losing this title, apart altogether from its becoming oppressive. This happens in the case of an alien government which continues to hold a people in subjection after they have reached political maturity and desire self-government. Here is a situation which has become common only in modern times and which, by reason of its infrequency in connection with colonial rule in the past, was not at all envisaged by moralists. It was recognised, however, by Dr. Walter McDonald, who was not otherwise noted for broad views on the subject of revolt. He writes: 'When a nation takes up arms to assert a rightful claim to complete independence, it does not oppose legitimate authority. For the acting government becomes a usurper *ipso facto*, the moment independence becomes due'.[1]

CONDITIONS FOR LAWFUL REVOLT

In other words, there is an ethical principle that justifies armed insurrection to secure independence when this is due. It rests essentially on the right to revolt against tyranny in the sense of absence of a legitimate title to rulership. And it is linked with no particular theory concerning the origin of political authority. It does not say that a government loses its authority whenever the people choose to withdraw their consent, nor that it is necessarily tyrannical if the people have never consented to it, or have given it only a forced consent. All it says is that, once it becomes due, a people is entitled to independence and an alien government which refuses to grant this becomes tyrannical, through losing its title, unless the people consent to its rule for the future. Such consent, as we have seen,

[1] W. McDonald, *Some Ethical Aspects of Peace and War*, London 1919, p 172. This principle is also defended in a tract on ethics published in India: D. Ferroldi, S.J., *Ethica*, Part III, *Social Ethics*, Ranchi 1948, pp 242-243.

is compatible with the Common Good Theory.

The principle of the right to revolt to secure independence when due can be invoked to justify the struggle in Ireland during the early decades of the 20th century. I am not concerned here with the morality of earlier Irish insurrections. They may or may not have been justified on different grounds, such as the permanent lack of a just title on the part of the government, or because it was tyrannical by reason of oppression. I am not concerned with these considerations here. What I do want to say is that, even if the British government had become the legitimate government of Ireland, it would have lost its title unless this were otherwise renewed by the people—through its refusing to grant legislative independence to Ireland after this had become indisputably due.

Of course, in addition to the justice of the cause, certain other conditions are necessary before revolt is morally lawful. They include the impossibility of getting rid of the tyranny except by armed force, proportion between the evil caused and that to be removed by the revolt, the serious probability of success and the approval of the community at large. It is a little disconcerting to an Irishman to find Don Luigi Sturzo, after he has listed these conditions, going on to say: 'And therefore we cannot hold the armed revolt of Ireland in 1916-21 to have been legitimate, even though historically justified and though all our sympathies as Catholics and as free men supported her claims. The Bishops of Ireland . . . were cautious and sought to further pacification, while the Holy See remained neutral'.[1]

Let us examine the conditions and their application to the Irish scene. First of all, as in the case of war in general, all peaceful means of settlement must have failed. Owing to the greater extent to which these methods are available in democratic States, it is less easy to appeal to arms under democracy than under autocratic regimes. History contains many instances of peaceful 'revolutions' that were effected by constitutional means. The sweeping changes in Germany in 1932 are a striking example of such. Parliamentary regimes give

---

[1] Sturzo, *op. cit.* p 210.

people many opportunities for expressing their views. A free press, free meetings, free elections—all these provide a framework which, in theory, seems to render appeal to arms out of the question. But then theory and practice are not always in harmony. Indeed in this matter the theoretical position is seldom or ever fully realised. In order that such be the case, it would be necessary for democracy to function perfectly. From the moment that public opinion, for whatever reason, is unable to manifest itself under legal forms, appeal to other methods is the only alternative.

The next condition is that the evil inflicted by the tyrant must be greater than that which will ensue from revolting against him. In regard to this even Sturzo has to be broad-minded. 'Who', he asks, 'can forsee the future? The Irish when they rebelled during the Great War could not know that they would obtain autonomy and independence at a relatively small cost, so that the evils might (according to a worldly, not a spiritual scale of values) be estimated as less than the advantages. On the contrary there are grounds for believing that the Spanish generals who promoted the *pronunciamento* of July 18, 1936, thought it would go through as on other similar occasions, with an exchange of volleys or even of cannonades. Instead it has led to the civil war, in which we see with horror the savage destruction of the country and the decimation of the people'.[1] At the time of writing this Don Sturzo was of the opinion that there was a complete lack of proportionality of means in the case of Franco's revolt. Which goes to show chiefly how delicate is this matter, how open to mistaken judgment and how necessary it is to weigh all the conditions together before coming to a practical conclusion as regards any concrete instance.

A further condition for lawful revolt is that there must be a reasonable hope of success. Here again one has got to be realistic. The circumstances will usually be so complex that there will be room for disagreement, even amongst prudent men, in assessing them. Moralists accept the principle that this condition is verified in circumstances in which a revolt, even though

---

[1] Sturzo, *op. cit.* p 209.

it cannot be an unqualified success, will be effective at least by intimidating the tyrant and inducing him to moderate his rule. Even the certainty of a moral victory may be taken to justify revolt, as it does in the case of a defensive war. But it must be added at once that such certainty will often be impossible to establish. To refer to Professor Leclercq again. Such questions, he says, cannot always be resolved by aligning principles. They demand a practical judgment that entails a certain intuition into concrete situations, and a spirit of decision and of courage that is more frequently found amongst men of action than amongst scholars. If there be cases in which, because of the slim chances of success, revolt is folly, there are also cases in which revolt seems folly at the beginning but is acknowledged as wisdom after success.[1]

He applies this to the case of Ireland. 'The revolt in Ireland in 1920 was greater folly (than that of Spain against Napoleon), because Ireland had no hope of aid from anybody and she chose a moment to revolt when victorious England dominated the world. This was truly the struggle of the pygmy against the giant, the repetition of the struggle, which every sensible man would have condemned, between David and Goliath. However, once again, the pygmy was successful'.[2] It is because of such examples that Pribilla asserts that 'active resistance will always be a gamble and will ever need brave men who will not shrink from danger'.[3] From this, he adds, 'there follows the

[1] Leclercq, *Leçons de Droit Naturel*, vol. II, p 199.

[2] In this connection a passage from Thomas Moore's *Memoirs of Lord Edward Fitzgerald*, (London 1897) is worth quoting: 'Of the right of the oppressed to resist, few, in these days, would venture to express a doubt; the monstrous doctrine of passive obedience having long since fallen into disrepute. To be able to fix, however, with any precision the point at which obedience may cease, and resistance to the undue stretches of authority begin, is a difficulty which must forever leave vague and undirected the application of principle; a vagueness of which the habitual favourers of power adroitly take advantage, and while they concede the right of resistance, as a general proposition, hold themselves free to object to every particular instance of it'—pp 373-374.

[3] Pribilla, *op. cit.* p 22.

important and limiting truth that the decision in such matters cannot come from the small man, who has neither the large view of the real situation nor the requisite means and contacts for the organisation of resistance'.[1]

Which brings us to the final condition, namely, that the identification of tyranny and the taking up of arms must not be done by isolated individuals or by one party only, but by the majority of the people or the people as a whole. We find this insisted on by all the traditional expositions. St. Thomas himself says that armed resistance must not be undertaken 'by private initiative but by public authority'.[2] There is a sense in which this principle is incontestable and in which its validity will always remain. Pribilla puts it well when he says that 'to stick a revolver into the hands of immature, over-excited youths'[3] is not in conformity with right thinking concerning revolt. Dr. Michael Cronin too expresses the same idea when he says that it would be unjust 'to drive people to resistance against their will'.[4]

To go further and demand that the clear consent of the majority of the people be forthcoming would be to seek a mechanical application of the principle that is impossible. 'In matters of this sort', wrote Dr. Murray in Aristotelian language, 'mathematical completeness is not required'.[5] The writers whom I have just quoted appear to forget this. It is unlawful, says Dr. Cronin, 'to initiate resistance unsupported by the mass of the people'.[6] And Pribilla speaks of the 'truth emphasised again and again in works of historical significance for our question, that the decision to resist and the conduct of the resistance are not matters for the individual but for the Estates of the Realm or similar bodies whose duty it is to represent the people and therefore to see that they get their rights. The individual comes

---

[1] Pribilla, *op. cit.* p 21.

[2] *De Regimine Principum*, Bk I, c. 6.

[3] Pribilla, *op. cit.* p 30.

[4] Cronin, *op. cit. loc. cit.*

[5] Murray, *loc. cit.* p 403.

[6] Cronin, *op. cit. loc. cit.*

in only as the executor of the general will and the defender of the *maior et sanior pars'.*[1]

With all due respect to Pribilla, it seems that he is being over-attentive to the lesson of history in this matter. The works of historical significance for the question were written in a different political framework from that which prevails today. Their writers were thinking against a background of monarchical regimes that were limited by their dependence on various public bodies.[2] This is certainly the case with St. Thomas and provides a complete understanding of what exactly he meant when he declared that revolt should not be undertaken without public authority. For, having said this, he adds immediately that the reason for it is because 'it pertains to the people to provide itself with a king. The king, instituted by the people, can be deposed by it without injustice, or his power can be limited if he abuse his royal authority tyrannically'.[3] Suarez is clearer still: 'If the legitimate king governs tyrannically, and if there is no means of defense open to the kingdom other than to depose and expel the king, the people as a whole (*respublica tota*) can

---

[1] Pribilla, *op. cit.* pp 21-22.

[2] See for example, Lessius, *De Justitia et Jure*, Bk II, 9, 4, 12: 'If the tyranny increases so as to appear intolerable and if no other remedy remains, then he (the tyrant) must first be deposed by the nation or *assembly of the kingdom* or some other possessing authority'. See also Suarez, *De Caritate*, D. 13, sect. 8, c. 2. And Mariana, *De Rege et Regis Institutione*, *passim*. 'Mariana's King', it has been remarked 'is a closely watched, suspect being. . . The "people" is the real sovereign— that is, in its representative assembly . . . likely at any time to regather into its hands that limited and qualified authority that conditionally it had given to its King'—F. J. Shirley. *Op. cit.* London, 1949, p. 168. Appeals to the ancient limitation of monarchs by *Parlements* were made by French Huguenot writers of the 16th century against the growing absolutism of the Valois kings. See Francois Hotman's *Franco Gallia*, Paris 1573 and 'Junius Brutus', *Vindiciae contra Tyrannos*, 1579. A full account of these writings is given in J. W. Allen, *A History of Political Thought in the Sixteenth Century*, London 1928. Also P. Mesnard, *L'Essor de la philosophie politique au XVIe siècle*, 2nd Ed., Paris, 1952.

[3] *De Regimine Principum*, Bk I, ch 6.

depose him by the public and mutual deliberation of the towns and the nobility (*publico et communi consilio civitatum et procerum*).[1]

The fact that Suarez upheld the Translation Theory of the origin of political authority has nothing to do with the special significance of what he says here. He is referring to the practice whereby the Estates of the Realm could intervene in the name of the people when a king became tyrannical. But where are the Estates of the Realm today? Gone are the barons and the guilds, the political power of the towns and the universities— what used to be called the 'natural' representatives of the people. In democratic regimes they have been replaced by members of Parliament, but Parliament is nowadays so closely associated with actual government that, *ex hypothesi*, these cannot play the part of effectively representing the wishes of the people when they are radically opposed to government policy. This is particularly so if what the people want is in contradiction with the system on which the representatives themselves are based. This was one of the troubles with the old Irish Party at Westminister, which was unable to decide, in the name of the Irish people, that the demand for Home Rule in Ireland should be prosecuted if necessary by force. We know that a way was found out of this impasse by the election, in 1919, of an independent Irish Dáil which assented to armed resistance. Indeed we have

---

[1] Suarez, *Defensio Fidei*, Bk I, vi, ch 4. It has been noted by E. Lewis (*Medieval Political Ideas*, vol. I, London 1954, p 271) that this right of the people as a whole represented the institutionalisation of a private right to disobedience to tyrannical commands that had been recognised from time immemorial. This is particularly true of later medieval thought which gave currency to the consent theory of political authority. 'The thesis that all power originated in the community', says Lewis, 'was easily extended to the idea that the community still retained the right to secure its own good government through the withdrawal of power from a tyrannical ruler: thus the doctrine of a private right of insurrection merged into the idea of a public right of deposition. Bodies which could be construed as exercising the latent rights of the community—the imperial electors or the estates—were accordingly regarded as agencies which might properly represent the community in the formal deposition of a ruler'.

here almost the only example in modern times of a revolt being backed by the Estates of the Realm. Leclercq says of it: 'One could find an application of the theory of St. Thomas in the revolution in Ireland, where the representatives of the people, regularly elected, took leadership of the revolt. But this case is quite exceptional'.[1]

Leclercq takes the bold step of declaring that the principle that revolt against tyranny is unjustified unless it is formally backed by the majority of the people, is generally inapplicable in modern times. Ultimately, he says, it is the individual conscience that must make the decision. Each person must satisfy himself as to whether the conditions for lawful revolt are verified and the revolt will take place if there is a sufficient number of one mind to make it possible. All the moralist can do is to insist that prudence be respected and that an endeavour be made to take all circumstances into account. This is not subjectivism or situation ethics, which would reduce objective morality to a matter of individual choice. Rather is the position that the extent of individual decision in the matter must be taken as representing an important element in fixing the objective morality of any particular revolt.[2] It is along these lines that justification might be found for the Irish revolt of Easter 1916.

[1] Leclercq, *op. cit.* vol II, p 196.

[2] Similar considerations motivated De Vareilles-Sommieres to write: 'It is not necessary that the majority of the citizens should act; even a minority, if it is sufficiently strong, has the right of defending and saving the country'—*Les fondements du droit*, Paris 1889, p 248. E. von Kuehnelt-Leddihn has pointed out that 'to the opponent of the theory of popular sovereignty (either in its Roussellian or in its Bellarminian form) there is no philosophical connection between rebellion and public opinion. Ninety-nine per cent of the population might be blissfully happy under a tyranny based on the torture and exploitation of one per cent . . . Nevertheless, the problem whether a rebellion supported by only one per cent of the population can succeed—at first glance a purely practical question—cannot be brushed aside. After all, even a just war can only be started if there is a chance of winning it. All intellectual virtues . . . have to be mobilised by the "lonely individual" in order to come to a *personal* decision . . . the individual, whom theology cannot provide in all situations with an elaborate and infallible casuistry. And here

In this connection it should be emphasised that what is said about the individual conscience is subordinate to the overriding authority of the Church. If ecclesiastical authority should declare that a revolt is unjustified, the individual Catholic cannot lawfully take part in it. This holds apart from all consideration of whether his own judgment that it is ethically warranted may be correct. In point of fact the Church has always been extremely careful about committing herself to a decision in this matter. While there are many examples of the Church intervening to declare a particular revolutionary movement or revolt unlawful, it is difficult to find a clear example of where ecclesiastical authority has explicitly favoured a revolt.[1] In his letter to the Irish Hierarchy, of 27 April, 1921, Pope Benedict XV wrote: 'In the political conflict in Ireland, the Holy See has taken for its rule, as in other difficulties of this kind, not to favour either of the two parties, a line of conduct to which it is always prudently bound by the past'.[2]

The Irish Bishops were guided by this directive. Professor Leclercq's analysis of the position which they adopted is interesting, both because it is at once the view of a foreigner and of an eminent ethician. He writes: 'From 1919 to 1921 the Irish bishops, in a series of declarations, protested the right of the

---

we face, finally, a mere fragment of that terrible responsibility which all of us have, not only towards ourselves and our kin, but also towards that seemingly never ending process affecting mankind with all its pitiless forces—that great drama of which God is the everlasting spectator —*history.*—*Liberty or Equality*, London 1952, pp 177-178.

The fact that the condition for lawful revolt which relates to the backing of the people originated during the hey-day of the Consent Theory of the origin of political authority is not sufficiently appreciated by present-day moralists.

[1] Once implanted, however, a *de facto* government 'even if established by a revolution or *coup d'état* . . . is always regarded by the Church as one that by restoring order, or at least by fixing power in responsible hands, can bring back calm, order and peace to the country, these being goods that deserve all support, over and above the interests of fallen royal houses or vanquished political parties, for order and peace are inestimable goods'—Luigi Sturzo, *Politics and Morality*, p 201.

[2] Letter *Ubi Primum*, 27 April 1921.

Irish people to govern themselves. But they avoided the consequences and concluded each time by inviting the faithful to be patient. In their collective declaration to Pope Benedict XV, of 21 June, 1921, they declared that "until repression ceases, and the right of Ireland to choose her own government is recognised, there is no prospect that peace will reign amongst us". These letters of the Irish Hierarchy give the impression that it approved of the revolt, without daring to approve of it explicitly'.[1]

He adds that much the same course was followed by the Mexican bishops, from 1926 to 1928, during the period of religious persecution in that country. They avoided pronouncing directly on the morality of the revolution, while approving of it implicitly by declaring that 'the laity have an unequivocal right of defending by force the inalienable rights which they cannot defend by peaceful means'.[2] Professor Leclercq concludes: 'These examples show sufficiently the prudence with which the ecclesiastical authorities venture on to this terrain . . . The practice of the Church shows that it is frequently preferable to leave it to individuals to decide for themselves according to the requirements of their consciences'.[3]

THE DUTY OF REVOLT?

What then of the duty of revolt? It is one thing for the individual conscience to decide that it is morally lawful to participate in armed revolt; it is another to decide that there is a duty to do so. And where there is question of duty, the Church surely cannot remain silent? As regards this matter,

---

[1] Leclercq, *op. cit.* vol. II, p 193. The 'collective declaration' here referred to by Prof. Leclercq, was the statement of the Irish Hierarchy issued after its June meeting at Maynooth in 1921. Cf *The Irish Ecclesiastical Record*, Fifth Series, vol. XVIII (1921), p 86. For the other declarations of the Irish Hierarchy from 1919 to 1920 see *The Irish Ecclesiastical Record*, Fifth Series, vol. XIV (1919), p 328 and vol. XV (1920), pp 150 and 424.

[2] Declaration of the Mexican Bishops to President Calles, May 1927.

[3] Leclercq, *op. cit.* vol. II, p 194.

some further distinctions seem necessary. The fact that, in the past, moralists did not treat of revolt precisely from the point of view of duty was probably due, in the first place, to the circumstance that they were busy with the more basic and pressing question as to whether—and under what conditions— revolt can ever be lawful and, in the second place, to the fact that the tyrannical abuse of power with which they were usually confronted was seldom of the appalling kind that has appeared in Europe during the 20th century. Indeed during the 19th century most revolts rested on anti-monarchical enthusiasm rather than on any moral consciousness that the regimes attacked were tyrannous by reason of lacking title to rule or by abuse of power. In such circumstances, it is understandable why moralists devoted little or no attention to the question of a possible duty to revolt.

As Pribilla puts it, since the Reformation, and more espe- cially since the French Revolution, 'Catholics and Protestants competed against each other, not without jealousy, to see which faith could commend itself as the more valiant support of the throne and defence against revolution. This competition quite certainly coloured teaching on the right to resist . . . (It) also formed part of the campaign against the revolutionary move- ments running through the nineteenth century. Moreover, many clutched at the hope, which proved delusive, that the safe- guards provided legally in the constitution would make the question quite unreal, or that the moral pressure of public opinion would suffice to restrain any excesses of those in power in the State'.[1] In other words, there was an inclination to place an almost total reliance on constitutional means as a method of redressing any grievances that people might have. Moralists were slow to admit that peaceful means for doing this can ever be exhausted. Even granted that they were in legitimate revolt against tyranny, in one or the other or both senses of the word, this consideration would have been sufficient for 19th century ecclesiastical authority to declare, as it did, for example, against the Fenians in Ireland. If, as was the case, Rome saw this movement as one of revolt against 'tyranny' solely in the sense

[1] Pribilla, op. cit. pp 26-27.

of a regime which was thought to lack legitimate title by reason of not yielding to the then emerging consciousness of a right to national self-determination, the attitude it adopted is all the more understandable.[1] But even where there was clear question of revolt against tyranny in the sense of the abuse of political power, the habitual attitude of 19th century moralists and ecclesiastical authorities was to maintain hope in the possibility of a betterment of affairs by peaceful means.

Their position is extremely well exemplified by Meyer, whose important work *Institutiones Juris Naturalis* was published in 1900. Having defined 'revolt' in the strict sense as a rejection of legitimate authority, he is emphatic that it is always contrary to the moral law. But having said this he finds himself grudgingly compelled to admit that what he calls 'active resistance' against tyranny can sometimes be allowed. However, the most he will say is that in itself it is *not against* the law of nature.[2] He was merely reflecting the general approach of moralists of the 19th century.

For these reasons we need not expect these moralists to treat of the question as to whether revolt can be a duty. But, to quote Pribilla again: 'All this belongs to the past. Meanwhile, all of us, Catholics, Protestants and Jews, have experienced such extraordinary misuse of political power that none of the earlier theologians or lawyers had, or could have, forseen it; and in the face of this misuse, we were in teaching and in practice helpless to the point of suicide. At the same time a new phenomenon appeared: a Terror was set up and power perverted, not by a monarch but by a Party or a would-be universal regime. Thus the whole question of the right to resistance has been set in a

---

[1] 'Never did the Popes of the last century approve of the revolts of Ireland, Poland and Latin America; indeed, in particular instances they blamed and condemned them . . . After the French revolution . . . (theologians) tended to the negation or quasi-negation of all legitimacy of revolt. Faced with the national and liberal revolutions, their fear of making any concession to the spirit of the age led them, in the name of legitimate power, to cast doubt on even the right of the Greeks to throw off the yoke of the Turks'—Sturzo, *op. cit.* p 197.

[2] '*Per se* it is not contrary to the natural law', *op. cit.* vol. II, p 524.

new light by the turn of events, and it must therefore be thought out afresh . . . In times like these, situations can arise in which it is not enough for Christians to pray and suffer; it falls to them as a solemn duty to drive back force with force, protecting and shielding themselves, their family and their nation from untold misery and injustice and the gravest dangers to faith and morals. They must beware lest through the weakness and cowardice of the good the power of the wicked should gain the upper hand in the world. And as the signs of the times continue to point to storms ahead, the faithful should be instructed about their duty of civil obedience, without anxious reserve, so that they may clearly understand not only the need for it but also its limits, and so that when occasion arises they will know their right and their duty'.[1]

THE LIMITS OF NATIONAL SELF-DETERMINATION

It is important to realise that the right to revolt for what I have called 'nationalistic' reasons is subject to the same limitations as is the right to national self-determination. Viability as a nation is not the only criterion whereby to decide whether independence should be pursued. Self-determination, like sovereignty, has an international resonance that is coming increasingly to play a part in national affairs.

I propose to show that in fact this consideration constitutes an ethical principle that places well defined limits to the right of self-determination. As such it limits the right to revolt in the name of nationalism. It is also relevant to the actions of existing States in that circumstances can arise when they have a moral duty, in their mutual interest, to subordinate national considerations to a new and wider political union.

I know of only one place in which this question is discussed. It is the collection of essays on *Some Ethical Aspects of Peace and War* by Dr. Walter McDonald, to which I have had occasion to refer in the earlier part of this book. Possibly because of the political temper of the time at which it was published,

---

[1] Pribilla, *op. cit.* pp 27-28.

what Dr. McDonald had to say on this subject was largely ignored and quickly forgotten. It will be profitable to present it once again, when public opinion as well as political thinking may be more receptive of it. Dr. McDonald based his whole position on what he calls the 'Principle of Development', which, as far as I know, owes its original elaboration to him. 'I beg to submit the following as an ethical principle, roughly outlined, and possibly needing amendment: A time may come in the development of peoples, when their interest requires them to combine, for advance and protection; and when this happens they do wrong to maintain separate independence'.[1] To this he added the principle, already established in relation to other matters in the field of social relations that such union, when called for by the common interest, may be secured if necessary by pressure.

Dr. McDonald claimed that the Principle of Development is more fundamental than and something which conditions the Principle of Self-Determination. If, he says, development 'here and there results in need of union, it results as surely in need of fission; and where this need is, there also will be the right'.[2] A nation may be entitled to independence in virtue of the principle of development and just as surely in virtue of the same principle may be obliged to union with others. Dr. McDonald adduced evidence for the principle from the realm of nature. 'It is not among nations only the law of Self-Determination holds, but in every form of life; wherein also we may see how it is conditioned. Everyone knows how strawberry-plants send out runners, with a tendency to develop roots at certain nodes; whereby, when these rootlets strike in a suitable place, new plants are formed. These, like colonies, draw sustenance, for a time, from the parent through the runner, till their own roots have well struck, when they rely more and more on these; the connection with the parent organism becoming gradually useless and disappearing at length. Sever it before the time when the new roots have struck, and what might have been a fruitful

---

[1] W. McDonald, *Some Ethical Aspects of Peace and War*, London 1919, p 81.

[2] *Op. cit.* pp 93-94.

plant will wither. So too, should bees swarm before the colony that leaves is strong enough to shift for itself; or at a time wherein shifts are vain which in other circumstances might have set it up, the colony will fail unless united with another stock. For such a colony, in such circumstances, the self-determination of complete independence is fatal. And so of men. One does not advise every immature or untrained lad to set up for himself; and even when a young man is entitled to marry and set up a home, he may not be in position to open business. For this one needs not merely strength of body and culture of mind, but opportunity'.[1]

He found similar examples in the domain of economics and labour relations. 'It seems, therefore, to be a law of life that self-determination is conditioned by development and environment; so that (i) any organism—whether vegetable or animal, individual or social—that sets up for itself prematurely, assuming more independence than its development in its condition of environment allows, is sure to fail and will have to pay the penalty; while (ii) the same holds of those which continue the struggle in isolation, after the time when, owing to change of environment, they are no longer in a position to maintain themselves without combining with others'.[2]

'This law of combination', says Dr. McDonald, 'seems to be far more imperative than is any principle of 'Self-Determination' permissive . . . The independence that served the states of ancient Greece left them later an easy prey to Roman power. From the fact that a number of independent Irish clans were so easily vanquished by the Normans, it follows that the independent clan system was then ruinous; but it does not follow that it had been so always, before the Irish had to face that powerful combination . . . Taken singly, any number of rods are easily broken; and *Divide et impera* is just as true in its way as *Sinn Fein*'.[3]

If one accepts this Principle of Development, one must also accept the conditioning which it entails for the right of Self-

[1] *Op. cit.* p 92.
[2] *Op. cit.* pp 95-96.
[3] *Op. cit.* p 95.

Determination. Very few were prepared, at Dr. McDonald's time, to admit a limitation to Self-Determination which, particularly during the period immediately after the First World War, was one of the most sacred tenets in the political canon. It mattered not that the Principle of Development, which sets limits to self-determination, is also the very justification of self-determination and revolt in the case of a nation whose independence is due. In so far as it confined the right of self-determination it was unacceptable. But the years have passed and the times have changed. To my mind, the chequered history of the efforts to uphold an absolute right of self-determination, which distracted statesmen during the inter-war period, is itself proof of the bankruptcy of the idea, unless it be conditioned by the Principle of Development. It provides adequate evidence for the validity of this as an ethical principle.

The form under which the principle of self-determination has been most frequently employed is that in which it coincides with the right to national independence. In this sense it means that each nation has a right to constitute an independent State and it is as old, or as young, as the principle of nationality. Without going into the question of the origins of modern nationalism, it will, I think, be admitted that national self-consciousness is a product of the 19th century. It reached its high point between 1848 and 1870, during which its expression in a series of plebiscites linked it with the process of the democratisation of the State and the basing of political life essentially on the will of the people. Nation States had formerly been built up from above; from now on they would reflect the unity of existing communities. Indeed it is possible to show that the idea of national sovereignty arose out of the idea of the sovereignty of the people which gained currency during the period of the rise of liberal democracy. 'People' became synonymous with 'nation' and European democracies developed hand in hand with nationalist movements. Towards the end of the century, due to the rise of an aggressive nationalism on the part of the larger European nations, less was heard of the principle of self-determination as a right of all nations. But it came into its own again during the course of the 1914-18 war.

Looking back over it now,[1] it seems that the Western Allies adopted their policy of defence of the rights of small nations only after the Russian Revolutionary Government proclaimed, in March, 1917, that its aim was to establish peace on the basis of 'the right of the nations to decide their own destinies'. This right, which was given recognition the following November in the Treaty of Brest-Litovsk, was ignored in practice when the 'liberated' States, that had been sundered from the Russian Empire by the Treaty, were overrun by German armies. It was this that led the Western Allies to include respect for the right of national self-determination in their peace terms. It emerged into premier rank in 1918 when Wilson prepared his Fourteen Points and Four Principles.

During the Peace Conference self-determination dominated the scene. When it ended, the Austrian and Turkish Empires had disintegrated into a host of national States that had first begun to appear on the scene as their parent powers succumbed to the disorder of defeat. It would be hard to know whether, in recognising them, the Allies were applying the principle of self-determination or were following the inexorable logic of fact. Indeed it has been shown[2] that, even at this time, they had numerous reservations about the absolute nature of the principle. It appears to have been upheld by each only on the occasions and to the extent that its results were acceptable or could not be avoided. The Italians, for example, insisted on the restoration of their former frontiers, regardless of the wishes or ethnic characteristics of the populations concerned. The French called for the enforced separation of the Rhenish Republic from Germany. The British did not contemplate putting the principle into practice in their own colonies and the Americans, despite Wilson's championship of it, described it as 'loaded with dynamite'.[3] Even Wilson's own sincerity of belief in his principle is cast into doubt by his rejection of the claim of Ireland to self-determination. Hunter Millar's *Diary* tells us of how he received an Irish delegation on the subject: '(Wilson) spoke of

[1] Cf A. Cobban, *National Self-Determination*, London 1945, *passim*.
[2] Cf Cobban, *op. cit.* pp 17-22.
[3] Robert Lansing, Wilson's Secretary of State.

the Irish question and said that he had been made very angry by a delegation of the Irish, who had visited him while in the United States, and had requested him to promise to ask the Peace Conference to make Ireland independent . . . Of course he had refused to promise anything about it . . . His first impulse had been, from his fighting blood getting up, that he had wanted to tell them (the Irish) to go to hell'.[1]

Even in those cases in which they were prepared to apply the principle of self-determination, the post-war statesmen ran into difficulties. Firstly, it proved impossible to set up the new States without creating new minorities. Secondly, and more fundamentally, there was no agreement on the conditions which a nation should satisfy before it could legitimately claim the right of self-determination. Language provided the test in certain cases, but it was soon found that there were so many exceptions to its possible employment that its practical value as a criterion diminished. The value of plebiscites was also lowered when it was realised that it was possible for a State to introduce large numbers of its nationals into a neighbouring territory and then claim it on the basis of self-determination.

The result was a minorities problem, which distracted Europe for years after Versailles. The most that could be done was to guarantee the minorities the civil rights and liberties of citizens of the national States in which they were included. The minority treaties, subsidiary to the Peace Conference, did exactly this, but it was much less than what the minorities wanted and marked a recession of the principle of self-determination into the background. Indeed, in 1920, the International Committee of Jurists of the League of Nations declared that 'Positive International Law does not recognise the right of national groups, as such, to separate themselves from the state of which they form part by the simple expression of a wish, any more than it recognises the right of other states to claim such a separation'.

In a fascinating book, entitled *National Self-Determination*, published under the auspices of the Royal Institute of Inter-

---

[1] Hunter Millar, *The Drafting of the Covenant*, I, 294; cited in Cobban, *op. cit.* p 22.

national Affairs by Oxford University Press (1945), Mr. Alfred Cobban has investigated the weaknesses of the right of self-determination as applied by the Peace Treaties, and has shown how it can be refashioned into a more defensible principle that would incorporate whatever validity its predecessor possessed. It is Cobban's view that the reason why self-determination received only a limited application in the peace treaties was that in the nature of things it could not be applied consistently. Understood as the absolute right of each nation to determine its own government, it was bound to run up against insuperable difficulties. In the first place, such a right would be possible only on condition that each nation had a determinate General Will—a conception about which even its original proponent was himself sceptical. In the concrete the will of the majority has to be followed, creating immediately the vexed problem of minority rights. In the second place, there is the difficulty of deciding on what is a nation. Even granted this, there is the further difficulty that the right of national self-determination, as understood in the past, assumed a coincidence between the cultural and political aspects of nationality that is by no means universally true. The thesis of their coincidence, worked out by German theorists of the 19th century, is being progressively weakened every day by the emergence of minority national movements in existing States. The Basque, Welsh and Flemish movements are just a few examples.

Cobban insists on the need for revising the conception of nationality that was taken for granted by the theory of self-determination. It is no longer possible to regard Europe (much less the world) as capable of being allocated between distinct nations, each with its own State. Some nations are too scattered to permit of this; others are too small to be capable of sustaining a State. Nationality too differs in kind. Here it may be political, there cultural, in other places a mixture of both. Finally, nationality is not a static thing; it is constantly changing—being built up or losing force. The theory of the nation-State, on which the principle of self-determination had its basis, was 'built on the assumption that national loyalties are exclusive', and on an idea of national homogeneity that 'is patently not true'.[1] Even in France several cultural nationalities exist side by side, which formerly coincided with autonomous States. In short, 'the multi-national State must re-enter the political canon . . . The attempt to make the culturally united nation-State the one and only basis of legitimate political organisation has proved untenable in practice. It was never tenable in theory'.[2]

Any other attitude leads to impossible conclusions, in particular regarding the right of secession. All the tests—national feeling, sufficient population, adequate resources, etc.—that may be proposed with a view to deciding when a section of an existing State can break away on its own, are, says Cobban, easier to draw up on paper than to apply in practice. The big difficulty is that, if the door were thus opened to seccession, it would be well-nigh impossible to prevent it being flung wide open. Granted the principle of seccession, Ireland and Britain, for example, would both have to face embarrassing questions. Cobban frames these accurately and pointedly. 'Why was it right for Ireland to claim independence from Great Britain, and wrong for Ulster to claim independence from Southern Ireland? And if the Ulster Protestants were rightly allowed to remain free from Catholic Irish rule, why should not the Catholics of Tyrone and Fermanagh break away from the remainder of the Six Counties'.[3]

Having demolished the idea of an absolute right of national self-determination, Cobban asks whether the idea of self-determination must be dropped altogether. His answer is firmly in the negative. For one thing, the idea has by no means lost its power over world opinion, nor has the sentiment of nationality lost its force. Self-determination in some form or another is inextricably connected with the realisation of natural rights. It is Cobban's contention that it can be a useful instrument for the reconciliation of conflicting interests if it be recognised as a right that is not absolute, but one whose exercise must be

[1] Cobban, *op. cit.* p 61.
[2] Cobban, *op. cit.* p 63.
[3] *Op. cit.*, pp 68-69.

limited in a way that is compatible with social life. Used in this way it can provide the key, not only to the implementation of the aims of the bigger nations, but to a satisfactory integration of provincial and regional nationalities in multi-national States. The nation-State, as heretofore understood, is not the only condition of the assurance of the rights of every nation. A form of self-determination must be hammered out, which, while it will not be inimical to the aspirations of the lesser nations—even regional—will neither conduce to a balkanisation of the world, which, in truth, would be its own *reductio ad absurdum*.

It is Cobban's view that, before one can say whether self-determination is necessary in any given case in the interests of national rights, one must determine what these rights are and whether they are compatible with membership of another and greater whole. He regards self-determination as a mechaism for the defence of these rights rather than as something with a positive value of its own, except where the desire for independent sovereignty is so intense and long-lived that anything else will leave the nation in question radically dissatisfied. Even in this case it should be employed only as a last resort. Where possible, regional nationalities should be catered for by regional governments, which would have care not merely over their non-political activities, but over that degree of government which, in modern times, is necessary to satisy their national aspirations. What powers they will possess should be dependent on the circumstances. If they demand their own language, for example, then they must have it and all official business of the State as a whole must be conducted in more than one language. The central government must be content with those powers that are necessary to enable it to fulfil its integrative functions adequately, namely, the preservation of order and the promotion, in the State as a whole, of the general temporal prosperity of its citizens.

These considerations hold, in certain respects, in Cobban's further view, of the relations between independent sovereign States. He is thinking particularly of international integration in economic matters. At the present day only the great powers can ambition economic self-sufficiency; for the smaller peoples economic nationalism is outdated. Not that the smaller States have no separate economic interests. Rather is the position that they are unable to further them in isolation. 'The true criticism of the economic policies of many small states in recent times has not been that they promoted the economic interests of their own peoples, but that they failed to do so'.[1] There must be no question of their being confronted with the dilemma of the past —poverty with independence or economic development at the price of political subjection. The only possible economic relation between a small State and a great one must not be, as it need not be, one of exploitation. But 'it must be recognised that the smaller nations, whether they are politically independent or not, are bound to rely economically on their relations with greater units. Such States as Luxemburg, the Central American and Caribbean states, or Eire, for example, cannot stand by themselves economically . . . Whatever the demands of self-determination, the smaller nations, if they wish to prosper, can only do so by integrating their economic policies into broader economic systems. It must be frankly recognised that the economic viability of most of the smaller nations is inevitably dependent on the policies of their greater neighbours. The one point we must emphasise is that considerations of political prestige, or the search for an illusory independence, ought not to be allowed to stand in the way of necessary economic connections. In the economic world self-determination is an irrelevant conception'.[2]

In military matters also some voluntary limitation of rights may be necessary on the part of the smaller powers. Indeed their prospects of continued independence seem to be linked with the strategic interests of the dominant powers. More precisely, their adequate defence seems to entail their participation in some form of multi-State alliance. If a condition of this means that bases have to be granted to another State, there is no adequate justification for refusing to allow this. 'It has always been possible for one government to maintain armed forces or to hold strategic points within the territory of another by treaty without any implication of inequality'.[3]

[1] Op. cit., p 161.
[2] Op. cit., p 163.
[3] Op. cit., p 171-172.

In short, the notions of absolute sovereignty and an absolute right to self-determination must be dropped. In so far as they render unattainable the economic and military collaboration which the present day demands, they are an obstacle to progress and peace. Cobban believes that the considerable measure of success that has attended the policies of the British Commonwealth and the Soviet Union towards their own members is due, in part at least, to their recognition—such as it has been —of the cultural and linguistic rights, the economic interests and regional autonomy of these. He ends his book by saying that 'self-determination is a matter of degree. The rights of nationality are not absolute: they vary with the internal and external circumstances of each nation'.[1] It is but another way of expressing what Dr. Walter McDonald defended in virtue of the ethical requirements of his Principle of Development. And the most convincing proof of the validity of Dr. McDonald's position is Cobban's unveiling of the inadequacy of absolute self-determination.

Dr. McDonald's approach is further strengthened—from an exclusively ethical viewpoint—by the teaching of Pope Pius XII on international affairs. At the very beginning of his pontificate, in his Encyclical *Summi Pontificatus* (20 October, 1939), he traced the evils of the time to a rejection of a universal moral law. From then on he never ceased to call for a return to this. Its specific requirement—international co-operation—began to figure in his discourses with his Christmas Message for 1941. There is need, he said then, for co-operation not merely within this or that party, this or that country, but amongst all peoples, humanity as a whole. The war ended, he returned to the theme, and his Christmas Message for 1948 contains an explicit rejection of absolute national self-determination:

'A convinced Christian cannot confine himself in an egoistic "isolationism", . . . as long as he is not ignorant of the deviations of intransigent nationalism, which denies or tramples under foot the solidarity between peoples, which imposes on each multiple duties to the family of nations. Catholic teaching on the State and civil society is founded on the principle that, by divine will,

[1] *Op. cit.,* p 182.

peoples form together a community, having a common type of object and common obligations. The Catholic Christian, convinced that every man is his neighbour and that every people is a member, with equal rights, of the family of nations, will associate himself willingly with the generous efforts . . . which help to remove states from the constriction of an egocentric mentality'. These ideas were repeated by Pope Pius XII in many other addresses of the period immediately before his death.

NATIONALITY AND POLITICS

Intransigent nationalism is an ethical monstrosity. In all truth it is also the greatest enemy of true nationalism, for it is founded on a false conception of nationality. 'Nationality' designates a certain character which a group of people have in common and which distinguishes them, as a group, from other groups. Fundamentally cultural in nature, it derives primarily from a common way of life. On its origin and cause there is much disagreement.[1] Some have traced it to what might be called 'metaphysical causes': nations have been created by God, they stem from laws of nature, or are the product of mystical forces in the universe. Others have linked it with 'physical causes': nations are due to climate, or food, or are the result of racial differences between peoples. Still others trace it to purely 'cultural causes': nations are fashioned by economic or social forces, are the fruit of political design, or, finally, are the by-product of a common language.

Almost all of these views have found reflection amongst Irish nationalists. P. H. Pearse opted for a metaphysical cause of nationality, though he did not hold the more extreme ideas involved in Herder's *Volksgeist*, Bluntschli's *Volkswille* or Grundtvig's *Folkaanden*. For Pearse nationality was a spiritual thing: 'I think that one may speak of a national soul . . . and that is not merely figuratively speaking. When I was a child,

[1] Cf Boyd C. Shafer, *Nationalism: Myth and Reality*, London 1955, pp 15-56.

I believed that there was actually a woman called Erin . . . This I no longer believe as a physical possibility, nor can I convince myself that a friend of mine is right in thinking that there is actually a mystical entity which is the soul of Ireland . . . But I believe that there is really a spiritual tradition which is the soul of Ireland, the thing which makes Ireland a living nation, and that there is such a spiritual tradition corresponding to every true nationality'.[1] As a result of this belief he held that 'like a divine religion, national freedom bears the marks of unity for it comtemplates the nation as one; of sanctity, for it is holy in itself and in those who serve it; of catholicity, for it embraces all the men and women of the nation; of apostolic succession, for it, or the aspiration after it, passes down from generation to generation from the nation's fathers'.[2]

James Connolly, as might be expected, adopted the Socialist thesis that nationality results from economic causes. With the coming of a classless society nationalities will disappear.[3] In the meantime, however, they play an important role in hindering the conquest of the world by a few big powers to the detriment of the emergence of the classless world order. Connolly did not at all agree with those 'doctrinaire Socialists' who argue 'that Socialism should not sympathise with oppressed nationalities or with nationalities resisting conquest'.[4] He managed to reconcile his belief in ultimate internationalism with an Irish nationalism, at least as a transitory stage. And so he could write that 'inspired by another ideal, conducted by reason not by tradition, following a different course, the Socialist Republican Party of Ireland arrive at the same conclusion as the most irreconcilable Nationalist'.[5]

Very different was the position of Thomas Davis, who saw nationality as fundamentally the product of language. His views

[1] P. H. Pearse, *The Spiritual Nation*, Dublin 1916, p 4.

[2] P. H. Pearse, *Ghosts*, Dublin 1916, p 4.

[3] This is an inference, rightly deduced I believe, from Connolly's attitude to the eventual emergence of a world language. Cf *Socialism and Nationalism*, Dublin 1948, pp 59-60.

[4] James Connolly, *Socialism and Nationalism*, p 59.

[5] *Ibid.* p 36.

on the subject resemble those of the 19th century German lin-
guist August Schleicher, for whom language was essentially a
material thing, taking its form from the organs of speech and
hearing of different peoples, which he conceived as varying in
a way that anatomists have been unable to confirm. 'The
language which grows up with a people', says Davis, 'is conformed to their organs, descriptive of their climate, constitution
and manners, mingled inseparably with their history and their
soil, fitted beyond any other language to express their prevalent
thoughts in the most natural and efficient way . . . A people
without a language of its own is only half a nation. A nation
should guard its language more than its territories—'tis a surer
barrier, and more important frontier, than fortress or river'.[1]
From this it follows that language, if not the main cause of
nationality, is an integral and indispensable factor in it.

The trouble with all such views is that they are one-sided,
though all have some modicum of truth. Nations are the fruit
of a many-sided process. Though they are not produced by inexorable 'natural laws', they are the product of nature in so
far as they mirror the different characteristics of peoples that
are due to it. Each nation too has a spirit of its own, but in the
sense only in which the term is used figuratively and not even
analogically. Nations likewise are somewhat conformed to their
physical surroundings, such as climate, and reflect, as well as
contribute, to the creation of the economic structure within
which they exist. The idea of race can also be connected with
nationality, although again only in the qualified statistical
sense in which the concept of 'race' has any validity. Last, but
not least, there is the role of the State, which can further
national unity in a variety of ways.

Perhaps the best way in which all these facts can be taken
together is by saying that nations are the products of history.
But this would involve a bigger mistake than those which it is
intended to remedy if it meant that history is something before
which peoples are entirely helpless. *The will of a people to
nationhood is of vital importance;* given time it can bring the

---

[1] Thomas Davis, Our National Language, in *Thomas Davis: Essays
and Poems*, Dublin 1945, p 71.

most diverse groups into solidarity. Nationality, says the Louvain Professor of Law, Jean Dabin, is as much a matter of
'willing' as of 'being'.[1] It may well be that Dabin's view is
coloured by Belgian experience, in which Flemish and Walloon
are welded together into the Belgian nation. At least it is the
Belgian contention that, despite the cultural differences which
may exist between people, life together in a political unity can
eventually establish similarities on which a new nation can take
root and prosper. The Swiss adopt a similar line of reasoning.
From this angle a sense of solidarity is the most important
thing in nationality; other spiritual and physical factors are
very secondary.

I feel that here is something which deserves careful ponder-
ing. It has never been popular with what might be called traditionalist thinkers. Charles Maurras, for example, categorically
rejected it: 'It is not our will that has made us French. We have
not willed our nationality, we have neither deliberated nor even
accepted it . . . the *patrie* is a *natural society*, or, which comes
absolutely to the same thing, a *historic* one. Its decisive characteristic is birth. We no more choose our *patrie*—the land of
our fathers—than we choose our father and mother'.[2] This is
an argument that has numerous weaknesses. Surely the child
of an Irish family that spends say two years in America is of
Irish nationality, though born abroad during this period? A
more telling objection is that Maurras's idea seems to imply
that nationality is a static thing, in the sense that it leaves no
room for the appearance of new nations or the transformation
of old ones, as a result of unity obtained—consciously or unconsciously—through political policies, or the accidental cultural accretion and even change which sociologists recognise
can flow from both social conflict and social co-operation. I am
convinced that, whatever else they may possess in common,
unless the members of a group are *conscious* of themselves as a
community, and *wish* to maintain the identity of that community, they cannot be said to be a nation. Indeed, in an existing

[1] Cf Jean Dabin, *Doctrine générale de l'état*, Brussels 1939, p 16
[2] C. Maurras, *Mes idées politiques*, Paris 1937, p 252.

nation, it appears that this very consciousness and will to unity are inseparable from many of the nation's other characteristics that are due to history and a common tradition.[1]

The will to unity, that is so essential to the idea of nationhood, can be present before the nation as such fully develops. Who will deny that, in the French State of the past, political life in common helped to generate a new nationality? It made for the fusion of the cultures of Normandy, Brittany, Provence and the Isle de France into a new—though not undiversified—national culture. If it is true that a common nationality helps to bring about a unified political structure, it is equally true that the latter can conduce to the former. Nationality is an ever-changing, evolving thing and to think otherwise is to be as unrealistic as one is politically myopic and sociologically uninformed. By all means it behoves a nation to be jealous of its traditions, in so far as they incarnate values that it would be the poorer for abdicating. But it would be running counter both to the lesson of history and sound common sense for a nation to seek to deny itself the benefit of all alien cultural influence or for a State in which more than one national strain is discernible not to work towards a synthesis of the good elements in each. Even in political groupings in which a federal structure is necessary, it should be regarded as but a political device that is transitory.

These considerations can be applied to the question of the partition of Ireland. There can be little doubt that much Southern thinking on the matter in the past has been dominated by a somewhat exaggerated nationalism. Linked to this has been a conception of national self-determination that would override the wishes of the minority in the North-East. One must confess that the policies erected on these bases have been un-

---

[1] 'We think of nationality as the will of the living members of the community; only on second thoughts do we realise that this contemporary generation, which monopolises with such assurance the visible scene, is but the fleeting incarnation of a force infinitely vaster than itself. It is the will bequeathed by the past that gives its incalculable momentum to the will of the present', Arnold Toynbee, *The New Europe*, London 1915, p 60.

successful, so unsuccessful indeed that doubt has arisen about the validity of the very bases themselves. At present a process of heart-searching is going on, a renewed effort to rethink the whole problem and to find a more satisfactory approach to its solution.

One can still find some echoes of the older approach. In his speech on partition before the Oxford Union in 1960, Mr. Lemass re-affirmed 'the simple truth that Ireland is one nation, in its history, in its geography and in its people, entitled to have its essential unity expressed in its political institutions . . . Ireland is, by every test, one nation. It is on that essential unity that we found our case for political reintegration'. But the body of his speech showed a realistic attitude to the factual division of the country and its people. One is forced to ask whether this division is merely an accident of history, or whether its source lies in deeper cultural forces. Many people feel compelled to accept the latter alternative, recognising a cultural cleavage between the Ulster Unionists and the Nationalists. The very dichotomy 'Unionist and Nationalist' itself speaks eloquently for the nature of the differences which prevail.

The truth seems to be that there is a cultural division between the people of Ireland. It is quite legitimate, as Mr. Lemass has put it, for the South to desire 'the reunification of the national territory', of that territory which was the fatherland of the Irish before the planters came and in the separated part of which hundreds of thousands of the more ancient stock still dwell. In this territory and this people Ireland is one. But territory alone does not constitute a nation and the ancient stock are only the bigger fraction of its present occupants. Geography and people in themselves do not suffice to produce a unified nation. And, as far as history goes, the Irish Question, Home Rule, Partition, give evidence more of disunity than of anything else.

Not that Ulster Unionists, on the average, are of British nationality, in the cultural sense of the term. Mr. David Kennedy has painted a revealing picture of their concept of loyalty: 'In a more primitive age, loyalty was a personal bond linking the subject to his chief or king. Personal loyalty on that plane went out with the Stuarts, and there was substituted for it loyalty to the will of the people made known through Parliament and expressed in the person of a constitutional monarch. But in the years 1912-14 the Ulster Unionist found himself in a painful dilemma. In 1912 the Commons passed the Home Rule Bill. In 1914 it was placed on the Statute Book with a stay of execution. After some wriggling on constitutional niceties Ulster appealed to a deeper level of subconscious loyalty symbolised by the Solemn League and Covenant, Foxe's *Book of Martyrs*, and a mythological figure on a white horse who seems to have galloped out of the mists of Celtic paganism. In the face of these tribal gods Ulster defied King and Constitution and set up a Provisional Government'.[1] The trouble is that the Irish Nationalist finds it difficult to placate these tribal deities. He too, of course, has his own national Pantheon that is equally difficult of acceptance by the 'Orangeman'. And unfortunately for understanding, both in North and South political symbols have become unduly associated with these 'national creeds'. As Mr. Kennedy has shown, even Catholic-Protestant co-operation in the North is difficult for Catholics under symbols of a crown and flag that are used as party emblems signifying loyalty to an ideology.

The essential barrier to Irish unity lies here. Even economic obstacles are secondary to it and too much should not be hoped from their removal. Too often we have been given to understand that they are the chief difficulty. Sir Horace Plunkett may well have been right in saying that 'the intensely practical nature of the objection which came from the commercial and industrial classes of the North who opposed Home Rule was never properly recognised in Ireland'.[2] But the recognition and answering of this objection would not close the cultural gap. This is something which only time can do and there are indications that its closing is not impossible. The tradition of the Milligans is not dead; of the Presbyterian minister Andrew Bryson, who initiated the collection of Irish manuscripts in the British Museum;

---

[1] David Kennedy, Whither Northern Nationalism, in *Christus Rex*, October 1959, pp 276-277.

[2] Sir Horace Plunkett, *Ireland in the New Century*, London 1905, P 77.

of another Presbyterian, William Nielson, who published an Irish grammar; or of Dr. MacDonnell, who founded a Harp School in Belfast and gathered a selection of Irish airs from Connaught. Many Northern Protestants show a vague interest in the Irish language; some amongst them have become its champions. There is an Ulster Protestant Gaelic Society to boot, while the Ulster Literary Theatre, which contributed in an important way to the Irish Literary Revival, still continues, though with less vigour than before, to provide plays of the kind that brought it support in the past from Protestant Nationalists like Roger Casement. The Scots-Gaelic background of many Unionist families has inspired an appreciation of Irish music and dancing, something for which the Belfast station of the B.B.C. also caters. On the other hand, many Catholic Nationalists get real enjoyment from certain Orange songs; even 'the Twelfth' has homely aspects for very many of them.[1]

All this shows that it is possible to narrow and even close the cultural gap between the older and more recent settlers in Ireland. Even if religious differences were to remain, a narrowing of divisions in secular culture would itself suffice, as is clear from the experience of other countries, to make for significant communal unity. As yet there is no such unity. In Ulster, says Mr. Kennedy, 'there are three distinct communities corresponding to the three main religious groups: the native stock, Catholic in faith and Gaelic in tradition; the Scots settlers, Presbyterian, but often of Gaelic stock; the Church of Ireland is the church of the English settlers who still regard themselves as a colony in an alien land. A process of attrition has eaten into all three but in the main the classification holds. The *Herrenvolk* mentality of the Ascendancy still regards the natives as second-class citizens, and Presbyterians promoted to privileged status have become infected with that mentality. But common ground in cultural activity is greater than politicians and publicists would have us believe'.[2] A nation is not a territory; it is a people.

[1] Cf David Kennedy, The Growth of a Community, in *Christus Rex*, April 1959, pp 112-114.

[2] Kennedy, *loc. cit.* p 114.

In the Ireland of today we have an ancient stock and more recent arrivals. Two nations? Or a nation still in the making? 'Ireland', said Mr. Asquith, 'is a nation; not two nations, but one nation. There are few cases in history, and as a student of history in a humble way I myself know none, of a nationality so distinct, so persistent, and so assimilative as the Irish'.

National unity can be promoted by political unity—of a kind that will respect the present cultural values of the mass of Northern Protestants and insure them due liberty of religious belief and expression. To this end, said Mr. Lemass in the Oxford Debate, an arrangement might be hammered out 'which would give them effective power to protect themselves, very especially in regard to educational and religious matters'. He then referred to the proposal that the question of Irish reunification might be considered on the federal basis which was outlined earlier. He agreed that this suggestion 'seems eminently practical and should effectively dispose of the apprehensions of the North of Ireland Protestant population about the consequences of reunification which they seem most to fear'. Indeed it might be argued that they would have a duty to accept it. If, as seems to be the case, the mutual material good of the two parts of the country demands their economic co-operation, that co-operation imposes itself morally in virtue of the Principle of Development. This also holds for political federation if it can be proved to be in the interests of a peace and harmony which does not sacrifice the legitimate interests of either side. Stormont must remember that 'there is no argument which could be advanced to justify giving to the Irish Partitionist minority the right to vote themselves out of the Irish State, that could not be applied with greater force to allow Co. Tyrone, Co. Fermanagh, South Down, South Armagh and Derry City the right to vote themselves in'.[1] If the remainder is not viable, there is no course open to it—even morally—other than union with a greater whole in which its economic and political interests will be safeguarded. Needless to say the same considerations apply in its own way to Southern Ireland as regards the ques-

[1] Mr. Lemass in Oxford Debate.

tion of uniting with greater wholes—economic and even political—to the extent that this necessary, or desirable, in the interests of the national or the international common good.

THE MORALITY OF STATES

It may be reasonably asked what kind of moral obligation is
in question here? On whom in particular does it fall? On the
State as a whole or on the individual statesman? It is a fact of
history and common observation that morality between States
is on a lower level than that between individuals. Lord Bryce,
in one of a series of lectures on international relations delivered
in America,[1] sought to explain the reasons which lie behind
this. Prominent among them is the fact that whereas an individual feels himself responsible to his fellow men, governments do
not commonly hold themselves responsible to anyone outside
the State. There is also the fact that their acts tend to be im-
personal, being the fruit of the collaboration of a large number
of men. Even when a government does have a sense of international responsibility, its power of decision is so divided between the executive, the legislature and the citizen body, that
it is all too easy for its individual members to shift the blame
for unconscionable measures from their own shoulders. Governmental responsibility, in modern democracies, is usually more
or less divided and, as Bryce says, 'wherever there is divided
responsibility there is a weaker sense of duty'.
    There is also, he adds, another important difference between
the morality of individuals and of States. The conscience of the
individual is kept awake to its duties by the law of the land,
in a way that does not hold for the State in international relations. Although the scene has changed, in this respect, since
Bryce's day, what he says is still true in an important sense.
Today a State could scarcely commit an act of aggression without arousing international protest of some kind. But there is

[1] Cf. Bryce, *International Relations*, Lecture VI, Popular Control of
Foreign Policy and the Morality of States, London 1922.

no law which positively outlines its duties as a member of the community of States. Should it decide to isolate itself from the problems of the world community, or even from those of its neighbours, it would be difficult to arouse in it a sense of failing in social justice. The individual man can be accused of selfishness and egoism in a way that is very difficult of application to the State. Only too frequently can statesmen be found who, however moral they may be in private life, are very prone to practise in the interests of the State the principle that the end justifies the means. If they succeed, they are hailed as great statesmen; if they fail, their wrong-doing is usually condoned as a mistake arising from misdirected patriotism.

The objective situation is as cold and clear as it is different from the picture just painted. When everything has been said that can palliate irresponsible action by statesmen, the fact is that they are subject to moral judgment. Allowing for the pressure of emergent necessities, which can limit their freedom of choice, allowing too for the undeniable division of decision-making in modern States, it still remains true that members of governments—to a greater or lesser degree—retain a personal responsibility for their actions as statesmen. Each one himself knows exactly the extent to which a particular policy has his assent and co-operation. And he is bound to see that, in so far as is possible, this assent and co-operation are guided by moral principles.

Morality is basically a matter for the individual person, as responsibility is always ultimately reducible to the freedom and rationality that are characteristic of man. States are moral in and through the men who guide their destinies. Hence the duty on statesmen to bring a moral outlook to bear on international questions in which their countries are involved. The Christian statesman should be especially conscious of this. The Catholic statesman in particular should remember that he is part of the Church active, and that the Church's policy for international justice depends on him for its furtherance and realisation. 'All Christians', writes Mgr. Dell' Acqua, ' . . . are invited to open themselves to these wider perspectives and to contribute, on their part, to the bringing about of a greater justice and charity.

It is necessary that all should be acquainted with what is accomplished by those Catholics who work on the international plane, with what they themselves can do to further this action, something which the Church awaits from her children in a world in which relations grow more extensive, without, for all that, becoming more human'.[1]

It must be accepted, of course, that statesmen are the trustees of the people and cannot exceed the authority which has been committed to them. In affairs of lesser importance they themselves are allowed to be the judges of the extent of their own power. Yet that circumstances can arise in which the will of the people should be directly consulted is the ground of the necessity of a device like the 'referendum'. We have already discussed whether this should always be used before a government can declare war in the name of the people. As we saw then the weight of the argument is against this. The same holds for democratic control of foreign policy. Not only are problems in this sphere continually changing and facts difficult to establish, but the whole thing is so unrelated to the average citizen's experience that his judgment on it is largely a matter of guesswork. What can be defended, however, is that measures of foreign policy should be decided in the open in so far as is possible.[2]

---

[1] Letter to the General Assembly of the International Conference of Catholic International Organisations, Bruges 8 April, 1957.

[2] 'There is often a certain soundness in the popular mind which may prove to be a guide safer than is any set of privileged persons. The people are not qualified to deal with every kind of matter, but when there is a plain issue, and especially if it is a moral issue, there is often seen a fairness and even a wisdom in the judgment of the people which we are not sure to find in the politicians. The people,—if not fevered by passion, for then they become dangerous—may have a more broad common sense view of what is not worth contending for than a group of officials, who may be steeped in traditions or prejudices. They may sometimes also have a clearer sense of what is just and reasonable and a greater willingness to settle disputes peacefully . . .; they condemned the Afghan war in 1878-9 as soon as an election gave them the opportunity, and they passed a like judgment on the South African War at the election of 1905. If public opinion is generally incurious or apathetic about foreign rela-

The most satisfactory way of consulting the people on foreign policy is by giving them adequate notice, through the
ordinary channels, of what the government is proposing to do.
Their reaction can then be measured and evaluated. To quote
Bryce again: 'Perhaps the chief gain to be expected from a fuller
popular control will be found in its fuller publicity. When the
ministers of a country have to submit their negotiations and
their treaties to the public judgment before the nation is committed to a certain course there may be a better chance of
avoiding ignoble or harsh and aggressive action. A people which
might be disposed to accept and ratify as a *fait accompli* what
had been already done, on its behalf, might refuse to approve,
when there had been full opportunity for public discussion,
negotiations or treaties likely to lower its credit in the eyes of
the world at large'.[1]

tions, that is partly because these topics have been so much withdrawn
from public knowledge as to receive less public discussion than they
require'—Bryce, *op. cit.* p 187.

[1] Bryce, *op. cit.*

CHAPTER FIVE

CATHOLIC TEACHING ON CHURCH AND STATE

THE charge that the Church is intolerant when she is in a position of strength in the State figures prominently in attacks on
Catholicism at the present day. Time was when the non-Catholic offensive on Rome was mounted primarily, if not exclusively, on theological grounds. Until the middle of the 19th
century, at least in the English-speaking world, with more or
less general agreement on the fundamental fact of the truth of
the Christian religion, objections to Catholicism tended to
centre on matters such as Transubstantiation and the Primacy
of the Pope. During the hundred years between then and World
War II, a certain shifting of position was made by opponents
of the Church. Objections came to be more philosophical in
nature, arrayed against the Catholic belief in the existence of
God, the immortality of the soul, free will and the like. Since
the last war, a further change is discernible. The charge now
made is that Catholicism is incompatible with progress in the
social and political domains—in particular, that it is out of
harmony with the democratic values of freedom and equality
which have latterly become so important in the secular world.

The defence of these values is one of the main preoccupations
of Western intellectuals today. It is ostensibly in the interests
of democratic liberties that American writers like Blanshard
have been fulminating against what they regard as the intolerance of the Catholic Church.[1] So effective has been their propa-

---

[1] Paul Blanshard, *American Freedom and Catholic Power*, 1st ed.
Boston 1949; new ed. Boston 1958, *Communism, Democracy and
Catholic Power*, British edition, London 1952.

198

ganda that we find Senator John Kennedy having to give assurances that, in the event of his becoming President of the U.S.A., there would be no question of his profession of Catholicism leading him to seek to undermine the system of separation of Church and State. He raised the matter himself on more than one occasion. 'There is one legitimate question underlying all the rest: Would you, as President of the United States, be responsive in any way to ecclesiastical pressures or obligations of any kind that might in any fashion influence or interfere with your conduct of that office in the national interest? I have answered that question many times. My answer was—and is—"No". Once that question is answered there is no legitimate issue of my religion . . . '.[1]

Despite his protests, many Americans continued to be suspicious of Catholic influence in politics were he to become President. In Ireland we have an analogous situation. Non-Catholic Unionists in Northern Ireland fear that one of the big consequences of a united Ireland would be Catholic intolerance towards themselves and their co-religionists. This attitude is there and cannot be denied. It was forcibly expressed at Garron Tower by Miss Mary McNeill and has found prominent place in Norman Gibson's pamphlet on partition. I will repeat it as it is outlined therein :

'Basically the Partitionist fears the exclusiveness of Roman Catholicism, its claims to absolute truth and the consequences that seem to follow from this position . . . As I understand it the Roman Catholic Church believes herself to be both the guardian of the faith and the protector of the faithful. In practice this appears to mean that in order to obtain conformity within a community to her moral and social teaching, she will as far as possible augment her own authority with the authority of the State . . . The Partitionist will be inclined . . . to ask what guarantee he would have that his religious freedom would be secure in a predominantly Catholic society. After all from the point of view of the Catholic or his Church the beliefs and practices of the Protestant are heretical and erroneous and must

[1] *New York Times*, 22 April 1960.

constitute a threat to the peace of mind and perhaps the loyalty of the faithful. It is, I hope, a fair statement of the case to suggest, then, that the claims of the Catholic and his Church make it difficult for them to tolerate what might be called the liberal society—the society which . . . leaves open to the individual as wide a field as it can for moral decision making . . . But to return to the Constitution. "The State recognises the *special* position of the Holy Catholic Apostolic and Roman Church as the guardian of the Faith professed by the great majority of the citizens". Putting aside any questions of theology which this statement might raise, the Partitionist is anxious to know what is meant by the "special position" etc. Does it confer any privileges or powers? What would it mean in a United Ireland? The Partitionist feels that no single Church should have any special privileges over and above the other Churches. He is of course aware that the present Constitution guarantees "freedom of conscience and the public profession and practice of religion . . . subject to public morality . . . to every citizen". But the value of this safeguard depends on who interprets what is meant by public morality and could mean much or little'.[1]

In view of this, it is desirable that some explanation be made available on the extent of the public tolerance of non-Catholic positions that can be accorded by a State with a predominantly Catholic majority. In its most fundamental terms, the question concerns the relations which, in Catholic teaching, should exist between the Church and the State. We must note immediately that on this important question there is a cleavage of Catholic opinion itself. Replies differ according as to whether those who provide them are liberal or conservative in their approach.

ESTABLISHMENT VERSUS SEPARATION

Some Catholics frankly assert that, in the Catholic State, i.e., the State in which Catholics have an overwhelming majority, the Catholic Church has a right to be established by law,

[1] Norman Gibson, *Partition: A Northern Viewpoint.*

as a result of which there must be considerable limitation on non-Catholics in the matter of freedom of religious expression and religious propaganda. In his *Belief of Catholics*, first published in 1927, the late Mgr. Ronald Knox freely admitted this: 'You cannot bind over the Catholic Church . . . to waive all right of invoking the secular arm in defence of her own principles. The circumstances in which such a possibility could be realised are sufficiently remote . . . Given such circumstances, is it certain that the Catholic Government of the nation could have no right to insist on Catholic education being universal (which is a form of coercion) and even to deport or imprison those who unsettle the minds of its subjects with new doctrines? It is "certain" that the Church would claim that right for the Catholic Government, even if considerations of prudence forbade its exercise in fact . . . And for these reasons a body of Catholic patriots, entrusted with the government of a Catholic State, will not shrink from repressive measures in order to perpetuate the secure domination of Catholic principles among their fellow countrymen'.[1]

One can find many expressions of similar views among Catholic writers. They are part of a defence of what is called the

---

[1] R. A. Knox, *The Belief of Catholics*, London 1927, p 241. A similar view was expressed in the Jesuit review *Civilta Cattolica*, for April 1948: 'The Roman Catholic Church, convinced through its divine prerogatives, of being the only true Church, must demand the rights of freedom for itself alone. Such a right can only be possessed by truth, never by error. As to other religions, the Church will certainly never draw the sword, but she will require that by legitimate means they shall not be allowed to propagate false doctrines. Consequently, in a State where the majority of the people are Catholic, the Church will require that legal existence be denied to error, and that if religious minorities actually exist, they shall have only a *de facto* existence without opportunity to spread their beliefs'—F. Cavalli, Le condizione dei Protestanti in Spagna. Of this Fr. J. C. Murray observed that 'it is probable that nothing has been written in decades better calculated to produce in the U.S. a blind reaction of total hostility to all things Catholic than the author's ruthlessly simplifying paragraphs on the Church's "unblushing intolerance"'.—J. C. Murray, Current Theology on Religious Freedom, in *Theological Studies*, Sept. 1949, p 414, n 26.

'union of Church and State', 'State religion' or the 'establishment of the Church'. Church establishment was quite common
in the 19th century. The Argentine Constitution of 1860 declared that the Government 'sustains the Roman Catholic and
Apostolic worship'. That of Peru in the same year said that the
Catholic religion was 'established . . . as the religion of the
nation'. Colombia in 1887 constituted it 'the religion of the
State'. As it was generally understood, such establishment
meant that non-Catholic cults were merely tolerated in and by
the State. The Constitution of Bolivia (1880) put this plainly:
'The State recognises and sustains the Roman Catholic and
Apostolic religion, permitting the exercise of other cults'. As
merely tolerated cults these others were usually subject to
political limitations; sometimes indeed cults other than the
established one were excluded altogether. Concordats with Spain
in 1851 and with the Republic of the Equator in 1862 expressly
stipulated that 'no other forms of worship than the Catholic
one should be tolerated' in the State. On the other hand, establishment frequently entailed material benefits for the Church,
the clergy drawing their incomes direct from the State. Just as
frequently it involved the Church in liabilities to the State which
sometimes hampered her spiritual mission. The need for State
approval in the appointment of bishops was one such disadvantage; there were others which need not detain us here.

Needless to say, there are many Catholics to whom the
system of 'establishment' is unacceptable in so far as it is identified with, or could involve, religious intolerance. They are more
than anxious to defend the view that it is no essential part of
Catholic teaching. The question was first raised in a practical
way in 1927 when there was a Catholic candidate for the
American Presidency—Al. Smith. Non-Catholic doubts about
his suitability were voiced in an *Open Letter* to Smith by the
New York lawyer Charles C. Marshall.[1] This expressed concern
lest a Catholic victory would weaken the structure of American
democracy. In particular it objected to 'certain conceptions
which your fellow citizens attribute to you as a loyal and conscientious Roman Catholic, which in their minds are irreconcil-

[1] In the *Atlantic Monthly*, April 1927.

able with that Constitution which as President you must support and defend, and with the principles of civil and religious liberty on which American institutions are based'. In brief, the charge was that, should Smith become President, the separation of Church and State would be endangered. Smith denied the imputation with the utmost vigour. 'Without mental reservation', he said, 'I can and do make that disclaimer. These convictions are held neither by me nor by any other American Catholic, so far as I know'. He went out of his way to defend the system of separation: 'The absolute separation of State and Church is part of the fundamental basis of our Constitution. I believe in that separation and all that it implies. That belief must be a part of the fundamental faith of every true American'.

Smith's reply to Marshall was that of an ordinary Catholic; it made no claim to be a philosophical exposition of the Catholic position. Indeed he weakened his case by giving the impression that he might not necessarily be reflecting the more common viewpoint of his Catholic co-religionists: 'You seem to think that Catholics must be all alike, in mind and in heart, as though they had been poured into and taken out of the same mould. You have no more right to ask me to defend as part of my faith every statement coming from a prelate than I should have to ask you to accept as an article of your religious faith every statement of an Episcopal bishop, or of your political faith every statement of a President of the United States'. While this was true in itself, it left the way open for the interpretation that at least some Catholics were anti-separation and, therefore, anti-democratic.

Heavier guns were called into action when Smith found a defender in Mgr. John A. Ryan of the Catholic University of America. Even before Marshall's letter, Mgr. Ryan had had a skirmish on the subject with the editor of the Unitarian *Christian Century*. He drew his points mainly from the volume *The State and the Church* which, in conjunction with Fr. Moorhouse Millar, he had brought out in 1922.[1] In this he had gone to pains to show that religious intolerance was no essential consequence

---

[1] John A. Ryan and Moorhouse F. X. Millar, *The State and the Church*, New York 1922.

of the Catholic teaching on Church and State. That Catholic theory favoured establishment he did not deny. What he contended was that establishment could take diverse forms. 'One observation may be made which is calculated to prevent much misconception and false reasoning on this subject. It is that the *principle* of union between Church and State is not necessarily dependent upon any particular form of union that has actually been in operation'.[1] In particular, the repression of non-established religions is no necessary part of it. It is not difficult to see what Mgr. Ryan had in mind. In England, for example, the Anglican Church is established, as a result of which it enjoys certain legal privileges. The Sovereign must be a member of the Church of England; twenty-six archbishops and bishops sit in the House of Lords and the due sentences of the ecclesiastical Courts are enforced by the State. But the Church is not endowed by the State nor are its clergy paid out of the national revenue. Neither is there any legal intolerance towards other Churches.[2] In somewhat the same way, one could have a Catholic State, in which Catholicism was established, without being involved in any interference with the religious liberties of non-Catholics.

But Mgr. Ryan carried his defence even further. It must not be thought, he said, that 'establishment' is so vital to Catholic interests that it must be sought in practice irrespective of circumstances. It has 'full application only to the completely Catholic State. This means a political community that is either exclusively, or almost exclusively, made up of Catholics'.[3] And Mgr. Ryan agreed with the German theologian Fr. Pohle that 'there is good reason to doubt if there still exists a purely Catholic State in the world'.[4] Hence what is desirable in theory is not always to be pressed for in practice. While 'establishment' must be defended *in abstracto*, in the concrete 'separation' must sometimes be accepted. Mgr. Ryan was here reproducing what

[1] Ryan and Millar, *op. cit.* p 34.
[2] See Cyril Garbett, Archbishop of York, *Church and State in England*, London 1950, pp 123-128.
[3] Ryan and Millar, *op. cit.* p 37.
[4] Article in *Catholic Encyclopaedia*.

is called the thesis-hypothesis distinction, which had been the stock in trade of Catholic apologists for three quarters of a century. The thesis represents the ideal in Catholic theory and expresses the way in which Church-State principles should be applied given the circumstances of an absolute Catholic majority. The hypothesis, on the other hand, expresses the extent of the application of these principles in face of less favourable *de facto* practical possibilities. Whenever the acceptance of the hypothesis is necessary, owing to the pressure of fact, one must still uphold the thesis as the ideal. In this way it is possible for Catholic theory to come to terms with a pluralist society in which equal status is accorded to all religious denominations.

Mgr. Ryan added a third argument in his effort to convince American non-Catholics that they had nothing to fear from Catholic claims. It was that there was no likelihood, in the foreseeable future, of America becoming so Catholic that any establishment of Catholicism as the religion of the State would become a practical proposition. His fellow-citizens, he said, should be 'sufficiently realistic to see that the danger of religious intolerance toward non-Catholics in the United States is so improbable and so far in the future that it should not occupy their time or attention'.[1]

He repeated all these arguments by way of supporting Smith.[2] He even went further and maintained that should establishment ever come, it would certainly involve no religious discrimination. In order to extenuate his reference to the latter possibility in his book he explained that it was written so as to face a possible extreme difficulty. 'I wanted to state the Catholic doctrine in all its rigour in order to forestall the charge of minimizing'.[3] We know that his efforts to secure Smith's election failed and we are told that his reaction to the affair was one of dismay. He mourned what he regarded as the bigotry and ignorance of American non-Catholics. 'There will be required', he wrote, 'a long, a comprehensive and an intensive campaign

[1] Ryan and Millar, *op. cit.* p 39.
[2] Cf F. L. Broderick, When Last a Catholic ran for President, in *Social Order*, vol. x, n 5 (1960).
[3] Letter to the New York *World*, 11 April 1927.

of education to enlighten those that sit in darkness'.[1] He did little, however, to make his views more acceptable to them. In 1941, with the co-operation of Fr. Boland, he published a new edition of his book (entitled *Catholic Principles of Politics*), which made no change in the presentation of his teaching on Church-State relations.

From 1947 on the attack on the Church on the grounds of being inimical to democracy has been pushed with new vigour by an organisation which calls itself 'Protestants and Other Americans United for the Separation of Church and State' (POAU).[2] It is centered on the implications of the Catholic thesis. Bypassing the situation of hypothesis, the charge is levelled that the Catholic ideal is for a society that would be undemocratic. We must content ourselves with a couple of examples of what is asserted. 'A discussion of "Democracy" does not occur in the Catholic Encyclopaedia . . . This is not to say that there are no democratic Catholics in America or elsewhere. It is simply to say that democracy is an idea foreign to the essential political ideology of the Roman Catholic Church-State'.[3] ' . . . The ideal of the Roman Catholic Church is church-state union wherever that policy results in the establishment of the Roman Catholic religion, while in areas where that is not possible it pursues a purely opportunistic policy . . . '.[4] Perhaps the most incisive statements of this viewpoint have been penned by Paul Blanshard. In his *American Freedom and Catholic Power* and *Communism, Democracy and Catholic Power* he has taxed Catholic theory on Church-State relations with intolerance. The Catholic position in relation to censorship of books, education and medical ethics has also come in for castigation as authoritarian.

[1] J. A. Ryan, A Catholic View of the Election, in *Current History*, December 1928.

[2] For a full account of the activities of P.A.O.U. see L. P. Creedon and W. D. Falcon, *United for Separation*, Milwaukee 1959.

[3] P.A.O.U., *Church and State* (February 1951), p 2. Quoted in Creedon and Falcon, *op. cit.* p 215.

[4] P.A.O.U., *Church and State* (March 1954), p 1. Quoted in Creedon and Falcon p 225.

It is not our business here to deal with the latter charges seriatim. They have already been refuted by American writers.[1] Our interest is rather in the central charge that the Catholic political ideal is radically and inescapably undemocratic. I think it is fair to say that this has been responsible, in large measure, for a reorientation of American Catholic attitudes on Church-State relations. I am thinking in particular, of the work of Fr. John Courtney Murray, S.J. While it is true that, even before the Blanshard onslaught and as far back as 1945, Fr. Murray was laying the foundations of a new approach to this question, there can be little doubt that he has been spurred to develop it in face of the severe criticism to which the older approach of men like Mgr. Ryan was subjected by Blanshard and to which, unfortunately, it seemed open in certain respects. Of course there were also stirrings in a new direction on the Continent of Europe, as witness the writings of Frs. Aubert and Rouquette, Frs. Hartmann and Max Pribilla, S.J.[2] Fr. Murray's thinking is contained in a multitude of articles, notably a series in *Theological Studies* of which he is editor. Many of them have also been brought together in the much-publicised book *We Hold These Truths*.[3]

It is Fr. Murray's contention that the thesis-hypothesis explanation represents an ambivalent attitude that is far from satisfactory.[4] In 1948, in a famous address to the Catholic

[1] See Currin V. Shields, *Democracy and Catholicism in America*, New York 1958; James O'Neill, *Catholicism and American Freedom*, New York 1952.

[2] R. Aubert, in *Tolérance et communauté humaine*, Paris 1952; R. Rouquette, in *L'Église et la liberté*, Paris 1952; H. Hartmann S.J., *Toleranz und christlicher Glaube*, Frankfurt 1955; French trans. *Vraie et fausse tolérance*, Paris 1958; M. Pribilla S.J., Dogmatische Intoleranz und burgerliche Toleranz, in *Stimmen der Zeit*, 144 (1949).

[3] J. C. Murray, *We Hold These Truths*, New York 1960.

[4] 'Heretofore the Catholic answer has been somewhat ambivalent. The American political idea and the institutions through which it works have been accepted in practice, rather completely and perhaps naively. At the same time there seems to exist an implied condemnation of the system in theory . . . The question now is, whether this ambivalent attitude is any longer either intellectually or morally respectable,

Theological Society of America,[1] he declared that it had out-
grown its usefulness. It would be a mistake, he said, to think
that that 'somewhat *ad hoc* theologumenon' supplies irrevocably and for all time the categories in which we must continue
to debate the problem of Church and State. 'For my own part',
he continued, 'I incline to think that the usefulness of this
particular distinction is increasingly outweighed by its tendency
to mislead, and that its categories are too facile to admit of
fruitful theological and political thought'. If, for example, one
were to say that the thesis is verified in Spain but only the
hypothesis in the United States, one would step off 'on the
wrong foot into a morass of futile controversy, that centers on
an irrelevance—whether the particular political form of the
Spanish State is in any sense part of some Catholic 'ideal'.' Fr.
Murray just cannot get himself to regard such a unitary pattern of political organisation as the norm for politico-religious
relationships. He is hyper-conscious of the non-unitary, the
pluralist, character of the social framework of the United
States. And he emphatically asserts that Catholic philosophy
must accept this as normal.[2] In practice, he urges, American
Catholics are its stoutest defenders; indeed such pluralism is
very much an American Catholic prejudice.[3] The only course

whether it takes proper account of the realities in the situation and of
the special affirmation of the human that America has historically made'
—*We Hold These Truths*, pp 182-183.

[1] J. C. Murray, Governmental Repression of Heresy, in *Proceedings
of the Third Annual Meeting of the Catholic Theological Society of America*,
Chicago 1948, p 37.

[2] 'The Catholic community faces the task of making itself intellectually aware of the conditions of its own coexistence within the American
scene. We have behind us a lengthy historical tradition of acceptance
of the special situation of the Church in America, in all its differences
from the situations in which the Church elsewhere finds itself. But it is
a question here of pursuing the subject, not in the horizontal dimension
of history but in the vertical dimension of theory'—*We Hold These
Truths*, pp 27-28.

[3] 'The American Catholic is entirely prepared to accept our constitutional concept of freedom of religion and the policy of no establishment
as the first of our prejudices. He is also prepared to admit that other

for the Church in America to adopt is frankly to admit that the system which obtains there is fully in accordance with the demands of Catholic Church-State theory.[1] In short, Fr. Murray maintains that establishment cannot properly be said to be the Catholic ideal for the United States. Separation and the pluralism which it reflects can be accepted unequivocally and without reluctance.

In this he could claim the support of American bishops, past and present.[2] In 1824 John England, Bishop of Charleston, exclaimed: 'May God long preserve the liberties of America from the union of any Church with any state'. In 1843 John Hughes, Archbishop of New York, described the Constitution of the United States as 'a monument of wisdom'. In 1909 Cardinal Gibbons piled praise on it: 'We know the blessings of our present arrangement; it gives us liberty and binds together priests and people in a union better than that of Church and State. Other countries, other manners; we do not believe our system adapted to all conditions . . . For ourselves, we thank God we live in America'. And in 1948 Archbishop John McNicholas stated firmly: 'We deny absolutely and without qualification that the Catholic bishops of the United States are seeking a union of Church and State by any endeavour whatsoever, either proximate or remote. If tomorrow Catholics constituted a majority in our country, they would not seek a union of Church and State . . . We hold firmly that our own constitutional provisions are the best for our country'.

prejudices may obtain elsewhere—in England, in Sweden, in Spain. Their validity in their own context and against the background of the history that generated them does not disturb him in his conviction that his own prejudice, within its own context and against the background of his own history, has its own validity'—*op. cit.* p 47.

[1] '. . . Under American conditions any other course but freedom of religion and separation of church and state would have been disruptive, impractical, indeed impossible'—*op. cit.* pp 59-60.

[2] Cf The Voice of the Church in America, in *America*, 24 September 1960; also Creedon and Falcon, *op. cit.* pp 226-229. For a general account of the background to the Church-State question in America see Jerome K. Kerwin, *Catholic Viewpoint on Church and State*, New York 1960.

It seems then that Fr. Murray is on very safe ground when he claims that separation is best for the Church in America. Only confusion can result from the kind of hedging acceptance that is accorded to it by the more wary approach of men like Mgr. Ryan. And there can be little doubt that the wide diffusion of Fr. Murray's ideas on this subject played no small part in Senator Kennedy's election to the Presidency. The climate of opinion of 1960 on the Church-State issue was very different from that of 1928. In a way which Mgr. Ryan would not have welcomed, those who sat in darkness had been enlightened by Fr. Murray's campaign of education. And yet can one say that the matter is now finished, that all is over in the great debate? There are many who continue to be confused. Who, they ask, is the greater prophet? An *America* symposium, prior to the election, gave proof of this. One of the contributors, editor of *Christianity and Crisis*, put the position plainly: 'Protestants and others will continue to be uneasy at certain points until they are convinced that the openness to the 'American experiment' represented by the thought of Fr. John Courtney Murray, S.J., is more representative of the Catholic Church in America than are the principles enunciated by Ryan and Boland in *Catholic Principles of Politics*'.[1]

One has to admit that there is an important cleavage of opinion between Mgr. Ryan and Fr. John Courtney Murray. Nor is this difference confined to American scholars. The German Jesuit, Fr. Hartmann, says that, when we begin to examine the problem of Church-State relations, 'we discover that there is no unanimity on the question in the Catholic world. One group of theologians defend the "Catholic State" as a direct conclusion from the Catholic faith's claim to truth; other theologians may reject it completely'.[2] An American Protestant writer puts it as follows: 'A . . . fact about Roman Catholicism that needs to be understood by Protestants is that the Catholic Church is divided from top to bottom in this country and abroad on matters of principle in regard to religious liberty.

---

[1] Wayne H. Cowan, in On Raising the Religious Issue, in *America* 24 September, 1960, p 707.

[2] Albert Hartmann, *op. cit.* p 173,

There is a traditional main-line position that favours the confessional Catholic state as the ideal type of relationship between Church and State. This view would limit the rights of religious minorities in a nation that has a very large Catholic majority . . . This position is often called the "thesis" and the adjustments of the Church to religiously pluralistic nations involve a second-best position that is called the "hypothesis" . . . It is important to realise that a very able and earnest attempt is being made by Roman Catholics in this country, with much support from Catholics in Western Europe, to change the principles as well as the practice in this matter'.[1] There is no defined dogmatic teaching on the part of the Church on the question; hence the differences of opinion that have arisen.

SCOPE AND TERMINOLOGY OF THE PROBLEM

It is necessary to be aware, from the very outset of discussion on these attitudes, that there are two separate questions involved. The first question is what is the due position of the Church in a State in which there is a large Catholic majority? The second is whether this position, whatever it may be, unavoidably entails intolerance towards non-Catholics? We will confine ourselves, in the present chapter, to the first question If we can succeed in isolating the essence of the Catholic claims, we can later address ourselves to investigating how it is realised.

What then does the Church demand of the State? To Fr. Murray's mind, relations between Church and State have always been and must continue to be governed by three principles: the freedom of the Church, harmony between Church and State and, thirdly, co-operation between them. These principles have to be brought down from the world of abstraction and given concrete application in different circumstances. The legal system of Church 'establishment' or the 'union of Church and State', was, he says, only one application, suited to the age of emerging national States and the ideological framework of

[1] John C. Bennett, *Christians and the State*, New York 1958, pp 264-267.

monarchical absolutism. It was an adaptation of the principles
to a particular historical context and does not represent a permanent exigence.[1]

In the present age a quite different application is necessary,
which is *aeque iure* as theologically valid as the system of establishment. It is demanded by the requirements of the democratic
State, which today 'presents itself with all the force of an idea
whose time has come'. In this context, it behoves the Church
to seek out what is good in the liberal ideology and to apply
her principles anew in the light of this.[2] Fr. Murray believes
that it is possible to do this. The principle of the freedom of the
Church is sufficiently respected by a constitutional guarantee
concerning the free exercise and propaganda of religion. That
of harmony between Church and State can be implemented
by the people themselves through freedom of association and
free political institutions, while co-operation between Church
and State can be effected by State protection of the Church's
freedom, the adequate fulfilling of its own temporal function
and the spiritual penetration of the political domain by a laity
conscious of its Christian responsibilities.

Fr. Murray maintains that it is only by way of an approach
such as this that the Church can reconcile the democratic attitude towards freedom, which is worthy of being preserved, with
her own perennial theological principles. The system of establishment is no longer useful. 'Like the theory of "the two swords",
it has had its moment of history'.[3] Fr. Murray contends that
there is need for formal recognition of this in the textbooks of
Public Ecclesiastical Law. Indeed 'the whole tradition needs
to be reviewed, not merely that segment of it which tends to

[1] J. C. Murray, The Problem of State Religion, in *Theological
Studies*, vol. XII (1951), n 2.

[2] 'The theological task of the moment is . . to explore, under the
guidance of the Church, the possibilities of a vital adaptation of Church-
State doctrine to the constitutional structure, the political institutions
and the ethos of freedom characteristic of the democratic State'.

[3] J. C. Murray, On the Structure of the Church-State Problem, in
The Catholic Church in World Affairs, Gurian and Fitsimons ed., Notre
Dame 1954, p 30.

dominate the ordinary manual *de jure publico*, whose separate existence as a treatise dates from the nineteenth century and reflects its anxieties'.[1]

From this it would seem that Fr. Murray is proposing the American solution for adoption by the universal Church. Indeed his purpose in *We Hold These Truths* appears to be not merely to defend it as the best for America but to hold it up to the world for admiration and imitation. Elsewhere in his writings he makes this explicit.[2] So much so that an *America* editorial couples his name with a suggestion that the American solution may, in God's providence, be instrumental in developing a general Catholic theology of toleration.[3] Fr. Murray himself has insisted that his views do not mean that he unreservedly defends separation. 'I am not', he says, 'implying that what is called "separation" of Church and State is today somehow the thesis'.[4] But one has to understand what exactly he means by separation. A Roman professor of the Public Law of the Church, Fr. Bender, O.P., has clearly described three different forms of it.[5] The first is what he calls 'pure separation', under which all Churches are treated as private societies and all are equally protected by the law. The second is 'hostile separation', under which the State seeks to deny to the Church the basic right to guide the moral life of her subjects as citizens. Thirdly, there is

---

[1] Murray, *loc. cit.* p 32.

[2] Cf J. C. Murray, Church, State and Religious Liberty, in *The Catholic Mind*, May-June 1959, pp 201-215.

[3] On Religious Toleration, in *America*, 24 September 1960, pp 694-695. Mr. Donal Barrington has the same thing in mind when he writes: "Many people await with eagerness the book in which Father Murray will work out the general principles of his political philosophy. Only then will the value of his thought to countries like our own, which seek to combine civil unity with religious integrity in a democratic community, be fully appreciated"—in *Hibernia*, February, 1962. While it is true that Fr. Murray writes as an American Catholic addressing his fellow Americans on the attitude of American Catholics to the American Constitution, his approach derives from *general* principles of political philosophy.

[4] J. C. Murray, Governmental Repression of Heresy, *loc. cit.* p 89.

[5] L. Bender O.P., *Chiesa e Stato*, Rome 1945, pp 46-47.

'partial separation', under which the Church, while being essentially considered as a private society, is conceded certain rights that are proper to a moral person in public law. It becomes clear quickly that what Fr. Murray is disclaiming is a partiality for any form of hostile separation. 'I understand the canonical essence of "separation" to lie in the denial or ignoring by the state of the unique juridical personality of the Church, and the consequent denial or ignoring of the fact that there exists, in an order higher than that of the state, an external spiritual authority that has an independent sovereignty over its subjects in all that concerns their spiritual and moral life even as citizens'.[1] This is more usually referred to by writers as the 'complete' separation of Church and State.

In certain respects, Fr. Murray's disclaimer is difficult to follow. On the one hand he proclaims that he is not defending a system of complete separation while on the other he is loud in his praise of the American solution which American political leaders have frequently described in terms which should be unacceptable to him. 'I believe in the absolute separation of Church and State', said Al. Smith, in an effort to convince Americans that he was a friend of the Constitution.[2] Similarly Senator John Kennedy recalled his fourteen years of public service 'supporting the complete separation of Church and State'.[3] Of course not all Americans see the situation in the same way. Mgr. Ryan, although he did not regard the Catholic ideal as verified in America, was disposed to think that the system of separation there was not 'complete'. He thought that the Federal government had never really adopted a policy of indifference towards all religion, whatever might seem to be the implications of the Constitution. The appointment by the President of an annual public thanksgiving day, the official employment of chaplains in the forces, the exemption of church property from taxation —these and other instances were cited by Mgr. Ryan as indicative of the fact that American separation is not complete. A

---

[1] Governmental Repression of Heresy, *loc. cit.* pp 89-90.

[2] Quoted by E. Duff, Church and State in the American Environment, in *Studies*, vol. XLIX (1960), p 236.

[3] *Loc. cit.* p 229.

similar view has been expressed from time to time by American judges.[1] And yet the American solution was described by Pope Leo XIII, in his Encyclical on 'Catholicity in the United States', as separation of a kind that was out of harmony with the Catholic ideal: 'It would be very erroneous to draw the conclusion that in America is to be sought the type of the most desirable status of the Church, or that it would be universally lawful or expedient for State and Church to be, as in America, dissevered and divorced. The fact that Catholicity with you is in good condition, nay, is even enjoying a prosperous growth, is by all means to be attributed to the fecundity with which God has endowed His Church, in virtue of which unless men or circumstances interfere, she spontaneously expands and propagates herself; but she would bring forth more abundant fruits if, in addition to liberty, she enjoyed the favour of the laws and the patronage of public authority'.

In virtue of this, certain of Fr. Murray's expositions of the Catholic teaching on Church and State seem at first sight to run counter not only to his own denial that he is defending 'separation' as a thesis but to the clear sentiments of Pope Leo XIII. He is certainly opposed to Church-State 'union'. Is this union, he asks, such an unalterable realisation of Catholic principles 'that any constitutional situation which deviates from it can be the object only of . . . a concession to the exigencies of an "hypothesis", prompted by expediency, and not the embodement of a "thesis", warranted by theological and political doctrine? Surely the answer must be no'.[2] For Fr. Murray, the system of pluralist separation is not at all to be regarded as hypothesis, 'the simple product of a factual state of affairs in which the Church is somehow shorn of power, compelled in expediency to make only minimal demands etc. On the contrary, it is thesis—the full development, by theological reflection and political experience, of the central datum of the distinction of the two powers and their hierarchic collaboration

[1] Cf Most Rev. John J. Wright, Secularism in America, in *The Catholic Mind*, vol. LVIII (1960), p 494.

[2] J. C. Murray, Contemporary Orientations of Catholic Thought on Church and State, in *Theological Studies*, vol. X (1949), p 229.

for the total good of man and human society. Anything less than this is hypothesis—a conditional state of affairs, arguing immaturity either in Catholicism or in politics'.[1]

Although defending pluralist separation as the Catholic thesis, Fr. Murray would not wish to describe it as the Catholic 'ideal'. He does not like the phrase 'Catholic ideal of Church-State relationships'. He maintains that it is false to think that any particular form of socio-religious organisation either constitutes or can constitute the Catholic 'ideal'. Ideal forms are never realised in practice.[2] For this reason, in so far as the Catholic thesis represents the Catholic ideal for Church-State relations, Fr. Murray's version of it, despite his protests, is not thesis. Still it is also clearly something different from the traditional hypothesis, which is essentially acceptable only as a compromise in abnormal circumstances.[3] A Spanish jurist—Fr. Sotillo—has thrown light on the distinction between Fr. Murray's position and that of the traditional thesis-hypothesis. Whereas the latter envisages the hypothesis as something to which the thesis should yield only by way of exception (*hypothesis particularis*), for the former it is assumed to be the natural and universal thing (*hypothesis generalis*) in view of the contemporary and future requirements of democratic States.[4]

It is not difficult to see that even the clearing of the ground for a new examination of the problem of Church-State relations is itself by no means an easy task. The terms 'thesis' and 'hypothesis', 'establishment' and 'separation' have become so subject to diverse interpretations that it is scarcely possible to speak of them at all in the abstract. This is especially true of 'establishment' and 'separation'. We have noted a usage of 'establishment'—indeed the most common one—of which the connotation implies some religious intolerance. But we have also noted

[1] Cited in Carrillo de Albornoz, *Roman Catholicism and Religious Liberty*, Geneva 1959, p 66.

[2] Cf J. C. Murray, Governmental Repression of Heresy, *loc. cit.* pp 37-38.

[3] Cf Bender, *op. cit.* p 102.

[4] L. R. Sotillo S.J., *Compendium Juris Publici Ecclesiastici*, 3rd ed. Santander 1958, p 211.

that it has been used in senses which do not imply this. 'Separation' too has been seen to be open to various meanings that do not coincide. In particular, complete or absolute separation is a very different thing from partial separation. Nor is it always easy to know in practice which form is actually incarnated in the varied and complex arrangements between the two powers. It will be better therefore if we eschew altogether the use of the terms 'establishment' and 'separation' and seek to uncover the basic Catholic teaching on Church-State relations free of the inevitable handicap which their employment would entail. Of course it will be impossible to avoid all reference to them, particularly when reporting the views of other writers. I wish to make clear, however, that the discussion which follows should not at all be understood as a balancing of the arguments for 'establishment' versus 'separation'.

The textbooks of Public Ecclesiastical Law are unanimous in demanding that the Catholic Church enjoy a specially favoured position in the State in circumstances in which this is a practical possibility. This claim is based on the consequences of certain presuppositions. As in the case of Fr. Murray's fundamental principles, these presuppositions are also three. The first is that there is an objective duty on society, as well as on the individual, to subject its official life and actions to God's law. The second is the truth of the Christian and Catholic religion and the third, which flows from the others, is that there is an objective duty on the State to have a special care for the Catholic Church. Given these, the textbooks draw the logical conclusion that, when it is possible to do so, Catholic statesmen have a subjective duty to give special recognition to the Catholic Church. This is the position adopted, for example, by Cardinal Ottaviani in one of the best-known manuals of Public Ecclesiastical Law.[1]

[1] Ottaviani, *Institutiones Iuris Publici Ecclesiastici*, 3rd ed. Rome 1947, vol. II, pp 46 *seq.*; L. Bender, *Ius Publicum Ecclesiasticum*, Bussum 1948, pp 169-200; N. Jung, *Le droit public de l'église*, Paris 1948; L. Sotillo, *op. cit.* pp 176 *seq.*; Cappello, *Summa Iuris Ecclesiastici, Publici*, 4th ed. Rome 1932; Cavagnis, *Institutiones Iuris Publici Ecclesiastici*, 2nd ed. Rome 1888.

Both Ottaviani and Murray have arguments for their divergent conclusions. In favour of the former there is an appeal to authority and tradition. No. 77 of the famous *Syllabus* condemned the proposition that 'In our day, it is no longer expedient that the Catholic religion should be treated as the sole State religion and that any other forms of religious worship should be excluded'.[1] Pope Leo XIII too, in the Encyclical *Immortale Dei*, said that 'States . . . are bound absolutely to worship God in the way which He has shown to be His will' and, in his Encyclical *Libertas*, he said that both 'justice and reason forbid the State to be atheistic; or to have the same attitude towards the various religions, as they say, and to bestow upon them the same rights indiscriminately, because this would lead to atheism'.

In an important address to the Lateran University on 2 March, 1953, Cardinal Ottaviani treated anew of these matters.[2] Raising the question of how the official Church attitude to them stands today, he referred to what he called 'the pendulum theory' of certain writers, to the effect that Church teaching takes account of the rhythm of history and that, as regards Encyclical letters, a distinction must be made between what is permanent and what is transitory by recognising the relevance of changing concrete circumstances. The Cardinal maintained that it is not allowable to apply this distinction to the fundamental principles of Public Ecclesiastical Law. At least he declared that such would not be allowable if it meant that these fundamental principles, as 'solemnly affirmed in the Encyclical letter *Immortale Dei*, are merely the reflection of historic moments in the past'. On the contrary, these principles are firm and unchanging. 'They were valid in the days of Innocent III and Boniface VIII. They are valid in the days of Leo XIII and Pius XII'.

But, passing from reasons of authority to those of internal cogency, the manuals of Public Law and Dogmatic Theology

[1] Cf Denziger, *Enchiridon Symbolorum*, n 1777.

[2] Ottaviani, Church and State: Some Present Problems in the Light of the Teaching of Pope Pius XII, in *American Ecclesiastical Review*, vol. CXXVIII (1953), n 5.

explicitly affirm that there is a major obligation on the State—
stemming from natural law—to acknowledge God as the source
of political authority, to 'worship' Him as He wills to be worshipped and to conform, in so far as it can, to His law.[1] For the
State too is a creature of God and, as far as is possible, must
acknowledge its dependence on Him. As a moral person it is
the subject of duties, though it can satisfy these only through
the medium of physical persons and the official acts of those
who have authority over it. In consequence of this, writers see
a theological necessity for the special recognition of the Catholic
religion, because the absolute obligation of the State to God
includes the hypothetical obligation of accepting the religion
that God may reveal.[2] This obligation becomes a subjective
one for Catholic statesmen who are aware of it and who are
in a position to respect it in practice without undue difficulty.
In view of the importance of the matter it is rather surprising
that the manuals do not devote more space to proving the point
that the State, as such, has an obligation to render worship
to God. The generality of them seem to regard this duty as
rather obvious and certainly not in need of elaborate proof.
They are usually satisfied to point out that religion provides
the moral basis for political life. A more relevant argument
is based on the social nature of man, by reason of which his
worship of God must take on a communal as well as an individual character, and not merely within a formally religious
community. The civil community also, as the most important
of all secular communities, must inevitably be concerned
with religious worship. So true is this that St. Thomas Aquinas,
in his *De Regimine Principum* (Bk. I, ch. 14), declares that
if the final end of human existence were a purely natural one,

---

[1] Cf also V. Cathrein S.J., *Philosophia Moralis*, 17th ed. Friburg
1935, pp 432-434; Ryan and Boland, *Catholic Principles of Politics*, New
York 1941, p 311; H. Rommen, *The State in Catholic Thought*, St. Louis
1945, p 366; R. J. Giguere, *The Social Value of Public Worship according
to Thomistic Principles*, Washington 1950, *passim*.

[2] Cf e.g. R. Garrigou-Lagrange, *De Revelatione*, 4th ed. Rome 1945,
vol. II, pp 411-425; J. M. Herve, *Manuale Theologiae Dogmaticae*, Paris
1949, vol. I, pp 520-535; P. Parente, *Theologia Fundamentalis*, Turin.

it would fall to the State—whose concern in such a case would embrace the ultimate end of man—to determine the form of religious worship by civil law.

Even as things are the State has the duty to promote the practice of religion, through ways and means that are within its proper competence. So deeply rooted in human nature is the need for the public and social expression of worship that the State would be acting contrary to its purpose of promoting the common good of its citizens if it ignored a matter of such vital importance to the individual. Its duties to religion, however, do not stop at this. In the name of sound politics, if in no other, it is bound to accord a special juridical position to the religion and religious organisation of its citizens. Once again, in the *De Regimine Principum* (Bk. II, ch. 16), we find a discussion of this and it is regarded as a first principle of politics by the Encyclicals of Pope Leo XIII.

The classic statement of the State's duties to religion occurs in the Encyclical *Immortale Dei*. 'This is the bounden duty of rulers to the people over whom they rule; for one and all we are destined, by our birth and adoption, to enjoy after this frail and fleeting life, the supreme and final good in heaven. To the attainment of this every endeavour should be directed. In as far, then, as on this depends the full and perfect happiness of mankind, the securing of this end should be of all imaginable interests the most urgent. Hence civil society, established for the common welfare, should not only safeguard the well-being of the community, but should have at heart also the interests of its individual members, and that in such a manner as not to hinder but in every way to render as easy as possible the possession of that highest and unchangeable good for which all should strive. For this purpose, care must especially be taken to preserve unharmed and unimpeded the practice of religion which is the bond connecting men with God'. And again: 'Nature and reason, which command every individual devoutly to worship God in holiness, because we belong to Him and must return to Him since from Him we came, bind also the civil community by a like law. For men living together in society are under the power of God no less than individuals are, and society, not less than individuals, owes gratitude to God, who gave it being and maintains it, and whose ever-bounteous goodness enriches it with countless blessings . . . It is a public crime to act as though there were no God. So, too, it is a sin in the State not to have care for religion, as something beyond its scope . . . '

One of the reasons for the reluctance of some Catholic writers to allow that the State should 'worship' God flows from an inability to see how this can fall within its scope. In the first place, they say that, as the State is not a physical person, it is incapable of the personal psychological activity that is essential to the profession of belief of any kind. In the second place, they urge that the State, as such, cannot be subject to an obligation to God, since it is not at all directed to a personal ultimate end, which constitutes the root basis of all moral obligation. Thirdly, they point out that the profession of faith involved in worship of the true God involves the exercise of a supernatural life in which the State is lacking.

These difficulties are based on radical misconceptions of the situation, which it is essential to get rid of immediately. There is no doubt that the State is quite unable to give assent to religion in precisely the same way as is the individual. But this does not mean that it cannot do so analogously. Just as we cannot deny that in some way—its own way—the State can know its own end and the means to it, its own nature and the rights which accrue to it, so also, it can be said that, in the same way, it can 'know' and can 'acknowledge' God. A moral person is capable of an act of will in a way that is analogous to that of a physical person. However, in the case of the State and religion the import of its recognition of God, by the very nature of the State, is inextricably related to the juridical framework of the religion of its citizens. In other words, it is a matter of the common good or, to put it differently, of the rights of men in society. For this reason it can be said to be of obligation on the State, even though the State has no personal ultimate end. The juridical requirements of the citizens provide a sufficient basis for the obligation as they do in the case of all similar duties of the State. The carrying out of it, of course, depends on the physical persons who govern the State; only through these can the State be said to have obligations in the full sense. Through these too the State can be put into a position which it is correct to describe as implying a 'profession of religion'. It is a mistake to think that, in order to attain to this, the State, *per impossibile*, would have to profess belief in the individual dogmas of religion in some such way as does a physical person. The profession of the true religion in this sense is neither possible to the State nor necessary as a means to its 'salvation' as a moral person. It is not open to the grace of appreciating revelation; it cannot possess the light of faith. But it does not follow from this that the State is entirely incapable of all forms of religious assent. It can effect such by way of giving special juridical recognition to religion, which it comes to adopt through the natural process of human logic arguing from the historical and social and political facts that are created by the situation of religion within it.

Pope Leo XIII made a short-circuit of considerations such as these when he issued his clear and peremptory statements on the relation of the State to religion. 'It is clear', he said in *Humanum Genus*, 'that those who would absolve society from all religious duty act not only unjustly but also with ignorance and folly'. And in the Encyclical *Libertas* he wrote that 'justice forbids, and reason itself forbids, the State to be godless; or to adopt a line of action which would end in godlessness—namely, to treat the various religions (as they call them) alike, and to bestow on them promiscuously equal rights and privileges'. In the Catholic State, he explained, the State must take special cognisance of the Catholic religion. In such circumstances, he wrote in *Vehementer nos* (11 July, 1906), 'that the State should be separated from the Church is an absolutely false and most pernicious thesis'.

The greatest difficulty which confronts the Leonine position is that of deciding on the mode and measure of the action of the State as regards religion. It has been suggested with reason that a fair criterion is to be found in canon 1325, n. 1 of the Code of Canon Law, which binds the faithful to profess their faith whenever their silence or way of acting would otherwise imply the negation of or contempt for religion. Following this it is suggested that, whenever the State expresses its ideological bases —as in a Constitution—it should not fail to give a special place to the religion of the people. In the same way, it should not ignore the place of religion in public life on the occasions in which important national celebrations are being held. Finally, and of greater importance, its laws should not contravene but should rather respect and protect the religion of the people. Pope Leo XIII summed up the duties of the State to religion under three heads in the following passage in *Immortale Dei:* 'All who rule, therefore, should hold in honour the Holy Name of God, and one of their chief duties must be to favour religion, and to protect it, to shield it under the credit and sanction of the laws, and neither to organise nor enact any measure that may compromise its safety'.

LIBERALS AND CONSERVATIVES

Fr. Courtney Murray is not ignorant of these arguments, yet he still denies the conclusion to which they lead. In an early article he even concedes the existence of an objective obligation on the part of the State to align itself with theological and moral truth.[1] It is the implications of the obligation that he sees differently. As I have already mentioned, he does not believe

---

[1] J. C. Murray, Freedom of Religion: the Ethical Problem, in *Theological Studies*, vol. vi (1945), p 266, n 9 b. In this article Fr. Murray writes :

'(1) The State has the obligation to acknowledge God as its author, to worship Him as He wills to be worshipped, and to subject its official life and action to His law.

(2) The State has the obligation directly to promote public religion and morality as essential elements of the common good . . . ' Note 9 b, referring to the above, reads: 'This absolute obligation includes also the hypothetical obligation of accepting a higher belief, law, and mode of worship, if God reveals them as His will; of this obligation we shall speak in a later article'. I am not aware that precisely such an article ever appeared.

that these can be incarnated in a sort of 'transtemporal' or 'ideal' system of 'establishment'. In Fr. Murray's view, the only permanent obligation on the State in the matter of religion is to ensure that it has freedom of exercise.[1] As a result, he would regard the system of legal recognition as being necessary only when and if it is essential to this freedom. He allows that when such systems were followed during the course of history, it was largely because, at the time, this was the best guarantee of the Church's freedom—something that is understandable when religion and its social framework are interdependent. But he insists equally that it should be reintroduced only if, in particular cases, the situation is such that the official profession of Catholicism by the State is necessary for the preservation of the Church's freedom. The State has no obligation to follow this course if it can otherwise afford the Church adequate liberty.

Such alternative is said to be possible in a democracy, at least of the type which prevails in America. I have already indicated the ways in which Fr. Murray thinks it can be done without any special recognition of the Church by the State. He is aware that Pope Leo XIII condemned the equal treatment of all religions by modern democracies and upheld the system of establishment of the Catholic Church that was common in Catholic countries at his time. But he argues that this opposition must be understood against its historical background. The Pope was really attacking the rationalism and denial of all authority that was characteristic of democracy as he knew it in his own time. In two long articles Fr. Murray has sought—not without success—to show that the context in which Pope Leo XIII issued his pronouncements on Church and State was that of 19th century liberal democracy on the Con-

---

[1] 'I am inclined to say that the only form of *cura religionis* on the part of the State that is inherent in the line of political relationship is the *cura libertatis religionis*, which, in the hypothesis of the founding of the Church, must extend itself to a *cura libertatis Ecclesiae*'—Murray, in *American Ecclesiastical Review*, vol. CXXIV (1951), n 5.

tinent of Europe.[1] He has shown that Pope Leo was preoccupied with a consciousness of the fact that, in nearly every European country, an organised campaign against the Church was being waged, in the name of liberty and democracy, by the Masonic and atheistic adherents of these new political ideas. The Pope believed in the existence of a vast conspiracy for the overthrow of religion and the Church, a belief that was only too well justi-fied by the behaviour of those governments that had effectively come under liberal influence.

For this reason, the idea of legal disestablishment in itself played only a minor role in Pope Leo's criticism of the systems of separation which were growing up in the Europe of his day. His real grievance was that the new system sought 'to drive God out of society', 'to strip society of its Christian form'.[2] The new democracy lent itself admirably to this policy. It possessed two marks, in particular, which were unchristian. The first of these was its monistic idea of absolute sovereignty—conceived as the omnicompotence of the people. Here, under a different form, was something which Christianity had once overcome, the pagan idea of exclusive political hegemony, which ignored all distinction between the State and society. It marked the be-ginning of the development of what, under the title of 'totali-tarian democracy', has been so well described by J. L. Talmon[3] and Lord Percy of Newcastle.[4] Side by side with this, and in fact part of it, was another mark, which was radically incompatible with Christianity. This was the elevation of democracy to the level of a quasi-religion, the investment of the State with many

---

[1] J. C. Murray, Leo XIII on Church and State: The General Struc-ture of the Controversy, in *Theological Studies*, vol. XIV, (1953), n 1; also Leo XIII: Separation of Church and State, in *Theological Studies*, vol. XIV (1953), n 2.

[2] Letter *Praeclara Gratulationis*.

[3] J. L. Talmon, *The Origins of Totalitarian Democracy*, London 1952.

[4] Lord Percy of Newcastle, *The Heresy of Democracy*, London 1954, also J. C. Murray, The Church and Totalitarian Democracy, in *Theolo-gical Studies*, vol. XIII (1952), n 4.

of the functions of the Church by according to it an unwarranted self-sufficiency—in short, by a secularisation of politics that was tantamount to its 'sacralisation'. In this context it can readily be seen that 'disestablishment' was part and parcel of a theological denial of the nature of the Church.

To sum up, Pope Leo XIII was confronted with a situation in which a newly introduced constitutional system calling itself the separation of Church and State—the kingpin of the new political structure—was being used to effect the 'consummation of a social apostasy' by which an anti-religious laicism sought to undermine Christianity. By reason of this, his teaching on Church-State relations had a polemical bias.[1] According to Murray, to the extent that this polemical stamp is to be found in Pope Leo's teaching, this teaching 'is dated and needs interpretation within the context of its own date'.[2] Its accents, as it were, must be recognised or one will be misled. Fr. Murray does not regard his stand in this matter as in conflict with the canons of interpretation which have been laid down by Cardinal Ottaviani. He takes his cue from a passage in Leo XIII himself: 'When one comes down from abstractions on to the solid earth of facts, one must indeed be careful not to deny the principles just established; they remain firm. However, in becoming incarnate in factual situations the principles are invested with a stamp of contingency determined by the environment in which they find application'.[3] The heart of the matter is to decide what the Pope regards as the principles. In a comprehensive

---

[1] 'It had been asserted that the individual free will was single sovereign over public life; that the 'people' were the ultimate sovereign over political life; that the Church was no sovereign at all, indeed, that the public power was sovereign over it. Consequently, the Pope's first and last affirmation is of the power of God. His first and last denial is of a power in man that could claim complete autonomy and autarchy, and still pretend to make sense'—J. C. Murray in *Theological Studies*, vol. XIV (1953), p 14.

[2] Murray, *loc. cit.* p 19. Cf also *Theol. Studies*, vol. XIII (1952), p 552: 'Immortale Dei therefore is frankly fragmentary, undisguisedly polemic, written with a very special enemy in view—an enemy with two facets, ideological and political'.

[3] Encycl. *Au Milieu.*

analysis of the relevant texts,[1] Fr. Murray claims to have proved that these principles do not formally and precisely relate to any special legal position but are rather concerned with the distinction between Church and State, the concomitant freedom of the Church, and the need for concord and co-operation between the two. This is his proposed solution to what he calls the 'doctrinal problem', which is 'to discern in their purity the principles that are at the heart of tradition'.[2]

Working from this, Fr. Murray would defend his statement that Pope Leo's teaching is 'dated', as saying nothing more than did Pope Pius XI when, in *Quadragesimo Anno*, he clearly indicated that, over the course of time, changed conditions necessitate a flexible application of Leonine teaching on economic matters as expressed in the Encyclical *Rerum Novarum*.[3] This is not to say that the letters of Pope Leo XIII are to be regarded merely as *livres de circonstances*. The position is rather, as Fr. Murray puts it, that the theologian must not remain 'simply the literal exegete of Leo XIII, as if somehow the total doctrine and practice of Church-State relations had reached their definite and ultimate stage of development in the Leonine *corpus*'.[4] This is all the more so if he is dealing with a pattern of democracy that is quite different from that criticised by Pope Leo. And such, it is claimed, is the Anglo-American democratic tradition. Its defenders—and they number many more than just Fr. Murray—are loud in proclaiming that this tradition was free from the two radical vices of 19th century Continental democracy—a monist totalitarianism in social life and a pseudo- religious concept of the State. Absolutism and the sacralisation of politics were largely unknown to the political philosophy from which sprang the American pattern of democracy. The natural law tradition—though weakened—was never abandoned in America as it came to be on the Continent of Europe. Nor has religion in America ever been subjected to the same attacks, under cover of political values, as in Europe. It is Fr. Murray's

---

[1] Murray, in *Theological Studies*, vol. XIV (1953), pp 187-214.
[2] Murray, in *Theological Studies*, vol. XII (1951), p 164.
[3] Cf Pope Pius XI, *Quadragesimo Anno*.
[4] Murray, *Theological Studies*, vol. XII (1951), p 164.

thesis that in America the system of Church-State relations must be understood against this general background. Whereas in Europe it was prompted by an equal disrespect for all religion, in America it stems from an equal respect for all.[1]

To return to the teaching of Pope Leo XIII, Fr. Murray insists that the Pope was not and could not be referring to America when he issued his sweeping condemnations of democracy. Positively, there are plenty of indications that the system which he was attacking was identical with Continental democracy. Negatively, it could not be said that the Church in America was in the 'precarious situation' which the Pope saw to be the effect of the European systems of separation. In any case, even if he did have America as well as Europe in mind, Fr. Murray would defend the argument that, in its twentieth century setting, the problem of the Church and democracy must be given a twentieth century answer. For even though it is true objectively that political society is bound to subject itself to God, this does not mean that it must necessarily establish the true religion. Between the truths of theology and the practical possibilities of concrete political reality there is a gap that must be spanned with the help of the virtue of political prudence. There may be circumstances in which it would be politically, and morally, foolish to attempt to give religion any special juridical place in the State. It is certain that 'an immediate illation from the order of ethical and theological truth to the order of constitutional law is, in principle, dialectically inadmissable'.[2] In the context of American democracy, he would regard such a step as totally unjustified.

The debate on the question still continues to exercise writers. It received a new impetus when on 6 October, 1953, Pope Pius XII delivered an allocution to the Union of Italian

---

[1] The First Amendment 'implies no denial of the sovereignty of God over both society and state, no negation of the social necessity and value of religion . . . It does not make the state a Church, nor does it establish a political religion . . . It is a legal rule, not a piece of secular ecclesiology'—Murray, in *Theological Studies*, vol. XIV (1953), pp 152-153.

[2] Murray, in *Theological Studies*, vol. X (1949), n 3.

Catholic Jurists that had a definite bearing on the the subject.[1] Admittedly the question was not dealt with *ex professo*, but it is closely connected with the subject of the address. In this the Pope envisaged the possibility that the international community may soon have to frame legislation to secure the formal toleration by all of the different religions and standards of morality of the various peoples which the member States embrace.[2] He imagined such a ruling as taking the following form: 'Within its own territory and for its own citizens each State will regulate religious affairs by its own laws. Nevertheless, throughout the whole territory of the community of States, the citizens of every member State will be allowed their own ethical and religious beliefs and practices, in so far as these do not contravene the penal laws of the State in which they are residing'.[3]

Failure to adopt such a course could create serious international difficulties. Islamic countries give rise to much resentment in this respect. Over their vast areas religious liberty is virtually unknown, the Church-State system forbidding conversion from Islam under heavy penalties. Only Palestine, Iraq and the Northern Sudan possess any procedure for the legal recognition of conversion to another faith. Although Christian and Jewish communities are allowed to exist, they are subject to

[1] Cf *Pope Pius XII on the World Community*, New York 1954.

[2] The Pope speaks of 'communities of States and peoples, whether already existing or only a goal to be achieved'. There has been some discussion on what exactly he meant by this, whether those 'already existing' envisaged the Council of Europe and the United Nations, and those 'to be achieved' a European or World Political Community. It is more probable that what the Pope had in mind was an ideal international community. See Ed. A. Conway S.J., Organisation of the World Community, in *Pope Pius XII on the World Community*, pp 18-19.

[3] In 1960 a study prepared for the United Nations recommended that governments ensure freedom of public and private worship and freedom to disseminate any religion if it does not impair the rights of other religions. The writer, Mr. Krishnaswami of India, called for U.N. endorsement of its proposals. With certain reservations these proposals exemplify the kind of ruling which the Pope had in mind. A summary of them under sixteen heads is to be found in *Social Action*, Poona, vol. x, n 8, pp. 340-343.

considerable economic and cultural discrimination. In Egypt a somewhat similar situation prevails. Islam is the religion of the State, in consequence of which non-Islamic creeds are subject to many disabilities. Conversion from Islam can mean the loss of inheritance of property, while if a Moslem woman becomes a Christian she becomes the ward of her Moslem relatives, even though she be married to a Christian and have borne children to him.[1]

It is easy to see how the continued existence of such religious discrimination could prove a barrier to the effective working of a world community. There are also difficulties which stem from the legal provisions of some Catholic countries. In certain countries of Latin America, and notably Colombia, there may be undue obstacles to Protestant missionary freedom. A concrete example of a different aspect of the kind of thing the Pope may have had in mind arose between Spain and the United States in 1954. In each of the countries in which the U.S. has acquired military bases, complicated arrangements have been necessary in order to define exactly the legal position of their personnel. As guests in the sovereign territory of a number of different States, American citizens find themselves involved in a variety of legal situations. Some of these are connected with matters of religion. In Norway, for example, it is necessary for Catholics to publish their marriages in the Lutheran Church. In Saudi Arabia there has been a total ban on Jewish and Christian marriages. Such laws could clash with the native rights of resident foreigners. Towards the end of 1954 it became clear that somewhat similar difficulties could arise for Americans in Spain. The civil law on marriage in present-day Spain refuses to recognise as legally valid any marriage involving a Catholic which has not been performed in conformity with the prescriptions of Canon Law. This is something quite different from the American situation, in which a Catholic can contract a valid civil marriage without regard to the regulations of the Church. At Christmas, 1954, it was reported in the American papers that an arrangement had been arrived at whereby U.S.

[1] See Cecil Northcott, *Religious Liberty*, London 1948, pp 13 and 88.

military chaplains should not perform any marriages in Spain which, though they might be valid according to the civil code of the United States, would not be recognised by Spanish law. It is clear that there was nothing seriously objectionable in this agreement; the legitimacy of the children was at stake, as well as the desirability of ensuring the goodwill of the Spaniards. Yet, despite this, there was an outcry against the agreement by many Americans. It is precisely as a method of avoiding such difficulties that Pope Pius XII raised the question of the international ruling on toleration which we are discussing.

The problem was whether Catholic statesmen could consent to this ruling, even if in a position to impede error if they so wished. The Pope answered that there is no simple solution. Two principles govern the matter. The first is that error in religion and morality has no objective right to exist or be propagated. The second is that, sometimes, in the interests of a higher good, the State may refrain from hindering the existence of such error.[1] Indeed, under certain circumstances, it may even be preferable for a State—in view of the higher good of itself, the Church and the international community—not to impede error or evil which it is in a position to repress. Hence those who rule over a Catholic people will have to act in accordance with what St. Thomas calls 'regnative prudence'. Catholic statesmen must be guided by 'a comparison between the evil consequences that stem from toleration and those from which the community of States will be preserved through the preservation of the formula of toleration'. Not that they can ever adopt any measure that would positively approve of what is clearly and objectively evil. But they can agree to a system which would tolerate it. In practice, the Pope said, they should seek the judgment of the Church when faced with making a decision of this kind. For it is a matter that concerns, not only the individual Catholic State, but the interests of the universal Church.

[1] 'Reality shows that error and sin are in the world in great measure. God reprobates them, but He permits them to exist. Hence the affirmation that religious and moral error must always be impeded, when it is possible, because toleration of them is in itself immoral, is not valid absolutely and unconditionally (*nella sua incondizionata assolutezza*)'.

It is clear from this that the Pope allows the possibility that Catholic States may co-operate in an international system of religious pluralism. The higher goods of political stability and peace may demand that they follow this course. Because of this, some commentators have thought that the papal address represents a corrective to Cardinal Ottaviani's position. Others claim that careful examination shows that there is absolutely no point on which the two documents contradict one another.[1] These point out that Cardinal Ottaviani was dealing with the question of religion and the State as an internal problem for a Catholic people. The papal address, on the other hand, had in mind the problems that can arise for a Catholic State in the matter of external co-operation with other States in formally agreeing to a rule whereby the different religious and moral attitudes of the citizens of each will be tolerated by all alike. And it simply leaves the way open for a practical acceptance of this by Catholic States. It is merely a realistic facing of facts in the interests of the international common good. There is nothing in it in conflict with Cardinal Ottaviani's insistence that, for its own citizens, a State with a Catholic majority should give special recognition to the Church. On the contrary, the Pope was careful to point out that the Church, 'in principle or as a thesis (*per principio, ossia in tesi*), cannot approve the complete separation between the two powers (Church and State)'. The Church can never give positive approbation to such a move, although, because of the conditions which prevail in any particular country, she may sometimes—and even frequently—allow it in practice.

---

[1] Cf Joseph Clifford Fenton, The Teaching of Ci Riesce, in *The American Ecclesiastical Review*, vol. cxxx (1954), n 5. It would be strange if the Pope were to deny that, in theory, the Catholic Church should receive special recognition in a Catholic State. For in earlier speeches he had held up the example of Italy and Spain, in which such a condition existed. See his Radio message to the Italian Eucharistic Congress in 1951 and Discourse to Spanish Religious in Rome in 1944. Also his Address of Welcome to the Spanish Legate to the Holy See in 1948 (*A.A.S.*, 1948, pp 554-555).

It is a *modus vivendi* in the interests of peace and the well-being of the Church.[1]

It is possible, of course, that the papal address was intended to be a call for moderation on the part of Catholics as regards expressing the theoretical demands of the Church in the case of circumstances which permit their realisation. For these circumstances are so seldom found today in any country that one could easily be unrealistic when speaking of them and could give the wrong impression concerning what the Church demands in general practice. In most areas of the world today the Church lives side by side with other religions and even with irreligion. In his address to the seventy-seventh German *Katholikentag* in 1956, Pope Pius XII squarely faced this fact. It entails, he said, that a system of co-existence has to be agreed to. This means that all the Church can ask for is freedom to live in the State, in conformity with her constitution and her law, looking after her members and freely preaching the Gospel of Christ. Such is 'the fundamental, indispensable condition for any sincere co-existence'. Co-existence along these lines might be regarded as the normal system of relations for the Church to adopt at the present day. In view of it, it could be said with some truth that Fr. Murray's approach to the question of Church-State relations is the better one. In support of it it is also said that, following action by the French Ambassador and others after Cardinal Ottaviani's pronouncement, it was declared that the Cardinal's views were those of his Eminence and not an official declaration. On the other hand, in July, 1953, the *New York Times* claimed that it had sought and obtained clarification on the subject of the Cardinal's teaching from 'a high Vatican source', to the effect that his views while being neither official nor semi-official were

---

[1] It is in this sense that some of the textbooks of Public Law describe tolerance as immoral in itself (*in se ipsa immoralis*). Thus Sotillo, *op. cit.* p 212. From this point of view it is nothing but the cessation of the exercise of the jurisdiction of the Church over those Christians who refuse to be subject to her. As such it can never be more than a means whereby greater evils are avoided. See N. Jung, *op. cit.* p 135.

'unexceptionable'—which report was taken up and given wide publicity by *Time*.[1]

A MATTER OF APPROACH?

In all this matter it would be well to note certain important points. In their own way the textbooks of Public Ecclesiastical Law are just as moderate as the professedly liberal articles of Fr. Murray. They by no means ignore the requirements of political prudence. They do not say that the special recognition of the Church is necessary—or even desirable—in all circumstances, but only in a State that has an absolute Catholic majority, due to which it can be effected peacefully and with the assent of most of the people.[2] It is true—and this is a difficulty —that they never define what is meant by 'absolute majority'. At least I know of no place in which such a definition can be found. That it means more than just a simple majority is probable; otherwise there would seem to be no point in adding the word 'absolute'.

What the books of Public Law really mean is that there can be no question of special recognition except in circumstances in which, owing to the great predominance of Catholics, it is generally acceptable and can be reasonably assured of tranquil working conditions.[3] In other words—when it is possible and

[1] Cf Fenton, *loc. cit.* p 341.

[2] For an account of the different ways in which the textbooks conceive such a situation see Sotillo, *op. cit.* p 225.

[3] Such would clearly be lacking if the giving of special recognition to the Church would create serious unrest among the people and make the laws relating to it difficult to enforce, thereby undermining the authority of the State. The same would be true if such recognition would only hinder the larger good of social progress, e.g. at the international level, or if its maintenance involved undue Statist authoritarianism. In the Encyclical *Libertas* Pope Leo XIII spoke of 'those who, while they do not approve the separation of Church and State, think that the Church ought to adapt herself to the times and conform to what is required by the modern system of government'. 'Such an opinion', he wrote, 'is

workable. If one is prejudiced one will regard this as expediency.[1] Reason says that it is good practical politics and eminently respectful of the virtue of political prudence. It certainly
means that the traditional teaching is just as moderate—in
practice—as is the liberal and that it does not entail an 'immediate illation' from the order of theological and moral truth to
that of political practice.

sound, if it is to be understood of some equitable adjustments consistent
with truth and justice; in so far, namely, that the Church, in the hope
of some great good, may show herself indulgent, and may conform to
the times in so far as her sacred office permits'.

[1] E.g. Charles C. Marshall, *The Roman Catholic Church in the
Modern State*, New York 1928. One does not even have to be prejudiced
in order to do this. A surprisingly forthright statement to this effect
is attributed to the French Catholic leader of the 19th century, Louis
Veuillot. 'When you are the masters', he is reported to have said to the
Liberals of his day, 'we claim perfect liberty for ourselves, as your
principles require it; when we are the masters we refuse it to you, as
it is contrary to our principles'—reported in Laveleye, *Le gouvernement
dans la democratie*, vol. I, pp 187-188; also Lecky, *Democracy and Society*,
London 1896, vol. II, pp 20-21. Fr. Max Pribilla, however, says that the
whole thing is a legend, that Veuillot never made any such remark and
that the idea originated in a sarcastic reflection of Macaulay in the
Edinburgh Review for July, 1835—Dogmatische Intoleranz und burgerliche Toleranz, in *Stimmen der Zeit*, 144 (1949), p 27 ff. French trans.
in *Unite chrétienne et tolérance religieuse*, Paris, 1950, pp 147 ff. While
this may well be true, it is quite certain that some contemporary
Catholics regard the thesis-hypothesis distinction as an instrument of
expediency. Fr. Murray puts no tooth whatever on this, while Mgr.
Charrière of Geneva and Fr. Augustin Leonard O.P., say straight out
that it is a piece of 'opportunism'. Cf Carillo de Albornoz, *op. cit.* pp 66,
14 and 17. The real facts of the situation are quite otherwise. There is
no question of the Church having two different measures in the matter
of its relations with the State, geared respectively to the rights of the
Church and the circumstances which prevent these being fully respected.
The Church's whole attitude is regulated by principle, on the one hand
that of the rights of truth and on the other the equally valid principle
that rights should be exacted only when there is adequate power to do
so. Hence instead of principles and practice in Church-State relations,
it would be better to speak of principles and the application of principles.

In my opinion, the difference between Cardinal Ottaviani and Fr. Murray is to some extent one of approach to the problem. Cardinal Ottaviani and the traditional expositions concentrate on the *objective duty*, which binds all States, to recognise the true religion when this is possible. They soft-pedal the 'when this is possible' clause, and write as if this duty were normally a subjective one, the circumstances which would make it such being pretty general. The so-called liberal approach of Fr. Murray and those who agree with him, on the other hand, is to concentrate attention on the 'when possible' qualification, to point out that it is seldom if ever verified in the multi-confessional world of today, indeed to regard it as something that can with safety be ignored. The whole structure of democracy is said to run counter to it, for democracy cannot countenance any legal provision that would favour one section to the exclusion of other sections of the community. This approach is dominated by the idea that democracy is a form of political organisation that is 'presently man's best, and possibly last, hope of human freedom'.[1] In face of it, the question of giving special recognition to any Church can at most be but purely theoretical.

All this might be summed up by saying that Cardinal Ottaviani's approach is primarily theological, that of Fr. Murray and his school primarily political. Cardinal Ottaviani's approach is centered on the respect which is due objectively to truth; Fr. Murray's is tailored to show that the Church respects human freedom, which is so important a value to contemporary democracy. If proof is needed that this is indeed the purpose of the Murray line, it is to be found in an article in the Jesuit review *Thought*, by one of Fr. Murray's ablest supporters, Fr. Gustave Weigel.[2] 'The controversy', says Fr. Weigel, 'concerns the proper formulation of the perennial Catholic doctrine on Church and State in order to bring out its compatibility with the American democratic system'. It is part of the product of what Fr. Walter Ong, S.J., in his most interesting *Frontiers of American Catholicism*, calls the 'defence mentality' that is cha-

---

[1] Murray, in *Theological Studies*, vol. XII (1951), p 163.

[2] G. Weigel S.J., The Church and the Democratic State, in *Thought*, Summer 1952.

racteristic of the American Catholic consciousness.[1]

This mentality is responsible for a 'passion for self-criticism and close inspection of the point at which Catholicism and the American way of life intersect'.[2] Referring in particular to the controversy with which we are dealing, Fr. Ong says that the Blanshard attack, which occasioned it, has, through stimulating men like Fr. Murray into writing, not merely convinced Americans in general that Catholics are not conspiring against American liberties, but has forced Catholics to a practical realisation 'that there are theological problems raised in terms of the reality which is America for which the answers cannot be found already framed in theology manuals'.[3] For although some attempts were made in the past to link the American way of life with Catholic thinking, notably as expressed by 'advanced' political writers such as Bellarmine and Suarez, they are not adequate to satisfy the requirements of the present generation. They are part of an older tendency to 'base an endorsement of the Church in America . . . upon the reduction of an issue to European components', which tendency, understandably, 'has a limited appeal to educated Americans who, pretty much in proportion to their education, are already oppressed by a sense of their permanent indebtedness to Europe'.[4] The American intellectual needs to have dogma 'presented to him, as historically present, as a deposit of truth which . . . has had a career in the dynamic process of history of which he feels himself a part'.[5] Fr. Murray's work is a response to this need.

As Fr. Weigel sees it, both groups have made an important contribution. That of Cardinal Ottaviani and the writers of textbooks of Public Ecclesiastical Law, is to insist on the truth that the Church, independently of history, has an ideal of society which is derived from a consideration of the nature of man, as

[1] Walter Ong S.J., *Frontiers in American Catholicism*, New York 1957; Cf also Thomas F. O'Dea, *The American Catholic Dilemma*, New York 1958 and John Tracy Ellis, *American Catholicism*, Chicago 1956.
[2] Ong, *op. cit.* pp 13-14.
[3] Ong, *op. cit.* pp 19-20.
[4] Ong, *op. cit.* p 21.
[5] *Ibid.*

redeemed by Christ, the founder of the Church. Because of this, Fr. Weigel calls these writers the 'static expositors' of Church-State relations. The contribution of the Murrayites, whom he calls the 'dynamic expositors', is, while not ignoring this truth, to stress the fact that it is not a pragmatic norm for government in the concrete, which must function in non-ideal situations. Between them, he says, clarification has been brought about. He makes sure to emphasise that this clarification was aided particularly 'by the insights of the dynamic theologians who showed that there was a dimension of Catholic thought which was *not sufficiently brought to light* by the manuals. The manualists do not stress the truth that the order of concrete government is an immediately practical order where prudence is the guiding principle, toleration a necessary instrument, and public order as productive of the common good *the dominant objective*'.[1]

It would be erroneous to adopt this viewpoint to the extent of maintaining that, basically, there is no conflict between the two positions. True, both sides agree that it would be a mistake to think that, in the concrete circumstances, the Constitution, for example, of the United States is fundamentally in error in its catering for religion, in such a way that Catholics should— here and now—seek to correct the situation by trying to modify that document. Both sides hold that prudence, which is enjoined by Catholic teaching, would forbid such action because of the turmoil which would ensue. The traditionalists add that the only change of circumstances through which such modification might be effected, would be a spectacular increase in the Catholic population to such a degree that the constitutional revision could be brought about with the assent of the vast majority of the people. This addendum, however, the progressives reject. They point out that it is exactly the point on which men like Blanshard base their charge that Catholic political philosophy is undemocratic. These do not deny the *fact* that American Catholics are loyal to American democracy, that they conscientiously fulfil their civic duties, or that they have no subversive scheme to change the American system of government.

---

[1] Italics mine.

What they do say is that, given suitable circumstances, the *logical* position for the Church to adopt is one that is incompatible with American democracy. It is in an effort to avoid this that the progressive theologians have developed their approach, which seeks, as it were, to erect the present *de facto* position of the Church in America into a *de jure* one that expresses the full theoretical demands of the Church in a framework of democracy that is regarded as universally valid and desirable, not merely at the present time but for the foreseeable future.

In assuming this task, they are catering primarily for the 'Americanisation' of the application—not the content—of Catholic teaching, a presentation for which so many American Catholics feel the need. As Fr. Walter Ong has observed in a more recent book,[1] apart from the work of a man like Isaac Hecker, the most radical departures in organisation and technique on the part of the Church in America have had so far only a pragmatic basis. No one has even recognised them as unique until recently. Personally, I would be inclined to go further and to suggest that one of the objectives of the contemporary 'liberal' school of American Catholics is to attempt to show that Catholicism is positively favourable towards democracy by 'canonising' the system of Church-State relations found in America.[2] It is interesting to note that Balmes looked

[1] W. Ong, *American Catholic Crossroads*, New York 1959.

[2] In point of fact the 'liberal' school goes far to satisfy not only Catholics but also secularists on the native character of American Catholicism. Fr. G. Weigel has pointed out a paradoxical role of religion in relation to present-day American society. American secularists, far from rejecting religion, tend to regard it as a good thing if it helps citizens to be better citizens. In so far as it fosters the virtues which the nation needs, it is acceptable. 'It seems, then', says Fr. Weigel, 'that the role of religion in America is to produce the virtues which the secular community needs . . . Yet is this the answer to the question of the role of the American Churches? Are the American Churches here to save America'?—*Faith and Understanding in America*, New York 1959, pp 47-48. In reply to his own question Fr. Weigel distinguishes between purpose and consequence, function and by-product. The true role of the Catholic Church in America is to save Americans rather than America; it should never set out to subserve purposes such as motivate the secularist. But it can

on the defence of the Consent Theory of political authority as performing a similar service in an earlier period.[1] And who can doubt that the same considerations play a part in explaining why the Consent Theory received the support of the American Archbishops Ireland, Hughes and Spalding?

Laudable as this purpose is, it should not be carried to extremes. By all means let us embrace unreservedly all that is good and ethically valid in democracy. Let us show too—as we can—that its finest values are incarnate, at least radically, in the Christian tradition. Let us be loud in proclaiming that the Church can look democracy in the face while adhering to the letter of her perennial teaching. This we may certainly do. But only because Catholic teaching, as I hope to show later, is of such a nature that it does not have to be accommodated to the democratic ethos. There is all the difference in the world between moulding Public Ecclesiastical Law to fit the requirements of democracy and showing that the latter, in fact, are not in conflict with the juridical implications of the one true Church. The Public Law of the Church rests basically on dogma. Indeed as a distinct science it only dates from the last century, prior to which its role was filled by the Church tract in dogmatic theology. The demands of the Church of Christ on the State are fundamentally doctrinal; they stem from the uncompromising source of theological truth.

certainly reap any advantages which its positions may secure per accidens by reason of their being acceptable to secular interests. One can readily believe that Fr. Weigel's distinction corresponds to the facts. It is never possible, however, entirely to exclude the contingency of a writer or writers getting caught up—whether consciously or unconsciously—in the task of presenting Catholicism in a way that will be acceptable to American secularism.

[1] Speaking of Bellarmine he writes: 'Whatever his motive may have been . . . this theologian, I say, explaining the doctrine of the Church on the Divine origin of civil power, does it in such terms that, while giving sacred guarantees for the good order of society, he does not infringe on the liberty of the people; this is the vindication of Rome against the attacks made upon her'—*Protestantism compared with Catholicity*, p 243.

Any approach that would even seem to turn the matter the other way around, would involve one in a highly dangerous game. I do not wish to suggest that Fr. Murray and his supporters are consciously engaged in such diversion. What I do feel is that there is a tendency in their approach to Church-State relations to begin from political and historical rather than from theological considerations. Admittedly, as I have noted earlier, this approach has the advantage of ensuring a regard for the relevance of temporal factors in the application of principle. Nevertheless, one cannot allow anything to obscure the fact that, where possible, the State has the duty to give what recognition it can to the truth of Christ as represented socially by the Catholic Church. It may be more popular, easy and attractive to be 'liberal'. But the hard fact remains that, in public as in private life, the truth of Christ demands acceptance and recognition. It has been, is and must continue to be the ultimate objective criterion of action, whether individual or social.

FREEDOM OR TRUTH

I am quite sure that Fr. Murray would vehemently protest that I have misunderstood and distorted his position. He would surely say that his approach is primarily theological. Does it not begin by enquiring how three principles—the freedom of the Church, harmony between Church and State and co-operation between them—can be preserved in a modern democracy?[1] From whence, however, does he derive these principles? I am well aware that he maintains that a proper understanding of Christian teaching in the past forces him to the conclusion that these are the doctrinal points at issue. But in this it seems to me that he tends to a one-sided interpretation of the central points

[1] Somewhat similar, though not exactly the same, principles have been adopted by E. McDonagh, Church and State in the Constitution of Ireland, in *The Irish Theological Quarterly*, vol. XXVIII (1961), p 138. See also Dr. McDonagh's contribution, Religious Freedom and the State, in K. McNamara Ed. *Christian Unity*, Maynooth 1962.

of traditional teaching on Church and State. He attaches prime
importance to the original Gelasian text, 'Two there are', which
laid the foundations of the ideas of Church-State distinction
and the freedom of the Church.[1] And he takes this as indicative
of the fact that the freedom of the Church is the central interest
to be secured by Church-State theory. In spite of his knowledge
of the work of Tellenbach,[2] he forgets that the Gelasian formulation of the theory of the two powers was a defensive measure,
designed to combat Caesaro-Papism.[3] It mirrored a preoccupation of the Church throughout the entire era of the Investiture
Conflict, but it is a serious mistake to think that it represented
the only point at issue. So much so that, in an appendix to his
work, Tellenbach has found it necessary to call attention to the
fact that many modern historians have misunderstood the relevance of the early medieval cry for the freedom of the Church.

In Tellenbach's view the aims of the Gregorian reformers
have been misconceived by modern research through being cat-
alogued in terms of our contemporary use of the word 'freedom'.
This has meant that they are usually expressed solely as demands by the Church to be free from the State; some have even
spoken of them as demands for separation. But how, asks Tellenbach, can this be reconciled with the demand for the supremacy
of the authority of the Church, which was also recognised by
the medieval ecclesiastics in consequence of their belief in unity
and of the role of the Church in the temporal domain? This too,
he says was part of their cry for freedom, for a 'freedom to' as
well as a 'freedom from'. In an effort to link the two the historian Hauck has maintained that, to the medieval mind, 'freedom
from others was thought of as dominion over others'.[4] In this
view dominion was demanded as a guarantee of independence,

---

[1] 'Two there are, august Emperor, by which this world is ruled on
title of original sovereign right—the consecrated authority of the priesthood and the royal power'—cited in *We Hold These Truths*, p 202.

[2] Gerd Tellenbach, *Church, State and Christian Society at the Time
of the Investiture Contest*, Oxford 1948.

[3] Cf Tellenbach, *op. cit.* p 34 *seq.*

[4] Hauck, *Kirchengeschichte Deutschlands*, vol. III, p 677. Cited in
Tellenbach, *op. cit.* p 183.

the Church seeking to be certain that its independence would be respected by its being supreme over the secular authorities. Tellenbach regards this as an overstatement. It has to be granted, of course, that certain medieval formulations of the claims of the Church were exaggerated and theocratic in the extreme. Such was the conception of the *plenitudo potestatis*, better known as the theory of 'direct power' or of the 'two swords'. Its best known exponent was Pope Boniface VIII in *Unam Sanctam*. Nobody has any hesitation about saying that this conception was time-conditioned and is long in the mortuary of ecclesiastical political ideas. It would be erroneous to regard it as expressing the essence of the medieval understanding of the relations of the Church to the State. What was primarily defended was simply the establishment of a right relationship between the spiritual and the secular powers. But this involved not merely freedom from undue influence but also freedom to carry out the mission of the Church. And while this, says Tellenbach, is primarily the conversion of the world, it 'necessarily involves the leadership of the world'. In other words, the fact that early Catholic teaching on Church-State relations takes the form of a call for the freedom of the Church is not in itself an adequate guide to the content of the demands of the Church *vis-a-vis* the State.

Which brings to mind again the encyclicals of Leo XIII, in which a similar emphasis on the freedom of the Church is to be found. Fr. Murray regards it as a repetition of the Gelasian position, needless to say in the sense in which he himself understands this. In at least seven encyclicals of Leo XIII can be found references to the freedom of the Church, which resemble much the Gelasian text. Fr. Murray says that he has counted over eighty occurrences of the phrase *libertas ecclesiae* or its equivalent in some sixty or more Leonine documents.[1] Elsewhere he says they number over a hundred, but adds that about a quarter of these have to do with the Roman Question.[2] This should have suggested that the Leonine references might not

---

[1] *Theological Studies*, vol. XII (1951), p 156, n 3.

[2] *Theological Studies*, vol. XIV (1953), p 191, n 57.

244   STUDIES IN POLITICAL MORALITY

at all have been intended to restate an ancient tradition in its
fulness. Nevertheless, speaking of *Immortale Dei*, Fr. Murray
writes: 'The core of the Encyclical is the splendid statement of
the ancient traditional doctrine of Gelasius I'.[1] It is built around
two propositions. The first of these is that human society is
from God through the instrumentality of the law of nature, the
second that the Church is from God through the law of Christ.
From these principles are said to follow the radical distinction
of the two societies and the primacy and freedom of the spiritual. True, 'the Leonine statement of tradition was uttered in a
particular historical context. Hence it reveals the accent which
the Holy See judged necessary to meet the needs of that context. This accent falls heavily on the freedom of the Church.
However, although Leo XIII chose this locus of accent for
immediately historical reasons, he actually chose the locus
which the genuine tradition itself demands as the proper
locus'.[2]

In this way Fr. Murray manages to escape a direct charge
of holding the 'pendulum theory' condemned by Cardinal Ottaviani. He regards the substance of what Pope Leo has said as
coinciding with the traditional teaching, which will always and
everywhere be valid. It is only in its overtones, directed exclusively at the conditions of his own time, that his utterances need
not be accepted verbatim. Pope Leo stood four square for the
liberty of the Church, its freedom from the ambit of the State.

What this forgets is that Pope Leo stood for much more
than this. He also called upon the State to fulfil its duties to
religion by giving special recognition, when possible, to the
Church. In one place Fr. Murray goes so far as to admit this,
saying that the Pope, in addition to his doctrine on freedom,
had another doctrine, that of public worship and a care for
religion on the part of the State.[3] He says he will deal with this
eventually but apparently has never done so. Canon Jacques
Leclercq, who is of much the same mind as Fr. Murray, is more

---

[1] *Theological Studies*, vol. XIII (1952), p 556.
[2] *Theological Studies*, vol. XIV (1953), p 191.
[3] *Theological Studies*, vol. XIII (1952), p 560.

forthright in his account of the extent of the Leoine teaching.
Pope Leo's full thesis, he says, requires more than official status
for the Church; it means 'submission to the moral magisterium
of the Church and the recognition of her full independence of
political forms', even those that favour her.[1] The Pope wanted
State care for religion all right, though not after the manner of
the Spain of Philip II or the France of the Bourbon restoration.
'Two there are' indeed—two points of emphasis in the Leonine
teaching, both of which must be taken into account. To concentrate on 'freedom' to the neglect of 'public religion' is to omit
one of the two from consideration. Nor is it the way in which
the accepted Public Law books of the Church approach the
question of Church-State relations. In face of this, and of an
inability to see when and where official teaching has done otherwise, I prefer to approach the problem in terms of what positive
recognition can and should be afforded by the State to Christian
truth. I regard the 'freedom' approach as paradoxically introducing a limiting element from the outset—begging the question, if you will, albeit unconsciously—due to the influence of
the contemporary political situation.

I do not wish, for one moment, to imply that Fr. Murray is
consciously trimming his sails to the democratic wind. On one
occasion Fr. Francis Connell of the Catholic University accused
him of trying 'to smooth the way toward a better understanding
of the Catholic Church on the part of non-Catholics in America',
I suppose by compromising or understating Catholic principles.[2]
'The suggestion is mistaken and injurious', said Fr. Murray. 'I
reject it'.[3] What I do say is that he gives ostensibly more weight
to political than to theological considerations. Considerations
of theory, of course, and not of party politics. Fr. Murray would
be the first to admit that, in this question, 'the initial stand-

[1] J. Leclercq, Etat chrétienne et liberté d'église, in *La Vie Intel-
lectuelle*, Feb. 1949, p 105.

[2] See F. J. Connell, The Theory of the Lay State, in *The American
Ecclesiastical Review*, vol. cxxv (1951).

[3] J. C. Murray, Freedom and Transcendence of the Church, in *The
American Ecclesiastical Review*, vol. cxxvi (1952), p 43.

point must be that of theory'.[1] But, as he sees it, 'initially and fundamentally' this theory rests 'not on the dogmatic assertion' of a theology of the Church's authority but on 'a philosophical explanation of the structure of the human conscience and of the State'. In other words, on an ethical and political basis. He does add that the problem cannot be wholly solved simply in terms of philosophy; it must at some stage 'be given a theological formulation'.[2] And he does formulate his stand for freedom in theological terms. When, he writes, 'the problem of freedom of religion appears on the theological plane as the problem of Church and State, the basic issue involved in it is the freedom of the human person, Christian and citizen, to live at peace in Christ and in society, that he may thus move straight on to God'.[3] And again: 'The whole of the so-called "institutional action" of the Church, whether in her mission to souls or in her mission in the temporal order, has no other ultimate focus than the protection, support, and perfecting of the freedom of man to reach his eternal destiny . . . No matter how the Catholic may judge the tactical value of this or that "institutional action" of the Church, universal or local, past or present, he is by no means inclined to mistake its final purpose, nor to suppose that it pursues any other goal than what Catholic phraseology calls "the good of souls" . . . Beyond these interests, which are identical with the purpose of the redemption, the Church has no other "institutional interests".'[4]

Despite this undeniably freedom-favouring theological viewpoint, Fr. Murray feels compelled to place more reliance on presenting the Catholic teaching on religion and the State in terms of the ethical and political formulations to which it lends itself. He thinks it is too difficult, in view of history, to get non-Catholics to accept the argument that the theological formulation in question is really Catholic. There is also the fact that Catholic and Protestant theologies of the Church are radically

---

[1] J. C. Murray, Freedom of Religion: the Ethical Problem, in *Theological Studies*, vol. VI (1945), p 229.

[2] *Ibid.*

[3] *Loc. cit.* pp 237, 238.

[4] *Ibid.*

divergent, in such a way as to make theological dialogue concerning relations of Church and State very difficult if not altogether impossible. 'Here, therefore, is our problem—a common
problem: While preserving intact our theological disagreement
(which has its own grounds), how shall we abolish mutual dis-
trust, and strengthen our social unity, civic amity, harmony of
action and mutual confidence in a common pursuit of the common good'.[1] His answer is of vital importance for an understanding of his entire *prise de position:* 'Briefly, I would put the
position thus: (1) we can reach an important measure of agreement on the ethical plane; (2) we must agree to disagree on the
theological plane; (3) but we can reach harmony of action and
mutual confidence on the political plane, in virtue of the agreement previously established on the ethical plane as well as in
virtue of a shared concern for the common good of the political
community, international and national . . . Our subsistent theological disagreements will cease to generate suspicion and
separation on the level of social life, when both sides have the
assurance that their opposing theologies of the Church are projected against a background of an ethic of conscience and a
philosophy of political life that are based on reason, that are
therefore mutually acceptable, and that are not destroyed by
the disagreements in ecclesiology. This ethic of conscience and
this political philosophy will stand guarantee that our respective
theologies can under no circumstances have such implications
in the temporal order as would be injurious to the integrity of
conscience, be it Catholic or Protestant'.[2]

A final argument in favour of the political approach is that
the problem of religion and the State can never be completely
divorced from the fact that it essentially involves a relation
to concrete circumstances and contingent realities of a social
as well as an individual nature.[3] To this extent it is an empirical problem of political science. In pursuit, therefore, of
the ethical and political perspectives of his problem, Fr. Murray
insists that 'we prescind from all the realities of the present,

[1] *Loc. cit.* p 240.
[2] *Loc. cit.* pp 240-241.
[3] *Loc. cit.* p 242.

historic, supernatural order, which are certified to us only by revelation and known only by faith. In particular, we prescind from the fact of Christ, on which the whole supernatural order of salvation is built. We leave out of consideration His teaching and His mission and His Church'.[1] The question of Church-State relations will resolve itself once we have clearly established our philosophy of conscience and the State. It will only remain for us to succeed in 'harmonising the order of reason with the order of faith—what we know with what we have been told by revelation. (Indeed) the essential part of the problem of religious liberty consists in harmonising the solution reached on the ethical plane in terms of reason and the natural law with the solution reached on the theological plane in terms of the Church and the law of the Gospel'.[2]

I have quoted from Fr. Murray at such length and so frequently only to prove the point that he does indeed approach our problem from the political rather than the theological end. There can be no gainsaying the worthiness of his motives in so doing, but one can have qualms about the success of the venture. It is undeniable that he does present a philosophy of liberty that must be acceptable to many outside as well as within the Church. What is open to doubt—and to me more than doubtful—is whether he has ultimately succeeded in fusing it satisfactorily with the demands of theology. In his own mind, of course, he has done so, but not everybody will be disposed to agree. The theologian and public lawyer will be prone to believe that he has given insufficient place to considerations relating to the nature of the Church. It is true too, as Fr. Weigel has noted, that this particular problem calls for very delicate handling. Even an abstract answer to an abstract problem can produce communal nervousness by the very fact that its expression is an event on a community.[3] Its meaning and relevancy in the group in which it is launched may be obscured by its use of a formula around which acrid debates have centered. Ways of avoiding this will certainly be sought by the dis-

[1] *Loc. cit.* p 242.
[2] *Loc. cit.* p 278.
[3] G. Weigel, *Faith and Understanding in America*, p 6.

cerning teacher and I have no quarrel with such an attempt in so far as it is possible. The question is whether the issue of religion and the State is of such a nature that it can legitimately be isolated—even temporarily—from theological considerations?

Even if it is not, there is room for taking circumstances into account. As far as papal teaching goes, one can readily admit that the popes themselves are ever ready to take account, not merely of speculative theory but of the practical repercussions which it will have in a given community at a given moment. Which explains what seems to be conflicting teaching given at different times by the same or successive popes. But to recognise the needs of a concrete situation is not the same thing as to give them predominance. Admittedly the nature of the question at issue is relevant. 'When dealing with a contingent set of circumstances', says Fr. Weigel, 'a question which seems merely abstract actually takes on a very concrete meaning, and the total question is not a purely speculative one. Existentialist factors predominate'.[1] Is this the case with the Church-State issue? It does involve empirical elements wherever it is raised. Though it may seem to be merely abstract, it is pregnant with concrete meaning and can in no way be said to be purely speculative. But surely this does not mean that existentialist factors predominate and must take priority in any effort to provide an answer to it? Fr. Murray would reply that he does not say that they should, that his approach to the question is essentially philosophical. My point is not to deny this but to query his relegation of theological factors to second place in the interests of meeting the existential situation. And if he counters this by saying that, in doing so, he is dealing with the question of freedom of conscience rather than precisely with that of Church and State, my answer must be that this distinction is inadequate, so inadequate indeed that one cannot answer the former question without *ipso facto* answering also the latter. Once again we are back to the importance of the theological element, which appears immediately the Church enters the scene.

[1] *Op. cit.* p 5.

It is quite impossible to provide an acceptable solution to the problem of Church-State relations by way of exclusive analysis of the nature and object of the State. To say that its domain is that of the temporal only is to hide behind an unexamined truth. For one thing the temporal is not identical with the natural; true happiness even in this life is possible for many only if they enjoy satisfactory conditions for the pursuit of their supernatural well-being. When the majority in a State are of such a kind can it rightly be said that their government should have no care for their interests in this respect? In such circumstances does not even the natural law demand that the State take cognisance—in what ways are open to it—of the supernatural order? One might go further, were it necessary, and argue that the law of Christ imposes direct duties on the State, in the matter. For reasons which will later emerge, I prefer to concentrate on the former approach, i.e., to maintain that in the case of a Catholic people the very requirements of democracy itself expect the State to take account, even if indirectly, of Catholicism.

Fr. Murray is not at all disposed to agree with this. Does it mean, he asks, that the American Constitution is in conflict with the law of Christ by reason of the fact that the American people have forbidden it to give any special recognition to religion? His answer, itself in the form of a question, is on the political plane and reflects its limitations. Would an affirmative reply mean 'that the American system of constitutional government, wherein the powers of the civil ruler are limited by act of the people, is directly in contradiction to the law of Christ? This would indeed be a ferocious bit of logic, ending in political nonsense—in a denial of the essence of Western constitutionalism, the doctrine of consent that is the centre of Christian political philosophy and that has received its legitimate development in the Anglo-American political tradition'.[1] Fr. Connell's comment was that if the meaning of this was that it is essential to a democratic form of government to show no special favour to the one true religion, he begged to differ. I share this viewpoint, although its political validity cannot be proved in its

---

[1] J. C. Murray, in *Theological Studies*, vol. CXXVI (1925), p 35.

entirety just now. But by way of comment on the last quotation I would prefer to point out that it is a merely political
answer to what is, in part at least, a theological problem.

It is impossible to escape the conclusion that, in his handling
of Church-State relations, Fr. Murray is over attentive to political factors. He is proud to be the first to try to pose this
problem against the background of American democracy.[1] And
he is critical of the traditional Public Law books which, he
hints, are absolutist in tendency because they 'never consciously
conceive the problem of Church and State in terms of a State
not organised on the monarchic and absolutist lines familiar to
Continental politics'.[2] One is forced to wonder whether his own
views are equally biased by reason of the fact of his viewing
the problem through democratic and American intellectual
spectacles? Somebody has remarked somewhere that it is a
characteristic of writers on Church and State each to defend
the system which pertains in his own country as being fully
Catholic. They may or may not be right in doing so, but it is
another matter when they begin to export their national systems. The Jesuit weekly *America* has maintained that the
American Catholic finds incomprehensible the fondness of some
Catholics abroad for interpreting American domestic affairs in
terms of the far less satisfactory history of Church-State relations
in their own lands.[3] The European in turn may be permitted
to examine the theological quality of the American product before assenting to the proposition that it is the best on the
market. Nor will he disregard a competent non-Catholic judgment on the matter. According to one such estimate, American
thinkers prefer 'to deal with juridical and political arguments
in favour of religious freedom, while European authors (with
the only exception of Maritain) study almost exclusively its
biblical and theological basis . . . We cannot help fearing that

[1] The Church 'has never consciously and adequately faced the problem, theoretical as well as practical, put to her by a state organised on
the constitutional and political lines proper to the tradition of Anglo-
American democracy'—*Theological Studies*, vol. cxxvi (1952), p 43.

[2] *Loc. cit.* p 45.

[3] *America*, 2 July 1960.

if the American tendency prevails, the deep theological meaning of religious liberty would be lost and also that the religious rights of man could suffer the same destiny as many other human rights or constitutional guarantees. We are indeed persuaded that religious freedom, although really a human right, is nevertheless on a higher level than the other human rights, as it is based directly upon the absolute relation of man to God'.[1]

Such is the comment of the study *Roman Catholicism and Religious Liberty*, published in the *Ecumenical Review* by the World Council of Churches. It can scarcely be said to minimise the theological aspect of the problem of Church and State, even if it does not conceive it in terms other than those of the religious *freedom* of the individual. A full and adequate approach to the problem demands not only this but also attention to the political implications of religious *truth*.

I would question therefore Fr. Murray's *preoccupation* with making the situation which prevails in present day multidenominational liberal democracies the touchstone for the conduct of the State in regard to religion. Admittedly it is the more common situation. Admittedly too it has to be the proximate standard in countries where a Catholic State is impossible. And even if one adopts the more common view that this consists of a State in which the 'quasi-totality'—or 'absolute majority' —of the people are Catholic, it is a rare enough commodity in the modern world. Yet it still remains true that the Catholic ideal for the State consists in a system which gives special recognition to the Church.

[1] Carillo de Albornoz, *op. cit.* pp 79-80.

CHAPTER SIX

THEORY AND PRACTICE IN CHURCH-STATE
RELATIONS

Fr. Murray is opposed to the State's giving special recognition to the Church because he identifies such recognition with the undesirable system of establishment that was so common in Catholic States in the past. This assumption pervades all his writing on the subject. What he is against is the concept of the 'union of Church and State', the 'religion of the State' or 'State-Church' idea. In one article alone, according to Mgr. Fenton of the Catholic University, the expression 'State-Church' occurs at least nine times, while there are some fifty-eight references to the 'institutionalisation' of religion in the State, to which Fr. Murray shows himself profoundly opposed.[1] His understanding of what it means to him appears clearly in the following, one passage out of many: 'The legal institution known as the state-church, and the later embodiment of Catholicism as "the religion of the State", represents an application of Catholic principles . . . to the complex political, social, religious, and cultural conditions prevailing in the modern State, as it appeared on the dissolution of medieval Christendom, took form in the era of political absolutism, flourished in the era of "confessional absolutism" under the royal governments in the "Catholic nations" of post-Reformation Europe, and sought reinstatement in the monarchic restorations of the nineteenth century'.[2]

[1] Cf J. C. Fenton, in *American Ecclesiastical Review*, vol. cxxiv, (1951), p 454.
[1] J. C. Murray, in *Theological Studies*, vol. xii (1951), n 2, p 161.

STUDIES IN POLITICAL MORALITY

REALITY AND MYTH

Why such a conception should be entirely identified with
every special recognition of the Church by the State is not at
all clear or easy to follow. As far as can be discovered, Pope
Leo XIII, who was such a champion of special recognition, was
not accustomed to use the phrase 'religion of the State' himself.
It seems that it occurs only once in the entire corpus of his
writings and then only in a passing reference.[1] The kind of
establishment involved in the religion of the State set-up that
Fr. Murray has in mind was equally abhorrent to the Leonine
way of thinking. For it was far from operating for the good of
the Church in every respect. It was this type of recognition of
the Church to which the younger Lammenais was opposed,
which would make of the Church a kind of Department of State,
at best a semi-State body or statutory corporation.[2] Its disadvantages to the Church of England have been listed comprehensively by a former Archbishop of York.[3] They are
summed up in the words 'State control'. Crown appointment
of bishops, oath of allegiance, Parliamentary decision on changes
of doctrine or worship, Royal calling of Convocations, secular
court of appeal for ecclesiastical matters and State influence in
the administration of Church property—these are some of the
disadvantages, and they are by no means all, that are commonly
incurred as a result of the establishment of the Church as the
religion of the State. Beside them the advantages of the system
pale into insignificance. The only advantage that Dr. Garbett
could find accruing from it in England is that it gives the
ministers of the Church a more enhanced status than they
would otherwise have. This, he says, makes their visitation of
homes easier and endows them with a spiritual authority which
they might otherwise find difficult to command.[4] It is not an
argument that will carry great weight with many Catholics,

[1] Letter to the Cardinal Vicar of Rome, 19 August 1900.
[2] Cf Vidler, *Prophecy and Papacy*.
[3] Garbett, *loc. cit.* pp 135-9.
[4] *Op. cit.* p 128.

particularly in countries like Ireland and America. Nor did it weigh either with Pope Leo XIII. He did not call for the 'establishment' of Catholicism, for Church-State 'union' or for a 'religion of the State'. All he insisted on is that in a 'Catholic state' or a 'Catholic nation' the Catholic Church should get special recognition in certain ways.

Fr. Murray will not agree even with this. He digs logical pitfalls in the way of such reasoning.[1] Surely, he muses, the argument cannot be moving in a circle: given a 'Catholic society', a State-Church (*sic*) is theologically necessary and a 'Catholic society' is one in which a State-Church exists! While he does not say that the argument is guilty of such a glaring fallacy, he does suggest that 'it seems to lurk beneath' it. 'The danger of begging the question is created by an attempt to transform an historical polemic argument into an abstract speculative one. The nineteenth-century polemic bore . . . upon a defence of the State-Church in the historic "Catholic nations", . . . which were considered such precisely because in them the Church was established by law. The polemic argument did not beg the question, because it knew what the question was—an historical one. The risk of circular argument arises when one evacuates the term "Catholic society" (or "State" or "nation") of its complex, concrete, and historical meaning, and attempts to give it a pseudo-abstract meaning by surrounding the term with a mist of indefiniteness'.[2] Out of historical context, the most intelligible content with which this term can be endowed is, he says, a purely statistical one. It is identified with a State with a Catholic majority. But this in turn is a pseudo-abstraction and is unreal and invalid as a pole on which to rest an argument, much less impose a constitution on a State. Constitutions are not adaptations to naked numerical facts of population. The only valid term of reference for law is 'the people' and this is a concrete, dynamic thing, growing in the moral soil of a country's history, moulded by experience and feeling and great leaders; it is an individuality, not a mere collectivity.[3]

[1] J. C. Murray, in *Theological Studies*, vol. XII (1951), n 2, p 174.
[2] *Ibid.*
[3] *Loc. cit.* p 176.

This is simply tilting at a man of straw. Admittedly one finds reference to a 'Catholic majority' in many descriptions of the kind of State in which the Public Law books say the Church should get special recognition. But it is intended merely as a handy rule of thumb, in which capacity I have employed it in these pages. It is not to be taken exclusively as a numerical criterion. Cappello, for example, speaks of the need for the population to be morally Catholic before the claims of the Church press in practice.[1] To employ for a moment the thesis-hypothesis terminology, the Catholic thesis applies only in a condition of things in which 'the people' is Catholic in outlook, in traditions, intentions and expectations. It is sometimes suggested that, at the present time, this is a purely hypothetical state of affairs, that in a divided Christendom and largely secularist world the 'Catholic State' is itself a condition of hypothesis, from a total or international point of view. In this connection it is worth recalling that, in its original employment, the thesis-hypothesis distinction was applied, not to international society but to 'a society' in given conditions.[2] It is further urged, however, that it is a mistake at the present day to argue upon the circumstances of any isolated country,[3] that today—in view of international developments—'it is not any more (as the thesis of the Catholic State seems to represent) a question of the welfare of a closed State'.[4] The answer to this is that contemporary needs can be met by measures such as those suggested by Pope Pius XII in his address to the Italian jurists, which does not, as we have seen, run counter to the duty of the Catholic State, in relation to its own people, to give special recognition to the Catholic Church. That such need not mean intolerance was implied by the Pope himself in the same address when he referred casually to the fact that the Church respected the rights of conscience 'after she became the State Church under Constantine the Great and the other Christian emperors'.

[1] Cappello, *Summa Iuris Ecclesiastici Publici*, n 324.

[2] See Mgr. Dupanloup's *La convention du 15 septembre et l'encyclique du 8 décembre*, Paris 1865.

[3] See Carillo de Albornoz, *op. cit.* p 19.

[4] Albornoz, *op. cit.* pp 51-52.

Yet another difficulty about accepting 'special recognition' for the Church in the Catholic State is made on the grounds that its purpose is to ensure the continuance of religious unity in the State, which, it is submitted, is not a political object. That the unity of the State is a political purpose is granted, but that religious unity may be made a means to this is rejected.[1] Religious unity, it is said, is not a necessary condition for State unity and no government can have a duty to preserve the religious unity of its people. But who ever said that, in Catholic Church-State theory, this is the reason for demanding special recognition for the Church? In thinking that it is, Fr. Murray, among others, has got a wrong slant on a fundamental aspect of the matter.[2] Whatever may be the object of the secular authorities, or the *per accidens* effects of the Catholic theory, the only interests of the Church are in the spiritual domain.

Special recognition of the Church may be necessary to secure these interests to the full in a State in which the vast majority is Catholic. It is not a question of seeking what *can* be secured from the State but what *ought* to be granted if the people's spiritual interests are to be adequately looked after in so far as their government is competent to do so. On the side of the State, this, in turn, reechoes its duty of doing whatever is necessary in pursuit of the political common good. It is simply erroneous to suggest that the limitation of the State to catering for the exigencies of public order means that it cannot grant special recognition to the Church.[3] And so far from true is it that this implies

[1] See J. C. Murray, in *Theological Studies*, vol. xiv (1953) n 2, p 205; also A Hartmann, *op. cit.* pp 243-244.

[2] 'Admittedly this concept may be a means to the preservation of a particular national unity or to the maintenance of the integrity of a particular national culture; as such, however, it cannot claim the patronage of the Church or of Catholic doctrine for national unities and cultures do not rank as ends or values proper to the Church, nor is her doctrine a means to them. The only proper point of reference is the freedom of the Church, which is the single necessary end that the Church directly seeks in her relations with political society'—J. C. Murray, in *Theological Studies*, vol. x (1949), n 3, p 425.

[3] 'I had supposed that in Catholic political philosophy the action

an absolutist political framework, that it is not merely in harmony with but demanded by democratic attitudes.

A final difficulty is lodged in this connection on the score that the Anglo-American brand of democracy places unique importance on the minimal intervention of the State.[1] In addition it is urged that democracy demands diversity, that the *consensus* on which it rests makes necessary the supposition of a multi-sided and variegated society. American writers have made a great deal of this aspect of democracy;[2] Fr. Murray has built it right into his Church-State theory.[3] It may be pertinent to note, as A. D. Lindsay has recalled, that this is a peculiarly Puritan contribution to political reality.[4] Their belief in the priesthood of all believers and experience of the working of democratic congregations caused the Puritans to adopt the political idea that government should be on a consensual basis, each group in society contributing what it had to say to the discussion, with government acting on agreements eventually arrived at. Even a little consideration, says Lindsay, shows how much the ideals of English and American democracy follow this Puritan pattern. In both countries they take for granted that there should be voluntary associations in society—religious, philanthropic, commercial—associations which the State may certainly regulate but which it does not create and of whose views it must take account. The Puritan contribution to modern democracy was an idea of equality 'which was compatible with, even welcomed and demanded differences'.

Whatever may have been its origin, this aspect of democracy

of the State was determined by the *exigencies* of public order; it is to do what necessarily must be done to preserve civil peace, not what possibly can be done without disturbing civil peace'—J. C. Murray, in *Theological Studies*, vol. x (1949), n 3, p 431.

[1] See M. Cranston, *Freedom: A New Analysis*, London 1953, chapters 1 and 4.

[2] E.g. T. V. Smith and E. C. Lindeman, *The Democratic Way of Life*, New York 1951, p 115: 'Democracies seek strength through diversity'.

[3] See J. C. Murray, *We Hold These Truths*, Part I, *passim*.

[4] See A. D. Lindsay, *The Modern Democratic State*, London 1943, vol. I, pp 117-121.

is hard political fact and must be faced as such. It does not at all disturb the Catholic political philosopher. When confronted with it our reply is that the special recognition demanded by the Church does not at all conflict with legitimate diversity. The big trouble with its critics is that they are prone to conceive it as coinciding with an intolerant establishment. The Church itself defends the idea that conditions favourable to truth must also be favourable to conditions freely to find and live the truth. A social order that hampers minorities as such and bans fair and free discussion is not favourable to the spread of truth itself. And it has been wisely remarked that the tendency to intolerance is so strong that in a land of homogeneous population the State should shield dissident minorities rather than concentrate on protecting the interests of the common opinion.[1] It must be admitted that, owing to the conditions which gave rise to them, papal documents of the past were not very preoccupied with this. Pope Pius XII has remedied the situation to a high degree. But when this has been said, it remains to be added that the traditional Catholic demands do not themselves run counter to the conditions of democratic diversity. The traditional demands are for conditions which favour the truth. While this always holds, the Church asserts that the conditions in question exhibit an altered content in the modern world from that of the past. 'If one wishes to formulate the thesis in complete fashion', says Canon Leclercq, 'let it be simply said that the duty of the State to favour the truth ought to be interpreted in the sense of the formation of social conditions favourable to this end, that its citizens may find the truth'.[2] There is nothing here in conflict with democracy of any brand.

THE CATHOLIC IDEAL

Fr. Murray eschews the use of the term 'ideal' when discussing the question of Church-State relations. It only remains for us to examine his criticisms of the concept. Some of these are

[1] Cf J. Leclercq, *loc. cit.* p 110.
[2] *Ibid.*

easily disposed of. When, for example, he says that 'no "ideal" realisations are possible in history; no application of principle can claim to be a *thesis*', one could have no option but to quarrel with this if it essentially meant that practice can never measure up to theory. The only truth it contains is the platitudinous one that a theoretical ideal, while remaining theoretical, cannot be reduced to practice. But, passing from this, Fr. Murray proclaims that it is impossible to see how any one application of Catholic principle is better than any other, at least in this particular sphere. The constitutional provision for religious freedom in the democratic State is as valid in its own historical perspective as was the legal institution of the State-Church in the post-Reformation monarchies. There is here no real objection to what we have called the ideal, but only a side-stepping of the true point at issue. What traditional theory regards as ideal does not necessarily cease to be such because of a philosopher's difficulty in reconciling it with his own views.[1] Particularly if his difficulty is due largely to the fact that he has misinterpreted the true significance of the ideal. In Fr. Murray's case there is abundant evidence that, whenever he speaks of the ideal, he has State religion—involving repression of dissent—in mind.[2]

[1] J. C. Murray, in *Theological Studies*, vol. XII (1951), p 165.

[2] ' . . . It is difficult to see why one institution is any less, or more, an adaptation of principle than is any other, why one should be considered more valid than the other, why one has greater right to claim the support of principle than the other'—J. C. Murray, in *Theological Studies*, vol. XII (1951), n 2, p 166.

'Does anyone know what a "Christian world" would be like that is not fashioned by great kings but by a genuine Christian people, whose historical experience has not been of subjection to the power and the tutelage by it, but of active participation in the power and control of it? Can anyone describe the spiritual reality of a Catholic majority that would be the historical product of an American future and not a relic from a European past? And if one cannot describe this spiritual reality, one cannot argue from it—not, that is, and remain faithful to the concrete Leonine manner of argument'—*Theol. Studies*, vol. XIV (1953), n 2, p 184.

In an ideal order, he writes, there would be no need for any guar-

THE CATHOLIC IDEAL

THE CATHOLIC IDEAL 261

However difficult it may be to conceive the ideal as realised in a predominantly Catholic America of the future, Fr. Murray's rejection of its implications rests on even deeper grounds. One cannot rightly speak, he says, of an ideal relationship between Church and State as if any such ideal could become existent and therefore a relevant subject of discourse. 'In what concerns religion, for instance, the order of existence is subject to the predestining decree of God, in consequence of which (however the matter may be explained theologically) not all men are among the elect. That is to say, the permanent, irremediable, existential, divinely willed situation of the human race is a condition of religious pluralism. The fact that (the so-called Catholic nations) should have found some sort of substantial religious unity does not represent the operation of some singly valid norm; as if unity alone were the norm, and as if the pluralism of dissent were somewhat abnormal. These small localised Christian unities were a matter of historical accident—providential, if you will, but accident nonetheless. And one does not project norms or ideals from a basis of historical accident, contingent in fact.'[1]

Much the same ideas, though in more qualified form, have been expressed by Fr. Gustave Weigel.[2] They bring us to the

antee of the freedom of the Church. 'No freedom needs legal guarantees unless it has enemies, who would damage or menace it. But in an "ideal" religio-social order, the freedom of the Church would have no enemies. (Hence)... in an "ideal" religio-social order there would be no such thing as legal establishment of religion and coercive treatment of dissenters. In such an "ideal" order there are *ex hypothesi* no dissenters; anyhow why should religion be legally established if it is already completely free, and secure in its public existence'?—*Theological Studies*, vol. XIV (1953), n 4, p 564.

[1] Murray, in *Theological Studies*, vol. XIV (1953), n 4, p 565.
[2] The final fruit of consideration of Church doctrine on Church and State, says Fr. Weigel, 'would it seems to me, be the tranquil recognition that the Catholic philosophy concerns an ideal framework, which, because of Original Sin, never exists anywhere in its purity. Historical environments are always removed from the ideal in varying degrees. In so far as a concrete situation recedes from the ideal, lawmakers and governors are objectively justified in tolerating conditions not of their

ultimate in debate on the Church-State question, to the philosophical and theological rock-bottom of the issue. Their greatest
exponent has been the philosopher Jacques Maritain, to whose
treatment of the matter we must devote some attention.

Maritain's position, like that of Fr. Murray, has undergone
development over the years; still his outlook on our subject
presents an extraordinary unity throughout his works on political philosophy.[1] Maritain builds his teaching on the twin foundations of 'immutable principle' and 'human liberty'. These he
unites by asserting that while the principles always remain,
their application changes in different periods of human history.
To forget this is to court disaster. The Christian philosopher of
politics must neither stubbornly stick to the past, nor yet sever
all connection with tradition. 'The true solution springs from
the philosophy of analogy. The principles do not vary . . . but
they are applied in ways which are essentially diverse, corresponding to one and the same concept only by a similitude of
proportion'.[2] One must not regard their application as falling
into a rigid univocal pattern; yet neither are their patterns of
implementation purely equivocal.[3]

Human history is an ever changing thing and political circumstances, systems and values are part of it. Though it is always dictated by the providence of God, it is only too prone to
produce what are deformities in the eyes of the Christian man.
One thing, however, is certain; there can be no undoing of what
is over in historical development; it is impossible to return to a

own making, which ideally would be suppressed or corrected. They must
not despise the ideal. Much less should they be guided by a false philosophy, but they may permit that degree of recession from the ideal
which is demanded for the common good, lest greater evils ensue or
greater goods be lost'—*Thought*, vol. XXVII, n 105, (1952) 183. Fr. Weigel
admits that such situations 'from a theological point of view, are not
ideal': *Pope Pius XII on the World Community*, p 29. But he seems to
accept them as universal, inevitable and normal.

[1] Cf A. Tamosaitis S.J., *Church and State in Maritain's Thought*,
Chicago 1959, *passim*.

[2] Maritain, *True Humanism*, London 1938, p 132.

[3] Maritain, *Man and the State*, London 1954, p 156.

past condition of things. The Christian realist must face up to this inexorable law and must seek to save what is good in historical deformities. In the knowledge that God can draw good out of evil, the Christian will try to turn them into assets. He can do this, Maritain thinks, only by recognising, accepting and uplifting the central characteristic—or dynamic image—of the age in which he lives. Every historical epoch tends towards some definite 'type'. It is this that is dominant in orientating its development and in providing the motive force in virtue of which it is moulded in a certain way. Although Maritain himself does not do so, one might call it the 'substantial form' of each age. Maritain calls it the 'concrete historical ideal'.[1] The Christian philosopher must have grasped this ideal, this climate of his time, if he is to be able to apply his unchanging principles in the proper way. In medieval Europe this climate consisted in a 'sacral' approach to things; man in general was the man of Christianity, of the Incarnation. During the Renaissance, the image of man began to change and the concrete historical ideal became, first, a Christian naturalism and later a purely rationalist humanism. Today it has almost become a crude materialistic paganism.

The root cause of this malady is seen by Maritain to lie in the bankruptcy of the Christian world.[2] The Christian world has failed because it dissociated the things of time from those of eternity. It allowed the secular to develop unvivified by the Gospel; spiritual and temporal go each its own way in an uneasy dualism. If it is to be saved, the temporal order must again be penetrated by Christian principles. But in striving for this we must not lose sight of historical changes. Our guide must be the concrete historical ideal of a *new Christendom* and not a now impossible ideal from the Christian past. Indeed the sacral

[1] *True Humanism*, p 121.

[2] Cf Maritain, *Religion et Culture*, Paris 1930. One must properly understand the sense which Maritain intends. 'A philosopher of culture who raises the question of the Christian world is not raising the issue of the truth of Christianity, but of the temporal responsibilities of Christians'. Cf also *True Humanism*, pp 33-34.

stamp, which was the reflection of the concrete historical ideal
of the Middle Ages, was, as it was effected, bound up with certain undesirable elements that are better forgotten. 'As it re-
ceded from the Holy Roman Empire and the medieval regime,
Western civilisation, even though deteriorating in other respects, as we know, freed itself from powerful impurities which
that regime in fact carried in its train; and it would be a strange
aberration for Christians to wish to come back to these impurities at the very moment when they have lost their historical
occasion for existence'.[1] On the contrary, 'the true substance of
the nineteenth century's aspirations, as well as the human gains
it achieved, must be saved'.[2] Hence in building up the new
Christendom, to which we should look forward, we must be
guided by a new concrete historical ideal of theocentric humanism. The realisation of this ideal lies in the future, but it is
necessary that we should begin to work towards it as from now.

In the context of this future historical ideal the traditional
and immutable principles which govern Church-State relations
will be applied in a new and analogous way. These principles
for Maritain are three: the freedom of the Church, the superiority of the Church and the co-operation of Church and State. He
adamantly refuses to accept the thesis-hypothesis dichotomy as
a suitable way in which realism and principle can be reconciled.
In so far as the thesis is conceived as *the* ideal in Church-State
relations—the absolute ideal independent of historical modification—Maritain objects that it is self-stulifying because, if it is
to be applied at all, it must be something existential. At best it
is but a misnomer for the way in which principles were once
applied in the far too idealised 'sacral' age of medieval Europe.
Medieval Christendom was characterised by the facts that everything was directed towards spiritual unity, that the temporal
played only a ministerial role, that external force was regarded
as capable of being legitimately employed for man's spiritual
good, that power in society was exercised from the top along
paternalistic lines and that the main aim of man and society

---

[1] Maritain, *Redeeming the Time*, London 1943, p 152.

[2] Maritain, *The Range of Reason*, London 1953, p 193.

was the construction of the Kingdom of Christ in this world. This was a fine historical ideal in itself,[1] but it is incapable of existing in the historical climate of the future.[2]

The concrete historical ideal of the new age must be marked, first and foremost, by pluralism, particularly in the religious sphere. Secondly, the domain of the temporal must be granted due autonomy; it must no longer be regarded as merely an instrumental agent but as a principal agent on a lower plane of activity. It pertains essentially to the secular sphere, though by 'secular' is not meant 'secularised' in the sense of indifferent to religion.[3] In this context, there must be full religious freedom; physical coercion must no longer be used in the service of God. Indeed temporal authority, having become closely dependent on the will of the governed, has to endeavour to respect all differences in the social scene. The society of the future will necessarily be a variegated one, a multiplicity of very different and sometimes clashing interests that must try to live together in fraternal community. Against this background our immutable principles must find new application.

That of the freedom of the Church is easily restated. The State must guarantee the Church her rights—not by serving the Church in any subordinate way, or by using force to secure her interests, but by respecting the rights of the Church to carry on her work while, at the same time, respecting the rights of others to do differently. While never *approving* what is contrary to natural law, the State must look to the temporal common good of all and sometimes even *permit* certain ways of acting that, in some measure, depart from natural law.[4] On this it is better to let Maritain speak for himself:

'There is a way of understanding this pluralist solution which would fall into the error of theological liberalism . . . Then one would think that human opinions of whatever kind have a right to be taught and propagated, and that, as a result,

---

[1] *True Humanism*, p 141.
[2] *Ibid.* p 203.
[3] *Man and the State*, pp 152-153.
[4] *Ibid.* p 167-168.

the body politic is bound to recognise as the proper juridical status of each spiritual stock the law worked out by that stock in conformity with its own principles. That is not the way I understand this solution. To me this solution means that, in order to avoid greater evils (that is of the society's peace and the petrification or disintegration of consciences), the body politic could and should tolerate within it—to tolerate is not to approve—ways of worship more or less removed from the true one: the practices of unbelievers are to be tolerated, St. Thomas taught; ways of worship and also ways of conceiving the meaning of life and modes of behaviour; in consequence, the solution means that the various spiritual groups within the body politic should be granted a particular juridical status. The legislative power of the commonwealth itself in its political widsom would adapt this juridical status, on the one hand to the condition of groups and, on the other to the general line of legislation leading towards the virtuous life and to the prescriptions of the moral law, to the full realisation of which it should endeavour to direct as far as possible this diversity of forms'.[1]

The principles of the superiority of the Church and of the co-operation of Church and State must also be applied in a new way. The State must continue to respect the primacy of the Church, but again, not by acting as an instrument for her spiritual mission, but by recognising that its own—autonomous—activity is concerned only with a part of man's wants, that man's spiritual needs are of a higher order than the material and that, even in achieving its temporal purpose, it needs the beneficial influence of spiritual values. Finally, the State must co-operate with the Church, not by granting her any specially favoured juridical treatment, but by the assiduous performance of its duties in its own sphere and by fostering amongst its citizens that spirit of liberty and brotherhood which is so essential if the Church's work is to prosper.[2]

---

[1] *True Humanism*, pp 160-161.

[2] In the future age which Maritain envisages the Church will not lose any of the essential rights she has claimed or exercised in the past. Rather will she 'renounce the *exercise* of certain of them, not because she is forced to do so, but voluntarily and by virtue of the consideration

Such, in brief, is Maritain's position. Although I have out-lined it within very narrow compass, the exposition is, I hope, substantially accurate. It is an attractive and strong position from many viewpoints. Its feeling for history and current realities is striking and praiseworthy. The charges that have been levelled at it in some quarters[1]—that it savours of the Hegelian dialectic—have, I feel, been answered.[2] Or at least, shall we say, they have not been clearly and absolutely estab-lished. The Marxist assertion that 'man makes his own history but he does not make it out of conditions chosen by himself' is a valid one; the trouble with Marxism is that it forgets the first part of the formula. Maritain retrieves the balance between freedom and determinism in a way with which nobody can reasonably quarrel. It will be granted by all that the application of Catholic principles on Church and State is not something that can or should remain static, or that the form which it is possible for it to take in concrete circumstances is not always one that leaves nothing to be desired. Historical reality makes it neces-sary for the Church to be content with that maximum that is relative to the historical context and therefore possible. One can call this the concrete historical ideal if one wishes.

The trouble with Maritain is that he seems to exclude the absolute ideal, to deny it not merely practical relevancy but even internal consistency and validity as a concept. He regards the traditional thesis—resulting from the nature of the Church and holding for all time at the theoretical level—as a false way of expressing the Church's demands of the State. Surely, he would say, the only ideal that means anything is that 'best' that

of the common good, the historical context having changed. She exer-cised in the past the right of making null and void a civil law which severely impaired the spiritual welfare of the people. She always pos-sesses this right in its root. If she made it emerge in actual exercise in the historical climate of today, this very exercise would harm the com-mon good both of the Church and of civil society. So by reason of justice (justice toward the common good both of civilisation and of the King-dom of God) does the Church give up the exercise of such a right'.

[1] E.g. A. Messineo S.J., in *Civiltà Cattolica*, (1956), pp 449-463.

[2] A. Tamosaitis S.J., *op. cit.* pp 56-73.

is attainable in given circumstances. Is not the Church frequently glad to accept less than what the thesis demands? Is
it not therefore permissible, he asks, 'to think that by not
demanding that Catholicism should be the State religion in
Portugal and renouncing all social and political discrimination
in her favour, the Church did not contradict herself, nor the
Syllabus, nor the Encyclical *Quanta Cura*, nor the Encyclical
Immortale Dei, nor the Encyclical *Libertas*? Is it possible to
regard as good and opportune the new solution which was thus
effected? Is it permissible to think that it gives us a practical
orientation that is especially valuable for our times, without,
of course, seeing in it, for this reason, the only possible lawful
solution, nor discrediting other solutions, by which the supreme
principles to which this solution remains faithful, are realised
otherwise'?[1] Why, then, he implies, should this new solution
be described in terms of the hypothesis as something grudgingly
accepted when nothing better could be attained? But who ever
said that a description of the 'new solution' in terms of the
hypothesis, rather than in those of the 'concrete historical ideal',
would not mean that this solution was 'good and opportune'—
in the circumstances? Properly understood, the hypothesis
means just that.

In actual fact, in at least one place Maritain himself admits
that the thesis-hypothesis presentation, though often incor-
rectly construed, can be interpreted in a satisfactory manner.[2]
And, in so far as he holds that the Church never loses any of
her rights in any circumstances but only renounces the use of
them if their exercise would harm the common good of her own
or of the civil society, are we not entitled to ask, in the words
of one commentator, whether such a position does not 'bring
us back to the classical solution of thesis and hypothesis, according to which the Church renounces the enforcement of her
rights on account of circumstances'?[3] Now if the hypothesis
remains, so does the thesis. What else, says the same com-

[1] *Raison et Raisons*, Paris 1947, p 269.
[2] *Man and the State*, p 141.
[3] Tamosaitis, *op. cit.* p 103.

mentator,[1] can be the meaning of the specification, added by Maritain, that the Church retains her rights in their roots.[2] In any case, to deny altogether the existence of an absolute ideal for the relations of the Church to the State, or to maintain that it is inherently impossible for practice ever to measure up to this, would seem to conflict with something close to the essence of Christianity. There is grave danger in tending to classify the absolute ideal with a utopia, as Maritain, in some places, does.[3] He regards a utopia as something that is an end term and resting place which, for that very reason, is not realisable in historical reality. The concrete historical ideal is quite otherwise. It is essentially a thing in process and, as such but only as such, can be realised. The new Christendom must conform to this. If Maritain means by this that the Kingdom of God in its fullness is not attainable in time, in that it is utterly impossible for the State ever to attain to the ideal of a relatively homogeneous and unified Catholic society in the peaceful and social profession of the religion of the true Church, I cannot see how he can escape the charge of being in error. What is more likely is that in an effort to get Christian minds away from being preoccupied with a thesis that is conceived in terms of the Christian Europe of the Middle Ages, he tends to exaggerate the incapability of existence of any such thesis in the historical climate that we have entered and that will endure in the foreseeable future.

[1] *Ibid.*, p 103.
[2] *Man and the State*, p 166, n 1. In *Man and the State*, pp. 155-165, Maritain maintains that his pluralist principle "would require of the State a juridical recognition of the moral codes" peculiar to any group in the State which represents "an asset in the heritage of the nation". He bases his demand for such recognition "on the exigencies of the political common good". But he insists that this should in no way infringe upon the basic rule of equal laws and equal rights for all citizens". In particular, the State should not "assist the Church by granting her favoured juridical treatment". He admits that a privileged juridical situtation is the ideal one for the Church but holds that the circumstances in which this might be realized are no longer possible in the modern world.
[3] *True Humanism*, pp 121-122.

He is much too dogmatic about this future. Who can say that, in God's providence, a time will not come for which the concrete historical ideal will be the application of what we have called the absolute ideal? Who can charter the ways of God's grace? One gets the impression that Maritain, in holding up to us the vision of a new Christendom, such as he conceives it, is just as inconsistent as was Marx when, while insisting on the ever-changing Hegelian process of history, he placed an end to its evolution, for practical purposes, in the stage of Communist Society. Maritain would defend his 'Christianly inspired modern democratic' pattern of society 'even if one single citizen dissented from the religious faith of all the people'.[1] Why? Apparently to ensure the kind of situation which Cardinal Manning described to Gladstone and which Maritain quotes as so significant: 'If Catholics were in power in England, not a penal law would be proposed, nor the shadow of constraint be put upon the faith of any man . . . If the Catholics were to-morrow the "Imperial race" of these Kingdoms, they would not use political power to molest nor shut one of their churches, or colleges, or schools. They would have the same liberty we enjoy as a minority'.[2] But would the organisation of society approaching our absolute ideal entail aught else? Does the special recognition of the Church, as I have termed it, entail aught else ? Even granting the fact that, as it was developed in practice, the sacral system of medieval Christendom frequently conflicted with genuine human liberties, the sacral ideal in itself, did not entail this. May we not hope and strive then for a situation, in which Catholicism, as the religion of the vast majority and perhaps all of the citizens, is recognised in such a way as accords both with the objective rights of truth and the subjective rights of human personality? 'I believe', says Maritain, 'in the possible advent of a new Christendom because my name is Jacques . . . James typified the second theological virtue'.[3] Surely Christian

---

[1] *Man and the State*, p 167.

[2] Manning, *The Vatican Decrees in their Bearing on Civil Allegiance*, London 1875, pp 93-94. Quoted by Maritain, *Man and the State*, p 181.

[3] Maritain, *Reflections on America*, New York 1958, p 191.

hope leads us to believe that even greater things than he envisages are possible? In the meantime we do what we can in the situation as we find it. The best attainable position for the Church in any situation—taking account of all relevant circumstances and due rights—undoubtedly constitutes the concrete historical ideal in that context. Traditional exposition would describe it as meeting the requirements of the hypothesis. But not, if rightly understood, an hypothesis 'reluctantly accepted' or accepted 'as a matter of expediency'.[1] That the hypothesis description has often been wrongly understood in this way is undeniable and provides much excuse for the attitude of Murray and Maritain to it. My plea is that 'abusus non tollit usum.'

I am in entire agreement with the endorsement, on the part of the commentator to whom I have already referred, of the view that on the question of tolerance in a pluralist society, 'Maritain proceeds with uncertainty'.[2] It is particularly regrettable that he has not discussed in greater detail and clarity the valid use of the thesis-hypothesis distinction that he admits is possible. Had he done so, we might find our views not so far removed from his. It may be, of course, that in this, as in other philosophical matters, Maritain deliberately seeks to avoid a mathematically precise mode of expression, so as to make possible a deepening and fruitful reflection by others. Speaking of this suppleness of language, which is necessary in philosophy, he says: 'If I were not afraid of scandalising the reader, I should say that in philosophy as in poetry verbal equivocations occasionally guarantee the most fertile and the truest intuitions'.[3] But at the end of it all I cannot see that he has disposed for good of the traditional thesis or 'absolute ideal' for the State, or has shown that the special recognition of the Church, in the sense which we here defend, is not desirable, given the circumstances which make it possible and in which alone it is demanded by Church-State teaching.

[1] *Man and the State*, p 167.

[2] Cf Tamosaitis, *op. cit.* p 102.

[3] Maritain, Introduction to M. J. Adler's *Problems for Thomists*, New York 1940, p ix.

THE THESIS-HYPOTHESIS DISTINCTION

Incorrect understanding of the thesis-hypothesis distinction must be carefully avoided. If this is done the main objections to it disappear. The primary source of misunderstanding is the idea that, according to the thesis, the Church is entitled to the assistance of the State in suppressing heresy and propagating the Gospel. According to the same view, the hypothesis is what the Church will tolerate in practice, but only very reluctantly as an evil to be borne. It was this understanding of the distinction that led an American bishop to remark that 'so many conditions for its accomplishment are lacking in every government of the world that the thesis may well be relegated to the limbo of defunct controversies'. One could heartily agree with his sentiments if the thesis were to be understood as just outlined. It appears, incidentally, that whenever American bishops have seemed to renounce the thesis, it is this interpretation of it that they have always had in mind.[1] Yet it is amazing with what regularity it continues to turn up in discussions on Church-State relations.[2]

[1] E.g. Bishop John Carroll: 'We have all smarted under the lash of an established church and shall therefore be on our guard against every approach to it'; Archbishop John Hughes: ' . . . that justly obnoxious union of Church and State'; Cardinal Gibbons: 'As a citizen of the United States . . . I proclaim ,with a deep sense of pride and gratitude . . . that I belong to a country where the civil government holds over us the aegis of protection without interfering in the legitimate exercise of our sublime mission as ministers of the gospel of Jesus Christ'; Cardinal Cushing: 'I have never met any ecclesiastical leader who desired the union of Church and State in this country. 'It is ridiculous to assert that, were Catholics ever to gain the balance of political power in the United States, they would be obliged by their principles to impose restrictions on the religious activities of their non-Catholic fellow-citizens'; Archbishop Karl Alter: 'I can categorically state that there is no doctrine of the Catholic Church which places upon its members the obligation to work for a change in respect to that religious freedom which is guaranteed to all of us by the Constitution of the United States'.

[2] E.g. J. Vialatoux and A. Latreille, *Cristianismo y laicidad*, San Sebastian 1950.

Undoubtedly this goes a long way towards explaining why the distinction came in for such criticism at the Fifth International Thomistic Congress (Rome, 1960). Canon Dondeyne of Louvain made a sweeping attack on it as being a survival from the Middle Ages and the *ancien régime*. If, he said, the Church did not accept the United Nations' declaration of the rights of man, she was cutting herself off from the main stream of modern social life. Another participant referred to the predicament of the missionary, who might easily find himself confronted with an Islamic State which appealed to the thesis-hypothesis distinction to exclude him from its territory. In general there was much support at the Congress for the idea that tolerance is something positive—an offshoot of justice—and should be accepted with more than reluctance.

Misunderstanding of the thesis-hypothesis terminology has been so common that one has seriously to consider whether it would not be a definite step in advance to abandon this terminology altogether. In this connection a look into history is helpful; it shows that the terminology is by no means sacrosanct. The distinction itself is old. One can find it in substance in St. Thomas,[1] while, in 1584, it was the centrepiece of a book on heresy by the Rector of the University of Louvain.[2] It became classical during the 17th century. The terminology, on the other hand, did not become the language of theology until the middle of the 19th century; prior to that it was used exclusively to illustrate the distinction between dialectic and rhetoric. Dialectic was said to deal with theses or questions in the abstract, rhetoric with hypotheses, i.e., taking account of concrete circumstances.[3] As far as theology goes, therefore, the terminology is not old. More important is the fact that, when it was first introduced into theological language, it had somewhat different overtones from what it has in many minds today. It first became famous by reason of its use by Mgr. Dupanloup in the well-known pamphlet in which he tried to rationalise the *Syllabus*

[1] *2a 2ae*, Q. 10 art. 11.

[2] Jean Molanus, *De fide haereticis servanda*, Cologne 1584.

[3] Cf J. Lecler, A propos de la distinction de la 'Thèse' et de 'l'Hypothèse', in *Recherches de Science Religieuse*, vol. XLI (1953), n 4.

of Errors. The *Syllabus,* as we mentioned earlier, had issued an absolute condemnation of the separation of Church and State. It was in this connection that Mgr. Dupanloup introduced the thesis-hypothesis: 'One must distinguish between absolute propositions and relative ones; for what might be admissable *en hypothèse* will often be false *en thèse'.*[1]

What has generally escaped notice is that, when he spoke of the thesis, it is the liberal thesis he had in mind and not the Catholic.[2] His point was that while certain opinions may be admissable in given circumstances, they are false if erected into absolute principles. He rejected the ideas of extreme Liberalism when thus universalised but he did not employ the distinction, as it has come to be understood by so many, to the effect that the Catholic thesis represents absolute principles and the hypothesis their mitigation in adverse circumstances. It has been said that Dupanloup's explanation of the Syllabus was honoured by a special Brief of Pius IX, who declared that the Bishop of Orleans had thereby joined the group of bishops who had condemned the modern errors in the same way in which the Pope himself had condemned them.[3]

There is room for some doubt about the purpose and meaning of the Brief. There can be no doubt that Dupanloup's pamphlet did a great deal to quiet the storm caused by the *Syllabus.* The question is whether it interpreted the Pope accurately. Some would see the approval in the Brief as noticeably guarded. The Pope associated Dupanloup with the other French Bishops who 'had reproved these errors in the sense in which we re-

---

[1] *La convention du 15 septembre et l'encyclique du 8 décembre,* Paris 1868.

[2] This interesting point has been noted by Fr. M. Bevenot S.J., Thesis and Hypothesis, in *Theological Studies,* vol. xv (1954), n 3.

[3] Some people, he says, 'want to make unrestricted freedom of worship into a universal ideal, one that is absolute and obligatcry at all times, in every country . . . The Pope does not think such an ideal to be the best, He has for himself and for the Church another ideal, and you must never ask them to make practical necessities that are merely relative into absolute truths, to transform regrettable facts and unfortunate necessities which are tolerated, into dogmatic principles'.

proved them ourselves'. In fact, of course, as far as the application of the distinction went, Dupanloup's position was a novelty.
It was certainly new to France. That it was not entirely acceptable to Rome was hinted at in the Pope's suggestion to him
that he should as competently expound the Encyclical *Quanta
Cura* as he had rebutted the critics of the *Syllabus*. In point of
fact the thesis-hypothesis distinction, when it was mooted for
the first time, had got no support at all from Pius IX. This had
been in October 1863, when it was enunciated in an article in the
Roman journal *Civiltà Cattolica*, by its editor Fr. Curci. The
Civiltà was a Jesuit organ which had been founded by Pius IX
to give a reasoned exposition of the papal point of view. Fr.
Curci's article had applied the distinction—as did Dupanloup
later—to the Liberal ideal of separation. While rejecting it in
theory, he admitted that, in the concrete, separation could be
acceptable to the Church. But the writer's thought showed a
tendency at times to slip imperceptibly into applying the distinction to the Catholic ideal. This is so when he wrote that 'the
universal maxim, while remaining true in itself, can only be
applied in part and in a very imperfect way; at times it cannot
be applied at all'.[1] Indeed he was disposed to the idea that separation is a kind of half-truth, which, although it cannot be
accepted if regarded as the ideal, can be adopted in certain
circumstances with alacrity because of the element of truth that
is really in it. We are reminded immediately of Montalembert's
compromise with Liberalism, which accepted the hypothesis as
normal and desirable under modern conditions. Fr. Curci had
been impressed by Montalembert's liberal speeches at the Malines Congress of 1863. And the *Civiltà* article, while critical of
Montalembert in certain respects, was meant to provide a
formula that would span the conservative-liberal split in the
Catholic ranks. For this reason it was not at all acceptable to
the Pope and led to the dismissal of Fr. Curci from the *Civiltà*.

In other words, the thesis-hypothesis distinction was open to
equivocation, because of which its introduction was not welcomed by Pius IX. For the same reason it is probable that he

[1] Bevenot, *loc. cit.* p 442.

was not too happy about its use two years later by Dupanloup. For whatever may have been the latter's interpretation of it, it was employed by Montalembert for the furtherance of a Liberal Catholicism that was unacceptable. You have succeeded, he wrote to Dupanloup, in making Pius IX give his blessing to Jacob in the place of Esau. For Montalembert, whatever might be said for the thesis as the absolute ideal, in the modern world it is outmoded and unreal. Circumstances are such as to make its abandonment desirable everywhere; it is no longer the concrete ideal of the age. One cannot avoid the feeling that, by reason of its openness to this interpretation, the thesis-hypothesis distinction—even as advanced by Dupanloup—was suspect by Rome.

It is worth recalling that a different way of expounding the papal position was put forward by the Dean of the Faculty of Theology of Paris, Mgr. Maret. It constitutes a kind of third party approach. It is in the domain of the thesis rather than in any sense of the hypothesis that Mgr. Maret sought to bring a solution to the problem at once in conformity with Catholic doctrine and liberal society. The end to be achieved, he said, is the kingdom of God amongst men, towards the realisation of which the union of Church and State as it had been known is only one of a number of means. Personally he was disposed to favour a moral rather than a political union, a 'union resulting from the reign of faith in minds and hearts', a union that does not require 'the sacrifice of the principles on which rest the majority of modern constitutions'.[1] In this way Mgr. Maret hoped that the thesis could be verified in the majority of modern States.

While Pope Leo XIII did not himself employ the thesis-hypothesis terminology, he does seem to have accepted the distinction. In *Immortale Dei* he expresses himself as follows: 'No one has any legitimate ground for accusing the Church of being an enemy of either just tolerance or healthy and justifiable liberty. While the Church considers that it is not right to put the various forms of worship on the same footing as the true

[1] Cf Adrien Dansette, L'Église et la liberté dans l'histoire du XIXe siècle, in *L'Église et la liberté*, Paris 1952, pp 207-208.

religion, it does not follow that she condemns heads of States who, with a view to achieving good or preventing evil, in practice allow these various creeds each to have their own place in the State. It is indeed the custom of the Church to take the greatest care to ensure that no one shall be forced to embrace the Catholic faith against his will, for, as St. Augustine wisely observes, a man can believe only of his own free will'. The remarkable thing about this usage of the thesis-hypothesis distinction is that the Pope's criterion for applying it is not whether Catholics are in such a strong position in the State as to be able to oppress non-Catholics. On the contrary, while affirming that the ideal is religious unity, he explicitly allows that a system of pluralism may have to be adopted by a State so as to ensure freedom of faith and avoidance of coercion'.[1]

This brief historical survey serves to show the variety of interpretations to which the thesis-hypothesis distinction can be submitted. It is unfortunate that the one that has received most attention and publicity can scarcely be said to be the most satisfactory one. In fact there can be no doubt that it were better forgotten; it does not at all provide a faithful reflection of the Catholic position, which we have gone to pains to show does not entail an intolerant Church-State union. This was implied by Pope Pius XII in his address to the Italian Catholic Jurists (6 October, 1953) in which he said that 'repression of religious liberty does not exist as a general principle, i.e., as a thesis'. A German writer, Fr. Hartmann, says that this papal statement 'may well be taken as a rejection of the "thesis" of the Catholic State'.[2] To which suggestion our comment can only be 'It depends'. To us it is clear that rejection of religious oppression does not mean the rejection of the thesis of the Catholic State in the proper understanding of this. For Fr. Hartmann, as for many others, 'the idea of the Catholic State becomes a 'thesis', i.e., a binding principle, when the limits it imposes upon religious freedom and its efforts to suppress religious errors in public life are declared to be essential to the ideal

---

[1] Cf Albornoz, *op. cit.* pp 72-73.
[2] Hartmann, *op. cit.* p 213.

order'. As we understand it, the special position which we claim for the Church in the Catholic State has nothing to do with such-like establishment.

And yet we must admit with Cardinal Lercaro that 'the distinction we make today between the "thesis" and the "hypo-thesis" tends to leave the modern mind perplexed. In seeming to distinguish between the ideal of tolerance and the concrete historical situations in which she has found herself, the Church appears to have sanctioned a policy which is based on compro-mise'.[1] If the source of the misunderstanding is the thesis-hypothesis terminology, there is nothing to prevent our dropping it. Not the least of the merits of our glance into history has been to show that the terminology in question was never official. If anything it was far from being unequivocally approved by authority; its wide adoption has been due entirely to its em-ployment by writers. But whatever may be our terminology we must continue to work for an ideal—that society explicitly and visibly profess belief in the true God and render worship to Him in the way that He wills.[2] The Church can never give up the hope that all the nations of the earth will publicly recognise the sovereign dominion of Christ the King. To this end, said Pope Pius XII, 'the Church does not conceal the fact . . . that she regards unanimity of action between herself and the State as an ideal'.[3] She wishes too that, in so far as is possible, this harmony be stable; hence her interest in institutional relations and juridical guarantees. In so far as she may seem intransigent it is because she attaches practical importance to the social rights of evangelical truth. She is also, of course, realistic, and is ready to allow adaptations of this principle in the interests of what it is possible to achieve in the concrete. But this itself is only further proof of her struggle for the principle; it is the principle itself which demands such application on the grounds

---

[1] Cardinal Lercaro, Religious Tolerance in Catholic Tradition, in *The Irish Ecclesiastical Record*, Fifth Series, vol. XCIII, (1960).

[2] Cf A. de Bovis S.J., L'Église dans la societé temporelle, in *Nouvelle Revue Théologique*, vol. 79 (1957).

[3] Allocution of 20 February 1946.

that a partial good is better than none. The Church does not
share the view that anything which falls short of her ideal must
therefore be repudiated in all circumstances. On the contrary
she is ready to accept a wide variety of social forms in which the
ideal can be reflected to a greater or lesser degree. One must not
think, said Pope Pius XII, 'that the Church assumes a rigid and
permanent form at any given moment and ceases to develop.
On the contrary, the Church is always leaning attentively over
mankind, listening to the pulse of humanity'.[1]

[1] Address of 6 October 1953.

CHAPTER SEVEN

THE SCOPE OF RELIGIOUS TOLERATION

IN discussing the question of religious toleration it is necessary immediately to distinguish between what is called 'public' and 'private' tolerance. Private tolerance is practised by ordinary individuals in their everyday lives. It is something quite independent of one's ability or otherwise to take practical steps to curb the evil with which one is confronted. It has been well described as a quality of mind which enables a man to endure attitudes other than his own without undue vexation. Public tolerance is something quite different. It is primarily related to a constitutional and legal position under which evil is, at least to a large extent, allowed to exist and is not crushed out by the power of the State.[1]

It cannot be stressed too strongly that doctrinaire intolerance forms no part of Catholic teaching. The Church does insist that, in private life, the individual that is true to his faith will be characterised by what writers call 'doctrinal intolerance'. In many respects this is very much a misnomer. It stands for the attitude of mind of the man who is sincere about his beliefs and, as such, is not open to what contravenes them. He is poles apart from the so-called liberal who refuses to respect intellectually the demands of truth as truth. The latter's attitude is that of the sceptic, of him who listens to all views but is interested in none, or, what is the same thing, regards all as possibly true. Such tolerance is clearly impossible for the Catholic. The true

[1] See Vermeersch, *Tolerance*, Engl. trans., London 1913.

280

believer must stand for doctrinal intolerance, for an inward acceptance of his faith and an outward profession of its tenets to the exclusion of others. Indeed it was precisely this uncompromising attitude which marked off Christianity from the beginning. The religions of Greece and Rome were religions without dogma. External ritual conformity was all that they required; if he offered incense to the gods, a man could believe what he liked. It was its opposition to this outlook that brought persecution on early Christianity. The true Christian is and must be intolerant as far as his own adherance to the teaching of his Church is concerned. But seeing that this in no way touches the liberty of others to do likewise, calling it intolerance can sometimes mislead.

Tolerance is essentially a practical entity, having a bearing on one's relationship with others. It is concerned with the extent to which one can bear with the championing by others of what one certainly knows to be wrong. Tolerance is a Christian virtue. Not of course that one should tolerate everything; tolerance does not mean endurance without limits. It is true that the Christian is bound to all men in charity, that he must try to understand the misguided and the motives for their behaviour, and seek to dissuade them gently from their erroneous or evil courses. But there is a point beyond which he will cease to be mild. Christ loved all men as did no other. He was gentle and understanding as was no other. Yet at times he struck out fiercely against evil. The true Christian too will love all men always, will be gentle and understanding as far as possible, but will by no means tolerate everything. In other words, one can love one's fellowmen and still be justly intransigent in certain circumstances. Charity knows no limits but there are definite limits to tolerance.

The difficulty lies in determining exactly what these limits are, or in other words, in delineating the proper scope of tolerance. In religious matters it means establishing the ambit of due liberty. There are certain points which and must be made at the outset. Religious liberty—in the sense of liberty of conscience—is upheld by Catholic teaching, on a basis

of philosophical, scriptural and theological arguments.[1] These
are emphatic that the dignity of the human personality requires
belief to be a free and internal act. They maintain, in addition,
that the supernatural order respects this feature of the natural,
that Scripture shows that God addresses Himself to man as a
creature capable of free obedience, that further, as a son of God,
man's freedom takes on a new aspect, and that there is an intimate connection between grace and liberty in the sense that it
is Catholic teaching that grace completes what is free activity.
Stemming from this—logically and inevitably—is the conclusion
that faith is a free gift on the part of God and a free acceptance
on the part of the human recipient. All effort to employ human
coercion to elicit religious persuasion is as ineffective as it is
also unjust. This is the teaching, not merely of contemporary
theologians, but of the Fathers of the Church as far back as
Lactantius and Tertullian.[2] In virtue of it it can be said that
the defence of religious liberty is part and parcel of Catholic
teaching.

PUBLIC TOLERANCE

This liberty does not at all consist exclusively in an inner
freedom that does not extend to what is called external liberty.
Modern writers express this by saying that, as man is a social
animal, inner freedom is void of real meaning if it cannot be
externated within human society. Some of them like to see in
this the social aspect of the metaphysical link between the personality and its transcendental destiny.[3] In face of history, however, it is somewhat difficult to get acceptance of this idea of a
public tolerance, as well as a private, in the Church. In fact the
fundamental reason why some Catholics play down the traditional teaching on the obligation of the State to give special
recognition to the Church is because reference to this teaching

---

[1] All these arguments have been well summed up in Carillo de Albornoz, *Roman Catholicism and Religious Liberty*, Geneva 1959, ch 2.

[2] Cf Albornoz, *op. cit.* p 67.

[3] Cf Albornoz, *op. cit.* pp 37-39.

—which is so readily assumed to be out of tune with democratic values—can, in their opinion, only strengthen the impression, already deep-seated in many non-Catholics, that the Catholic Church is intolerant towards other religions. In thus moderating Catholic teaching they are both right and wrong. They are right in so far as the situation of the Church over most of the world today must be what Pope Pius XII called co-existence with error. But they are wrong, I believe, in their understanding of what the special recognition of the Church must necessarily entail.

To determine this, it is necessary immediately to distinguish between the order of theology and the order of civil law, between the ecclesiological and governmental domains. It is a matter of theological truth that the Catholic Church is the one true Church. In consequence, it can be said that, in God's eyes, no one is free to reject or ignore it. In themselves these truths are entirely supra-political; they pertain to a different domain from and cannot be touched by civil law. It was in forgetting this and in assuming the principle that one religion is as good as another that Liberal Democracy—especially in Europe—was guilty of its most grievous error. In doing so, it set the State up as a religious authority, capable of making what in reality is a theological decision. But, for the same reason, the order of civil law has no power to decide that the Catholic Church is the one true Church of Christ. It pertains to the very nature of the political order that it recognise that citizenship, as such, is compatible with multiple religious adhesions, and that religious affiliation in itself must be free and outside the jurisdiction of the State. In an important sense, therefore, religion is something which is entirely beyond the ambit of the State.

But here it is necessary to introduce a further distinction. The order of government—the 'State'—can have a number of senses, depending, more or less, on the context in which the term is used. In the first place, it can mean a commonwealth of persons, a collection of individual citizens in one community. In the second place, it can mean the constitutional form of such a commonwealth, an abstract system of social organisation. In the third place, it can mean the actual institutions of government that are erected under this constitution. Fourthly, it can mean the authorities—the rulers themselves—who staff the system. Now it is quite clear that, in the second and third of these senses, the political order is quite incapable of touching the theological in any formal way. That is, no constitution and no legal institutions can worship God; they are incapable of this by reason of the fact that they are not rational beings. On the other hand, in the sense of the collection of citizens or the collection of rulers, the State is undoubtedly capable of such worship. In these cases, however, the situation is really that each citizen, qua citizen, and each ruler, qua ruler, can render personal acts of worship to God. As far as the State in the sense of the constitutional and legal framework is concerned, no such theological attitude is possible, and it was this which I had in mind when, in the previous paragraph, I drew the distinction between the orders of theology and politics.

Yet when this has been said, it must still be remembered that the constitutional and legal framework of the State can have material relevance to the religious persuasions of both citizens and rulers. It is vital to understand how this can be. Though the contrary is frequently assumed, the act of establishing Catholicism as State religion was never intended either as a theological decision or as a religious act—a profession of faith on the part of the State in the one true Church. Fr. Courtney Murray himself will be the first to grant this.[1] The act of recognition of religion is always a legal act, setting up a juridical institution and, because of that, pertains to reason, not faith. It simply buttresses the public status of religion by obliging both rulers and citizens to respect it in the external forum.

There is room for variation as regards how this status is established. During the *ancien régime*, when it was widely introduced by Catholic States, it took a fixed pattern, involving a stipendary clergy, governmental veto over the appointment of bishops and State enforcement of certain Church decrees. It would be a mistake, however, to think that it must always and necessarily take this form. History has shown in fact that many

---

[1] Cf J. C. Murray, in *Theological Studies*, vol. XII (1951), pp 171-172.

aspects of this system were detrimental to the well-being of the Church. Indeed the present set-up in Czechoslovakia provides abundant proof that much of it can be adopted even by an anti-religious regime. The Czechoslovak Communist Law of Church Affairs of 14 October, 1949, makes provision for State payment of all clergy in the country, State approval of ministers of religion, the defraying by the State of their travelling and other expenses, the provision of social allowances and pensions for the clergy, State responsibility for the regular outlay of churches, supervision of their property by a State Office for Ecclesiastical Affairs and, finally and logically, punishment of the clergy by the State for any infringement of the law relating to Church matters.[1]

Such a system, even when used in a way that is beneficial to the Church, is not essentially entailed by Catholic teaching. In 1941, in their *Catholic Principles of Politics*,[2] the American writers Ryan and Boland declared the Catholic ideal for Church-State relations to consist in some kind of admission on the part of the State of the existence of God, the recognition of Catholicism as the religion of the State, the invitation of the blessing of the Church on its work and the ceremonial participation of the Church in important public functions. In addition, they thought that it meant that representatives of the State should attend the important religious events of the Church, that the State should sanction specified Church laws and that it should afford special protection to the rights of the Church and of Churchmen against unjust attack. This is clearly a much less extensive form of recognition than that which was in vogue in the 'Confessional State' of post-Reformation Europe. It shows immediately how historically circumscribed is Fr. Murray's idea of 'State religion' when he writes that this concept as it has appeared in the nation States of post-Reformation Europe, 'asserts that the State as such makes public profession of Catholicism as its one and only religion; and by consequence it asserts that no citizens may make public profession of any other reli-

---

[1] Cf Ehler and Morrall, *Church and State through the Centuries*, London 1954, pp 615-617.

[2] Ryan and Boland, *Catholic Principles of Politics*.

gion. In further consequence, the coercive power of the State
is brought to bear to inhibit the public profession or propaganda
of other religions'.[1] Seeing that he believes that the juridical
recognition of religion by the State inevitably implies these assertions, it is understandable that Fr. Murray should think that
emphasis on it at the present day is responsible for a situation
in which 'in the popular mind the Church, which is the home of
freedom and the last bulwark of the rights of man, has become
identified, not with freedom but with governmental coercion.'[2]

How wrong he is in this belief becomes evident on examining
Cardinal Ottaviani's exposition of the Catholic position. About
this the Cardinal stated emphatically: 'If there is any certain
and indisputable truth to be found among the general principles
of Public Ecclesiastical Law, it is the truth that the rulers in a
State composed almost entirely of Catholics, have the duty to
influence the legislation of the State in a Catholic sense. Three
immediate implications follow from this duty:

(1) The *social*, and not merely the *private* profession of the
religion of the people;

(2) The Christian inspiration of legislation;

(3) The defence of the religious patrimony of the people
against every assault that seeks to deprive them of the treasure
of their faith and of their religious peace'.[3]

FREEDOM OF BELIEF AND OF WORSHIP

Let us examine these requirements in some detail. Of the
first Cardinal Ottaviani himself says simply that States cannot,
without serious moral offence, conduct themselves as if God
were non-existent. The question is how the requirement can be
met. It is certain that it is not met merely by the State allowing

[1] J. C. Murray, in *Theological Studies*, vol. x (1949), p 424.

[2] J. C. Murray, in *American Ecclesiastical Review*, vol. CXXIV (1951),
n 5.

[3] Cf. Church and State: Some Recent Problems in this Light of
the Teaching of Pope Pius XII, *American Ecclesiastical Review*, vol.
CXXVIII (1953).

Catholic citizens to perform acts of religion in groups as well as individually. The State itself must, in some way, profess the religion of the people. In discussing this duty writers are too ready to assume that it is fulfilled primarily by incorporating into a written constitution a statement to the effect that the Catholic Church is accorded a special position in the State. The reason for this is that the majority of them identify this special position with one form or another of the union of Church and State which was established by written constitutions in 19th century regimes. It is clear, however, that a constitution need not necessarily be a written one. In the case of an unwritten constitution how can the special position be guaranteed? The fact is that, whether written or unwritten, the function of a constitution is to guard the principles which regulate the formulation of laws and to preserve the heritage of the people from which it springs. In a Catholic State the important thing is that the authorities accept Catholic teaching as an inspiring criterion of its laws and institutions. It is certainly more important that the State in fact should formulate its prescriptions in accordance with Catholic doctrine than that it should pay lip service to a written formula and ignore it in practice. For it is well known that the letter of a constitution can be disregarded by people who are not animated by its spirit. Needless to say, the rights of the Church should be guaranteed rather than that respect for them be left entirely to chance. The point is that an unwritten constitution can do this just as effectively as can a written one. Quite a few jurists even consider it better, as being less rigid and more adaptable to the ever-varying needs of society.[1]

The essential thing is that the constitution—whether written or unwritten—of a Catholic State should effectively confer a special position on the Church. How it can do this is the further question. We have already seen that neither a constitution nor any legal instrument is able, as such, to perform an act of faith or worship in the strict sense. How then can our

[1] See T. I. Jimenez et Urresti, *Estado e Iglesia*, Rome 1958, p 248 *seq.*

STUDIES IN POLITICAL MORALITY

first requirement be fulfilled? It can be done, it seems to me, by the observance of such things as having a special Mass on the opening of Parliament and by having religious ceremonies on other important State occasions. I do not think that the requirement is necessarily met by the provision of a chaplain's service to the armed forces, the exemption of the Church (Church buildings, convents, cemeteries) from taxation, or even the taking of an oath by high officials before assuming office. Each of these could be subjected to an interpretation that would exclude their being regarded as manifestations of the social profession of the religion of the people. Many of them can be found in States—e.g., the Phillipines—which simply cannot be regarded as assigning special recognition to the Church. Indeed the Phillipines provides a good example of a State whose official life is permeated with the philosophy of religious indifferentism. On one occasion President Quezon, himself a practising Catholic, made explicit assertion of this: 'As an individual, I worship my God in accordance with my own religious belief. But as the head of the State I can have no more to do with the Catholic Church than I can with the Protestant denominations, the Aglipayans, the Mohammedans or any other religious organisations or sects in the Philippines'.[1]

When the head of State, *in this capacity*, assists at Mass, the whole situation assumes a different resonance. The special position of the Church in the State is being catered for. It should be carefully noted, however, that in such a State, there is nothing to prevent a non-Catholic from being nominated even to the supreme post in the land. Nor is there anything to prevent the State, as such, being represented, when necessary, at non-Catholic religious functions. While remaining free in his own beliefs, a non-Catholic, even in the highest office, would be bound to act in accordance with the constitution.[2] It should be added that the recognition of the Church which is demanded

[1] Quoted in A. A. Olalia, *A Comparative Study of the Christian Constitution of States and the Constitution of the Philippine Commonwealth*, Washington 1944, p 78.

[2] Cf Jimenez et Urresti, *op. cit.* p 250.

in the Catholic State is verified by respect not just for one but for three requirements.

It is debatable whether a declaration that the Catholic religion is the official religion of the State should be enshrined in an article of a written constitution where this exists. As we have already seen, one can argue that the State, when giving utterance to its basic ideology, should not omit to state where it stands as regards religion. However, in an article which appeared some years ago,[1] Dr. Alfred O'Rahilly declared that in a State in which all the material rights of the Church are otherwise respected by the constitution, nothing more is required in the way of securing a specifically Catholic constitution, 'unless certain people wish to introduce some pious rhetoric into that document'.[2] To seek to do this, he thinks, would merely be to campaign for a 'futile embellishment' of the constitution.

In his pamphlet *The Church, the State and the Constitution*,[3] Mr. Donal Barrington expresses somewhat similar views. The Church, he argues, is concerned with the supernatural life of man, the State with his temporal welfare. The Church occupies her position in society in virtue of her own inherent rights and privileges, which the State simply cannot touch. The State does not and cannot 'place' the Church in this position; it does not and cannot 'confer' her privileges on her. Indeed 'to attempt to do so would be the height of insolence'. He thus goes further than saying that an article of a constitution that would recognise the true Church as such is nothing more than empty verbiage. It is at best an error, at most an arrogant claim. I cannot but wonder, however, whether this misses the point at issue. Surely a constitution could legitimately introduce an article which, while reflecting—though not constituting—the dogmatic position, would recognise Catholicism as the official religion of a State the vast majority of whose citizens were Catholic? Surely too, to do this would be more than word-spinning? Indeed, in

[1] A. O'Rahilly, in *The Standard*, 9 July 1954.

[2] *Ibid.*

[3] D. Barrington, *The Church, the State and the Constitution*, Dublin 1959.

an important respect, it seems necessary in order to avoid anomaly. For if, in a Catholic State, the duty of social profession of
the religion of the people is to be carried out as indicated
earlier, ought not the statesmen who observe it have the official
backing of a constitutional provision which would formally
make them representatives of the State when so doing?

It should be realised that, even if such formal recognition
were entailed by our first requirement, it would in no way interfere with the belief and worship of non-Catholics. There is no
denying that, in previous ages, religious establishment was used
as a political instrument to enforce religious homogeneity in the
State. This was so, in its own way, in the pagan Roman Empire,
when freedom of conscience was recognised only to the extent
that the individual might follow his own persuasion provided
he rendered at least external cult to the gods of Rome. It was
a principle too of the early German Protestant principalities
and also, as we know so well, of England under Elizabeth and
Cromwell. Indeed it was the Reformation that first introduced
into Christian Europe the idea that religious error—qua religious—should be forcibly suppressed, a programme which the
Reformers adopted even in areas in which they were but a
powerful minority. Catholicism has never held that conscience
can be forced, or that belief and worship should be anything but
free as long as they are in good faith. The many examples of
intolerance with which Catholic regimes have provided us were
due either to the fact—which unfortunately was only too common—that Catholic rulers found it hard to accept the good faith
of apostates, or to the fact that apostasy constituted a pragmatic danger to the State. It is true that there have been individual theorists who have preached religious intolerance as a
principle, but—as we shall see later—they did not express the
mind of the Church. At any rate, there can be no doubt that
the fulfilling of the first requirement laid down by Cardinal
Ottaviani would not conflict with the rights of non-Catholics
to practise their own religion.

Turning now to the second requirement, Cardinal Ottaviani
says in explanation of it that what it is opposed to is moral and
religious indifference on the part of the civil law. The State,

he says, and here he quotes Pope Pius XII, must draw inspiration from sound moral and religious principles. Of course there can be no question of its being formally grounded on revelation. The framing of legislation must always be the work of human reason. Yet just as it is possible to construct a general philosophy that is in harmony with religious truth, so also it is possible, while remaining true to the rational method of jurisprudence, to construct a body of civil law that is in harmony with Catholic attitudes. For the most part this is achieved by respecting natural law in legislation that is hammered out by the State through the right use of reason and entirely independently of authoritative Church direction. Where inspiration can be derived from Church teaching is in cases where the natural law is obscure and concerning which the Church, as its guardian, has authoritatively interpreted it. In such cases, the law of a State which is seeking to respect our second requirement, will be based, not precisely on Church teaching, as such, but on the natural law as presented by the Church, with her long experience and many students in the field of its elucidation. In following this course, the civil law remains faithful to its own canons. It is true that objection may be raised by a non-Catholic minority that has adopted a different view of the content of the natural law on the issue involved. But on what legitimate grounds, may we ask? Remember that there is question here of a State in which the vast majority of the people are Catholic and question, therefore, of legislation that must be geared to serve the interests at least of the majority. In such circumstances, if the Catholic interpretation of natural law is not to be followed when there is a difference of opinion, which interpretation has the right to this? Practical politics alone points to the answer.

If, as a result of this, certain limits are placed on the freedom of action of non-Catholics, it is hard to see how they can have any legitimate grievance. They themselves will admit that some limits to human freedom are necessary in every political community, which limits increase in number, up to a point, with the degree of civilisation which the community attains. It is generally admitted, for example, that public morality demands limits to free speech; there is no right to indiscriminate scandal-mongering. There is international unanimity too, amongst civilised peoples, that there must be certain limits to freedom of religion. Forms of worship that would entail, say, ritual prostitution, human sacrifice or cannibalism, are rightly proscribed.[1]

[1] In India, in 1802, Lord Wellesley prohibited under severe penalties the sacrifice of children by drowning, which took place annually at a great religious festival. It was found necessary to repeat such legislation as recently as 1870. Similarly the human sacrifices once performed before the images of Kali were abolished, while in 1829 the suttee was suppressed, whereby Hindu widows were immolated on the funeral piles of their husbands. Cf Lecky, *Democracy and Liberty*, London 1896, vol. I, p 442.

In 1882 the United States began a long struggle for the ending of polygamy, when the Edmunds Law provided that it should be punishable with a fine of 500 dollars and a term of imprisonment of up to five years. Lecky describes this as 'a striking illustration of the extreme energy which democratic communities can throw into repressive legislation'—*op. cit.* p 456. The matter was definitively settled by the Supreme Court in 1878 by its decision in the Mormon cases. To the Mormon plea that a plurality of wives was a religious duty, the Court replied that this was long odious to Western civilisation and therefore no proper part of religion in the constitutional sense that is guaranteed by the Bill of Rights. Cf Wm. O. Douglas, *An Almanac of Liberty*, London 1954, p 140.

The same thing is illustrated by blasphemy laws. In the United States there were convictions for blasphemy in 1811, 1822, 1834 and 1921. They were based on the fact that the blasphemies either overlapped with obscenity or attacked the interests of the majority of the people. Cf Douglas, *op. cit.* p 175. An interesting example of the latter eventuality is to be found in the judge's summing up in the case of an English trial for blasphemy in 1908. The judge observed that, while 'a man was free to think, to say, and to teach that which he pleased about religious matters', if he made 'a coarse and scurrilous attack on doctrines which the majority of the people held to be true, in a public place, where passers-by might have their ears offended and where young people might come, he would render himself amenable to the law of blasphemous libel'. In a similar case of 1911 another Justice commented as follows: 'If the decencies of controversy were observed, even the fundamentals of religion might be attacked without the writer being

Even in secular matters, it has been found necessary to curtail the citizens' freedom, and this even in the most democratic States. At the present day, in face of Communist penetration, countries like the U.S.A. have been forced, in the interests of self-defence, to adopt such measures. Unless they are prepared to stand and watch their democratic institutions being corroded from within, by infection from the rival ideology of Communism, they have to take steps to preserve the ideological minimum which is necessary to make possible the survival of democracy. And they seek to do this by a campaign, not only against the overt *behaviour* of Communists, but even by attempting to weed out *allegiance* to Communism, at least on the part of the higher State officials. Hence the probing into Communist infiltration into the civil service and the trade unions. Hence too the many safeguards that are being taken to maintain secrecy in matters of defence, with the multiple and harrassing regulations that this involves for the press, broadcasting, photography and even travel.[1]

The action of the State which sees to it that its legislation satisfies Cardinal Ottaviani's second requirement, is doing nothing more nor less in the domain of morals than democratic States have found necessary in a variety of domains. If the freedom of some people is curtailed by reason of this, it is only because the interests of the majority make it necessary. As a consequence, it is hard to see how the criticism can be substantiated that it is undemocratic procedure for a State, the majority of whose citizens are Catholic, to give legal sanction to what is called the indirect power of the Church or to recognise the provisions of Canon Law in so far as it may.[2] The majority

---

guilty of blasphemy. A man was free to speak as he pleased on religious matters, but not as to morals; but when they came to consider whether he had exceeded the limits of fair controversy they must not neglect to consider the place where he spoke and the persons to whom he spoke. A man was not free in any public place to use common ridicule on subjects which were sacred'. Cf Hypatia Bradlaugh Bonner, *Penalties upon Opinion*, London 1934, pp 119 and 122.

[1] Cf J. R. Wiggins, *Freedom or Secrecy?* New York 1956, *passim*.
[2] Cf L. Bender, *Chiesa e Stato*, Rome 1945, p 64.

of textbooks of Public Law assume that the implementation of
our second requirement must mean that the State, either by
its constitution or through concordat, actually bind itself in
some way to respect the directives of the Church relating to
matters that indirectly pertain to the sphere of religion or
morals. And it is quite true that Catholic States in the past
did commonly follow some such arrangement.

The important thing is that the directives of the Church be
respected by legislation; how this is acomplished is a matter
of secondary importance from the point of view of the Church.
M. Magnin has remarked that 'in its interventions the Church
never intends to get entangled in concrete details of political
tactics or in legislative refinements, which can vary in accordance with the juridical institutions of diverse countries'[1]. All
the Church insists on is what is called the due subordination of
the State.[2] Its position is summed up under four heads: the
supremacy and independence of each power in its own domain;
the need for concord and mutual help between them; the right of
the Church to prevail in case of juridical conflict; and actual
respect for the indirect power of the Church.[3] Due subordination
does not therefore mean that the Church seeks to subject the
State to the dominion of its own direct power. It is a long time
since any Churchman laid claim to temporal as well to spiritual
power on the grounds that both belonged by right to the Church
in virtue of its very nature. The days of Innocent III and Boniface VIII are long past.

Since the time of Bellarmine the claim of the Church in the
temporal domain has been regularly expressed in terms of the
indirect effects of the spiritual power. This is the accepted ap-
roach of the textbooks to the subject. It has lately come in for
a serious battering, not in the least from the pen of Fr. John
Courtney Murray. The indirect power, he maintains, is really a

---

[1] E. Magnin, *Libertés et devoirs politiques des catholiques*, Paris 1932.
Cited in N. Jung, *Le droit public de l'église*, Paris 1948, p 126.

[2] Cf L. Sotillo, *Compendium Iuris Publici Ecclesiastici*, Santander
1958, p 252.

[3] Cf A. Ottaviani, *Institutiones Iuris Publici Ecclesiastici*, vol. II,
3rd ed., Rome 1948, p 106.

concealed claim to temporal power in that its direct and immediate consequences are temporal. They are temporal things that are willed directly as means to spiritual ends; the spiritual is reached in and through the temporal. And 'temporal effects', he says, 'remain temporal; they do not become spiritual by being referred to a spiritual end'.[1] He charges the Bellarminians with failing to get away completely from the medieval structure of society in which two powers functioned in harmony in 'one society'. At best theirs was a transitional theory from the Church-State of the Middle Ages to the Church and State dualism of today.[2] In short, Fr. Murray contends that an indirect power means a claim to jurisdiction by the Church over the State and is inextricably bound up with the system of union of Church and State to which he is so utterly and rightly opposed.[3]

Defenders of the theory of the indirect power reject this charge, as resting entirely on a misconception of what they

---

[1] J. C. Murray, Governmental Repression of Heresy, in *Proceedings of the Third Annual Meeting of the Catholic Theological Society of America*, Chicago 1948, p 45. De Lubac calls the Bellarminian theory 'a bastard compromise, and an untenable one, between the theory of direct power and the theory of directive power'—*Le pouvoir de l'église en matière temporelle*, in *Revue des Sciences Religieuses*, vol. XII (1932), p 335.

[2] Bellarmine's theory, he says, 'was too much fashioned on a set of facts that had ceased to be facts, and hence had lost theological validity. More concretely, his particular theory is not so much a theory of the two powers or of Church and State, as a theory of the two powers within the 'one society' that medieval Christendom knew. On the other hand, his theory was buttressed by a firm political philosophy of the political power as natural in its origin, end, and functions. And to this extent his theory looked forward into the age in which the State, as we know it, was coming of age. This is why I call this theory transitional'—*loc. cit.* pp 43-44.

[3] His difficulty is with the manner in which it achieves harmony between Church and State, 'though the agency of a jurisdiction of the Church over the State itself. In other words, to the concept "religion of the State", there has been related a particular concept of the so-called indirect power that is Bellarminian in its connotations'—Murray in *Theological Studies*, vol. X (1949), n 3, p 423.

stand for. They admit that the power is a true jurisdiction, whether legislative, judicial or coercive. But they insist that it is really a spiritual power. Its purpose is to subserve the spiritual mission of the Church by consulting the spiritual welfare of men. It affects temporal things only accidentally, in so far as they have some relation to religion and therefore the salvation of souls.[1] However sincere this defence, it would seem that the theory of indirect power could at least be easily abused even in the interpretation of its theoretical meaning. The point at issue is how the sovereignty of the State can be preserved while demanding its due subordination to the Church? The concession of juridical superiority to the Church in any matter in virtue of its unilateral prerogatives is something that cannot be accepted by the modern sovereign State. Deadlock has been avoided through the instrumentality of concordats which bilaterally agree to certain arrangements in matters of mutual interest. But the claim of the Church, with which we are dealing here, can urge in relation to many matters that were not covered or even envisaged by concordat. When this occurs are we to hold that the sovereignty of the State must yield before that of the Church? There is not much point in saying that the State is free and sovereign within its proper order if the Church claims the right to define the limits of her own order, in such wise as to define indirectly those of the State. Should the State ignore this, can the Church infringe its sovereignty by declaring its laws invalid and freeing its citizens from obedience? There can be no doubt that at times the theory of the indirect power has been formulated in unsatisfactory ways such as this.

The better formulation would seem to be one in terms of two absolutely distinct sovereignties that are exercised over one and the same subject. Or, more accurately, sovereignties that are exercised on two formally different subjects that are ani-

---

[1] Cf Ottaviani, *op. cit.* n 305; also Hergenrother, *Kirche und Staat*, p 209: 'The indirect power of the Church in matters temporal in general, and in relation to the dethroning of princes in particular, is not a temporal but a spiritual power. It is exerted in matters temporal only in so far as they intrench upon religion, and in this way cease to be purely temporal'.

mated by one and the same physical person. That of the Church bears on the personality possessed in virtue of Baptism, that of the State on the personality possessed through citizenship. In case of conflict a man must prefer the interests which relate to the attainment of his spiritual welfare and which pertain to his canonical rather than to his civil personality.[1] There is no question of Church law having an immediate repercussion on the juridical validity of civil law. Rather it operates through the person over which it has competence. The Church does not touch, nor can it touch, the personality of man precisely as a civil subject. It has no power whatever in this domain. The formulation of the Church's power which is here advanced does not at all imply even an indirect power in temporal matters of a kind that could abrogate the juridical character of civil law. It presumes the principle that no force that is extraneous to the sovereign order of the State can limit or weaken that order in any respect. At the same time it preserves whatever of value there is in the theory of the indirect power, particularly the fact that it implies the use of genuine power or jurisdiction. It is not therefore to be confused with the theory of what is called 'directive power', which would regard the directives of the Church relating to temporal matters as merely moral counsels. This theory is unacceptable in that it does not impose obedience to these directives; their only force is to create a duty in prudence.[2] Because of this the theory is rejected by the majority of authors. Real power of jurisdiction, says Cappello, entails necessarily the duty of obedience,[3] and he refuses to allow that directives on temporal affairs are not binding. Our theory looks upon them as real commands that are addressed by the Church to the canonical personality. It is the sovereignty of the Church that prevails when they are followed, but it prevails directly as sovereignty over its own subject which in this case dominates the civil personality.

Something very like this was put forward by John of Paris

---

[1] See P. Giuseppe di Mattia, *Il concetto guiridico di sovranita nel diritto ecclesiastico e civile*, Rome 1959, p 47 *seq.*

[2] Cf N. Jung, *op. cit.* p 124 *seq.*

[3] *Op. cit.* p 310.

in the latter part of the 13th century. Maintaining the exclusively spiritual character of the Church's sovereignty, he also
insisted on the illegitimacy of an illation from the order of
dignity to that of causality on the grounds that the temporal
should be instrumental to the spiritual. The intervention of the
Church in the temporal was interpreted by John as a purely
spiritual action which is exercised over the conscience of Catholics. In this way it can guide and admonish civil rulers and, if
they are incorrigible, can clarify the conscience of the people
to the extent of declaring that they are no longer bound to
obey. The effects of this are certainly temporal effects but
it is equally certain that they are produced indirectly or, as
John puts it, *per accidens*, through the exercise of a purely spiritual power in its own order. They flow from a genuine jurisdiction that is exercised *in* the temporal without, however, being
exercised *over* the temporal in any way.

Fr. Courtney Murray has adopted John of Paris's theory and
has incorporated it into his own approach to Church-State
relations.[1] But acceptance of it does not by any means involve
one in accepting also a general position such as Fr. Murray's.
Fr. Francis Connell, who is at serious difference with Fr.
Murray's central ideas, has given evidence of being open to
accept this view of the nature of the Church's intervention in
the sphere of the temporal. What is important, he says, is that
the State, in fact, recognise the interests of the Church when
they are at stake. 'Whether this obligation of the State should
be called "direct" or "indirect" is a matter of little consequence
as long as the idea itself is properly understood'.[2] The theory
which we have been defending has the advantage of being in

---

[1] See Murray, John of Paris and the Indirect Power, in *Theological
Studies*, vol. x (1949), n 3; also Murray, *Government Repression of Heresy*,
loc. cit. pp 52-62. In the latter article Fr. Murray writes: 'What the
Church aims to do is to animate from within these rational structures
and processes (i.e. of the State) with her own spiritual energies in order
that they may be rational in act and achievement as in design. She does
not aim to alter the finality of the State, but to enable the State to
achieve its own finality as determined by its nature'—pp 65-66.

[2] Cf *American Ecclesiastical Review*, vol cxxv (1951), pp 10-11.

harmony with the importance which the Church places on the lay apostolate and, in particular, on what is called Temporal Action of Christian Inspiration.[1] It satisfies both the preoccupations of contemporary Catholicism and the jurisdictional interests of traditional Church-State teaching.[2]

There is no difficulty about accepting this while continuing to resist the essential elements in Fr. Murray's approach to Church-State relations. In fact these are such as to create the suspicion that Fr. Murray finds it difficult to effect an entirely satisfactory welding of the theory to them. In particular, it is hard to see how he preserves intact the hierarchical and institutional aspect of Church authority. This emerges, for example, when he criticises Fr. Connell for being a 'man of the right', who 'instinctively conceives the problem of Church and State in terms of the Church understood solely as the spiritual power, not as the *communitas fidelium*, the Christian people'.[3] He would prefer to substitute a free and dynamic action of the individual Christian for an ordination of things by way of the guidance of authority. Of course he is entirely right in stressing the fact that Christian Temporal Action is something spontaneous on the part of Catholic laymen. So much so indeed that it is often stated that they alone are responsible for it. It is certainly not something which stems from the authoritative direction of the Church to the extent that this decides on its nature in the concrete. As far as the practical organisation of secular life is concerned, the layman has an independent field of action. All this is true and needs emphasis. But it is also true that the principles on which rests the Christian conception of life are the special province of the Church as teacher. Not only this—the Church has the authority to forbid any particular application of them which it considers

[1] Cf Y. M. J. Congar, Les conditions théologiques d'un pluralisme, in *Tolérance et communauté humaine*, Paris 1952, also Yves de Montcheuil, *For Men of Action*, London, 1957 and J. Newman, *What is Catholic Action?* Dublin 1958, pp 130 seq.

[2] The theory has been advanced in a doctrinal dissertation completed at the Lateran University by a stout defender of the central points of the traditional approach—Mattia, *op. cit.*

[3] Murray, in *Theological Studies*, vol. XIII (1952), p 47, n 15.

to be wrongly conceived. And while its authority may bear on the conscience of the individual, it is nonetheless an aspect of the spiritual power of the institutional Church.[1]

From the point of view of the end result it does not seem to matter a great deal whether or not this power of the Church is constitutionally guaranteed. In the context of modern democracy it is better that it should not. One can wholeheartedly agree with Fr. Murray when he says that this power should be exercised in a manner consistent with historical circumstances, that it is out of tune with the contemporary mind for the Church to try to exercise it through constitutional recognition and backing, and that she should rather address herself to the consciences of the citizens who, by their collective action, can see to it that the government follows a course that is unobjectionable.[2] As I have said, given a Catholic people that is true to the Church, the result should be the same no matter what system is followed. But let us be quite definite that a legal guarantee of respect for the directives of the Church is not in conflict with any fundamental principle of democracy in the

---

[1] It might be noted also that Fr. Murray's views tend to regard the State, not as *societas perfecta* or temporal power, as such, but as 'a rational force employed by the body politic in the service of itself as a body'. It is simply 'a set of institutions combined into a complex agency of social control and public service'. Because of this it is easy to understand why he should interpret the John of Paris theory as meaning that 'in these perspectives the action of the Church would be rather on the conscience of the community than on the actual bearers of governmental authority'—*Theol. Studies*, vol. x p 424. Fr. Murray's concept of the State has been criticised by implication by Mgr. George Shea's article, Catholic Orientations on Church and State, in *The American Ecclesiastical Review*, vol. cxxv (1951), pp 405-416. The fact is that the 'action of the Church' is both on the conscience of the community in general and on that of the government authorities, as authorities, in particular. These, as the agents of the temporal power, are especially open to direction by the spiritual power in matters which touch on the secular domain which they control.

[2] Cf A Church-State Anthology, Victor R. Yanitelli, in *Thought*, Spring 1952, p 6.

case of a State in which the vast majority is Catholic. It must be remembered that on Catholic theory itself it should be discontinued if circumstances arise in which the majority no longer want it.

FREEDOM OF PROPAGANDA

We come now to the third and last requirement, namely, that the State should protect the religion of the people against assault. This implies that the Catholic State will place some limitation to the propaganda of non-Catholic interests. In doing so it is merely protecting the majority of its citizens in a matter which they hold sacred and of the highest importance. To a certain extent, such action by the State causes no difficulty. There can be no genuine objection to the limitation of propaganda which—even on human evidence—is false, but which uses insidious methods to ensnare the unwary. The modern panoply of propaganda methods, as used by many contemporary 'isms' to play covertly on the irrational in man through emotional suggestibility, is something against which the citizens have a right to be protected, in every domain, that of religion included. This is a duty which—though hitherto neglected, despite the vogue of unscruplous advertising—will undoubtedly come to the notice of statesmen in the future, due to the entry on the scene of the 'hidden persuaders'.[1]

Difficulty arises only when there is question of 'straight' propaganda—in our case in the interests of non-Catholic beliefs. As regards this, at first sight, the Catholic position would seem to be one of intolerance. 'Reason revolts', says Cardinal Ottaviani, 'at the thought that, out of deference to the demands of a small minority, the rights, the faith, and the conscience of the quasi-totality of the people should be spurned, and that this people should be betrayed, by allowing the enemies of its faith to introduce division among its members, with all the consequences of religious strife'.[2] And Pope Pius XI once declared

[1] Cf Vance Packard, *The Hidden Persuaders*, New York 1957.
[2] *Loc. cit.*

in face of Fascism that it should be 'clearly and loyally understood that the Catholic religion, and it alone, according to the
Statute and the Treaties (i.e., the Lateran Treaty and Concordat with Mussolini's Italy), is the religion of the State, with
the logical and juridical consequence of such a situation, especially with reference to propaganda'.[1] He added that, as a result,
full liberty of propaganda, which can easily trick unenlightened
minds, is inadmissible.

Are we here faced with an indefensible requirement, one
that is unacceptable to democracy and that must be classed as
intolerant? Before rushing to conclusions we should pause to
think. Propaganda, as Martin Buber would say, is concerned,
not with the 'I' alone but with the 'I and Thou'. What is called
the right to propaganda is not just a right whereby an individual
may express his views; it is directed at getting other people to
adopt them. In considering it, therefore, the interests of two
sides have to be safeguarded, the right of the individual to the
free expression of his views and beliefs, and that of his hearer
to the protection from assault of what he holds sacred. But then,
when the matter has been thus reduced, we are left without any
special right to propaganda that is distinct from the ordinary·
right to free expression. Nor, in the many charters of human
rights to which our times have given birth, can I find any unqualified 'propaganda right' listed. Not even the most extreme
defenders of liberty will claim that such exists. The classic plea
in modern times for unfettered liberty of expression was that
of J. B. Bury, which caused a stir in 1912.[2] But Bury does not
claim that untrammelled propaganda is a 'human right'. His
defence of it is based—proximately at least—on non-moral
grounds. Its justification, he says, 'rests on no abstract basis,
on no principle independent of society itself, but entirely on
considerations of utility'.[3] Taking up Mill's earlier treatment
of the question, in his work *On Liberty*, Bury restates the

[1] Letter of 30 May 1929 to Cardinal Gasparri, in *Osservatore Romano*,
3 June 1929.

[2] J. B. Bury, *A History of Freedom of Thought*, New edition, London 1952.

[3] Bury, *op. cit.* p 187.

argument that freedom of propaganda is grounded on the permanent interests of man as a progressive being, who needs to have the kind of certainty about received opinions that can only be secured by the fact that they have been fully canvassed and have not been shaken. We may be permitted to reproduce Bury's argument in full:

'The progress of civilisation, if it is partly conditioned by circumstances beyond man's control, depends more, and in an increasing measure, on things which are within his own power. Prominent among these are the advancement of knowledge and the deliberate adaptation of his habits and institutions to new conditions. To advance knowledge and to correct errors, unrestricted freedom of discussion is required. History shows that knowledge grew when speculation was perfectly free in Greece, and that in modern times, since restrictions in inquiry have been entirely removed, it has advanced with a velocity which would have seemed diabolical to the slaves of the medieval Church. Then, it is obvious that in order to readjust social customs, institutions, and methods to new needs and circumstances, there must be unlimited freedom of canvassing and criticizing them, of expressing the most unpopular opinions, no matter how offensive to prevailing sentiment they may be. If the history of civilisation has any lesson to teach it is this: there is one supreme condition of mental and moral progress which it is completely within the power of man himself to secure, and that is perfect liberty of thought and discussion. The establishment of this liberty may be considered the most valuable achievement of modern civilisation, and as a condition of social progress it should be deemed fundamental. The considerations of permanent utility on which it rests must outweigh any calculations of present advantage which from time to time might be thought to demand its violation'.[1]

Bury goes on to attempt to link this with moral values. 'Once the principle of liberty of thought is accepted as a supreme condition of social progress, it passes from the sphere of ordinary expediency into the sphere of higher expediency which we call justice. In other words it becomes a right on which every man

[1] Bury, *op. cit.* pp 191-192.

should be able to count. The fact that this right is ultimately based on utility does not justify a government in curtailing it, on the ground of utility, in particular cases'.[1] At the very best, all that this proves is that society has a right to progress through the free expression of views. If this is the case, it follows that society has also the right to curtail such expression, in so far as society believes that what it would really cause is regression. Instances of this may be exceptional, but the conclusion itself is inescapable. And this is just what contemporary democracy has done in curtailing the expression of Communist ideology. So much so that H. J. Blackham, in an Epilogue to the 1952 edition of Bury, is compelled to admit that 'social progress is no longer possible by *laissez faire;* it is a difficult possibility, which depends on our rational control'.[2] And although Blackham, I am sure, would not subscribe to this, the curtailment of non-Catholic propaganda by a Catholic State is but an eminent example of such rational control. It is demanded by good politics in the interests of peace and the tranquillity of the majority of the citizens. That most broadminded prelate, Bishop Charrière of Lausanne, Geneva and Friburg, has imagined what would otherwise result. 'Let us suppose, for example, that at the door of the church in one of our most completely Catholic villages, some sectarian group were to distribute coarse tracts attacking the divinity of Christ, the Eucharist, the Blessed Virgin or the Church. How can one guarantee that this could take place without provoking violent reaction? The natural response of people who are insulted in what they hold to be most sacred must be reckoned with. Religious liberty gives no one the right to indulge in any kind of provocation whatsoever'.[3]

A word is necessary here on the Universal Declaration of Human Rights adopted by the General Assembly of the United Nations in 1948. Article 19 declared that 'Everyone has the right to freedom of opinion and expression; this right includes freedom to hold opinions without interference and to seek, receive and impart information and ideas through any media and re-

---

[1] Bury, *op. cit.* p 195.
[2] *Op. cit.*
[3] Cf *The Catholic Mind*, July-August 1958.

gardless of frontiers'. What is here called the right to receive and impart information is the same thing as a right to propaganda. The background to its adoption by the United Nations is interesting.[1] In the debates concerning it two opposed tendencies were evident. The one insisted on the necessity for curtailing freedom of expression and of propaganda; the other was opposed to any such limitation in time of peace. The former was championed by the Eastern bloc, led by the Soviet Union, the latter by the Western representatives, in the persons particularly of the United States and British delegates. The attitude of the West, which prevailed, was coloured by the fact that what the Eastern bloc was defending was really a conception which conferred a monopoly of propaganda on the State. The West wished to curb the vicious use to which this has been put in modern times by dictatorial and totalitarian regimes.[2] In addition it argued that what was being drawn up was a list of rights of the individual man that abstracted from those of the State. In this perspective the rather absolute statement of the Declaration concerning a right to propaganda takes on a different and more acceptable character.

A number of contributors to a symposium on the Declaration, sponsored by UNESCO, were careful to point out that any such right does not exist *in vacuo*. A definition of the relation of the individual to the society in which he lives must go hand in hand with a declaration of rights.[3] And all rights presuppose obligations. The 18th century tended to forget this and to be one-sided in treating of rights, laying stress on the rights of the individual to the neglect of society. And yet, even the declaration of 1789 supposed acceptance by the individual of the idea that liberty can be curtailed by law and that freedom of speech is subject to 'responsibility for any disturbances of public

[1] See K. Kada, *Liberta di religione, di stampa e d'associazione: Esame storico-critico degli articoli XVIII, XIX e XX della Dichiarazione Universale dei Diritti dell'Uomo*, Rome 1959, *passim*.

[2] Cf Jacques Driencourt, *La propagande, nouvelle force politique*, Paris 1950, ch 7.

[3] Cf E. H. Carr, The Rights of Man, in *Human Rights: Comments and Interpretation*, Jacques Maritain ed., London 1949.

order'. Then again, it would be a mistake to treat all propaganda in relation to the right to give and get information. One of the symposiasts stated frankly that it is an error today to regard freedom of information as an extension of freedom of expression, which itself proceeds from freedom of thought. It lags, he said, behind the concept of modern political sociology, which recognises that contemporary media of communication are only to a limited degree the organs of the expression of opinion. They are more properly regarded as pre-conditioning or satisfying opinion, either preceding it or following it but not expressing it. The techniques of modern media of communication belong to the field of mass psycho-sociology rather than to that of individual psychology. They constitute an industry that is only to a minor degree dependent on the views of individual producers. Here is a social fact of which any attitude towards propaganda must take account.[1]

A further consideration flows immediately from this. It is that any inclusion of the right to information among the rights of man must mean 'more than seeking a mere increase or improvement in the knowledge available to the public. It involves a radical reconsideration of the function of information. It means that the products, the methods and even the organisation of the news industry must be reassessed from the point of view, not of the interests or prejudices of those who control its production, but of the human dignity of those who henceforth are justified in expecting of it the means of free thought'.[2] It cannot be allowed to exploit the minds of the masses. As an extension of the right to education, the characteristic of information must be 'availability' rather than 'militancy'. And even at that it must be related to needs. Everybody cannot have a right to access to all sources of information in all circumstances, nor do all groups need the same information. There must be a realistic assessment of the interests of the people coupled with a recognition of their historical and sociological relativity. 'Recognition that the right to the expression of opinion must be conditioned

[1] Cf Rene Maheu, *The Right to Information and the Right to the Expression of Opinion*, in Maritain, *loc. cit.*

[2] Maheu, *loc. cit.* p 219.

to the historical perspective of a particular democracy, is not sacrificing a human right to reason of State. On the contrary, that right is thus given its full meaning by refusal to sacrifice to an abstract concept the merits and chances of success of a concrete undertaking. Nor is it a question of limitation from outside . . . What is meant is the self-imposed restraint inherent in liberty, which is known as the sense of responsibility'.[1]

The favourable attitude of democracy towards freedom of propaganda does not mean that the State can permit the propagation of anything and everything. The essential difference between authoritarian and democratic regimes as regards propaganda is that whereas the former allow it only in so far as it serves the overriding interests of the State, the latter permit what might be called 'private' propaganda.[2] The 'pressure group' has come to be looked upon as a characteristic feature of democracy in America and the British Commonwealth. It simply is not tolerated in authoritarian States, which look upon a plurality of ideas and interests as inimical to the well-being of a collectivist system in which community interest is absolute. No ideological opposition to it can be allowed. For the democratic State the problem is the inverse of this: How is the government to take effective account of private propaganda so as to remain in real contact with the wishes of the majority of the people? Public opinion is the very nerve centre of the democratic form of the exercise of political power. And, as we have seen already, what is today the opinion of the minority may tomorrow be that of the people as a whole. Opinion therefore ought to be pre-eminently free, for, in a real sense, it is the repository of sovereignty. Democratic government has the strict duty of tolerating opinion that is opposed to its politics at any given moment.[3] Even in the defence of democracy itself it would run counter to its own principles if it were to ban all propaganda that was anti-democratic. This defence must consist largely in engaging in counter propaganda, not indeed—as with the Communists—by way of preaching a better world to be enjoyed in a

[1] Maheu, *loc. cit.*
[2] Cf Driencourt, *op. cit.* p 241 *seq.*
[3] Maheu, *loc. cit.*

hypothetical democratic future but by reminding people of the present advantages of the democratic way of life which they know. But it must combat, even by exclusion, the kind of insidious propaganda that would lead to anarchy and revolution through deceiving the people.[1] Its duty of protecting the society of which it has care imperatively demands that this be so.

The Catholic State will adopt the same approach to religious propaganda as it will towards propaganda in general. It will not be intolerant towards the propagation of a religion that is not that of the majority of the people just because it is a minority religion. Nor will it curb this even if its ethos is foreign to the traditions of the people, provided the methods used in propagating it are unexceptionable. But it will limit propaganda, even in matters of religion, that inevitably constitutes a threat to the peace. The most liberal Catholic writers allow this; it is part and parcel of the nature of democracy.[2] But although an erroneous

[1] Cf Driencourt, *op. cit.* p 241 *seq.*

[2] See, for example, Hartmann, *Toleranz und christliche Glaube*, Frankfurt 1955, p 246; J. C. Murray, *Governmental Repression of Heresy*, *loc. cit.* Lecky writes as follows in *Democracy and Liberty*, vol. I, pp 440-441: 'There is a broad and intelligible distinction between the right of freely expressing religious or political opinions in churches or meetings to which one is obliged to come, in books or papers which no one is obliged to read, and the right of expressing them in the public street, which all men are forced to use, and which are the common property of all. The first and most essential form of liberty is the liberty of performing lawful business without molestation and annoyance, and this liberty is most imperfectly attained when it is impossible for men, women or children to pass through the streets without having attacks upon their religious belief thrust upon their attention. In most countries such street controversies are rigidly suppressed. Where they are permitted, they ought surely to be deemed a matter of tolerance, and not of right; to be regulated in each case according to special circumstances. Some years ago it was the habit of a Protestant missionary society to placard the walls throughout the Catholic provinces of Ireland with questions and arguments subversive of the Catholic faith, and missionaries might be seen driving along the roads throwing controversial leaflets to every peasant and into every turf-basket as they passed. In my own judgment, such a method of propaganda ought not to have been

conscience has no natural right to propagate its error,[1] the Catholic State, qua State, must confer a civil right on it to do so to the extent that it does not injure the temporal common good. In the Catholic State this will mean, in fact, that no religious propaganda will be allowed that employs slander or makes open attacks on the religion of the majority.

The Catholic State which lives up to its obligations in this matter need create no embarrassment for the Church or for individual Catholics. One hears it suggested sometimes that a broadening of attitude towards freedom of propaganda is necessary if the Christian State is not to create difficulties for ministers of the Gospel in the mission fields among peoples who are hostile to the spread of Christianity. In face of intense opposition in many countries, Christianity, it is said, can only expect liberty for itself by demanding it for all.[2] This argument has been applied to the Catholic State by Pribilla in his plea for tolerance, on the grounds that the Church's missions are widely scattered in Protestant, Mohammedan and pagan lands, and that the treatment of non-Catholic religious propaganda in

permitted, and it is probable that most of those who disagree with me would admit the principle for which I am contending, if the arguments that were disseminated had been directed not against Catholicism, but against Christianity'.

[1] In a discussion on the rights of conscience Fr. Murray writes: 'It is, of course, always understood that the . . . erroneous conscience can claim no rights when it issues in acts that are repugnant to the law of God. For this reason, I include . . . no "right of irreligious propaganda", and no "right of association for anti-religious purposes", etc. In no sense are these things rights of conscience, that follow from obligations of conscience'—in *Theological Studies*, vol. VI (1945), p 276.

[2] Cf Cecil Northcott, *Religious Liberty*, London 1948, p 82. There are certain countries which forbid entrance to Christian missionaries. They include Tibet, Afghanstan and Saudi-Arabia. Anti-missionary feeling flares up in Egypt pretty regularly and in Turkey evangelism is disapproved and medical and educational institutions restrained from doing anything either publicly or privately that can be supposed to influence the minds of those who benefit from them towards a change of religion. See Northcott, *op. cit.* pp 73, 88 and 91.

Catholic countries has an inevitable repercussion on the freedom of Catholic propaganda elsewhere.[1] While this is true, I think that no genuine objection can be raised to Catholic theory on the subject of religious propaganda. Nor does the Church claim any privileges for her own missions that she refuses in principle to grant to non-Catholic religious bodies. She will even allow, in theory, that the work of Catholic missions may be curbed by the State if it offends in any of the respects which we have mentioned. It is unlikely that this is ever true in practice of her work, although the same cannot be said for non-Catholic missions in certain Catholic countries. In theory she can agree with and in practice fear nothing from the following words of Mr. Nehru: 'Unless a given faith proves a menace to public order, or its teachers attempt to thrust it down unwilling throats of men of other persuasions, there can be no justification for measures which deprive any community of its rights'.[2]

Of course debate will always rage as to how theory is implemented in practice and, in this respect, the Catholic State is no exception. What needs to be emphasised is that there is no such thing as 'the Catholic State' in the concrete; there are Catholic States that try to apply the principles in their own circumstances. Purely political factors can also intervene to cloud the picture. For this reason one must not make the mistake of judging Catholic theory on religious toleration in terms of the extent of public tolerance that is found in any particular Catholic State. For the same reason, it is no part of our purpose here to defend the position adopted in any given State, for example, Spain. Let us allow a Spanish writer to speak for himself. If, he says, the Spanish situation 'is the only regime compatible with the common good—that is, the order, the welfare, the cordial ideological unity of Spaniards—it is a just and

---

[1] Cf M. Pribilla, Dogmatische Intoleranz und burgerliche Toleranz, in *Stimmen der Zeit*, vol. 144 (1949); French trans. Intolérance dogmatique et tolérance civile, in *Unité chrétienne et tolérance religieuse*, Paris 1950, p 164.

[2] Reported interview, Ecumenical Press Service no 79. August 1946. Cited in Northcott, *op. cit.* p 84.

Catholic regime'.[1]

Nobody claims that Spain is a democracy, but then democracy is not the only form of just government. And it is not for us to judge whether the Spanish measures concerning religious propaganda are demanded by the concrete situation. Article of the *Fuero de los Espanoles* runs as follows :

'The profession and practice of the Catholic religion, which is the official religion of the Spanish State, shall enjoy official protection. None shall be molested for his religious beliefs nor for the private exercise of his cult. No ceremonies or external manifestations other than those of the State religion shall be permitted'. If the most democratic States are entitled to make efforts to preserve the ideological minimum necessary for their well-being, who can deny that Spain, emerging from a civil upheaval, has the right to follow an analogous course. And if, in seeking to preserve their unity and stability from being undermined in the future, the Spaniards adopt rather extreme measures, who has the right to tell them their business? In feeling that they require a much stronger ideological unity than say, the United States, the Spaniards, remarks Dr. O'Rahilly, may be wrong. He himself, he says, would oppose any such policy in Ireland. 'But', he adds, 'I feel that the Spaniards are the best judges as regards their own country, its needs and possibilities. In thus acting they are dealing with their own concrete situation as Spaniards, not as Catholics. They are not implementing any Catholic dogma, nor are they inspired by "the most rigid Catholic claims"—as if the rest of us were watering down our religion. I cannot discover any general principle with which to condemn the Spaniards. Nor, as far as my knowledge goes, can I find any accompanying violation of natural rights. There is some restriction as regards the externation of non-Catholic cults. This would probably exist in any case. Could you imagine an Eucharistic procession in the streets of Belfast'?[2]

[1] P. G. Lopez S. J., La democracia como régimen politico-cristiano, in *Razón y Fé*, vol. 134 (1946), p 166.

[2] A. O'Rahilly, in *The Standard*, 9 July 1954.

REALISM AND CIVIL LIBERTIES

At this point it may be objected that, while the legal restriction of religious propaganda may be acceptable within the framework of an authoritarian regime, it is entirely repugnant to a democratic society. It is an objection which does not stand up to examination. Recent legal history in the United States has shown that, even in a democratic country such as this, with freedom of speech guaranteed by the First Amendment, realism has compelled a curtailment of religious freedom in certain respects. The words themselves of the First Amendment are eloquent: 'Congress shall make no law respecting an establishment of religion, or prohibiting the free exercise thereof; or abridging the freedom of speech, or of the press; or the right of the people peaceably to assemble and to petition the government for a redress of grievances'. But it has been found necessary so to narrow what is meant by 'freedom of speech' that things detrimental to the common welfare might not go uncurbed.

Examples might be quoted from many domains.[1] To begin with, in the matter of obscene literature, the Supreme Court has indicated[2] that State legislatures are not prohibited from taking action against certain publications, provided their enabling statutes are drawn up so as not to violate the First Amendment directly. The freedom of the press is being narrowed more and more.[3] During 1953-54, for example, the press was excluded from over twelve hundred committee meetings of Congress, over five hundred Senate committee meetings and some seventy meetings of joint committees. Armed services committee meetings are most frequently closed, as also are those of the Foreign Relations Committee of the Senate. In the same way, the press is excluded from many judicial proceedings, or is barred from publishing certain kinds of evidence. Pre-trial

---

[1] Cf Walter Berns, *Freedom, Virtue and the First Amendment,* Louisiana State University 1957, *passim.*

[2] In Winters v. New York.

[3] Wiggins, *op. cit.*

publicity is particularly hindered, as being likely to prejudice a fair trial of the case. In twenty-eight States cameras are excluded from court. Information on military matters is almost impossible to get, so extensive is the net of 'top-secret', 'secret', 'confidential' and 'restricted' material. In 1953, this was broadened still further to cover non-military matters of 'strategic' importance.

Nor is there untrammelled freedom to print what one knows. Although there is no licensing or prior censorship (in peace time) of publications in general, the Atomic Energy Act involves a kind of previous restraint and censorship by prohibiting the publication of news regarding nuclear energy that has not first been cleared. As regards radio and television, it is evident that some sort of licensing had to be introduced, because channels for broadcasting are limited and have to be allocated. The situation was one that the First Amendment could not have envisaged. The Communications Act of 1934 gave the government power to make any rules required in this connection, and it is interesting to note that the Communications Commission (which the Act set up) stopped a radio station in 1941 from advocating the political cause of the licencee. Finally, the Post Office exercises a wide control. At one time 'prohibition' propaganda would not be carried through the mails. At present the Post Office has statutory authority to declare mail unacceptable which violates the Espionage Act, advocates treason, or is obscene.

It is noticeable that the most common type of limitation of the press in the United States occurs in what is regarded as of importance for national security. For a long time the same was true of speech in general. In a famous case, brought under the Espionage Act of 1917,[1] Justice Holmes laid down the criterion which was to be followed: 'The question in every case is whether the words used are used in such circumstances and are of such a nature as to create a clear and present danger that they bring about the substantive evils that Congress has a right to prevent'. By this a big area of discussion was placed beyond

[1] Schenck v. United States. 249 U.S. 47 (1919). Cf Berns, *op. cit.* P 49 *seq.*

the reach of government and, until recently, whenever free speech came into conflict with any claims other than national security, it was certain to emerge triumphant. The result of this, notably in a number of cases which concerned the activities of the Jehovah's Witnesses, was that municipalities were prevented from 'defending' themselves against 'invasion' by those who would set up phonographs outside private houses, denounce the religious beliefs of the inhabitants and distribute defamatory literature amongst them. So much so that Justice Jackson was driven to comment although in a somewhat different context: 'There is a danger that, if the Court does not temper its doctrinaire logic with a little practical wisdom, it will convert the Constitutional Bill of Rights into a suicide pact'.[1] Literal interpretation of the First Amendment had become unrealistic.

As one writer has put it, such strict interpretation meant that if someone wanted to preach his religious opinions on another's doorstep, his freedom to do so could not be abridged in the interests of privacy. In fact his freedom of speech would be upheld even if he insisted in preaching through a loudspeaker on a Sunday afternoon when the rest of the population wanted to doze in the sun. In the opinion of Justice Douglas, expressed in relation to a case involving the distribution of literature from door to door by the Jehovah's Witnesses: 'This form of religious activity occupies the same high estate under the First Amendment as do worship in the churches and preaching from the pulpits'.[2] Professor Corwin's reply was sarcastic: 'In other words, the right of religious enthusiasts to solicit funds and peddle their doctrinal wares in streets, to ring doorbells and disturb householders, and to accost passersby and insult them in *their* religious beliefs, stands on the same constitutional level as the right of people to resort to their own places of worship and listen to their chosen teachers! If, as is generally understood, one man's right to swing his fist stops just short of where another man's nose begins, a somewhat similar rule must be

---

[1] Terminiello v. Chicago, 337, U.S. 1 (1949). For an account of the cases involving the Witnesses see W. Gellhorn, *American Rights*, New York 1960, pp 45-55.

[2] Berns, *op. cit.* p 75.

presumed to hold in the field of religious activities'.[1] Indeed
Justice Jackson felt so indignant yet impotent before a case in
which the Witnesses had harassed the people of a town on Palm
Sunday, using phonographic equipment, that he protested:
'How then can the Court today hold it a "high constitutional
privilege" to go to homes, including those of devout Catholics
on Palm Sunday morning, and thrust upon them literature
calling their church a "whore" and their faith a "racket"?'[2]

Two recent decisions have changed the situation. The
first ruled the constitutionality of an ordinance which forbade
the use of any kind of sound track 'which emits therefrom
loud and raucous noises' in city streets.[3] Despite the protests
of Justice Black that the First Amendment gives free use
of 'all present instruments of communication', as well as others
'that inventive genius may bring into being', Justice Frank-
furter declared: 'So long as a legislature does not prescribe what
ideas may be noisily expressed and what may not be, nor dis-
criminate among those who would make inroads upon public
peace, it is not for us to supervise the limits the legislature may
impose in safeguarding the steadily narrowing opportunities for
serenity and reflection. Without such opportunities freedom of
thought becomes a mocking phrase'.[4]

The second decision ruled the constitutionality of a city
ordinance against house to house peddling, which had been
challenged by mass circulation magazines. Of this Justice Black,
dissenting without effect, remarked: 'Today's decision marks a
revitalisation of the juridical views which prevailed before this
Court embraced the philosophy that the First Amendment gives
a preferred status to the liberties it protects'.[5] In other words,
freedom is no longer 'preferred' as it was before, because of the

---

[1] E. S. Corwin, *The Constitution and What it Means Today*, Prince-
ton 1948, pp 200-201. Cited in Berns, *op. cit.* p 84.

[2] Douglas v. Jeannette, 319 U.S. 157, 180 (1942).

[3] Kovacs v. Cooper, 336 U.S. 77 (1949). See however a somewhat
contrary decision in Kunz v. New York, 340 U.S. 290 (1951). Gellhorn,
op. cit. pp 49-51.

[4] Cited in Berns, *op. cit.* p 65.

[5] Breard v. Alexandria, 341 U.S. 622 (1951).

anomalous consequences to which this had given rise. The law has been compelled to make a distinction between what can and cannot be allowed in the interests of public order. For speech, as Justice Douglas has said, 'may strike at prejudices and pre-conceptions and have profound unsettling effects as it presses for acceptance of an idea'.[1] Personally he was of the opinion that in doing so it may 'best serve its high purpose'; there will be occasions when reasonable men will look on the matter in a different light.

Even though subsequent decisions may have left the final position somewhat doubtful, these cases have at least established the principle that an exaggeratedly liberal attitude towards. civil liberties can be as damaging to the State as it is unrealistic. Undoubtedly it is a difficult and delicate matter to establish a proper balance between individual liberty and the protection of the common good. It is so easy to confuse the maintenance of the latter with its compulsory pursuit, in a way that easily conflicts with fundamental democratic values. As the Supreme Court put it on one occasion: 'Those who begin coercive elimination of dissent soon find themselves exterminating dissenters'. Jacques Maritain has pointed out frequently that a primary aim of the democratic State should be the creation of unity through common adherence to the democratic charter. For the very sake of attaining this practical unity, inner differentiations must be allowed to work themselves out through a system of pluralism. All this is very true in its place. Nevertheless, a democratic society cannot blind itself to the fact that some degree of social coercion is necessary, even in the domain of the expression of ideas whether they be secular or religious in nature.

In relation to political liberty, the United States has not only made some *speech* illegal, but has actually passed a statute that forbids even the advocacy of seditious *ideas*. This—the Smith Act of 1940—was ruled constitutional by the Supreme Court in a case in which it had been invoked against some members of the Communist Party.[2] This decision, giving back-

[1] Terminiello v. Chicago.
[2] Dennis v. United States, 341 U.S. 494 (1951).

ing to an Act which had declared: 'It shall be unlawful for any person to knowingly and wilfully advocate . . . the desirability . . . . of overthrowing or destroying any government in the United States by force and violence', means in effect that the political *tenets* of Communism were outlawed, as these cannot be divorced from defending the necessity of civil strife.[1] That this case 'represents the end of a one-way street for our liberal justices', is the summing up of one authoritative American commentator.[2]

To get back to Catholic theory, Cardinal Ottaviani's third requirement of the Catholic State is only a guarantee of what sound politics would itself enjoin. It was under the pretext of public order that Mr. Asquith, then Prime Minister of England, forbade the Procession of the International Eucharistic Congress through the streets of London in 1908. He seemed to believe that it might occasion a repetition of the sort of disturbance that occurred during the Gordon Riots of the 18th century. No one can deny the State a wide discretion in such matters. It is on this theoretical foundation that the case for the Spanish law on religion rests. Discussion as to how Catholic is Spain, how necessary for political unity are the measures adopted etc., is secondary, though for too long it has occupied the premier place in foreign comments on the Spanish situation. In a real sense too, our third requirement is also secondary. On Catholic theory itself, it rests on the desirability of preserving the tranquillity of at least the majority of the citizens in the possession

---

[1] Cf Berns, *op. cit.* pp 203-204.

[2] Berns, *op. cit.* p 206. The possible dangers in the Dennis decision have been discussed in Walter Gellhorn in his *American Rights*, pp 74-78. He points out that in the Yates case (1957) the Supreme Court curtailed the effect of its former decision. As the law now stands, the advocacy of the forcible overthrow of the government is not prohibited as long as it is not accompanied by any effort to instigate action. Justice Harlan for the majority made a distinction 'between advocacy of abstract doctrine and advocacy directed at promoting unlawful action' and interpreted the Smith Act as intending to preserve that distinction. The result of the decision has been a notable falling off in the number of convictions of Communist leaders under the Smith Act. Cf Gellhorn, *op. cit.* p 82.

of their faith. It is entirely subordinate to a condition of things in which the majority are Catholic and, in itself, is independent of the choice of means by which a government will endeavour to maintain the public order. It is simply a guarantee, required by the Church, that the general duty to maintain order, by which all governments are bound, will be observed in the Catholic State so as to preserve the peace of the Catholic people in a matter which the Church has been appointed exclusively to promote at the supernatural level.

In themselves, therefore, the three requirements that are entailed by Catholic theory are not open to the accusation of intolerance. No intolerance towards non-Catholics, as such, is necessarily involved in any of them. In themselves they place no limits to the non-Catholic's freedom of belief, while as regards freedom of expression and of propaganda only those limits are demanded that are regarded as necessary also in secular matters even by the most democratic States. Methods of meeting the requirements are something entirely distinct from the requirements themselves and should always be examined *in concreto*. The charge that Catholic theory is opposed to 'liberty' means nothing, for liberty, like 'goodness', is an unfinished term as far as the order of human attributes is concerned. Even 'liberty of opinion', without explanation, means little. It is concretised in liberty of 'thought', 'expression' and 'propaganda'. Liberty of thought is something internal and invisible; it cannot be interfered with very easily. The nearest approach to controlling it has been by way of the use of drugs, a practice which our own times have unhappily witnessed.[1] Liberty of expression, on the other hand, is essentially manifested externally. It is the liberty of making public one's private opinions. Liberty of propaganda adds to this the idea that the purpose of expressing one's views is to influence others and to try to win them over to one's own position. Every aspect of the exercise of human liberty is included under these three heads. Freedom of speech, of religious practice, of the press, of education—all are manifestations of one or other of the three.

It is important to note that these three forms of liberty of

[1] Cf Charles Morgan, *Liberties of the Mind*, London 1955, p 10.

opinion are by no means rigidly distinct.[1] Liberty of thought, for example, is usually taken to cover not only the internal elaboration of ideas, but their private expression in individual and family life. It is not always easy, however, to decide exactly where these domains end and yield place to public life and public expression. What if one invites friends—possibly numerous friends—to one's private discussions and meetings? It may be said that such sessions remain private unless they are formal affairs, begun, let us say, on the sounding of a gong. But what difference is there, in this matter, between the sounding of a gong and the striking of a clock at the time when the session is to begin? In the same way, the public expression of opinion can very easily verge on propaganda. Indeed some people would say that simple expression is the most effective of all propaganda. One can influence others by being openly what one is, as much as, if not more than, by seeking to convert them. Thus a newspaper that is professedly addressed only to members of a particular Church can have a propaganda value by way of its indirect effect on others. Or again, an imposing church edifice is mute witness to the faith which erected it. In modern times nearly every aspect of liberty of expression can become, through publicity, a kind of propaganda. Hence there is no hard and fast distinction between the three forms of liberty of opinion. Because of this, difficulties are bound to arise in any effort to apply the three requirements which we have been discussing. But such problems concern the question of the application and not that of the nature of the requirements themselves.

From what we have been saying it should be clear that the Catholic teaching on public tolerance of religion is complex and full of nuance. Its most evident feature is its difference from that of a secular liberalism which would have the State equally indifferent to all religion. If the Church demands that the State should give special recognition to Catholicism, it is because she is acutely conscious of the demands of truth, as truth, in the social as well as in the individual domain. It should be noted carefully, however, that our defence of the Catholic State which

---

[1] Cf Jacques Leclercq, *Leçons de Droit Naturel*, vol. II, Louvain 1948, pp 57-59.

complies with this is based on political rather than on religious considerations. Our thesis has been that what is proximately a political duty on the State is at the same time of obligation for theological reasons. We do not argue to the theological situation from an analysis of the political, but we do defend the demands of theology on the State by marshalling political reasons that lead to the same practical outcome. I freely admit that one finds textbooks of Public Ecclesiastical Law that seem to think that Catholicism is recognised by the Catholic State precisely under the aspect of its being the true religion. With due respect I suggest that this is not the position. As the true religion Catholicism has rights *vis-a-vis* the State; it is on account of this that the Church will have none of secular liberalism. But, as in personal ethics, the duties which are correlative of such rights press in practice only when it is possible to implement them. In the case of the State and religion this possibility is constituted by a fabric of political reality which forms the exclusive criterion for the governance of civil society. If the public temporal good demands the special recognition of Catholicism, then the State not only can but ought to accord this. But in doing so it fulfils—objectively—what is a *theological* as well as a political duty. And simply because Catholicism is the one true religion, there can never be an objective theological obligation on any State to give such special recognition to any other religion.

This is not to say that the State cannot accord them some recognition or that it ought not to do so for political reasons. There is certainly no question of Catholic theory—if properly understood—involving the imposition of civil disabilities on non-Catholics on the facile grounds that unbelief has no rights. Again I admit that one sometimes comes across expositions of Public Law in which this, or something very like it, is expressed. To accept such suggestions at their face value would mean forgetfulness of the fact that faith is a gift of God. No, the only implications of the Catholic theory for non-Catholics concern the public and external aspects of their religious life.[1] In this domain

---

[1] Cf Sotillo, *op. cit.* p 220.

it is clear that the ordinary principles of politics demand that the interests of the majority get special recognition. Pribilla's comments on this deserve attention as he generally adopts the most tolerant attitude possible: 'Religious liberty does not at all mean that the majority must capitulate before the minority. Respect for the subjective conviction of others does not exclude a resolute defense in face of attacks against our own convictions. In practice it is inevitable that the religion of the majority enjoys advantages and is able to express itself more easily in public life. This is the natural consequence of given conditions. But it does not suffice in order that the minority should have a complaint of being harrassed and oppressed. For the same reason, it goes without saying, and requires only the most elementary tact to see, that a religious minority should not wound the religious sentiments of the majority by an indiscreet and noisy propaganda. Both the one and the other, majority as well as minority, ought to seek to make the struggle for the truth a struggle of minds, not a bout of fisticuffs, and to avoid everything that resembles an exposition of denominational passions. . . . If necessary the State ought to intervene so that the spiritual rivalry of the different denominations be channelled into forms that correspond to rules of law universally admitted and which bind out of consideration for the common good. Naturally it has also the right to protect itself by opposing excess, brutality and violation of public order'.[1]

Our whole point is that while the action of the State is dictated by the demands of public order, affairs of religion can and do come under this. It is a basic ethical principle, grounded on the interests of conscience itself, that harmony should exist between social organisation and the moral and religious persuasions of the individual. For which reason even Fr. Murray says that 'with reference to errors and evils that affect the social order, the State cannot assume a position of "neutrality" . . . It is, therefore, morally obliged to assume the position that atheism and actions contrary to the Natural Law have no rights in the social order, and that they can claim no freedom of public ad-

[1] Pribilla, *loc. cit.* pp 168-169.

vocacy or practice. To this position it is further compelled by its obligations to the common good . . . To spread disbelief in God or immoral practices is to undermine the social order . . . Obviously, the State has no mandate to convert the atheist or the secularist; on the other hand, it has no juridical obligation to give him free rein in the public life of the community; for it has a mandate to guard the juridical order and the common good. And this mandate gives the State the right to restrict the propaganda of atheism or secularism and the practice of immorality'.[1] It is in virtue of similar considerations that the Catholic State has the juridical duty to take special cognisance of the religion of the majority.

Religious minorities can have no legitimate quarrel with this and certainly not on the basis of religious intolerance. Immunity from differential treatment in the social and political domain is not a right of conscience in the strict sense. If it does exist it is strictly a political or civil right that is accorded in view of the circumstances which obtain in a State. As such it is subject to the juridically recognised exigencies of the common good. In the predominantly Catholic State it must yield to a special catering for the interests of the majority. Of course unjust discrimination is never lawful, but all discrimination is not necessarily unjust and differential treatment as regards the public status of different religious groups is certainly not unjust in itself.

THE RIGHTS OF THE MAJORITY

From the viewpoint which I have adopted it can be seen that the Catholic teaching on public tolerance is coincidental with that of democratic thinking on the rights of the majority. Catholic theory can find much to agree with in the statement of the Protestant—Vattel—on the place of religion and liberty of conscience in the State. As a piece of political philosophy it can certainly not be contradicted in its broad outlines and is also in harmony with the basic principles of Public Ecclesiastical Law. ' . . . Liberty of conscience is a natural and inviolable

---

[1] J. C. Murray, in *Theological Studies*, vol. VI (1945), pp 268-269.

right. It is a disgrace to human nature that a truth of this nature should need to be proved. But we should take care not to extend this liberty beyond its due bounds. A citizen has only the rights of never being obliged to do anything in religious affairs, and not of doing outwardly whatever he pleases, though it may proceed from his regard to society. The establishment of religion by the laws, and its public exercise are matters of State, and are necessarily under the jurisdiction of the public authority. If all men ought to serve God, the entire nation, in its national capacity, is doubtless obliged to serve and honour Him. And as it ought to discharge this important duty in that manner which appears to the nation to be the best, the nation is to determine the religion it would follow . . .

'That which shall have the approbation of the majority shall be received, and publicly established by law; by means of which it will become the religion of the State. But it is asked, if a considerable part of the nation insists upon following another religion, what does the law of nations require in this respect? Let us first remember that liberty of conscience is a natural right; and that there must be no constraint in this respect. There remain then two methods to take; either to permit this part of the citizens to exercise the religion they profess, or to separate the society, by leaving them their fortunes and their share of the country that belonged to the nation in common, and thus form two new States instead of one. The last method will appear no ways proper; it would weaken the nation, and thus would be contrary to the regard that ought to be felt for its safety. It is therefore of more advantage to take the first, and thus establish two religions in the State. But if these religions are too incompatible, if there be reason to fear that they will produce disturbances among the citizens and disorder in affairs, there is a third method (whereby) each partly has its separate government within itself, but they unite in foreign affairs, and form only one and the same republic . . .

'But if a new religion spreads, and becomes fixed in the minds of the people, as it commonly happens, independently of the public authority, . . . it will be then necessary to reason, as we have just done in the case of choosing a religion, to pay attention to the number of those who follow the new opinions, to remember that no earthly power has authority over conscience, and to unite the maxims of sound politics with those of justice and charity'.[1]

One does not have to accept an exclusive concept of 'established' religion in order to be able to follow the lines of Vattel's thought. Indeed his interesting reference to the possibility of having more than one 'established' religion shows that his concept of 'establishment' cannot have been exclusive. What he primarily wants to ensure is the place of religion in public life, which he regards as intimately related to the temporal common good. That the religion of the people receive special recognition is the main point which he wishes to establish; all his other suggestions are subsidiary to this. One wishes that he had given an explanation of how more than one religion could get such recognition or how different grades of recognition could be worked out. On these points he leaves us uninformed while much of what he does say in explanation of 'establishment' is too Erastian for Catholic theory. But one thing at least is clear and of relevance to the matter of the present chapter. It is that there would be no unjust discrimination in matters of religion. 'Religion', he says, 'is of extreme importance to the welfare and tranquillity of society, and the prince is obliged to have an eye to everything in which the State is interested. This is what calls him to interfere (sic) in religion or to protect it and defend it. He can interfere only upon this footing and consequently he can use his power against none but those whose religious conduct is prejudicial or dangerous to the State and cannot punish pretended crimes against God . . . Let us remember that religion is no farther an affair of State than as it is exterior and publicly established'.[2]

Catholic theory is saying no more and no less than this when it insists that in the Catholic State the religion of the people should get special juridical recognition. It may be asked, however, whether my interpretation of Catholic theory in this matter really accords with what has been the teaching of the

---

[1] E. Vattel, *The Law of Nations*, English trans. London.

[2] *Op. cit.* p 54.

textbooks. Surely, it may be urged, the Catholic claims are based on the truth of the Catholic religion, insistence on the juridical recognition of which means asking the State to take on a doctrinal role that is foreign to its nature and inevitably involves a confusion of the spheres of Church and State. I have no doubt that one can find Catholic expositions of this matter in which such an approach is adopted. Nor do I deny the fact that, in the minds of critics, it is regarded as *the* Catholic position. What I am denying is that it represents the tradition of the Church which, by and large, permits of the other interpretation. Fr. Castelein, S.J. lived and wrote at the time of Pope Leo XIII when the Catholic 'thesis' was a criterion of orthodoxy. What has he to say of the content of the Catholic ideal? According to this, he writes, Church and State 'each by its own authority and enjoying its own autonomy passed its own laws and pursued its own end . . . The ecclesiastical authority positively ordained both internal and external acts so that all would be imbued with the true faith and the practice of the supernatural virtues; the civil authority ordained only certain external acts and that in a negative way, prohibiting anything that might do public damage to the true faith and religion, something that can be reduced to damage to civil peace and prosperity. The State did not therefore proscribe the public profession of heresy as formally contradicting Catholic doctrine and impeding the salvation of souls, but only in so far as contradicting the social ideology or foundations of social ideology which the State judged necessary for the peace of the people and the temporal prosperity of society. Hence the State did not coerce Catholic citizens into the true and integral practice of the Catholic religion, nor did it proscribe any sins, even the most grievous, which were prohibited by divine or ecclesiastical law, but only certain external crimes that were contrary to civil order'.[1]

For Castelein it was the interests of civil order that not only permitted but demanded that the Catholic State 'by reason of its function is strictly bound efficaciously to impede any public

[1] V. Castelein, *Philosophia Moralis*, Brussels 1899, pp 533-534.

activity which, by its very nature, tends to destroy the true faith and religion'.[1] For the same reason he taught that the State in a mixed society should allow anything that did not contradict the principles of natural religion.[2] It cannot be legitimately objected that, by adopting this course, the State is assuming the role of judge of doctrine. Zigliara, who also wrote during the Leonine period, had an answer to this charge ready to hand.[3] The State, he says, has no authority as regards doctrine, but this does not prevent it from having the ability to discern what, in religious matters, is contrary to the public interest. Just as a private individual can defend an innocent person from attack by a manifestly unjust aggressor, without being constituted judge in the matter, so too the State can have a right and duty to protect the religion of the majority of the people against assault.

Of course this Catholic teaching by no means implies that in the Catholic State the majority can oppress the minority. Secular exponents of majority rule sometimes give the impression that the government represents the force of the majority of the people, to be used in whatever way the majority wishes. As if the government had the right to say to the minority, in A. D. Lindsay's way of putting it: 'You see now that there are more of us than of you. We intend to have our way. Are you going to come quietly or not?'[4] This is indeed the Marxist notion of democracy, in which government is conceived as the instrument by which the dominant class represses all the others. Real democracy does not look upon the relations of majority and minority as thus constituted on a basis of force. It defends the right of the minority to turn itself into a majority and when it can do so to assume the reins of power. It has been well pointed out that in a democratic government the majority is never a determinate majority but a majority which depends on the results of election.[5] In this connection the opinion has been ex-

[1] *Op. cit.* pp 532-533.

[2] *Op. cit.* p 534.

[3] Zigliara, *Summa Philosophica*, Paris 1891, vol. III.

[4] A. D. Lindsay, *The Modern Democratic State*, Oxford 1943, p 199.

[5] Lindsay, *op. cit.* p 200.

pressed that democratic government is difficult where a State is divided into a permanent majority and minority.[1] This is not the way to view the situation. It assumes that majority and minority are necessarily competing interests, each with an exclusive 'will' of its own. It is better to view them simply as social aggregates arithmetically related to each other in a way that must be taken into account when arriving at political decisions. On a whole lot of matters until the count is made there is no way of knowing what the majority interest will be. Religion is certainly an important part but it is by no means the whole of public life. And if the majority-minority method suffices for democratic procedure in other domains, there is no adequate reason why it should be suspended, much less reversed, in a State in which the majority interest is a quasi-permanent one in matters of religion.

Not that majority rule is insensitive to the interests of the minority, in any domain that of religion included. Indeed its only security of tenure is that which stems from its attending to as many sectional interests as it can reconcile with the general welfare. So that democracy could very well be described as the rule of groups in that the majority principle is a way of ensuring sensitivity to the widest possible range of interests.[2] No government can ignore sectional claims altogether; on the way it treats any of them may well depend whether it will stay in power. Yet for the same reason neither can it ignore their relative strength; it must pay special attention to the interests of the majority in any given matter. It is therefore necessarily involved in the business of discrimination, of treating sectional interests according to a scale of inequality.

Realistic democratic government is compelled by facts to a conception of democracy that is neither 'mystical' nor 'literal', to employ Walter Lippman's descriptive terminology.[3] It does not just pay lip service to the mystique of 'equal treatment'

[1] *Ibid.*

[2] Cf S. I. Benn and R. S. Peters, *Social Principles and the Democratic State*, London 1959, p. 338; also F. A. Hayek, *The Constitution of Liberty*, London, 1960, p. 106 seq.

[3] Cf W. Lippmann, *The Public Philosophy*, New York 1956.

while in practice ignoring minority interests. Nor yet does it adopt a false and abstract literal view of the complete equality of all sections of the community. It takes account of the fact that, as there are differences of station between individuals, there are differences of social relevance between the various sectional interests in the community. There is a lot of loose talk about the equality of all men and the consequences of this for social living. Although, as we have seen earlier, he does not seem to have applied the concept adequately in his own thought on Church-State relations, M. Maritain has explained that the only true equality between individuals and communities *inter se* is a proportional equality which takes cognisance of differences.[1] If the enslavement of men is anti-Christian, egalitarianism is pseudo-Christian; it sees only the essential equality among men, forgetting the individual for the abstract species. Christianity takes account of man in the concrete. It is because of its certainty of the community in nature of men that it also insists on the hierarchy which exists within this essential community and on the particular inequality on which it is based. Hence its insistence that 'as regards social life it is important to say at once that here also . . . there are and have to be both equality and inequality . . . Equality is primary inasmuch as—taken as equality pure and simple—it is concerned with the fundamental rights and common dignity of the human being, and, taken as equality of proportion, it is concerned with justice'. As long as fundamental rights and common dignity are safeguarded, the treatment of individuals and groups in accordance with their differences is justifiable. It is interesting to note that the liberal-minded Charles Morgan has given full support to these views as expressed by Maritain.[2]

It is the task of genuine democracy to recognise inequalities in so far as they are compatible with essential community of social life. There is a wealth of contrast, says A. D. Lindsay, between democracy in which differences are welcomed when

[1] Cf J. Maritain, *Principes d'une politique humaniste*, New York 1944. Trans. in *The Social and Political Philosophy of Jacques Maritain*, London 1956, pp 81 *seq*.

[2] Cf C. Morgan, *Liberties of the Mind*, pp 195-202.

they can be reconciled with fellowship and democracy in which differences of any kind are deplored.[1] He recalls how de Tocqueville, in his *Democracy in America*, disliked and disapproved of the democratic temper that envies any kind of pre-eminence, denies all standards of excellence and equalises all only by degrading all. Christian democracy does not involve such levelling; it does not turn on a demand for equal conditions for everyone. Its main interest is that each individual and section of the community shall count and shall be enabled to make his own contribution within the framework of the general interest. In short what it means by saying that all shall be treated equally is that 'none shall be held to have a claim to better treatment than another, in advance of good grounds being produced'.[2] This is the only sane meaning for the phrase 'equality of legal personality', which clearly should not mean that all individuals and societies should enjoy exactly the same rights and duties. All it signifies is the general rule that each legal personality is equal to every other in terms of basic legal capacity. It leaves open the question of what precise rights and duties each legal personality has in fact—or, what is the same thing—to what extent they are unequal.[3]

It is certain then that democracy is forced to take account of relevant social differences within the community. At which point the question is immediately raised as to what constitutes a relevant difference? And even when agreement is reached on this, there is room for further debate as regards the consequent degree of differential treatment which is entailed. Even admittedly relevant differences of social condition will justify only a limited degree of discrimination. The trouble with the *ancien régime* was not that it approved of discrimination but that many particular forms of its discrimination were unjust. There can be no valid objection to egalitarianism in so far as it meant the abolition of these, such as tax-exemptions and a property-owning franchise.[4] That it is not always easy to decide what

---

[1] Lindsay, *op. cit.* p 260.
[2] Benn and Peters, *op. cit.* p 110.
[3] Benn and Peters, *op. cit.* pp 122-123.
[4] Benn and Peters, *op. cit.* p 144.

are relevant differences or what should be the degree of differential treatment are internal problems for democratic political science. All I am interested in here is in showing that democracy recognises that there are differences and that the State has to face up to them in practice. Once this is granted it is seen that democratic progress consists as much in creating distinctions that conditions seem to justify as in eliminating those they do not.[1] The principle of equality is simply that there is a presumption against treating anybody differently until grounds for due distinction have been shown.

Democratic theory is therefore in harmony with the general idea that there has to be some discrimination in public life. As long as the fundamental rights of minorities are respected, it is quite candid about giving preference to the interests of the majority. Now this is all that Catholic theory on Church-State relations involves when it asks for special recognition of the Catholic Church in the Catholic State. There is no question whatever of religious intolerance springing from an unjust discrimination. Indeed the hypothesis, should conditions change and Catholics become a minority, is clear indication that Catholic theory is fully in accordance with the pattern of thinking that is characteristic of democratic majority rule.

[1] Benn and Peters, *op. cit.* p 115.

CHAPTER EIGHT

DEMOCRACY—TRUE AND FALSE

THERE was considerable flurry some years ago after the publication by an American writer of an elaborate attack on the political influence of the Catholic Church in Ireland. In *The Irish
and Catholic Power*[1] Paul Blanshard applied to Ireland the thesis
for which he had already acquired notoriety in his previous
books, *American Freedom and Catholic Power* and *Communism,
Democracy and Catholic Power.*[2] The gist of his argument is that,
while the political democracy of the Republic is genuine,[3] there
is an unofficial Church-State alliance in Ireland,[4] such as permits
'ecclesiastical dictatorship and political democracy to live side
by side without any sense of incongruity'.[5]

MR. BLANSHARD'S ARGUMENT

Though the Church in Ireland has no political party, it has,
says Blanshard, 'a program for the control of great areas of
modern life which belong to democracy'.[6] He instances elementary education, freedom of thought, domestic relations, law and
medical hygiene. He regards this control as a 'compromise with
democracy'[7] and believes that it is important to show it up for

[1] Paul Blanshard, *The Irish and Catholic Power*, Boston 1953.
[2] Paul Blanshard, *American Freedom and Catholic Power*, London
1951. *Communism, Democracy and Catholic Power*, London 1952.
[3] Blanshard, *The Irish and Catholic Power*, p 48.
[4] *Op. cit.* p 49.
[5] *Op. cit.* p 4.
[6] *Op. cit.* p 6.
[7] *Op. cit.* p 7.

what it is before Western eyes, lest any other State be tempted to accept this 'most advanced form of church-state relationship'. For Ireland, he says, is represented by Catholic apologists 'not only as the last bastion of Christian civilisation in Europe but also as the last bastion of a system of church-state relations which democracy needs for its moral welfare'.[1] It is held up as a model to other Catholic countries, 'the world's best showpiece of Catholic tolerance in a Catholic society', but one which he believes 'lacks many of the basic ingredients of freedom'.[2]

As an American, Mr. Blanshard regards it as his mission to lay bare the fallacies in this conception of democracy. In his own words: 'I believe that America has a lesson for the West in the field of church-state adjustment, a lesson of tolerance and good will derived from the practice of separating church and state, and that this lesson is flatly contrary to the gospel of church and state which is preached by Irish Catholicism. The two philosophies cannot both be right for the democratic world . . .'.[3] There is question, he believes, of choosing between two alternatives, the American system of Church-State separation or the Irish one of partial Church-State union under a democratic government.[4] Presumably he has no difficulty about choosing, nor, in his opinion, should anybody who is 'opposed to all bigotry and to all denominational special privilege'.[5] Any man who is averse to using 'sectarian advantage for political power'[6] cannot but reject the Irish system as inimical to democracy.

Secondly, as a descendant from a Protestant grandfather of County Down, Mr. Blanshard regards it as his mission to defend the 'preference of the Northern Irish people' to remain politically cut off from the South.[7] The attentive reader will notice that his argument somewhat changes here. He is well aware that

[1] *Op. cit.* p. 6.
[2] *Op. cit.* p. 7.
[3] *Op. cit.* p. 9.
[4] *Op. cit.* p. 11.
[5] *Op. cit.* p. 11.
[6] *Op. cit.* p. 11.
[7] *Op. cit.* p. 245.

the system of Church-State relations that is traditional in Britain and the Commonwealth involves a Church-State mixture that is unknown in America.[1] For this reason he is unable to say that Northern Irish Protestants are attracted by a British system of separation of Church and State. And so he shifts his ground, saying that they are keenly aware that 'Southern Irish democracy' is not 'as advanced or complete or mature as that of the British welfare State'.[2] But logic, perhaps, is out of place in this context. For immediately afterwards he is back again on the old refrain, agreeing with them in this choice to remain outside the Southern 'Catholic clerical State', in which choice 'the people of Northern Ireland are acting as the great majority of the American people would act under similar circumstances'.[3]

There is little need to dwell at length on Mr. Blanshard's specific charges regarding 'clerical' interference in temporal affairs in the Republic. Similar charges which he had earlier made against the Church in America have been ably and comprehensively dealt with.[4] Many elements in the replies hold also in the case of Ireland. Of course the claim may be made—as with Salmon's book *The Infallibility of the Church* (1888)—that until a book in reply to Blanshard's reflections on Ireland appears, his criticism must be regarded as valid. The argument is clearly a poor one, although in the case of Salmon it inspired Dom Butler's book over sixty years later. There seems little need to pay Blanshard such a compliment, if the known views of Southern Protestants themselves are to be counted for anything in deciding whether the Republic is a genuine democracy. In 1946, Mr. Childers, Parliamentary Secretary to the Minister of Local Government, replied to a charge made by the Northern Protestant Minister for Home Affairs to the effect that Southern Protestants are 'not happy' and 'do not prosper'. Mr. Childers is reported as saying that 'this was an entirely baseless allega-

[1] *Op. cit.* p 8.
[2] *Op. cit.* p 245.
[3] *Op. cit.* p 245.
[4] E.g. James M. O'Neill, *Catholicism and American Freedom*, New York 1952; Currin Shields, *Democracy and Catholicism in America*, New York 1958.

tion . . . The Protestants of the 26 counties lived in an atmosphere of complete tolerance, their share in industrial and commercial activity far exceeding the proportion of their numbers, and in connection with all government and local appointments where examinations were held, there was no religious test whatever'.[1] As late as 1959 we find the Protestant Senator, Professor Stanford, reiterating and even strengthening these sentiments: 'In this country there is full justice for minorities, and we have good reason to be thankful to be living here where justice prevails'.[2]

We may disregard Mr. Blanshard's extravagant criticisms of the role of the Church in Ireland in matters of education, censorship etc. Scarcely a month passes that they are not put forward—in one guise or another—from quarters not particularly noted for friendliness towards the Catholic Church. And Catholic replies, of all sorts, abound. I am more concerned with the fundamental, philosophical criticism that the Irish system is out of tune with Anglo-American democratic ideology. I hope I have already shown that the pattern of Catholic theory on Church-State relations in general is eminently in harmony with religious toleration and a genuine respect for religious liberty. I hope too, in a final chapter, to make clear that an arrangement on the Irish model is quite acceptable to Catholic principles. Mr. Blanshard is right in thinking that it might be held up to Catholic countries as an example which they could follow with safety. But if this is so, does his criticism not mean—in essence—that Catholic political philosophy, even in its most acceptable application, is unacceptable to American-type democracy?

For Mr. Blanshard, in fact, it means that Catholicism is at loggerheads with 'democracy' simply speaking. In his other books we are left in no doubt about this. In *American Freedom and Catholic Power* he has argued that the kind of tolerance accorded by Catholic principles represents a medieval rather than a modern conception. 'The hierarchy's undemocratic con-

[1] *The Irish Times*, 16 March 1946.
[2] Quoted by Mr. Lemass in Oxford Debate, *The Irish Times*, 16 October 1959.

ception of tolerance goes back to a medieval conception of limited freedom . . . a Catholic treatise on freedom frequently resembles a communist treatise on democracy. In such a treatise the standard meanings of words are often reversed or modified to fit a prefabricated conclusion that "true" freedom comes to men only through the Roman Catholic hierarchy'.[1]

Like so many of Blanshard's charges against the Church, this statement contains a truth which he twists out of its proper significance. It is quite true that the Catholic conception of tolerance does go back to a medieval conception of the nature of freedom. But not in the way, or with the implications, suggested by Blanshard.

LIBERTY AND CHRISTIANITY

One of the most important consequences of Christianity was its introduction into the world of a conception of religious tolerance which presented a grave challenge to the Roman State. I have already referred to the ancient pagan attitude towards freedom of opinion. In both Greece and Rome it was limited only to the extent that one could not externally deny the religion of the State. This was satisfied by outward conformity to the established cult, after which one was quite free to practice other cults if one wished. A problem had been caused in this respect by Judaism. Based on the idea of one God and one true religion, Judaism was out of harmony with the Roman system. It was essentially and uncompromisingly exclusive. But Judaism had not much influence and could be ignored. Centred, as it was, in a small region on the confines of the Empire, and being in no way anxious to make converts outside the chosen Hebrew people, the Roman authorities could afford to waive the law in its regard. With Christianity things were different. Although at the beginning it was regarded as but a dissident Jewish sect, its differences from Judaism were soon to make themselves manifest. Christianity, it appeared, was not merely exclusive but universal. It considered adoration of any

---

[1] Blanshard, *Freedom and Catholic Power*, London 1951, p 269.

god other than the God of Christianity as itself an offence against God. Moreover it would not be satisfied with any and every kind of worship of God. That alone was regarded as adequate which He Himself had signified as acceptable to Him. In other words, only Christian worship sufficed. Lastly, it had to be orthodox Christian worship. In later times this came to mean that non-Catholic Christian worship was excluded.

In addition to this, Christianity took upon itself the task of converting the whole world to the Christian faith. This means that it worked, not only for its own diffusion, but for the disappearance of all other religions. It was these characteristics of exclusiveness and universality that brought it into sharp conflict with the Roman government. If Christianity had but introduced one more god to the scene, then, presumably, all would have been well. But its principles entailed something quite different—the unseating of the pagan gods from their pedestals. The social effects of this would be disastrous for the State, particularly at a time when Emperor-worship was practised. As a result it is not surprising that Christianity should have quickly run into difficulties with the Roman authorities. Because of the close connection between the official religion and civic life, the Christian had to abstain from public solemnities. This led to his being regarded as an 'enemy of the State', as the long history of the persecutions shows clearly.

With the triumph of Christianity came an inevitable social reorganisation. Doctrinal error was now regarded as a form of corruption against which the citizens of the State had to be protected. It became part of the mission of the Christian State to defend its people from the evil influence of heretics. As the modern State fights disease in the name of 'preventive medicine', so the Christian State sought to prevent the spread of unbelief. Yet the Church never demanded or agreed to the idea that the true religion should be forced on people unwillingly. As early as the days of St. Justin Martyr we find her teaching that religious belief is essentially a free act of adhesion to truth.[1] In other words, the Church fully respected infidelity that was rooted clearly on a basis of good faith. It is true, of course, that,

[1] *Apology*, ch II.

from time to time, we find Christian rulers imposing the faith with violence. But this was an abuse that had no official ecclesiastical approbation. Thus Alcuin upbraided Charlemagne for forcibly baptising the Saxons. In brief, the attitude of the Christian State towards religion can be summed up under two main heads. First of all, it regarded as a duty the protection of the Christian faith. Secondly, but subordinate to this, it respected the genuine convictions of infidels and heretics.[1]

But let us examine the situation a little more closely.[2] To what extent did liberty of religion exist under the Christian States of the high Middle Ages? Liberty of internal belief, as might be expected, was allowed to all. As regards liberty of expressing it, a distinction was made. The Christian was not only free to worship publicly; he was bound to do so or be punished. For, knowing the truth and having given his adhesion to it, he was regarded as guilty of a crime if he failed to live up to it in his external actions. This attitude of the State was due to its conception of the extent to which it should co-operate with the Church. It meant that, in principle, the coercive power of the State could extend to punishing every breach of Christian morality. In practice it was far from being applied thus widely; rulers judged what was best in the circumstances. But the principle was always there and provided the basis for the punishment of heretics and apostates. For although sincere unbelief was generally respected, it seems that it was commonly thought that sincerity was a somewhat scarce commodity when there was question of apostasy, heresy or schism. Non-Christians, on the other hand, were allowed liberty of religious worship to the extent that it did not injure public Christian order. A great deal of seemingly harsh medieval legislation against the Jews can

---

[1] Cf. Pope Gregory IX, *Letter to the Bishops of France*, 1233: 'As for the Jews, Christians ought to conduct themselves with the same charity that they would desire to see used toward Christians who live in pagan countries'; Pope Innocent III, *Letter to the Archbishop of Soles:* 'It is contrary to the Christian religion that a man be forced to become and to remain Christian against his will and despite his opposition'.

[2] Cf J. Leclercq, *Leçons de Droit Naturel*, vol. III pp 64-71.

be explained as being necessary under this head. The law, for example, that they should stay indoors on Good Friday was undoubtedly prompted by the interests of public order. It was a police measure on the lines of the Organic Articles of the Napoleonic Concordat. Indeed its purpose was as much to protect the Jews from the Christians as to safeguard the latter from Jewish insults. This, of course, was also avoided and the avoidance of it was regarded as a duty on the State. Non-Christians were forbidden to attack or insult the faith. In consequence, it is only natural that liberty of propaganda is something that was especially forbidden to them.

In short, while the religious liberty of non-Christians in good faith was, in itself, respected, the medieval system placed definite limits to liberty of religious expression in so far as this might threaten or disturb the ideological framework of the Christian State. Tolerance there was, but within definite limits.

Medieval Christendom realised that full human freedom was no more attainable on earth than was full and perfect union with God. Yet man's aim must be to narrow the distance which separates him from the attainment of full freedom. Tellenbach, in his famous work *Church, State and Christian Society*,[1] tells us that the Middle Ages considered it acceptable that even among men on earth those who were spiritually more advanced should have some power over those who stood in need of guidance. And it was assumed—though not always rightly—that the existing gradations in society were a reflection of this. Within this structure freedom was conceived in terms of a social system in which each part was independent of all else except that to which it was immediately subordinate. There were particular freedoms rather than a freedom universally enjoyed. As Gierke puts it, in the Middle Ages 'an abstract conception of freedom . . . is lacking'.[2] There was the *libertas* of the serf, free from all but his particular overlord. There was the *libertas* of a monastery, free from the rule of the diocesan bishop, but subject to other ecclesiastical authority. There was the *libertas* of a people entire, free

---

[1] Gerd Tellenbach, *Church, State and Christian Society*, Studies in Medieval History, III, Oxford 1948.

[2] O. Gierke, *Political Theories of the Middle Age*, Cambridge, 1900.

from the rule of anyone except their king and bound to him only in so far as he fulfilled his duty to them.

We have here a further aspect of the medieval conception of freedom—its positive content. In this it differed fundamentally from the Roman conception, for which freedom was a negative thing, the absence of limitations, and therefore the same for all. In the medieval conception the positive content of freedom was more important than its negative aspect, independence. It meant the possession of certain rights. The *libertas* of a monastery, for example, consisted in the totality of its subjective rights, its status. For this reason the terms *libertas* and *privilegium* were interchangeable. The *privilegium* of a person or body meant its rights. Each person and body had its own *privilegium*, its proper *libertas*, its own proper *status*. There was an endless differentiation of privilege and, therefore, of status and liberty. Yet at bottom the possessors were all on the same level and their liberty was essentially the same. Indeed in medieval times there was frequent mention of the 'freedom' of serfs and even of slaves, just as much as that of their lords and masters. The rights of all had a similar legal structure and the differences between them were only quantitative. In particular, privilege did not mean an exception to law. As Tellenbach has put it: 'A privilege does not—as one might suppose from the modern use of the term—create exceptions to a generally prevailing law; rather it is the precise formulation of an actual and concret subjective right, that is, a *libertas*'.[1] The law was a system of 'to each his own'. It was the charter, as it were, of the rights of individuals and, for his reason, was a reflection of the natural law.

Such was the medieval conception of freedom. Those who wish to convince themselves can find abundant proof in Tellenbach's work. It was a notion of freedom as bounded by definite limits. And it is a notion that has not been forgotten by Catholic Christianity, although its concrete realisation has been altered since the Middle Ages. The question before us—raised by Blanshard and many critics of Catholicism—is whether it is compatible with the pattern of life that is known as 'democracy'.

[1] *Op. cit.* p 121.

THE MEANING OF DEMOCRACY

Though it ranks high among the most frequently used terms
at present, the meaning of 'democracy' is very far from clear.
It has somehow acquired a kind of mystical connotation, an
emotionally charged content, relating to what people regard as
important social values without being at all sure of what exactly they mean. This is particularly true of the man in the
street, who, mostly unthinkingly, declares himself an upholder
of 'democracy'. But it is true too of public figures and philosophers, whom one might expect to have clarified their ideas on
the matter. What seem at first sight to be the most diverse
political regimes are at one in claiming the label 'democratic'.
The vogue of democracy has become so sacred that, all over the
world today, to appear to reject it means to court ostracisation.

This vogue of democracy, coupled with the fact that it has
found the most divergent adherents, prompted the Norwegian
philosopher, Arne Naess, to undertake a comprehensive investigation into its meaning. The result has been the publication by
Oslo University Press in 1956, of *Democracy, Ideology and
Objectivity*, the only complete analysis of which I am aware in
what might be called the semantics of 'democracy'.

In an appendix Arne Naess gives a chronological list of
definitions—or what he calls 'definitoid statements'—on democracy. They range from a definition attributed to Solon in
the 6th century, B.C. to one proposed by President Truman in
1949. Over three hundred definitions in all are included—
'normative', expressing what their framers thought the term
should connote; 'descriptive', expressing the actual use to which
the term is put; and 'real', intending to cover the essential
points in the order of fact which the term purports to convey
in the order of ideas.

Despite the aids to clarity which he has brought to his task
and which frequently reveal coincidences in seemingly opposed
definitions, Arne Naess has to admit that it is utterly impossible
to regard 'democracy' as anything other than an equivocal
term. The only common element that can be found in the many

concepts of democracy is that it is a form of government or political system that is careful to respect the rights of the people. But beyond this 'genus' level there is nothing but diversity. 'Precisations' of what is understood as catering for the rights of the people yield extremely different ideas of democracy. From such have stemmed 'Athenian democracy' and 'Medieval democracy', 'Economic democracy', 'Liberal democracy' and 'Soviet democracy'. In the City States of Greece democracy was conceived as the political system whereby the people governed themselves directly. For understandable reasons this system of collective decision was never widely adopted; it is quite impracticable in the larger State. Modern times have seen the introduction of what is called 'indirect' democracy, by which the people—or the majority of the people—is said to govern itself through elected representatives. The more recent system of Soviet—or proletarian—democracy is something new. Stalin described it as 'democracy for the working people'.[1] Of course if the working people constitutes the whole population of the State, there would be no difference between proletarian democracy and direct or indirect democracy. And we know that, in Marxist theory, the process of history should eventually lead to the disappearance of all but the working class. But in such circumstances—also in Marxist theory—the State should disappear, except perhaps for some administrative apparatus. As long as the State as a form of government remains in existence, the description of democracy given by Stalin needs explanation. Stalin himself evaded doing this, but it was done with particular clarity by his predecessor Lenin: 'Democracy is a State which recognises the subordination of the minority to the majority, i.e., an organisation for the systematic use of violence by one class against the other'.[2] Democracy, in other words, means the dictatorship of the proletariat.

Whatever else this concept of democracy may entail, it is clearly a different concept from that of government by the people as a whole. The idea of oppression, which is essential to Lenin's notion of democracy, is quite foreign to the system of

[1] J. Stalin, *Leninism*, London 1946, p 579.
[2] V. Lenin, *The State and Revolution*.

representative government as conceived elsewhere. It is true that the majority system, which has emerged as the most common form of representative government, means that the minority has little say in practice. This is a difficulty that has defied adequate solution, but it does not necessarily involve the oppression of the minority. That is certainly not involved in the *theory* of representative democracy. Stalin might say, as he did say, that, in the capitalist countries, democracy means the dictatorship of wealth. But, as far as theory goes, there is no room for any dictatorship within its framework. The theoretical difference between it and the system of Lenin and Stalin is so great that one has to draw a rigid distinction between what have come to be called the Western and the Eastern concepts of democracy.

This in itself should be sufficient to warn us of the need for distinctions when speaking of democracy. It should be sufficient to put us on our guard when faced with glib assertions such as those of Blanshard that Catholic political philosophy can never go further than reaching an uneasy compromise with the 'democratic' way of life. It is so easy to use the word 'democracy' as suits oneself. Of course, it is the Western concept that Blanshard has in mind, or what is generally known as 'Liberal Democracy'. It will be profitable, however, to examine what this means more clearly. Perhaps it too is an equivocal, or analogous, concept, or a genus concept with more than one species?

One of the most striking characteristics about the protagonists of 'Liberal Democracy' is their uncritical acceptance of the idea that it is a univocal concept. The cause of this may not lie entirely with themselves, for it is also almost universally accepted by their antagonists. For Blanshard, Liberal Democracy is gloriously univocal, as are its concrete realisations in England, France and America. In this, as I say, he is but re-echoing the accepted thesis of contemporary Liberal philosophers. One of the most recent defences of Liberal Democracy—by the Italian Massimo Salvadori[1]—gives us a clear idea of what the concept

---

[1] Massimo Salvadori, *Liberal Democracy*, London 1958. See also J. Salwyn Schapiro, *Liberalism: its Meaning and History*, New York 1958, *passim*.

is believed to entail: 'Liberal democracy is the correct expression with which to designate democracy as the organisation of Liberty. Its significant feature is the way in which liberty and equality are interwoven with the aid of solidarity . . . The founders of the American Republic, the revolutionaries in France and the reformers in Great Britain were able to see the intimate relationship between liberty, equality and solidarity realised in the democratic state'.[1]

For Salvadori—and his self-styled Liberal colleagues—Liberal Democracy is associated both with a sceptical rationalism and something which approaches libertarianism in conduct. 'Liberty', says Salvadori, 'exists in the measure in which individuals can reach decisions through the use of their own critical reasoning powers, and in the measure in which they can act on the basis of the decisions reached'.[2] Liberty cannot be beholden to truth. Indeed in Salvadori's belief, there is no such thing as truth; for anyone to proclaim that he knows the truth is but arrogant assertion. Experience shows the limited range of reason and anything that is discovered by means other than reason is unproved. Nor have traditional ideas any relevance for the present. Whatever principles and concepts may have had validity in the past are no guide to the later problems of a dynamic world. Education in liberal democracies must aim at the development of the individual's reasoning powers; it must entirely eschew indoctrination of any kind. Needless to say, this 'new' education—of Dewey and Russell—has no place for morality and religion. The democratic State thus conceived is a secularist one. Its chief function is the maintenance of unlimited liberty in the realm of ideas, while, in the practical order, its ordinances will be so self-restricted as to allow as much freedom of action as possible. It is an officially godless

---

[1] Salvadori, *op. cit.* p 6. Cf also *ibid.* p 32: 'First in Great Britain, then across the Channel and across the Atlantic, the forerunners of liberalism (a small but dynamic and influential group) defined the institutions of a free commonwealth, of a society composed of free citizens. To advocate these institutions was the programme of liberals in Europe and in the Americas . . . '

[2] Salvadori, *op. cit.* p 17.

political construction, indifferent to all but men's right to think and say what they like and to do what they like in so far as that is compatible with the essential framework of social living.[1] This is the system which Liberals call democracy, and which they trace to the common heritage of the English, French and American revolutions.

It is a curious irony that those who lived at the time of these revolutions had a different story to tell. If we take up contemporary accounts of the French and American revolutions, what we are struck by is contrast rather than comparison. Such an account is to be found in the *Letters of Publicola*, published by John Quincy Adams in 1791. Its purpose was to show the profound difference between the spirit of liberty in America and that which animated the revolutionaries in France. 'Happy, thrice happy the people of America . . . whose principles of religious liberty did not result from an indiscriminate contempt of all religions whatever, and whose equal representation in their legislative councils was founded upon an equality really existing among them, and not upon the metaphysical speculations of fanciful politicians . . . ' In Adams's view the only thing common to the French and American political scenes was the word, empty of content, 'Republic'. It was Adams who, in 1801, when Minister of the United States of America to Prussia, translated into English an essay by the Prussian man of letters Frederick Gentz, *The French and American Revolutions Compared*.[2] Published originally in 1800 in Berlin, Gentz's essay is the greatest indictment ever penned of those who would confuse the origins

---

[1] Cf also Schapiro, *op. cit.* p 12: 'In general, liberals have been rationalists. As a consequence they have developed what may be called a secular attitude toward religion. In their view, a religion is an opinion to be tolerated like all other opinions; and a church is a private institution to be accepted like all other institutions. Liberalism has advocated freedom of non-belief as well as of belief. To achieve complete religious freedom required the secularisation of public life. Everywhere, liberals generally have advocated separation of church and state; secular, public education; civil marriage; and laws permitting divorce'.

[2] Frederick Gentz, *The French and American Revolutions Compared*, Chicago 1955.

of democracy in America and France.

Whereas the American revolution was the revolt of a harried people in defence of prescriptive rights, that of France, says Gentz, marked a new departure in the conception of man and society. It was a break with the past, occasioned by a radical dogma of liberty, whose authors regarded themselves as men with a mission, not merely to France but to the world entire. The American was, in a real sense, a revolution prevented, that in France a revolution merely started.[1] The first Congress of all the colonies, which met in Philadelphia in 1774, was moderate, in the extreme, in its demands: 'We ask only for peace, liberty and security. We wish no diminution of royal prerogatives; we demand *no new rights*'.[2] This is a far cry from claims to an abstract liberty such as were made in France. As Gentz puts it: 'The revolution of America was . . . a revolution of necessity . . . (It) exhibited a model of moderation in defence (whereas) the French one displayed an unparalleled example of violence and inexorable fury in attack'.[3]

[1] *Ibid.* p 47: 'The American revolution was from beginning to end, on the part of the Americans, merely a *defensive revolution;* the French was from the beginning to end, in the highest sense of the word, an *offensive revolution*'.

[2] Cited in Gentz, *op. cit.* p 51.

[3] Gentz, *op. cit.* p 56; Cf also *ibid.* p 60: 'The American revolution, at every stage of its duration, had a fixed and definite object, and moved within definite limits, and by a definite direction towards this object. The French revolution never had a definite object; and in a thousand various directions, continually crossing each other, ran through the unbounded space of a fantastic arbitrary will, and of a bottomless anarchy'. Also p 70: 'As the utmost precision of object, and consequently of principles and of means, distinguished the American revolution through its whole duration, so the utmost want of precision in the object, and consequently of perpetual mutability in the choice of the means and in the modification of principles has been one of the most stubborn, one of the most essential, and certainly one of the most terrible characteristics of the French Revolution'. And p 73: 'For the ambition (of the French revolutionists) . . . the theatre, which France offered to their thirst for destruction, was too small; they wished to tear the world from its poles, and commence a new era for the human race'.

In no domain does the difference between the resultant American and French systems of democracy come up more clearly than in that of the place of religion in society. The shrewd de Tocqueville—himself so sceptical about the value of many aspects of American life—gave special place and praise to the American—and British—achievement in having succeeded in combining religion with the political institutions of democracy. The character of Anglo-American civilisation, he says, 'is the result (and this should be constantly present to the mind) of two distinct elements, which in other places have been in frequent hostility, but which in America have been admirably incorporated and combined with one another. I allude to the spirit of Religion and the spirit of Liberty'.[1] He could not help contrasting the American scene with that in his native France, in which religion had been ousted from the official life of the nation. The reason lay in the forces of inspiration which had moulded the respective societies—in France, rationalistic, secularistic, anti-clerical; in America, positively Christian, if undenominational.[2]

Nor do those who have given us a description of England after the Glorious Revolution paint a picture of secularism such as is entailed by the democracy of Salvadori or Blanshard. One such account is that by the Genevan, De Lolme, whose essay

[1] Alexis de Tocqueville, *Democracy in America*, first published in 1835 and 1840. New York 1956, p 47.

[2] See de Tocqueville, *op. cit.* pp 144-145: 'It must never be forgotten that religion gave birth to Anglo-American society. In the United States, religion is therefore mingled with all the habits of the nation and all the feelings of patriotism, whence it derives a peculiar force . . . In the United States, Christian sects are infinitely diversified and perpetually modified; but Christianity itself is an established and irresistible fact, which no one undertakes either to attack or to defend. The Americans, having admitted inquiry, are obliged to accept in like manner a great number of moral truths originating in it and connected with it. Hence the activity of individual analysis is restrained within narrow limits, and many of the most important of human opinions are removed from its influence'.

The Constitution of England was published in French, in Amsterdam, in 1770.[1] It contains a lucid survey of the rights and liberties of the English people seen as deriving from their system of government and body of laws. There is no reference to any abstract notion of liberty. On the contrary, De Lolme contrasts the moderate and limited nature of the revolution of 1688—and indeed of every revolution that had occurred in English history—with the intemperate zeal for an undefined ideal of liberty, which caused revolutions elsewhere to be so barren of results. In ancient Greece and Rome, the Florence of Machiavelli, France, Spain, Denmark—'public commotions ended by treaties, in which . . . the grievances of the people, though ever so loudly complained of in the beginning by those who acted as their defenders, were, in the issue, most carelessly attended to, or even totally disregarded . . . But, if we turn our eyes towards the English history, scenes of quite different kind will offer to our view; and we shall find, on the contrary, that revolutions in England have always been terminated by making such provisions, and only such, as all orders of the people were really and indiscriminately to enjoy'. De Lolme saw the revolution of 1688 as but the completion of what was begun by Magna Charta, continued by the confirmations of this under Henry III, still further strengthened during the period of the Plantagenets and—after the Tudor interval—later maintained, right down through the Petition of Rights under Charles I and the additional guarantees of the reign of Charles II.[2] De Lolme certainly would have been the last to regard democracy in Eng-

[1] J. H. De Lolme, *The Constitution of England*, English trans. London 1821.

[2] Cf also Henry Hallam, *The Constitutional History of England*, p 131: 'It were a strange misrepresentation of history to assert, that the constitution had attained anything like a perfect state in the fifteenth century; but I know not whether there are any essential privileges of our countrymen, any fundamental securities against arbitrary power, so far as they depend upon positive institution, which may not be traced to the time when the house of Plantagenet filled the English throne'.

land as the fruit of the forces which were later to produce it in France.[1]

THE FATHERHOOD OF LOCKE

The fundamental reason for the disposition of later historians to identify the British, French and American traditions of democracy has been their belief that all three owed a common inspiration to John Locke.[2] They could be guilty of no greater mistake. It is true that Locke was the apologist of the English Revolution, but it is essential to understand exactly what this means. Though it is seldom recognised, it means no more than that Locke was the philosopher of a rebellious aristocracy, who wanted no change beyond the fashioning of a limited monarchy under which real power would be vested in themselves. Locke's *Two Treatises on Government* (1690) provided this. Historians of political theory are accustomed to point out that, as this was *published* after the revolution had been accomplished, its purpose was to justify the pattern which the revolution had taken rather than to expound fully its author's own views on politics. It is suggested that Locke's broader personal views can be glimpsed in the *Second Treatise*, in which, it has been said, he

---

[1] Even Schapiro is forced to admit that 'French liberalism was formulated in a different manner and proclaimed in a different spirit from that of British liberalism. Unlike the lattter it had no deep historic roots, no tradition of freedom that "slowly broadens down from precedent to precedent" . . . Its ideas . . . were universal in spirit, abstract in character, and revolutionary in application'—*op. cit.* p 50.

[2] E.g. Salvadori, *op. cit.* p 120, who says that Locke 'expressed the position of the majority of those who were responsible for the transformation both of Great Britain and of the American colonies after 1688'. Some Catholic writers hold a like opinion. Thus: 'Locke . . . developed a theory which was to be used as a prophetic vindication of two more revolutions in the eighteenth century (in addition to the English revolution of 1688), those in America and in France'—Thomas P. Neill, *The Rise and Decline of Liberalism*, Milwaukee 1953, p 49: parentheses mine.

'writes throughout with his eye on Hobbes',[1] the great enemy of popular sovereignty. And it is assumed that a full understanding of Locke the democratic revolutionary can be had only by combining the *Treatises on Government* with the later *Letters on Toleration*. It is difficult to maintain these views any longer, since the appearance of Mr. Peter Laslett's compelling demonstration that the *Two Treatises* was *composed* by 1683, at the latest, and was really a tract, on the side of the Whig Exclusionists, to combat the ideas of Filmer's *Patriarcha*, which had become a powerful weapon of the established monarchical order after its publication in 1680.[2] That the *Two Treatises* is a defence of 'aristocratic revolution' has been confirmed by Mr. Brian Farrell, who has shown conclusively that, in the *Second Treatise*, Locke leans rather heavily on Richard Hooker, the Elizabethan author of *The Laws of Ecclesiastical Polity*, in which stress was laid on the importance of consent to all forms of government and on the supremacy of law as against the claims of the absolute monarch.[3] In doing this, Mr. Farrell points out, Locke was in fact being conservative. He was en-

[1] C. E. Vaughan, *Studies in the History of Political Philosophy before and after Rousseau*, Manchester 1939, ch IV.

[2] Cf Peter Laslett, The English Revolution and Locke's Two Treatises of Government, in *The Cambridge Historical Journal*, vol. XI, no. I. According to Laslett, Locke's *Two Treatises*, is regarded traditionally as being 'a wonderfully effective justification of what the people of England had done in the year before its appearance . . . It gave coherence to their new constitution, it crystallised their social and political beliefs, it rationalised their Revolution then as it rationalised the American and French Revolutions which came after. Statements like these are a standard feature of all the history books and the works on political theory . . . This belief has never been seriously doubted . . . Nevertheless, it is quite untrue . . . What Locke wrote did justify the "Whig Revolution of 1688", if that phrase can be permitted at all . . . What cannot be maintained is that the original conception of the book was to justify a revolution which had already been consummated'.

[3] Brian Farrell, *The Influence of Richard Hooker on John Locke's Second Treatise of Civil Government*, Unpublished M.A. Dissertation, University College, Dublin 1956.

deavouring to show that Whig ideas meant a return to a more constitutional form of government. And he was glad to be able to use Hooker for the propagandist purpose of showing that there existed a respectable English political tradition which regarded political power as a trust. Undoubtedly Locke was more 'radical' than Hooker. He developed an elaborate theory of resistance—whereby the people could press their rights—of a kind that was quite impossible in the days of the Elizabethan. But it is poles apart from the kind of popular revolutionary democracy which was to appear in France in the following century.

Nor is there any trace of rationalist secularism in the *Two Treatises*. We get an engaging account of the origin of the State —out of an aboriginal condition in which men were free and equal, and by way of a contract whereby a government was set up to ensure respect for men's natural rights. We get an account too of the consequent functions of government—the securing of the life, liberty and property of the citizens. Thirdly, we get an account of the structure of government, in that Locke laid the basis, if he did not actually moot, what is today called the Separation of Powers. Most of this was acceptable to the nobility whom Locke served. They may not have liked his account of a State of nature in which all men were originally equal; indeed at the beginning they did not receive his work with much enthusiasm. Still his insistence on limited government and especially on property was such as to win their favour before long. The former idea served to provide backing for their retention of power from the King, while the latter was suitable comfort for a landed gentry. Hence, though Locke may have said nothing directly in defence of aristocracy, he has been rightly termed by Acton 'the philosopher of government by the gentry'. His was no paen of a universal abstract liberty and the common man benefitted only acidentally from his vogue. De Lolme was right when he declared that English revolutions have always been terminated by making provisions which 'all orders of the people', and not merely the few, could enjoy. But it is also true that, as far as the commoners went, these liberties were involuntarily secured by the action of an aristocracy that was interested merely in gain for itself. This was true of the barons at Runnymede; it was true too of the aristocratic rebels of 1688. They had to extend the privileges which they had won to some supporters outside their own ranks, supporters who, by reason of their growing power and financial influence, it was necessary to keep on their side. Hence it was that the freedom of the aristocrat came to be conferred—accidentally—on merchant and farmer.[1] For all that, Locke is still the apologist of the propertied classes. What his *Treatises on Government* offered and found acceptable in England was a parliamentary system through which these classes could exert influence.

In short, to call Locke the protagonist of French-type revolution is to play fox and geese with the facts of history. In this respect, Mr. Peter Laslett's conclusion to his 'revisionist' article on the chronology of Locke has an important bearing on the viewpoint which I am developing here. The political scientist, says Mr. Laslett, may find in this revision 'grounds for being critical of one of his accepted concepts, so useful and so inclusive as to be a general category, the concept of Revolution. The name Revolution, in the sense in which we use it, was born in England in 1688-89 . . . Because of what happened in England then, and because of the view which contemporaries so soon took of it and which historians immediately elaborated, we talk of the English Revolution, the French Revolution, the American Revolution, . . . We do so because we associate sudden political changes with total transformation, political and social . . . But as we have said, the phrase itself has become meaningless. Locke was no revolutionary in any case, in the conventional sense. How can we go on associating him with 'The English Revolution', whatever that may mean, now that we know that he wrote in anticipation of events? Perhaps it is time we abandoned the phrase itself and the system of muddled and superficial generalization which goes with it'.[2]

Locke, however, was also the author of a famous *Letter*

---

[1] Cf C. Northcote Parkinson, *The Evolution of Political Thought*, London 1958, p 117.

[2] Peter Laslett, *loc. cit.* p 55.

concerning Toleration (1689), in which was outlined, for the first time, the liberal thesis that the State should not favour any Church or religious group. Ostensibly based on the need for tolerance, in the absence of which Locke himself had to leave the country (1684), in reality it laid the basis of the lay, godless State. 'All the power of civil government relates only to men's civil interests, is confined to the care of things in this world, and hath nothing to do with the world to come'.[1] But if we are to search for the main influence of these ideas of Locke, it is to France rather than to America or England that we must turn. Jean Jacques Rousseau it was who most extensively adopted and elaborated them. Locke's influence on Rousseau is very marked. It was Locke who inspired the *Discourse on the Origin of Inequality* (1775) in which Rousseau followed the thinking of the *Two Treatises on Government*. It was from Locke too that he derived the idea of the Social Contract, which led to his own treatise, with that title, of 1762. And it was from Locke's *Letter concerning Toleration* that Rousseau got the germ of what he was to build into the idea of a godless liberal democracy.

For Rousseau carried Locke to his logical extreme. On Locke's reference to political power as residing in the community (the aristocracy) Rousseau erected the sovereignty of the people as a whole, with a general will that is absolute and can do no wrong. On Locke's *Letter* he also erected—and with greater ease—the idea of 'Civil Religion' for which his name has become notorious. Locke had mooted the divorce of politics and religion. But he had also—and quite inconsistently—refused toleration to Catholics and atheists. Of the Catholic Church he had said: 'That church can have no right to be tolerated by the magistrate, which is constituted upon such a bottom, that all those who enter it, do thereby *ipso facto*, deliver themselves up to the protection and service of another prince (the Pope)'.[2] All this was transformed by Rousseau, who saw that there would be no inconsistency if religion were exclusively a civil affair, if the State required belief in a God of reason and in the sanctity of the social contract and of the laws. 'These are the positive

[1] Locke, *Letter Concerning Toleration*, London 1800, p 19.
[2] *Letter Concerning Toleration:* parentheses mine.

dogmas' and 'whoever dares to say "Outside the Church there is no salvation" ought to be driven from the State, unless the State be the Church and the Prince the Pontiff'.

It is not difficult to see the influence of Locke in all this, little though Locke himself might have liked it. We can find it too in Condillac's *Essai sur l'origine des connaissances humaines*, in Sieye's *Essai sur les privilèges*, in Mirabeau's *Essai sur le despotisme* and Bayle's *Traité de la tolérance universelle*. We can find it in Helvetius, Cabanais, Voltaire and Holbach, Turgot, Diderot, D'Alembert, Condorcet and Destutt de Tracy.[1] The *philosophes* and *encyclopaedists* were Locke's pupils. But outside France his germinal secularism was not so widely accepted. In America the ideas of Locke that received general approval were more or less confined to his *Treatises on Government*. His limitation of the power of the State was accepted; so also his doctrine of the separation of powers and his defence of private property. His *Letter on Toleration* had much less vogue, though Locke did have some part in the drawing up of the Constitution of the State of Carolina in 1669.

It would be fatal to think that Locke had little influence on American thought. I do not wish to create this impression for a moment. The *Two Treatises* was avidly read by the political leaders and 'the great Mr. Locke' quoted reverently.[2] And not only by men like Franklin, Hamilton and Jefferson, but by the property owners,[3] the educationists[4] and the general philosophers. The *Two Treatises*, though seldom explicitly cited, was an important influence at the Constitutional Convention of 1789; it underlay the assumptions of the participants that the people had a right to determine their own constitutions. It was required reading for law students at the University of Virginia and its effect on popular thought is reflected in 'hundreds of

[1] Cf M. Siegnobos, *A History of the French People*, p 274.

[2] Cf Merle Curti, The Great Mr. Locke, America's Philosopher, 1783-1861, in *The Huntington Library Bulletin*, no. 11, pp 108-151.

[3] Cf Paschal Larkin, *Property in the Eighteenth Century, with special reference to England and Locke*, Cork 1930, p 145 *seq*.

[4] Cf P. F. Butts and L. A. Cremin, *A History of Education in American Culture*, New York 1953, pp 55 seq.

election sermons . . . and Fourth of July orations'.[1] Liberal educationists were influenced by Locke's *Some Thoughts concerning Education*[2]; his *Reasonableness of Christianity* became the bedside book of American rationalists,[3] and his *Essay Concerning Human Understanding* an established philosophical textbook. The *Letters on Toleration* too were used frequently by Unitarian apologists to defend themselves against the attacks of the orthodox. Yet it is interesting to note how soon the thought of Americans in general began to sift the cockle from the good grain in Locke. Mr. Merle Curti has provided us with a wealth of evidence on this[4]—Calvinistic Yale warning its students against Locke at the beginning of the 18th century; the growing realisation, as the century wore on, of the irreligion which he could be made to subserve; then, early in the 19th century, the dropping of his books as texts and the general appearance of a positive revolt against Locke that was intensified through associating him with the rationalism and materialism which had lain at the root of the excesses of the revolution in France.

Whatever Americans may have felt about Locke during the ferment of their revolution, once they had time to think they became quite definite about what they would accept of him. Of course there were always some who were ready to employ his ideas to further radical programmes. His uncalvinistic conception of human nature was found eminently suitable to provide backing for the work of the many humanitarian social reform groups which began to appear on the American scene during the 19th century. He had admirers too who tried to dissociate him from Rousseau and to bring about a general come-back of his influence. To an ever greater extent, however, he came to be appealed to only for specific purposes—by the opponents of slavery, for example, who were prepared to launch a revolution to end it, or, anomalously, by critics of the emerging aristocratic tendencies which began to manifest themselves

[1] Curti, *loc. cit.* p 136.
[2] *Loc. cit.*, pp 110-114.
[3] *Loc. cit.*, pp 114-119.
[4] *Loc. cit.*, pp 116-129.

in American life. More anomalously still, we find some Churchmen arguing from the Lockean pattern of American government that religion had an indispensable role to play in fashioning public opinion if the country was to be saved from the
forces of secularism. There was certainly no cult of Locke under
the trappings of liberal indifferentism in which Rousseau had
wrapped the *Letters on Toleration*.

RELIGION AND ANGLO-AMERICAN DEMOCRACY

The truth is that America did not need such liberalism.
Americans, as de Tocqueville remarked, were 'born free'.[1] The
main thesis of Louis Hartz's *Liberal Tradition in America*[2] is
that as America never developed the objectionable marks of a
feudal society, it never developed a tradition of reaction and
extreme revolution. It took an *ancien régime* to inspire Rousseau,
a *régime* which the American States never knew. The South
provided the nearest approach to this, yet it never kindled the
brand of bourgeois passion nor the frustrated intellectualism of
the Continental liberals. The European liberal on the Rousseau
model needed enemies in order to exist; in America they were
not to be found. An established religion, on the old model, was
lacking, amid the high degree of religious diversity of the colonists. Indeed religion itself, in the shape of New England nonconformity, was fiercely opposed to any 'political church'.[3] It

[1] *Democracy in America*, Boston 1873.

[2] Louis Hartz, *The Liberal Tradition in America*, New York 1955.

[3] Cf Hartz, *op. cit.* p 40-41. One must be careful, however, not to
carry this argument too far. During the century and a half that preceded
the Revolution European ideas on Church and State were transplanted
to America. The early colonists naturally and inevitably assumed that
it was normal practice for State and Church to be in some way associated. That was the way things were in their countries of origin. In the
Catholic countries of the Old World the Church was established, while
in England and the Lutheran States Church and State were so closely
united that at times the Church came near to being a department of
State. In Geneva there flourished a Puritan Church-State. It is not sur-

was for this reason that de Tocqueville wrote that the 'great advantage' of America was that it did not have to endure a democratic revolution'.[1] Undoubtedly the men who made America had known oppression; it was because of it that they had fled the old Continent. They were in a way revolutionaries by doing so, but as Hartz has said, they were revolutionaries with a difference. It was one thing to remain at home and fight oppression; it was another to leave it all far behind. These men established liberty in the New World, but their doing so generated no crusading intensity, no frenetic seizure by an abstract

prising, therefore, to find that in New Spain, New France, New Netherland and New England the co-operation of the State with religion was introduced. But there were striking differences between the forms which this co-operation assumed. The Catholic colonies not only supported the Church but suppressed dissent. In New Netherland, although the Dutch West India Company maintained an established Calvinist Church, it extended toleration towards the private practice of other creeds. The English colony of Virginia had been settled for the express purpose of bringing the true worship of God, as understood by Anglicanism, to the American natives who lived in 'miserable ignorance' of it. Hence the establishment there of the Church of England, with compulsory attendance at its services, the payment of tithes for its upkeep and the imposition of the oath of supremacy. In the New England colonies the Puritan settlers introduced varying degrees of State religion, from the theocracy of New Haven and Massachusetts Bay to the relative tolerance of Plymouth and Connecticut. In America as elsewhere general tolerance grew slowly. Rhode Island, under the influence of Roger Williams, initiated a 'livlie experiment', in 1663, of separating the Church from the State. It had been anticipated in this since 1649 by the Catholic Government of Lord Baltimore in the proprietary province of Maryland. In face of Protestant assumptions to the contrary it is ironical that it was a Catholic source that introduced the first Act of Toleration of dissent. Through the influence of this and of like measures in Pennsylvania and elsewhere, through the growth too, it must be admitted, of rationalism and scepticism among some, the various establishments gradually disappeared in the American colonies. They still existed, however, although with waning strength on the eve of the American Revolution. See Evarts B. Greene, *Religion and the State; The Making and Testing of an American Tradition*, New York 1941, *passim*.

[1] *Democracy in America*, Boston 1873, vol. II, p 123.

concept of liberty, no desire to sweep away all tradition.

On the contrary, they wished to preserve what was good in the European ideas and values that they had brought with them. The fact that theirs was the freest society in the civilised world gave them what Hartz—a Liberal himself—calls 'an appearance of outright conservatism'. Their legal system was built on Blackstone's natural law, for which reason John Adams penned the word 'Fool' to a page of Condorcet, on which the latter had claimed that American institutions had been planned rather than had grown out of tradition.[1] This is not to say that European Liberalism had no effect whatever on America. The secularism of Locke, for example, is evident in the Virginian disestablishment of the Anglican Church in 1786. There were men, like Jefferson—who was responsible for this Act—that were deeply infected by rationalist Liberalism. Jefferson was nothing if not an agnostic. In one letter he can protest that he is 'a materialist',[2] in another that he is nevertheless no atheist,[3] in still another that he cannot accept the idea of a triune God[4] and yet that he regards himself as a 'real Christian'.[5] Jefferson stood four square for the godless State. There was also, of course, Tom Paine, than whose Liberalism it would be hard to find a more extreme. These there were and many of their kind; the question is to plumb the depth of their influence.

I have already said that it is far too readily accepted that these Lockean extremists were the makers of American democracy. In the words of a contemporary Liberal, democratic Liberalism in America 'has its primal source' in the ideas of Jefferson.[6] The truth, in fact, is otherwise. That Jefferson and his like had great influence is undeniable. I have referred above to the Virginian Act for the separation of Church and State, on the occasion of the passing of which Jefferson made a speech

[1] Cf Hartz, *op. cit.* p 49.
[2] Letter to W. Short, 1820, in *Thomas Jefferson on Democracy*, Selected and Edited by S. K. Padover, New York 1954, p 120.
[3] Letter to Adams, 1823, Padover, p 120.
[4] Letter to Adams, 1813, Padover, p 117.
[5] Letter to C. Thompson, 1816, Padover, p 122.
[6] Schapiro, *op. cit.* p. 80.

on secularism. Yet its passing did not mean an acceptance of secularism, although Jefferson's eloquence had undoubtedly helped it through. The fact was, as Hartz says, that in the American climate of tolerance, the separation idea had emerged long before he began to speak. He played his own tune to the dance of American democracy, on a different key to the basic theme and, more often than not, striking a note of disharmony.[1]

[1] Cf Hartz, *op. cit.* p 39: 'Despite the European flavour of a Jefferson or a Franklin, the Americans refused to join in the great Enlightenment enterprise of shattering the Christian concept of sin, replacing it with an unlimited humanism'.

The first State constitutions—beginning with that of Virginia in 1776—contained declarations of religious tolerance which extreme Liberals have interpreted as meaning that the State as such was neutral towards all religion. They could scarcely have shot far wider of the mark. What is true is that there was an intention to block the general establishment of Anglicanism which some British politicians had projected for the colonies. There was even a fear that, following the concession to the Catholic Church in Canada made by the Quebec Act (1774), Catholicism might be established in some of the New England States. At least in 1775 a 'Gentleman on board the Fleet at Boston' had written home to the effect that 'the Romish religion is going to be established in America . . . (and) that they have begun with Canada'. What the revolutionary constitutions sought to avoid was an establishment of religion of this sort, with its paraphanalia of tithes and suchlike privileges. Only a minority were logical to the extent of opposing any form of establishment of any religion. Church establishment in one form or another continued after the Revolution in many States. It is clear, therefore, that the revolutionary constitutions, while promoting religious liberty for all, did not expect the State to be wholly neutral in matters of religion. And the Continental Congress regarded the individual State as exclusively competent to decide for itself what should be its attitude as regards religion. *This is the meaning of its famous reply to a query from the Papal Nuncio in Paris concerning its attitude towards the appointment of a Catholic bishop in the United States. It said that it had no authority either to give or to refuse consent, 'these powers being reserved to the states individually'* (Cf E. Humphrey, *Nationalism and Religion in America,* 1774-1789). 'I hope that Congress will never meddle with religion', said John Adams; 'Let every colony have its own religion without molestation' (*Works,* IX, 402). Hence the First Amendment to the Constitution passed

The same story is true of Paine. The most that can be said is that the letter of American democracy sometimes corresponds with his jargon; its content derived from a different source. One could be misled by the revolutionary Constitutions of 1776, which, as Franklin reported, evoked the 'rapture' of the extremists in Europe. Did they mean that the secularism of Paine was being accepted? Frederick Gentz has the answer and we can let him speak: 'When Paine's work appeared, in the year 1776, the American revolution had long since assumed its whole form and conscience, and the principles which will forever characterise it stood firm . . . And what a contrast between the wild, extravagant, rhapsodical declamation of a Paine, and the mild, moderate, and considerate tone in the speeches and letters of a Washington'.[1]

What then of the apparent extremism of the Constitutions? Gentz again supplies us with the answer: 'It is true that most of the constitutions of the United States are preceded by those idle *declarations of rights*, so dangerous in their application, from which so much misery has at a later period been derived upon France, and the whole civilised world. Much, however, as it were to be wished, that the legislators of America had disdained this empty pomp of words, that they had exclusively confined themselves within the clear and lawful motives of their resistance . . . and within the limits of their uncontrovertible rights, yet it cannot escape the observation of those who attentively study

by the Federal Convention in Philadelphia (1787), laying down that 'Congress shall make no law respecting the establishment of religion, or prohibiting the free exercise thereof'. It was intended to have no effect on the legislation of the individual States. On all this matter see the excellent account by E. B. Greene, *Religion and the State*, New York 1941.

[1] Gentz, *op. cit.* p 66. Gentz is here referring to Paine's first pamphlet, entitled *Common Sense*. Cf also pp 54-55: 'I will not deny that his (Paine's) celebrated work had influence among certain classes of people, and so far contributed to promote the revolution. But to judge the spirit and principles of the American revolution by this work would be as unjust as to confound the efficaciously active heads in the English revolution of 1688 with authors of some popular lampoon against the house of Stewart'.

the history of their revolution, that they allowed to these speculative ideas no visible influence upon their practical measures'.[1]
Hartz too admits that Paine 'found himself curiously out of
tune' with the political climate of America, in which his rationalism 'found a cool reception'.[2]

No, the Lockean extremism of Rousseau found outgrowths
but took no substantial roots in America. Lip-service rather
than example was paid to its secularism, in which respect Locke
is but a 'national cliché'.[3] In England likewise it was mainly
the *Treatises on Government* rather than the *Letters Concerning
Toleration* that found acceptance. It would be more accurate
to say that Locke's contemporaries in England exercised discrimination in what they accepted from the *Letters*. They were
quite ready to accept their inconsistent attitude of intolerance
towards Catholics, as the Test Act and the Penal Laws showed
so well. But they were not prepared to embrace their doctrine
of the lay State.[4] They had resolutely set their minds against
all such extremism, after experiencing the radicalism that had
emerged out of the Civil War. The moderate men, the men of
property, the religious men, had seen enough of this already in
the anarchism of the Levellers and the communism and atheism
of the Diggers.[5] They accepted from Locke only what justified
what they stood for; the rest they left to Paine and Rousseau.

The most interesting insight into Locke's role in the English

---

[1] Gentz, *op. cit.* p 63.

[2] Hartz, *op. cit.* p 73.

[3] *Op. cit.* p 140.

[4] Christopher Dawson has maintained that, despite the Penal Laws,
the Revolution of 1688 'marks the end of the attempt to base society on
a religious foundation, and the beginning of the progressive secularisation of the English State'. That it marked the end of 'political religion'
is undeniable; in theory, at least, the State would no longer enforce
any belief. But this is a different thing from the secularisation of the
State, the complete divorce of religion and politics of which Locke wrote
in his *Letter* and which was so avidly practised in post-Revolutionary
France.

[5] Cf David W. Petergorsky, *Left-Wing Democracy in the English
Civil War*, London 1940, *passim*.

intellectual world of his time is provided by the use to which his ideas were put in Ireland by the planter and Protestant ascendancy. Between 1728 and 1878 no less than twenty-six editions of Locke's works or commentaries on them were printed and published in Dublin.[1] His *Treatises on Government* had to be read by all Senior Sophisters in Trinity College. The same was true of his epistemological *Essay Concerning Human Understanding*.[2] But the *Letters on Toleration* are nowhere to be found. The Protestant ascendancy were prepared to welcome Locke's ideas in so far as they served to butress their own property and position. They could also embrace his metaphysics, as yet unaware of the pernicious spirit of scepticism with which it was infected and which was later to bear fruit in the halls of Trinity.[3] Nor would they have been averse to the intolerance towards Catholics that was such a manifest, if paradoxical, feature of Locke's *Letter*. But they would have nothing to do—overtly and consciously—with the secularism of Locke, to say nothing of his ideas on popular sovereignty as interpreted by Rousseau. Indeed when it later became evident that this was largely responsible for the revolution in France, they took great pains to see that nothing like that should happen in Ireland.

They had good reason for taking precautions to this end. Had not Wolfe Tone introduced Rousseau to Ireland? Were not the principles of '89 in the air? Paine's *Rights of Man* was being read and was being linked with the ideas of Locke. Something had to be done and done quickly. Bastide tells us that the *Treatises on Government* was actually banned by Trinity College at the time of the French revolution. But it would be better still to clear Locke's name of liberal ideas. And so in 1789 we find

---

[1] For a list of these see R. S. Devane, *The Failure of Individualism*, Dublin 1948, p 127.

[2] Cf R. B. McDowell, *Irish Public Opinion*, 1750-1800, London 1944, p 164, n 7. Cf also W. McNeill Dixon, *History of Trinity College*, p 79. It is interesting to note that Locke's *Essay* was also the main philosophical text used in Maynooth College at this period.

[3] As early as 1696, however, a letter from Molyneux to Locke gives evidence that the influence of the latter's rationalism was beginning to be felt amongst Irish Protestants.

Dr. Elrington of Trinity producing a special edition of the *Treatises* for the students. Its declared object was to draw a distinction 'between the system of Locke and the theories of modern democrats'. When Locke spoke of 'the people', said Elrington, he meant 'only those who were possessed of such property as was sufficient to secure their fidelity to the interests of the State'. It was unfortunate that the 'venerable advocate of political freedom' should have expressed himself so 'unguardedly' as to leave himself open to being cited in support of the ideas of people like Paine.[1] Indeed a notable fellow of Trinity described Paine as 'Locke gone mad'.

Paine in truth was Locke gone mad, Locke carried to excess by the *philosophes*. Neither England, nor its replica Protestant Ireland, would have anything to do with such a man. They accepted from Locke only such ideas as provided solace in their 'great possessions' and gave the species of democracy to their parliamentary system. This was the Liberalism which they learned from Locke and not that of Rousseau and Paine. It was because of this that British Liberalism during the 19th century became preoccupied with the economic freedoms of the men of property. Even a glance at the liberal literature of this period is sufficient to show how far removed the greater portion of it was from the kind of problem which agitated the political liberals of the Continent.[2] So much so that a liberal like Salvadori is driven to protest that 'liberty is not synonymous with free trade, free enterprise or *laissez faire*, although there is a close connection between the structure of the economic system and the possibility of choice which is the practical manifestation of liberty. The identification with economic *laissez faire* made by nineteenth century dogmatic economists of the classical school . . . was most harmful to the cause of liberal democracy in Europe . . . It is an insult to liberty to be reduced to the

---

[1] Cf McDowell, *op. cit.* p 164. For the influence of Paine's rationalism in Trinity College during this period see *Trial of John Burk of Trinity College before the Board of Senior Fellows*, Dublin 1794.

[2] Cf *The Liberal Tradition*, Edited by A. Bullock and M. Shock, London 1956.

level of an economic institution'.[1]

Salvadori might have included the Benthamites in his con-demnation. They too—though in a different way—were re-sponsible for the economic slant of 19th century British Liberal-ism. Although their criterion of right was the interest of the community—the greatest happiness of the greatest number—they had little difficulty in reconciling this with economic Liberalism. The interests of the community became 'the sum of the interests of the several members who compose it', each and all being best secured in a free 'natural' order in which 'nothing ought to be done or attempted by government'.[2] It was a happy practical compromise, which gave satisfaction to the Old Whigs, but which created unease and discontent in the ranks of the masses for whom such liberty meant only the free-dom to work in misery. Was it the need for further compromise or the influence of imported Hegelian philosophy that was re-sponsible for the change which came in towards the end of the century? Both factors, I am sure, played a part. With Green, Ritchie, Hobson and others, English Liberalism began to adopt a more positive conception of freedom. Individualists and Lib-erals these men still remained, but they ceased to regard the State as 'an opposing element to the individual'.[3] They began to look on liberty as more than 'the mere removal of compul-sion'; it consisted in the 'capacity of doing or of enjoying some-thing', in the interests of which 'it is the business of the State . . . to maintain the conditions without which a free exercise of the human faculties is impossible'.[4] Thus the way was opened for Lloyd George and for Keynes, for Beveridge and—shall we say it—for Bevan.

I am not interested here in tracing the growth of Welfarism from Liberalism. I am concerned only with showing how, with the help of ideas accepted from Locke, an economic Liberalism

[1] Salvadori, op. cit. p 21.

[2] Jeremy Bentham, Introduction to the Principles of Morals and Legislation, London 1948, p 126.

[3] D. G. Ritchie, The Principles of State Interference, London 1891.

[4] T. H. Green, Liberal Legislation or Freedom of Contract, in Bullock and Shock, op. cit. p 180.

rather than a political one was to be Britain's *métier*. The history of Britain during the 19th century shows very little trace of those Lockean ideas which had such success in Continental Europe. In fact political liberty was preached—and with considerable vehemence—only when Liberalism began to yield before a growing Statism in which the more discerning saw a threat to genuine individual liberty. Herbert Spencer believed that such Statism was a betrayal of Liberalism and produced his *Man and the State* (1884) to prove his point. He put no tooth on the expression of his conviction—later endorsed by Belloc and others—that the new developments presaged a 'coming slavery'. It was these same developments that had earlier drawn from Mill his essay *On Liberty* (1859), to this day regarded by extreme liberals as one of their classics. In reality it is a stumbling-block, were they disposed to see it thus. It is Mill's turning his back on the Utilitarianism of his youth, on the Benthamite Liberalism of his father, on the democracy of Locke as interpreted in England. The admirers of Locke just cannot have it both ways. We may grant them that Mill's essay is a song on the theme of Rousseau's Locke, but to the extent that this is so, it is a vindication of the thesis that the concept of liberty of the *Letters on Toleration* had not been accepted in England.

Nor was Mill entirely satisfied with this concept. He made a brave effort to provide a new criterion for the intervention of the State, which would satisfy at once both individual liberty and the need for State control to promote the conditions in which liberty could thrive. To this end he invented his distinction between actions that are 'self' and 'other' regarding: 'The only part of the conduct of anyone for which he is amenable to society, is that which concerns others. In the part which merely concerns himself, his independence is, of right absolute'. The distinction, of course, is so vague as to be impossible of application and it did nothing to hold up the trend towards Statism. Mill himself modified his own individualism towards the end of his life, in a work *On Social Freedom* which was still unpublished at his death. Its sub-title is 'The Necessary Limits of Individual Freedom Arising Out of the Conditions of Social Life'. Gone is the contempt of the essay *On Liberty* for 'the despotism of custom', which 'is everywhere the standing hindrance to human advancement'.[1] Mill now recognises the need to distinguish 'those restraints which must be borne for the sake of our moral and social culture, from those which arise from abuses in our social system'. He sets limits 'beyond which we cannot hope to extend our freedom without doing away with those conditions which render life valuable to us'.[2]

The one figure who remained true to Locke—as interpreted by Rousseau—was the Whig leader Charles James Fox. Sheridan, Grey, Erskine and Macaulay echoed his views—on an abstract liberty of speech and behaviour such as was advanced in France. Byron put them into verse. They have lingered on into the present in Russell and Laski. 'The view which I am concerned to urge', says Laski, 'is that from the standpoint of the State the citizen must be left unfettered to express either individually, or in concert with others, any opinions he happens to hold . . . He is entitled, further, to use all the ordinary means of publication to make his views known . . . (This) is a right that lies at the basis of freedom'.[3] In upholding it the State must be neutral towards all religion: 'No citizen enjoys genuine freedom of religious conviction until the State is indifferent to every form of religious outlook from Atheism to Zoroastrianism'.[4] But British democracy in general has never trod this road. It has been tolerant enough to allow Mill and Fox and Laski to voice their opinions, but it has never practised—at least in its fullness—the secular Liberalism which these have preached. British democracy has been surprisingly traditionalist. Paradoxically—as is Britain's fashion—it has combined Liberalism and Conservatism in a tradition whose values it is important to maintain. Democracy in America has followed a similar pattern uniting genuine liberty with a respect for religious and moral values.

Who was responsible for this balanced moderation? The answer is: the men who stood for freedom within limits, for a

[1] J. S. Mill, *On Liberty*, p 126.

[2] J. S. Mill, *On Social Freedom*, New York 1941, p 35.

[3] H. J. Laski, *A Grammar of Politics*, p 120.

[4] *Op. cit.* p 119.

liberty that is beholden to its Creator, for a political order which, though independent of religion, is linked to it by way of respect and co-operation. This is the tradition of Burke and Acton in England and in America of John Adams and Orestes Brownson.[1] To these Anglo-American democracy owes its peculiar character.[2]

CONSERVATIVE LIBERALISM

Edmund Burke is the outstanding representative of this tradition. In party politics Burke began as a Whig. Essentially anti-despotic and anti-imperialistic, he gave full support to the American Revolution and its principles. In economics he followed the Liberalism of Adam Smith and in religious matters was against the disabilities of Catholics. For these reasons he found Whiggism attractive. But he took an emphatic stand against the principles of the French Revolution. And, as time went on, he found himself compelled to abandon Whiggism in politics, when the Whigs, after the advent of Fox's leadership, tended more and more to accept the French version of Liberal Democracy. This was something to which Burke could not reconcile himself. But a liberal he always remained—not a liberal in the extreme Continental sense of the word, but in the moderate sense of Conservative Democracy. It is, I suspect, because of the difficulty of associating Conservatism with Liberalism that Burke's position has been understood by so few. In all probability it is also the reason why it represents a theoretical outlook that has only been partially realised in political practice. It is much easier to gain a following for ideas that are simple and exaggerated than to secure adequate support for moderate and qualified views.

[1] Due to Acton's influence Newman invited Brownson to a professorship at the Catholic University, Dublin.

[2] Cf Schapiro, *op. cit.* p 40: 'During the nineteenth and twentieth centuries English conservatives have not been reactionaries; once a reform was enacted they accepted it as part of the national system. And English radicals have not been revolutionists; they sought to accomplish their objectives by constitutional methods'.

The big problem for Burke was how to remain a lover of liberty and yet reject the extremism of Liberal Democracy. He solved it by recognising that liberty must be limited, that there is a true and a false idea of liberty. Extreme Liberalism, he saw, inevitably brings political chaos, from which society must be protected in the interests of genuine liberty itself. But he was far from being an out and out Conservative, of the kind that was so typical of 18th century England.[1] There is no shallower criticism of Burke, Augustine Birrell tells us, than that which accuses him in his later years of apostasy from liberal opinions. Rather is it that Burke 'is ever asking himself . . . how are men to be saved from anarchy'.[2]

The pivotal points of Burke's political philosophy are God, the natural order and the Church. Basic to all is the fact that man and the State are God's creatures and are consequently bound to submit themselves to His ordinances. For Burke this is a *sine qua non* of political sanity. It means that men have obligations that are 'not a matter of choice'.[3] 'There is an order', says Burke, 'that keeps things fast in their place; it is made to us and we are made to it'. It is an order of things that must be respected by government, despite the limitations on freedom of action which this entails. 'Society requires . . . that . . . the inclinations of men should frequently be thwarted, their will controlled, and their passions brought into subjection. This can be done only by a power out of themselves'[4]—a system of government that is guided by moral principles rather than the counting of heads. 'When we know that the opinions of even the greatest multitudes are the standard of rectitude, I shall think myself obliged to make these opinions the masters of my conscience'.[5] Not till then can government abdicate its right and duty to interpret the natural order for political ends.

The realisation of this order needs the sustaining help of

[1] Cf Colin Clark, English and American Conservatism, in *The Tablet*, 9 October 1954.
[2] A. Birrell, *Obiter Dicta*, 2nd Series, pp 188-189.
[3] Cf Appeal from the New to the Old Whigs, in *Works*, III, 79.
[4] *Reflections on the French Revolution*.
[5] Tracts on the Popery Laws, in *Works*, VI, 32.

religion. In Burke's view, it was because of their atheism that the Continental liberals were so prone to excesses of violence. 'Their morality', he says, 'has no idea in it of restraint, or indeed of a distinct settled principle of any kind. When their disciples are thus left free and guided only by present feeling they are no longer to be depended upon for good or evil'.[1] The good statesman must be guided by the truths of religion. Indeed Burke's idea of him resembles the medieval conception of one consecrated, as it were, to fulfil his task. 'Religion is so far, in my opinion, from being out of the province of a Christian magistrate, that it is, and it ought to be, not only his care, but the principal thing in his care'.[2] As a result of this, he was bound to support Church establishment. This he did, without quali-fication. Of course the Church whose establishment he defended was the Church of England. But as Russell Kirk has pointed out so well: 'His Church is an idealised Anglican establishment, but more than Anglican. There is something classical about it; something Catholic, too, so that bigots (including the old Duke of Newcastle) whispered that Burke must have been educated in the Papist seminary at St. Omer'.[3]

Indeed it is fair to say that Burke's political philosophy has much in common with Catholic thought. It coincides, in particu-lar, with the Catholic conviction that liberty must be ordered and that moral principles cannot be decided by ballot. Burke's position as regards Church establishment is also Catholic, not only in maintaining that the State must stand in deference to true religion, but in believing too that this can be done without placing religious minorities under any legal disadvantage. For, despite his advocacy of the established Anglican Church, Burke was insistent that Catholics and Protestant dissenters should not be subjected to disabilities because of their beliefs. He was poles apart from the Tory of his time who, though he might not persecute these, as his predecessors had done, regarded it

---

[1] Letter to the Chevalier de Rivarol, 1791. Wentworth Woodhouse Papers; cited by Russell Kirk, *The Conservative Mind*, New York 1953, p 29.

[2] Speech on the Petition of the Unitarians, in *Works*, VI, 115.

[3] Kirk, *op. cit.* p 31.

as important to prevent them from holding public offices or military commissions.

Burke held that freedom of opinion—especially of religious worship—is one of the fundamental rights of man. He was always a champion of genuine natural rights. But on no account would he subscribe to the rationalistic Liberalism contained in tracts such as Paine's *Rights of Man*. Rights do not derive simply from democratic constitutions; they are based ultimately on God and the moral law. Because of this, it is essential to the idea of rights that they be limited by the general pattern of morality. There is no such thing as a right to freedom to do wrong. Burke turned a deaf ear to Paine's entreaties to him from Paris to introduce into England 'a more enlarged system of liberty'. In Burke's view 'the pretended rights of these theorists are all extremes; and politically false. The rights of men are in a sort of middle, incapable of definition, but not impossible to be discerned. The rights of men in government are their advantages; and these are often in balances between good and evil, and sometimes between evil and evil . . . Men have no right to what is not reasonable, and to what is not for their benefit'.[1] There are no such things as absolute rights. The up-shot of it all is that freedom must be limited. If not voluntarily curbed, it must be restricted by the State. Indeed such 're-straints on men as well as on their liberties, are to be reckoned among their rights'.[2]

Burke's respect for genuine liberty was immense; for this he must always be classed as a true democrat. 'Far am I from denying in theory, full as far is my heart from witholding in practice, (if I were of power to give or to withold) the *real* rights of men. In denying their false claims of right, I do not mean to injure those which are real, and are such as their pretended rights would thoroughly destroy. If civil society be made for the advantage of man, all the advantages for which it is made become his right. It is an institution of beneficence; and law itself is only beneficence acting by rule. Men have a right to

[1] *Reflections on the French Revolution.*
[2] *Ibid.*

live by that rule; they have a right to do justice'.[1] In all Burke's works, remarks Russell Kirk, this passage is perhaps his most important contribution to political thought.[2] It contains a pen-picture of what he understood by true democracy.

Rather similar views were held during the following century by Lord Acton. First impressions are that Burke and Acton had little in common; in a number of places Acton criticised Burke. For example, he praised Carlyle's *French Revolution* for having, as he said, 'delivered the English mind from the thraldom of Burke'. Russell Kirk, in his study of the 'Conservative Mind', could find no room for Acton among conservatives of the calibre of Burke. 'Acton', he says 'would have hanged Robespierre and Burke on the same gallows'.[3] In reality there are fewer differences between Acton and Burke than has been believed by the generality of historians of political ideas. One of the reasons for this, undoubtedly, is that, until relatively recently, Acton has been much under-studied.[4]

Though he was primarily a historian, whose political philosophy was by way of commentary on history, it is possible to distinguish a number of political views that are characteristic of Acton. If Burke can be said to be a Liberal Conservative, Acton was a Conservative Liberal. He is usually claimed as a liberal *pur sang*. But he was certainly not an extreme Liberal in the Continental mould. Acton's Liberalism was a qualified one but, as Burke was, he has been frequently misunderstood. He was too Catholic and conservative for the extreme Liberals, and too much associated with Continental Liberal Catholicism

[1] *Ibid.*

[2] Kirk, *op. cit.* p 48.

[3] *Ibid.* p 11.

[4] The first full length study of Acton did not appear until 1935, thirty-three years after his death. Published in Germany, it had little influence in Britain and America. Two limited English studies appeared in 1942 and 1945 respectively. In 1952, however, two important works on Acton were published: *Lord Acton: A Study in Conscience and Politics*, by Gertrude Himmelfarb and *Acton's Political Philosophy*, by G. E. Fasnacht. Lionel Kochan's *Acton in History* (London 1954) deals with Acton the historian rather than the political philosopher.

for British Catholics. To understand him one has to balance his views *inter se*.

About his love of liberty there can be no doubt at all. It often led him to a condemnation of conservative thought which, in many of its representatives, was associated with a haughty intolerance. There are plenty of sentences in Acton which, if taken in isolation, would damn him immediately in the eyes of Kirk, the Conservative. Such, for example, is his reference to 'the moral error of the Conservatives',[1] or his sweeping statement that 'a close chain of prejudices and errors connects the Conservative of today with the legitimist and the absolutist, with the Royalist of the seventeenth century, the persecutor of the sixteenth . . . '.[2] But on examination we find that by 'Conservatives' here he meant the type of Tory whom Burke also loathed. He would have accepted the better things in Conservatism, including its support for the idea of religious influence in political life. It is true that he advocated 'a free Church in a free State', but here again his purpose should be discerned. What he was opposed to was the system of Church-State relations that had been also attacked by the younger Lammenais, on the legitimate grounds that it meant domination of the Church by the State.[3] His private papers show that he did not like being called a Liberal Catholic.[4] He would have welcomed an established Church that was not a State-Church like that of the restored empire or the ancient City States. In fact he would have welcomed the medieval version of the Christian State, by which truth was respected without interfering with genuine liberty. While editor of the *Rambler* he said this in effect, when, after the appearance of Mill's essay *On Liberty* in 1859, he felt it necessary to state explicitly that the idea of liberty which he defended was not an unlimited one.[5] He had no time for the unrealistic *concept* of freedom, the unrealisable individualism

[1] *The French Revolution*, p 122.
[2] Add. Ms 4949, cited in Himmelfarb, *op. cit.* p 207.
[3] During his study in Munich under Döllinger, Acton had come to be influenced by the Liberal Catholicism of Montalembert.
[4] Cf Himmelfarb, *op. cit.* p 230.
[5] Cf Political Thoughts on the Church, in *The Rambler*, XI, 1859.

of the Continental liberals and their English counterparts. They exhibited, he said, an 'abstract, ideal absolutism, which is equally hostile with the Catholic and with the English spirit. Their democratic spirit poisons everything it touches . . . The influence of these habits of abstract reasoning, to which we owe the revolution in Europe, is to make all things questions of principle and of abstract law . . . and the consequence is, that a false and arbitrary political system produces a false and arbitrary code of ethics'.[1] On the other hand, he regarded the principles of the American Revolution as acceptable, since they devised a host of checks and balances to democracy.

There is a definite analogy between the political principles of Acton and Burke. Acton's reference to Carlyle as having liberated the English mind from the thraldom of Burke is the kind of sweeping statement which he was so easily disposed to make but which can always be countered by another to the opposite effect, made in a different place or on a different occasion. Not that he was given to contradicting himself, but that his position was essentially the reconciliation of extremes in a middle view that was moderate and balanced. He had studied Burke intensely in his youth and, as a result, it is not surprising that he should have been influenced by him. 'My first literary impressions', he tells us, 'were the recommendation of Bacon's Essays, Burke, Newman'.[2] It was Döllinger who deflected him from the shallow Liberalism of Macaulay towards Burke who, at least at one period, became for him the great sage of politics whom he proposed as a teacher for Catholics. In the writings of Burke's last years, he wrote, 'whatever was Protestant or partial or revolutionary of 1688 in his political views disappeared, and what remained was a purely Catholic view of political principles and of history'.[3] And although in his own

---

[1] *Freedom and Power*, p 246; cf also *The French Revolution*, p 97.

[2] Letter to Döllinger, cited in Himmelfarb, *op. cit.* p 69. On the political philosophy of Newman—also a combination of Liberal and Conservative elements—see Terence Kenny, *The Political Thought of John Henry Newman*, London, 1957, *passim*.

[3] Review of McKnight's History of the Life and Times of Edmund Burke, in *The Rambler*, IX (1858), p 273.

later years he came to reject many aspects of Burke's practical politics,[1] there is no evidence whatever to show that he rejected the kind of mixture of Conservatism and Liberalism that was central to Burke.

Burke and Acton, each in his own way, had considerable impact in the shaping of the British democratic tradition. Though Burke never became the official leader of a party, much less Prime Minister, his influence on Parliament must not be minimised. His big contribution was the shaping of opinion on the question of liberty. His central thesis that, while liberty must be upheld it must be kept from passing out of bounds, had a profoundly moderating effect on political tempers in a revolutionary age. Acton too, by his literary efforts and lectures, had a powerful effect on the politicians of his time. He himself was identified with no political party. 'The best Conservative', he once said, 'is an American Republican, the best Liberal is a divine'.[2] He himself would gladly have been both. His influence was not on parties but on personalities, one of the greatest of whom was Gladstone and who, incidentally, was also influenced by Burke.[3]

In a general way it is true to say that the Gladstonian tradition is one of the basic pivots of modern British democracy. It is a tradition of balance, of middle of the road attitudes, of limited democracy and liberty within reason—the tradition of Burke and of Acton. This tradition is neither exclusively Conservative nor exclusively Liberal, but a complex fabric into which each is interwoven. In a real sense it demands both for its maintenance, for at its root it is a compromise—as are so many things English—between liberty and the demands of prescription. It is no wonder at all that J. H. Laski had to confess that democracy, as he understood it, is not to be found in British political life.

---

[1] I feel that Miss Himmelfarb has made too much of Acton's specific criticisms of Burke, to which the latter, by the way, was by no means always open.

[2] Add. Ms 4952, cited in Himmelfarb, *op. cit.* p 171.

[3] Cf. W. E. Gladstone, *The State in its relations with the Church*, 2 vols. London, 1841.

It is only too true—of course—that the tradition has been sullied. With the passage of time, the Liberal element has become predominant. It tended to do so even in Gladstone's day, despite his efforts to preserve his party from the spirit of Fox. Conservatism, on the other hand, went into a downward trend. One of the first of its principles to be whittled away was that of Church establishment. Though affirmed as late as 1910 by Lord Hugh Cecil, the link had been weakening for some time. The beginning of this can be seen, not in the abolition of the intolerant Test Acts, which had required M.P.'s to be Anglicans, but in the Gorham Judgment of 1850, which made it clear that it was the secular courts rather than the bishops that had the last word in theological disputes. Gladstone himself had been worried about this. His worst fears were to be realised in the present century when the relations between Church and State became quite paradoxical. As Colin Clark has put it: 'One would have thought that this element of Conservative doctrine was rapidly going by the board when the leadership of the Conservative fell to a Presbyterian, Bonar Law. But nobody seemed to mind. After all, the same Monarch has to fulfil the duties of being an Anglican in England and a Presbyterian in Scotland. The real disintegration of this doctrine came with Baldwin. Himself partly of Nonconformist descent, he made it quite clear that he regarded Nonconformity as quite as good as Anglicanism and frequently appeared upon Nonconformist platforms . . . The old liberal voters came over to the Conservative *en masse*, and by 1931 not much of the Liberal Party was left. Not much either of what used to be regarded as Conservative principles'.[1]

There were some who strove to halt this trend. Arthur Balfour wrote books and made speeches against the 'process of social degeneration which we must perforce recognise, and which, pending a satisfactory analysis, may conveniently be distinguished by the name of 'decadence'.'[2] But the battle he fought was a lost one. The headlong rush towards liberty and equalitarianism was carrying Britain ever nearer to the secu-

[1] C. Clark, *loc. cit.*
[2] Cited in Russell Kirk, *op. cit.* p 345.

larist paradise which today is known as the Welfare State. W. H. Mallock tried too and failed to stem it. The ear of the young was cocked in a different direction. In Cambridge the influence of Moore was dominating, causing the future men of the nation, as Keynes has told us, to repudiate 'all versions of the doctrine of original sin . . . (and) respect for traditional wisdom or the restraint of custom'.[1] Belloc and Chesterton were voices in the wilderness.

RECALL TO SANITY

That a reaction to this has now set in is very noticeable. It is due in large measure to the need for closing the ranks against the menace of Còmmunism, for an enlightened Conservatism that will not baulk at true progress, yet, at the same time, will be perspicacious about change. T. S. Eliot's writings on culture and Christian society give evidence of this. It is coming more and more to be recognised that, if society is to be stable, it cannot do without the pervasive influence of religion. As Russell Kirk has put it, the mastery of Fabian and naturalistic thinkers over the English mind has been shattered. Herbert Butterfield and John Betjeman and Colm Brogan and C. S. Lewis represent a renascent and vigorous Conservatism.

In America a similar Conservative trend is even more evident. Notable writers, like Clinton Rossiter[2] and Russell Kirk[3] have been recalling Americans to the conservative elements in the nation's tradition and in the men who were responsible for maintaining it. It is not as easily done in America as in Britain, partly because political philosophy has been less formally elaborated in America, and partly because America has never been faced as has Europe with problems relating to freedom as a value.[4] Freedom has been an accepted thing in America since Washington; it is an institution to be enjoyed

[1] J. M. Keynes, *Two Memoirs*, London 1949, pp 99-100.
[2] Clinton Rossiter, *Conservatism in America*, New York 1956.
[3] Russell Kirk, *op. cit.*
[4] Cf Berns, *Freedom, Virtue and The First Amendment*, pp 19-20.

rather than an ideology to be defended. It is for this reason that
Louis Hartz can say that there has never been a Liberal Movement in America.[1] It is for the same reason that Rossiter and
Boorstein[2] can say that a Conservative Movement has also been
absent. All of which is another way of saying that the American
political tradition represents a happy combination of Liberalism
and Conservatism. The truth of this becomes more striking
when we find both Hartz and Rossiter appealing to the same
facts and figures as examples of each of these viewpoints.

Why then the appearance of Rossiter's book which, as its
publisher's claim, is 'an eloquent appeal for a new conservatism
to sustain the Republic in the troubled years ahead?' Perhaps
it is because there have been signs in recent American history
of a tendency towards a Liberalism of the more extreme variety, a tendency which, in the courts at least, is now coming,
as I have earlier indicated, to be resisted. More likely the reason
is to provide American Conservatism with a conscious philosophical foundation, in the absence of which it is exposed to
every wind that blows.[3] For the curious thing about America is
that, while its political practice has always contained strong
conservative elements, its political tradition is assumed to be
avowedly liberal. Jefferson and Franklin and Jackson and their
like are assumed to be real fathers of the American Way of
Life. Small wonder that we find an American Professor declaring that 'there has altogether been too much' of this and that
America needs a history 'written from a sanely conservative
point of view'.

Rossiter has sketched the outlines which it might take. It

[1] L. Hartz, *op. cit.* p 45.

[2] Daniel Boorstein, *The Genius of American Politics*, Chicago 1953.

[3] Rossiter's big complaint is that American political life at present
is lacking in any formal philosophy. In his *Parties and Politics in America*
(Cornell 1960), pp 135-6, he writes: 'One has only to study the activities
of Congress on such matters as civil liberties and support of the arts
to realise that neither Jefferson nor Burke stalks the halls of Congress,
and that the essential Democratic-Republican division is between a
visceral, self-serving, bread-and-butter liberalism and a visceral, self-
serving, bread-and-butter conservatism'.

is not just a history of the warped Conservatism of 19th century America, which was unduly centered in the defence of property to the cry of '*Laissez Faire*'. What Rossiter calls for is a realisation of the better elements of Conservatism in the American past. It is not to be confused with a temperamental Conservatism that is blindly opposed to change; with possessive Conservatism, that is preoccupied with the defence of status and power; or even with the practical Conservatism of the John Birch Society that is so evident in America, but which has no roots in speculative thought. What he champions is a high philosophical Conservatism, which consciously protects the valuable aspects of the established order and tradition against 'careless tinkering' and the irresponsibility of abstract liberty.[1]

Taking its principles from Burke's 'first and greatest statement' of it, this Conservatism, this 'philosophy peculiar to the Atlantic community',[2] is well aware that man is a composite of good and evil. It is aware of the need for curbing his tendency to put his freedom to ill purpose and, while being careful to respect the dignity and personal equality of all men, it is satisfied that the right to justice, which is all that man can legitimately claim, is compatible with orders and classes and some discrimination. The true Conservative sees society as an organism, a cellular, differentiated growth, with roots in the past. He sees that the future of society depends on the care with which it is tended and on the conditions by which its development is guided. While stoutly defending representative government and the political institutions of democracy, he is ever aware of the need for guidance, for balance and limitation to popular sovereignty. He is not deceived by the slogan of abstract 'liberty'; his concept of human rights is a concrete one. While he recognises, for example, the right to freedom of con-

[1] Cf Rossiter, *op. cit.* p 9: 'Awareness, reflection, traditionalism, and at least some degree of distinterestedness—these are the qualities that distinguish the genuine conservative from all others who bear this label. He is a rare bird in any country, an even rarer one in this; and as he is rare, so is he precious'.

[2] Rossiter, *op. cit.* p 16.

science, he insists that it is 'matched by the duty to think wisely and worship decorously'.[1]

True Conservatism, in particular, 'promotes public and private morality, without which freedom cannot long exist. In league with church and family, it strives to separate men's virtues from their vices and to keep the latter under tight rein. It does all this by encouraging or at least protecting organised religion, by supporting the means of education, by enacting laws against vice, and by offering a high example of justice and rectitude'.[2] Religious feeling is 'the mortar that holds together the mosaic of Conservatism'.[3] The Conservative is constantly reminding himself of Burke's remark that man is 'a religious animal' and that of Disraeli that 'the spiritual nature of man is stronger than codes or constitutions'. Yet 'none of these statements, be it noted', says Rossiter, 'is in any sense an apology for clericalism'. Though he is not a Catholic, nobody could surpass Rossiter in his outline of the Conservative—and Catholic—attitude to Church-State relations. 'The Conservative is probably happiest when he has an established church to serve and to defend, yet he honours his nation's traditional solution to the problem of church and state. Like other men, he has his own ideas about the exact nature of that solution. As he is not a clericalist, so he is not a secularist; he suspects men who call too loudly and angrily for an "unbreachable wall between church and state". In any case, he cherishes religious feeling, and thus institutionalised religion, as the foundation of stability, cement of unity, patron of morality, check upon power, and spur to compassion; in fine, as the greatest of all civilising forces'.[4]

But have no doubt about it, this Conservative is a genuine democrat; he is ever ready to uphold the true concept of freedom. What he wishes is that his critics would 'stop confusing liberty with Liberalism,'[5] and realise once and for all that many of the values that are credited to Liberalism are part and parcel

[1] *Op. cit.* p 39.
[2] *Op. cit.* pp 34-35.
[3] *Op. cit.* p 43.
[4] *Op. cit.* pp 44-45.
[5] *Op. cit.* p 55.

of the Conservative tradition. His difference with the Liberal
is largely a matter of 'mood and bias'. Where the latter is disposed to give free rein even to the excesses of liberty, the former
insists that this cannot be done without destroying the foundations of liberty itself. Liberty, he knows, can only exist under
the 'rule of law'. He knows too that the 'higher law of God is
its very basis and that democracy needs to be strengthened by
religion.[1] The West, says Rossiter, needs such an outlook if it
is to survive, threatened, 'as was Burke's England, by an enemy
armed with ideas as well as guns'.[2] How different is this from
Salvadori's shallow concept of Liberal Democracy, which hates
Communism but cannot raise the forces to resist it.

[1] 'The liberties we talk about defending today were established by
men who took their conception of man from the great central religious
tradition of Western civilisation, and the liberties we inherit can almost
certainly not survive the abandonment of that tradition'—Walter Lippmann.

[2] Rossiter, *op. cit.* p 245. Cf also p 282.

CHAPTER NINE

PATTERN OF A CHRISTIAN CONSTITUTION

WHAT conception of democracy, if any, is to be found in the Irish political tradition? Until the present century we need not expect to find any well worked out speculative ideas on this or any other political system. The conditions for such intellectual ferment were not present. Nevertheless, it must be said that Ireland felt the impact, even in the ideological sphere, of the American and French Revolutions. Although, ostensibly, the chief effect of the American Revolution was to cause the formation, in 1778, of the Irish Volunteers for the purpose of defending the coasts against attacks by French and American ships, in reality, as Dr. Madden, biographer of the United Irishmen, has put it, 'it may be asserted, without fear of contradiction, that it was something less than loyalty alone and something more than the fear of invasion, that animated Ireland, and arrayed its spirit in the volunteer associations, when the voice from America was shouting "Liberty".'[1]

THE BIRTH OF A TRADITION

Indeed a year had not passed before the new, 'independent', army was pressing for political demands not unlike some of those which had caused the American revolt. Nor were the English authorities insensible to them and, for once, showed that they had learned from the mistake which they had made

[1] R. R. Madden, *The United Irishmen*, Dublin 1842, vol. 1, p 45.

in America. The 'Free Trade or This' slogan, which decorated the cannon of Napper Tandy's Dublin Volunteers, procured a considerable measure of commercial freedom as well as the eventual recognition of the parliamentary independence of Ireland (1782).

The further effort to secure parliamentary reform, which followed, was taken in the same spirit of liberty and constitutional democracy. It led to a *rapprochement* between Catholics and Protestants, for, although the Volunteers were Protestant officered and largely Protestant in composition, they could not afford to alienate the numerically stronger Catholics. But the liaison was ill-conceived and did not prosper. Dr. Patrick Rogers has given us a full account of the half-hearted efforts which the Volunteers made to secure Catholic Emancipation.[1] The controversies amongst the Protestants themselves regarding the wisdom of such a measure, the wavering of the National Convention (1783) in face of opposition from the government and the final shelving of the issue by the National Congress of 1784, show that the championship of the Catholic cause by the Volunteers had been motivated very largely by expediency. There were some, like the Earl Bishop of Derry, who do seem to have been imbued with a genuine democratic spirit. But the Protestants as a whole were more limited in their ideals. Both Northern and Southern saw the need 'to throw out . . . some conciliatory idea'[2] to gain the political support of the Catholics. That the franchise should be extended to them was an acceptable suggestion provided that government rested securely in Protestant hands. But the real aim was better representation for Protestants, a change in the inequitable system under which, in 1783, out of a House of Commons of 300 members, only 72 represented the Protestants of their constituencies, the remainder being nominated by peers and influential commoners. Northern Protestants in particular, having got rid of their religious disabi-

[1] P. Rogers, *The Irish Volunteers and Catholic Emancipation*, London 1934.

[2] Grattan at the Dungannon Convention, 1782, cited in Rogers, *op. cit.* p 67.

lities,[1] were now ambitious to become part of the Lockean-type democracy.

It would be a mistake to think that the struggle for their own religious liberty, just concluded, had fashioned these into champions of what today is known as religious toleration. As J. C. Beckett of Queen's University has pointed out,[2] the aim of this struggle had not been that every man should be allowed to serve the State, irrespective of his religion. It was concerned less with individuals than with a community, its main plank being that Presbyterians should be allowed full civic rights because of their role in maintaining the English and Protestant position in Ireland.[3] This outlook had not radically changed by 1783. Not that the dereliction of Catholic claims arose from a want of liberality on the part of the bulk of the Volunteers. Thomas Russell has protested that this was not the case. Rather it arose, he tells us, from 'their placing too great a confidence in *their leaders*, who were men of the first lordly and landed interests in Ireland, and who shamefully and meanly deserted the people'.[4] Government of the people, but not by the people as a whole, was the limited ideal which these Protestant leaders set

[1] Cf J. C. Beckett, *Protestant Dissent in Ireland*, 1687-1780, London, 1949.

[2] *Op. cit.* p 15.

[3] There was nothing in this struggle, says Mr. Beckett, 'about the rights of individuals and the abstract justice of universal toleration and equality . . . The Presbyterians had no inclination to tolerate Quakers, nor did they consider that the privileges which they asked for themselves should be extended to the Roman Catholics, whose inveterate hostility and potential insurrection they put forward as an argument in favour of their own further emancipation', *op. cit.*

[4] Cf Madden, *op. cit.* p 165. It should be noted carefully, however, that all the leaders were not of this kind, as is clearly demonstrated by the *Letter* of William Todd Jones to the Volunteers of Belfast 12th July 1784, in *Tracts on Catholic Affairs*, Dublin 1792. See too the thanks expressed by a Catholic Meeting in Londonderry (15 November 1792) to the Volunteers of Antrim and Down and to 'all those virtuous and generous Protestants, both in and out of Parliament, for their spirited and manly exertions in favour of the much injured Catholics of Ireland'—in *The Northern Star*, 1-5 December 1792.

themselves. Let a Belfast resolution of 1784 speak for itself: 'That the gradual extension of suffrage to our too long oppressed brethren, the Roman Catholics, *preserving unimpaired the Protestant Government of this country*, would be a measure fraught with the happiest consequences, and would be highly conducive to the security of civil liberty'.[1] It was this, rather than democracy or nationalism, that was their motive force. As it was, the failure of the Volunteer movement to enlist the support of the Catholic masses led to its eventual neutralisation and suppression by the Government. Into its place stepped the Whig Club, introduced by Charlemont, which stood for Lockean democracy of the purest kind—constitutional government on the part of an ascendancy unencumbered by Catholics. It paid lip-service, but little more, to the idea of an Irish democracy which would include Catholics and Protestants on equal terms.[2]

By now, however, new ideas were stirring; the French Revolution had taken place and its principles were attracting the attention of many Irishmen. As early as May, 1791, we find a Northern Protestant, resident in Dublin, suggesting that more radical measures than those of the Whig Club—which did 'nothing more than eat and drink'[3]—were necessary if genuine political liberty was to be attained. This was Dr. William Drennan, one of the more intellectual leaders of the later United Irishmen.[4] In Dublin too Wolfe Tone chaffed at the bit. He had been impressed by the fact that the failure of the Volunteers to

---

[1] Historical Collections relative to the Town of Belfast, p 298, cited in Rogers, *op. cit.* p 155.

[2] Cf Resolution of 16 March 1790: 'That no person ought suffer civil hardships for his religious persuasion, unless the tenets of his religion lead him to endeavour at the subversion of the State'. Dr. Madden says that this was meant to be hostile to Catholics and manifests the 'sneaking spirit of bigotry' of the Whig Club. *Op. cit.* vol. III, p 76.

[3] *The Drennan Letters*, Ed. D. A. Chart, Belfast 1931, p 54.

[4] 'I should much desire that a society were instituted in this city having much of the secrecy and somewhat of the ceremonial of Freemasonry . . . A Benevolent Conspiracy—a Plot for the People—no Whig Club . . . The Brotherhood its name—the Rights of Man . . . its end', *op. cit.* p 54.

accomplish reform had been because they had separated themselves 'from the great mass of the people who could alone give
them effective force'.[1] He was convinced that unless the Dissenters and Catholics combined against what he called the Protestants, who were in control of the government, reform could
never be accomplished.[2] It was to secure this union that he
wrote the pamphlet, signed 'Northern Whig' and entitled *An
Argument on behalf of the Catholics of Ireland*.[3] It led to his invitation to Belfast to meet a group interested in his proposals, out
of which meeting came the Society of the United Irishmen
(October, 1791).

The United Irish movement has been commonly presented
by history books as a great crusade for national and religious
liberty. I shall confine myself to citing only one such view. The
founding of the Society, says Rosamond Jacob, 'marks the day
when descendants of British planters in Ireland first became
Irishmen. Their fathers had usurped that name, calling themselves the Irish nation while they held that nation in slavery.
But in their sons, fired by the sight of despotism overthrown
in France, real democratic principles had wakened, and democratic principle broke the barriers that held them aloof from the
conquered race. They saw that it was the Catholic people who
were Ireland, and they stood up to demand freedom for them
as the first step towards a united nation'.[4] This is the generally
accepted interpretation of the movement, but, in fact, the objective truth is much more qualified.

Was it zeal for the rights of Catholics that fired its founders?
There is no compelling evidence for thinking that it was. Tone
tells us that, when he wrote his pamphlet, he himself was not
acquainted with even one Catholic.[5] He was matched in this by
his confrères in the North. About the Catholics in general, he

---

[1] Wolfe Tone, *Autobiography*, vol. I, p 47.

[2] Cf *op. cit.* pp 40-41.

[3] *Cf op. cit.* p 51.

[4] Rosamond Jacob, *The Rise of the United Irishmen*, London 1937,
p 66.

[5] *Autobiography*, vol. I, p 52.

wrote in his diary, 'they knew wonderfully little in Blefescu (Belfast)'.[1] Indeed it is clear that he met with considerable opposition in Belfast to the idea of an alliance with the Catholics that would entail their enfranchisement.[2] In so far as this was agreed to, it was, as Tone had said in his pamphlet, because no reform was thought to be *practicable*, efficacious or just that did not include the Catholics.[3] One must be reserved about the extent to which justice was considered. Tone himself seems to have included Catholic liberties under the Rights of Man, whose praises he had begun to sing and which he wished to see realised in Ireland. Some of the others, like Nielson, seem to have had a genuine belief in the justice of the Catholic cause.[4] But there can be no doubt that the attitude of many of the leaders was that of Drennan: 'The Catholic cause is subordinate to our cause, and included in it. For, as United Irishmen, we adhere to no sect'.[5]

What then was the dominant cause? The securing of political unity in the interests of the nation? Here again the answer must be qualified. Tone tells us what his own objects were and they *seem* at least to have been motivated by national aspira-

[1] *Op. cit.* p 77.

[2] Cf *op. cit.* pp 87 and 98.

[3] Cf *An Argument on Behalf of the Catholics of Ireland*, Dublin 1791, p 15: 'No reform is practicable, efficacious, or just, which shall not include Irishmen of every religious persuasion'. Cf also declaration of the preparatory committee of the Dungannon Convention, in Madden, *op. cit.* vol. III, p 82.

[4] 'Our efforts for freedom have hitherto been ineffectual and they deserved to be so, for they have been selfish and unjust, as not including the rights of Catholics in the claims we put forward for ourselves', cited in Madden, *op. cit.*. vol IV, p 5.

[5] The Society of United Irishmen of Dublin to the Volunteers of Ireland, in *The Northern Star*, Dec. 15-19 1792. Drennan in chair. It is probable, however, that most of the people who took this attitude were Peep of Day Boys rather than United Irishmen. That many of the United Irish leaders must have had the Catholic cause genuinely at heart is suggested by the fact that from 1796 on thousands of the Defenders in the North came into the United Irishmen.

tions.[1] But it is hard to know whether it was really patriotism or personal hatred of England that launched this adventurous and ambitious man on his chequered political career. The influence of nationality on his movement as a whole is at best obscure. One can assemble many references to 'the nation' from the documents of the period and it might, and has, been argued that the cement of the United Irishmen was a national consciousness. It is hard to say how far this was the case. The Volunteers too had appealed to the interests of the nation[2] and were commonly referred to as 'patriots'. Yet we know what they understood by 'nationality' and 'patriotism', something much more limited than these terms usually connote today. The United Irishmen's pledge, devised by Drennan in 1791, also referred to 'the Irish nation'.[3] But it is clear from one of his letters, written only a few months previously,[4] that he too was

---

[1] 'To submit the tyranny of our exerable Government, to break the connection with England . . . and to assert the independence of my country—these were my objects. To unite the whole people of Ireland . . . to substitute the common name of Irishmen, in place of the denominations of Protestant, Catholic and Dissenter—these were my means', *Autobiography*, vol I, p 51.

[2] Cf Resolution of the First Ulster Regiment at Armagh, 28 December 1780, cited in Rogers, *op. cit.* p 55.

[3] Cf *The Drennan Letters*, p 66. Note also: 'Fellow-Citizens—We speak to you with much earnestness of affection, repeating with sincerest pleasure, that tender and domestic appellation which binds us into one People. But what is it that has lately made and must keep us One? Not the soil we inhabit, not the language we use, but our singleness of sentiment respecting one great political truth, our indivisible union on the main object of general interest—a Parliamentary Reform. This is the civic Faith for which this Society exists'—United Irishmen of Dublin to their Catholic Countrymen, 7 June 1793. Cited in T. W. Moody, The Political Ideas of the United Irishmen, in *Ireland Today*, vol. III, no. 1, January 1938.

[4] Cf Madden, *op. cit.* vol. 1, p 197. 'In four words lies all our power, *Universal Emancipation* and *Representative Legislature*'—*Report of the Trial of Archibald Hamilton Rowan*, Dublin 1794, p 15. 'Universal emancipation and representative legislature is the polar principle which guides our society'—Address from the Society of United Irishmen in Dublin to the Delegates for promoting a Reform in Scotland (1792), in

thinking, not so much of national unity, as of a unity which would mean that 'men who differ in their creed may form a sound part of the same civil constitution'—in other words, political unity. And when the people of Belfast issued their address to the people of Ireland, it was to appeal for a restoration 'to us THE PEOPLE, what, we for ourselves, demand as our right, our due weight and influence in that estate, which is our property, the Representation of the people in parliament'.[1]

Apart from a few instances, such as the Sheares proclamation,[2] which was framed in the intemperate language for which John was notorious, the references of the United Irishmen to 'the nation' must be understood as generally meaning 'independent State'. It was a matter of the people as a whole acquiring full political rights rather than a quest for the national independence of a unified country—the same ideal as led also to the Society of United Englishmen[3] and in Scotland to one of similar name, the ideal which had caused Fox in England, in his effort to turn the Whig Club extremist, to give the famous toast, for which he was dismissed from the Privy Council, 'The Sovereignty of the People of Great Britain'.[4] It was inter-

---

Report of the Committee of Secrecy of the House of Commons, London 1799. 'Two objects interest the Nation—A Plan of Representation and the means of accomplishing it'—James Napper Tandy, signatory to Resolution of Society of United Irishmen of Dublin (1791), Dublin 1792.

[1] Cf Madden, *op. cit.* vol. II, p 168.

[2] Cf Madden, *op. cit.* vol. I, p 111. This society reproduced verbatim, in its constitution, the original declaration of the first club of United Irishmen. Introduction to *Report of the Committee of Secrecy of the House of Commons*, London 1799. Also Thomas Cooper, *A Reply to Mr. Burke's Invective against Mr. Cooper and Mr. Watt in the House of Commons*, Manchester 1792, appendix.

[3] Cf Jacob, *op. cit.* p 202.

[4] Cf Madden, *op. cit.* vol. I, p 114. Dr. Moody has given a good explanation of the United Irishmen's concept of nationality: 'The French revolutionary conception of the nation was a fraternal union of people, whose principle of association was neither blood, nor religion nor even language but rather a consciousness of common interests, common achievements and common ideals. Ireland's past was anything but rich in the traditions of such a unity. The United Irishmen faced the fact

national rather than national in inspiration, as the relations between these various societies bear out.[1] Drennan's wish that the Belfast procession of 1792 to commemorate the French Revolution should be headed by 'four flags, for France, America, Poland and Ireland,'[2] and which, as we learn from Tone,[3] was fulfilled, was indicative of the spirit that then prevailed in Ireland. The impression grows that the United Irishmen were not a nation in revolt, but a people in arms for purely political purposes, which, if achieved, would have laid the foundation on which an all-Ireland Irish nation might have been built.

Whatever views may have been later developed by individual members, the Society of United Irishmen, as originally constituted, did not have in mind the establishment of an Irish republic. Tone has told us that his own object at the time was rather 'to secure the independence of my country under any form of government, to which I was led by a hatred of England, so deeply rooted in my nature that it was rather an instinct than a principle'.[4] Nielson has recorded that the original object of the Society was 'equality of representation, without distinction on account of religion' and that 'the ideas of a republic, and separation, grew out of the severities practised by the Government upon the people'.[5] This is also clear from the first declaration of the Society in Dublin, which demanded an equal representation of the people in parliament,[6] and from the form itself of the United Irish 'test', in which the same aim was proposed for acceptance by the members. Indeed in 1793 we find a convention in Dungannon declaring its 'attachment to the

---

. . . and they called on Irishmen of whatever class, religion or origin to unite to make Ireland's future altogether different from her past. A common belief in political freedom rather than any mystical or romantic conception of nationality was to be the basis of this union'—loc cit. pp 20-21.

[1] Cf Jacob, op. cit. Ch vi: The International Brotherhood.

[2] The Drennan Letters, p 89.

[3] Autobiography, vol. i, p 102.

[4] Ibid. p 55.

[5] Cited in Madden, op. cit. vol. iii, p 167.

[6] Madden, op. cit. vol. ii, p 305.

form and original principles of the British Constitution', 'disapproval of republican forms of government, as applied to this kingdom' and a demand for 'a complete parliamentary reform as essential to the peace, liberty and happiness of the people'.[1] Even by the time of Emmet's leadership, there was a cleavage of opinion as to whether an independent republic was desirable or whether the country should be united to France.[2]

It would certainly be a mistake to think that the masses of Northern United Irishmen were animated by motives of national patriotism. In a letter to Dr. Madden, following the publication of the latter's first two volumes, one of their leaders, James Hope, confirms this.[3]

SPIRIT OF THE FRENCH REVOLUTION ?

The basic drive of the movement seems to have sprung from the influence on the leaders of the principles of the French Revolution. I have already referred to Drennan's desire, before the founding of the United Irishmen, for a Brotherhood which would defend the Rights of Man, in 'communication with leading men in France'.[4] He had not long to wait before his wish was realised. By 1792 a 'National Guard' had been formed in Dublin, whose badge was a harp surmounted by a 'cap of liberty' and whose members were known as 'citizen soldiers'. Provincial 'directories' on the French model were also set up.

[1] Madden, *op. cit.* vol. III, p 83.

[2] Cf Madden, *op. cit.* vol. VII, p 68.

[3] 'When writing of Ulster, you would require an extensive view of the influence with which patriotism had to contend—sectarian, mercantile and landed—to a greater extent than in any other part of Ireland . . . The mass confided in the writers and the speakers . . . Neilson, McCracken, Russell, and Emmet were the leading men in that struggle, with whom I was in closest intimacy. They were men—Irishmen—than whom I have met none more true. The cause of Ireland was then confined to a few individuals. The masses had no idea of the possibility of managing their own affairs', cited in Madden, *op. cit.* vol. V, pp 221-222.

[4] *The Drennan Letters*, p 54.

Was it because of this that Grattan described the United Irishmen as 'a blasted Jacobin society'?[1] Was it because of it that
Napoleon declared that 'the principles of the Irish leaders, when
he investigated the business, appeared to him too closely allied
to those of the Jacobins'?[2] Although the answer must be qualified, it is partly in the affirmative. It was not for nothing that
Whitley Stokes left the Society in 1793, saying that his sense
of religion was repelled by the free-thinking of the movement.
Jacobin influence was certainly at work—in the intercourse
with Priestly[3] and Muir[4] in England, but above all due to the
writings of Paine. The influence of Paine on the United Irishmen
is quite extraordinary, much more so than is commonly realised.
Himself an 'extra-mural' member of the Dublin Society,[5] Paine
was so cultivated in Ireland that at one time he thought of
visiting Belfast.[6] Newell, the informer, claimed that the *Rights
of Man* was frequently read at meetings of the Society.[7] It was
certainly described as a 'work of genius' by Charlemont, who

[1] *Irish Parliamentary Register*, vol. XIV, p 83, cited in Jacob, *op. cit.*
p 214.

[2] Tone, *Autobiography*, vol. II, p 341.

[3] Cf *The Drennan Letters*, pp 391 and 394.

[4] Cf Jacob, *op. cit.* p 196. Cf also Address of the United Britons to
the United Irishmen (1798), in *Report of the Secret Committee of the House
of Lords*, 1798, pp 33-35. The suggestion that the Corresponding Society
in England (based on much the same principles as the United Irish
Society) was associated with the Illuminées in France was made by
Arthur Young in his *Enquiry into the State of the Public Mind amongst
the Lower Classes*, Dublin 1798, p 8. The same charge appears in *An Address to the People of Ireland on the Present Alarming state of the Kingdom*,
Dublin 1798, pp 12-13. For an account of Price and Muir see respectively
The Northern Star, Oct. 13-17, 1792 and *The Press*, Dec. 16 1797. On the
influence of Illuminism on the United Irishmen see Appendix A to H. B.
Pollard, *The Secret Societies of Ireland*, London 1922.

[5] Cf Richard Hayes, *Ireland and Irishmen in the French Revolution*,
London 1932, p 289.

[6] *The Drennan Letters*, p 129.

[7] Private Memoranda taken from Newell by Pelham, predecessor of
Castlereagh.

scattered it amongst members of the Whig Club throughout the country.[1]

The United Irish leaders were affected in varying degrees by all this. The French Revolution was welcomed by Tone as 'glorious and successful';[2] with a little wine inside he could join in the radically worded toast: 'The spirit of the French mob to the people of Ireland'.[3] Even when assistant to the Catholic Committee, he had a hankering for 'Rights of Man, French Revolution, No bishops, etc., etc.'[4] And yet I feel that Tone was less influenced than were some of the others by the principles and philosophy of the French. 'I sought for aid', he says, 'wherever it was to be found',[5] though in seeking it he had to put up with much that did not attract him. His exasperation gets out of control now and then, as when he denounces Paine's *Age of Reason* as 'damned trash'.[6] He seems, however, to have accepted some of Paine, whom he later met and liked and described as having done wonders for the cause of liberty.[7] Liberty indeed was his own first love; he would have accepted anything that would conduce to its furtherance. 'Right or wrong, success

---

[1] During the 1790's almost all of Paine's writings were published— sometimes in more than one edition—in Dublin. *The Rights of Man*, which was published in the city in 1791, was distributed at a penny per copy throughout the country by the Whig Club, to the extent of 20,000 copies. Cf Musgrave, *Memoirs of the Rebellion in Ireland*, (Dublin 1801), pp 112-113. *The Age of Reason* was also distributed gratis. Cf Musgrave, *op. cit.* p 156. In addition, Paine's lesser known tracts were published as follows: *Letter to the Abbé Raynal on the Affairs of America* (1782); *Letter to the Earl of Shelbourne on his Speech respecting the acknowledgement of American Independence* (1791); *Letter to Mr. Secretary Dundas in answer to his Observations on The Rights of Man* (1792); *Agrarian Justice* (Cork, no date, after 1795); *The Decline and Fall of the English System of Finance*, Dublin 1796. A Life of Paine was also published: Francis Oldys, *The Life of Thomas Paine*, Dublin, 1791.

[2] *Autobiography*, vol. I, p 38.

[3] *Ibid.*, p 127.

[4] *Ibid.*, p 110.

[5] *Autobiography*, vol. II, p 357.

[6] *Op. cit.* vol. I, p 246.

[7] *Op. cit.* vol. II, p 189.

to the French, they are fighting our battles and if they fail, adieu to liberty in Ireland for another century'.

Dr. Drennan was more intellectually convinced by French principles. There is evidence in his letters that he was well versed in Locke[1] and in Rousseau,[2] in Mirabeau[3] and, needless to say, in Paine. As a result, it does not surprise us that he thought that Christianity was 'not much beyond man to discover'.[4] In the case of Lord Edward Fitzgerald, the link with the Revolution was of a more emotional nature. The cousin of Fox and friend of Sheridan,[5] he was immediately attracted by the 'political excitement'.[6] Like Tone, he too visited Paris and lodged with Paine,[7] as the emissary, it seems, of the United Irishmen to the Revolutionary Government. He was soon a member of the Jacobin Club,[8] and it does not surprise us to find him a signatory to an Irish address to the National Convention, in which the latter is congratulated for having carried on its wars 'for the triumph of Truth and Reason'.[9] The brothers Sheares were more deeply infected with rationalism, of the kind that had created secular democracy in France. Their library was said to have been a magnificent collection[10] and there can be little doubt that it included at least some of the writings of the *philosophes*. But they too made personal contact with the Revolution, becoming associated with Robespierre himself[11] and attending meetings of the various political societies in Paris. The Castlereagh Papers describe John at this time as

[1] Cf *The Drennan Letters*, p 93.

[2] *Op. cit.* pp 60 and 215.

[3] *Op. cit.*, p 94.

[4] Cited in R. B. McDowell, *Irish Public Opinion*, 1750-1800, p 177. Cf also *The Drennan Letters*, p 232.

[5] Cf T. Moore, *The Memoirs of Lord Edward Fitzgerald*, London 1897, p 107. First published in 1831.

[6] Moore, *op. cit.* p 126.

[7] Cf Moore, *op. cit.* p 128.

[8] Cf Hayes, *op. cit.* p 103.

[9] Cited in Hayes, *op. cit.* p 101.

[10] Cf Madden, *op. cit.* vol. II, p 20.

[11] Cf Madden, *ibid.*, p 16; also Hayes, *op. cit.* p 105.

'the firebrand of all the exiled patriots in Paris'.[1] In religious
matters he was said to be 'sceptical as to revelation'[2] and re-
minds us rather forcibly of Jefferson.[3] He seems to have believed
in a deistic universe, in a 'sacred Power, whatever by thy name
and nature'.[4] Finally, there was Arthur O'Connor, who adopted
the Revolution without any reservation. Bitterly anti-Catholic'[5],
he eventually settled in France, became the son-in-law and dis-
ciple of Condorcet and ended his life as editor of a rationalistic
review of religion.

In all of these the Revolution made its converts; even its
rationalism and secularism found reflection at times in their
recorded words and actions. And yet it is interesting as well
as important to note how they sometimes diluted their acceptance of it. It is impossible to say whether Tone's criticism of
religion is directed at religion itself or only at particular manifestations of it.[6] He certainly rejected the extremism of Robespierre.[7] So too did the Unitarian, Drennan,[8] who emphatically
protested his religion such as it was. Indeed Drennan came to
be entirely disillusioned with the Revolution as the imperialistic
designs of Napoleon became clear to him; he tells us that he

[1] Cf Hayes, *op. cit.* p 105, note 9.

[2] Madden, *op. cit.* p 125.

[3] 'An infidel I have lived and will die, Who verily think it a fraud,
Three persons should gather and jumble together, And make up all but
one God', cited in R. B. McDowell, *Irish Public Opinion, 1750-1800*.

[4] Cited in Madden, *op. cit.* vol. III, p 224.

[5] Cf Lecky, *Ireland in the 18th Century*, vol. IV, London 1909, p 256.

[6] Cf *Autobiography*, Vol. II, pp 217, 289, 300, 303.

[7] *Ibid.*, p 343.

[8] Cf *The Drennan Letters*, 80 and 232. In 1749 Hamilton Rowan
wrote to his wife from Paris as follows: 'I own to you candidly, when it
is of no avail, that my ideas of reform and of another word which begins
with the same letter are very much altered by living for twelve months
in France, and that I never wish to see either the one or the other procured by force. I have seen one faction rising over another and over-
turning it; each of them in their turn making a stalking horse of the
supreme power of the people to cover public and private massacre and
plunder, while every man of virtue and humanity shuddered and skulked
in disgraceful silence'.

reversed the latter's picture in his bedroom, 'placing his head where his heels were'.[1] His action was symbolic of the thoughts of many, after the death of Hoche had ended their hopes for a French invasion. Lord Edward seems to have been always in good faith as far as the secularism of the Revolution was concerned. He died in the hope that 'God would receive him for having contributed to the freedom of his country'. There were others for whom the same must be said—Neilson, who wrote from prison to his wife that 'all my experience, the result of all my most profound thinking, leads me more and more to attach myself to the Christian system of extinguishing animosities';[2] Thomas Russell, of whom it was said that his 'belief in Christianity was a strong and vital principle which influenced every act of his life' and who wrote before his execution: 'I trust for pardon and mercy through my Saviour',[3] and Jackson, who occupied his last days writing a reply to Paine's *Age of Reason* and in whose pocket, after his death—unfortunately by his own hand—was found a scrap of paper, on which was written a few words from Psalm Twenty-five: 'Turn Thee unto me O Lord and have mercy upon me'. Even John Sheares did not die, as he had proclaimed himself, an infidel.[4] These things speak more eloquently than could collected works; they are living—and dying —proof that the political philosophy of these men, although coloured strongly by Rousseau's idea of the Sovereignty of the People, recoiled from the extreme and unqualified secularism which is essential to Roussellian Liberal Democracy. Had they lived, the majority of them would probably have ended like Robert Emmet[5] who, at his trial, castigated France as 'the enemy of freedom in every part of the globe'.[6]

[1] *Ibid.* p 318.

[2] Cf Madden, *op. cit.* vol. III, p 275.

[3] Madden, *op. cit.* vol. VI, p 253. For his final address see Madden, *op. cit.* vol. VI, pp 261-264.

[4] Cf Madden, *op. cit.* vol. II, pp 193-194.

[5] Madden describes Emmet's abortive revolt as part and parcel of the system of the United Irishmen, *op. cit.* vol. VII, p 115.

[6] Speech from the dock, as reconstructed by Madden, *op. cit.* vol. VII, p 240. This account of Emmet's speech has been endorsed by T. A. Emmet, *The Emmet Family*, New York 1898, p 160.

It would be difficult to prove that the United Irishmen sought the creation of a State that would be indifferent to religion on the lines of the model to be found in France. It is beyond question that they argued for the ending of the establishment of the Church of Ireland and of the various consequences by which this was attended. But one could easily misunderstand their purpose in so doing. At his examination before the Secret Committee of the House of Lords, Thomas Addis Emmet was charged by Lord Glentworth with intending to destroy the Church. 'Pardon me, my Lord', replied Emmet, 'my intention never was to destroy the Church. My wish decidedly was to overturn the Establishment'. 'And have it as it is in France', interjected Lord Dillon. 'As it is in many parts of America, my Lords', explained Emmet.[1] At a similar interview Dr. McNeven pointed out that unless religion can do without State support, there is little to be said for it as religion.[2] Both maintained that there was no question of replacing the Protestant Establishment by a Catholic one constructed on the same lines. They claimed that not only Catholic opinion[3] but sound political philosophy precluded this.[4]

If the extent of the influence of Roussellian democracy on the leaders is difficult to delineate, it is even more so in the

---

[1] Cf Madden, *op. cit.* vol. IV, p 86.

[2] *Ibid.* p 260.

[3] *Ibid.* p 93 for Emmet's views on this; p 261 for McNeven's views.

[4] 'The destruction of religion is one thing', said O'Connor, at his examination, 'the destruction of establishment is another; the great and just principle upon which the Union is formed is the most perfect freedom for all religions alike. We are of opinion that the present monstrous Protestant establishment in Ireland is a grievous burthen on all the people of Ireland; highly unjust to those who are not of the Protestant religion, and highly injurious to the Protestant religion itself; for we are convinced it would work a very desirable change in the Protestant clergy of Ireland, if they were made to owe their maintenance to a faithful discharge of their functions, instead of obtaining it by a base and disgraceful cringing to patrons, and that if there was no other objection to tithes than their being an endless source of discord between a Christian ministry and the people, they might be abolished', cited in Madden, *op. cit.* vol. IV, p 333.

case of the rank and file of the United Irishmen. There is some evidence of popular zeal for it in the North. Tone tells us that *The Rights of Man* was the 'Koran of Blefescu',[1] in which there was a flourishing Jacobin Club. In 1791 the anniversary of the French Revolution was celebrated in Northern Ireland as nowhere else outside France. In the Belfast procession a portrait of Mirabeau followed the flag and one of the banners carried a slogan suggestive of religious indifference: 'Superstitious jealousy, the cause of the Irish Bastille: let us unite to destroy it'.[2] Financial support was forwarded to France;[3] parents christened their children after Revolutionary leaders;[4] trees of liberty were planted[5] and messages of congratulation sent to Paris. Kilrea witnessed the gruesome spectacle of a guillotine being manufactured, to be stored away for the day of the coming revolution in Ireland.[6]

But there was by no means unanimous support for this enthusiasm. Dr. Drennan, writing shortly afterwards, found it

---

[1] *Autobiography*, vol. I, p 77.

[2] Cf Moore, *The Memoirs of Lord Edward Fitzgerald*, p 156. At the banquet which followed, the Revolution was toasted. *The Northern Star* for 11-14 July 1792, gives a list of the toasts. They include 'The Constituent Assembly of France', 'The French Army', 'French Liberty', 'The Glorious Revolution of France'. Cf also *The Northern Star* 31 March-4 April 1792 and 27-31 October 1792. On 21 April 1792 Mirabeau was toasted at a Catholic meeting in Belfast. Cf *The Northern Star*, 18-21 April 1792. The same paper for 14-18 January 1792 carried an article entitled 'The Rights of Men and of Citizens' in which the then current French ideas were expounded on liberty, security, property and resistance to oppression. See Homer Calkin's article La propagation en Irlande des idées de la Revolution Française, in *Annales Historiques de la Revolution Française*, April-June 1955. Mr. Calkin is also the author of *Les invasions d'Irlande pendent la Revolution Française*, Paris 1956.

[3] Cf Hayes, *op. cit.* p 12.

[4] Cf James Winder Good, *Ulster and Ireland*, Dublin 1919, p 45.

[5] Cf Unpublished letter of Dr. Drennan, no. 625, referred to in *The Drennan Letters*, appendix, p 200.

[6] Cf Samuel McSkimin in his *Annals of Ulster*, cited in Good, *op. cit.* p 46. Cf. also Ireland and the French Revolution, in McDonell, *op. cit.*, ch. VIII, *passim*.

necessary to sound a note of caution 'for even here there are
enemies to the French Revolution'.[1] The address sent to France
from Belfast is particularly illuminating. In effect it was an
appeal to the French to put a restraint on their actions, and to
avoid divorcing democracy from religion—the kind of address
which, despite the hysteria, was only to be expected from the
majority of the God-fearing people of Belfast: 'We trust that
you will never submit the liberties of France to any other guarantees, than God and the right hands of the people . . . We
beseech you as men, as legislators, as citizens, and as soldiers,
in this your great conflict for liberty, for France, and for the
world, to despise all earthly danger, to look up to God, and to
connect your councils, your arms, and your empire, to his
throne, with a chain of union, fortitude, perseverance, morality
and religion. We conclude with this fervent prayer: That as the
Almighty is dispersing the political clouds which have hitherto
darkened our hemisphere, all nations may use the light of
Heaven: that, as in this latter age, the Creator is unfolding in
his creatures powers which had long lain latent, they may exert
them in the establishment of universal freedom, harmony and
peace'.[2] To which the rationalist French could only reply that
'our efforts will be favoured by the God of liberty',[3] whatever
they meant by that.

The impact of the Revolution on the Catholic masses is more
difficult still to understand. Again we find the vogue of Paine
who, although he was not translated into Irish, seems to have
been known rather widely to the common people. We read, for
example, that in Mayo 'the new political doctrines . . . have
pervaded the lower classes' and that a French invasion 'would
be joined by the peasantry of Connaught'.[4] We learn too that
'in County Cork Paine's works are read by the boys of almost
every school', although the addendum that 'in most houses they
now supplant the Psalter and prayer book'[5] makes it clear that

[1] *The Drennan Letters*, p 92.
[2] Cf Madden, *op. cit.* vol. I, pp 191-194.
[3] *Ibid.* p 196.
[4] *H.O. Papers*, cited in Hayes, *op. cit.* p 15.
[5] Cf Hayes, *op. cit.* p 8, note 12.

the writer was not speaking about the Catholics. Still, if we can judge from the anti-Paine pamphlets published in Cork in these years, his following in the South must have been considerable.[1] In Dublin, for every pamphlet that appeared attacking Paine's defence of the French Revolution,[2] another was sure to be published on the opposite side, by way of objecting to Burke's intransigent furtherance of the war with France.[3] Indeed pam-

[1] William O'Connor, *Candid Remarks on Paine's Age of Reason*, 1795; T. D. Hincks, *Letters originally addressed to the Inhabitants of Cork, occasioned by the Circulation of Mr. Paine's Age of Reason*, 2nd ed. 1796; James Bourke, *An Answer to a Late Pamphlet entitled Paine's Age of Reason*, 1797.

[2] Wm. Smith, *The Rights of Citizens, being an examination of Mr. Paine's principles touching government*, Dublin, 1791; *A Defence of the Constitution of England against the Libels that have been lately published on it, particularly in Paine's Pamphlet on the Rights of Man*, Dublin, 1791; *Remarks on Mr. Paine's Pamphlet called the Rights of Man*, Dublin, 1791; *The Rights of Citizens*, Dublin, 1793; John Adams, *An Answer to Paine's Rights of Man*, Dublin, 1793; Wm. Jackson, *Observations in Answer to Mr. Thomas Paine's Age of Reason*, Dublin, 1795. Whitley Stokes, *A Reply to Mr. Paine's Age of Reason addressed to the Students of Trinity College, Dublin*, Dublin 1795; Henry Hunt, *Caution to the readers of Mr. Paine's Age of Reason*, Dublin, 1795; J. Anketell, *Strictures upon Paine's Age of Reason*, Dublin, 1796; *The Speeches of the Hon. Thomas Erskine on the Trial of Thomas Williams for publishing the Age of Reason written by Thomas Paine*, Dublin 1797.

[3] Joseph Priestly, *Letter to the Right Honourable Ed. Burke occasioned by his Reflections on the Revolution in France*, 1791; R. Price, *Observations on the celebrated pamphlet of the Rt. Hon. Edmund Burke*, 1791; Benjamin Bousfield, *Observations on the Rt. Hon. Edmund Burke's Pamphlet on the subject of the French Revolution*, 1791; George Rous, *A Letter to the Rt. Hon. Ed. Burke in Reply to his Appeal from the New to the Old Whigs*, 1791; M. Depont, *Answer to the Reflections of the Rt. Hon. Ed. Burke*, 1791; Capel Lofft, *Remarks on the Letters of the Rt. Hon. Ed. Burke concerning the Revolution in France*, 1791; *A Letter to the Rt. Hon. Ed. Burke in Reply to his Reflections on the Revolution in France*, by a Member of the Revolution Society 1791; *An Answer to the Rt. Hon. Ed. Burke's Reflections on the Revolution in France*, by an Irishman, 1791.

phlets of all kinds on the French question abounded.[1] The popular press gave particular prominence to French ideas. The *Union Star* was definitely Jacobin in tendency, while *The Press* of Dublin, edited by Arthur O'Connor, devoted a section of each number to events in France. Sometimes it called outright for a French-type insurrection in Ireland.[2]

It would be imprudent to suppose that any considerable

[1] Cf also Richard Price, *Discourse on the Love of Our Country, containing the Declaration of Rights of the National Assembly of France*, Dublin 1790; Wm. Hamilton, *Letters on the principle of French democracy*, Dublin, 1792; Rev. F. McCarthy, *Funeral Sermon preached at a Solemn High Mass celebrated on 12 November for Marie Antoinette, Her Late Most Christian Majesty*, Cork 1793; Sir Laurence Parsons, *Thoughts on Liberty and Equality*, Dublin, 1793; T. McKenna, *An Essay on Parliamentary Reform and on the evils likely to arise from a republican constitution*, Dublin 1793; William Preston, *Democratic Rage, or Louis the unfortunate*, Dublin, 1793; *A Series of Letters containing an account of the massacres in Paris in 1792*, Dublin, 1793; *Memoirs of General Dumourier*, Dublin 1794; *Robespierre's speech to the National Convention of France*, Belfast, 1794; *Kingly Government asserted*, by an Irishman, Dublin, 1794; M. Mallet Du Pan, *Considerations on the Nature of the French Revolution and on the Causes which prolong its duration*, Dublin 1794; *Speech of the Rt. Hon. Charles James Fox in the House of Commons, 24 March, against war with France*, Dublin 1795; John Moore, *A view of the causes and progress of the French Revolution*, Dublin 1795; W. Staveley, *An appeal to light or the tenets of the deists examined and disapproved*, Belfast, 1796; *Letters on the subject of an invasion*, Dublin, 1796; *A plain address to the people of Ireland on the possible event of a French invasion*, Dublin, 1796; *French Fraternity and French Protection as promised to Ireland and as Experienced by other Nations*, by a Friend of the People, Dublin 1798; John Caspar Lavater, *Remonstrance addressed to the Executive Directory of the French Republic against the Invasion of Switzerland*, Dublin, 1798.

For an account of the literature of this period see Irish Controversialists and the French Revolution, in McDowell, *op. cit.*, ch. ix. A comprehensive, though by no means complete, bibliography of pamphlets published in Dublin at the time and also to be found in McDowell, *op. cit.*

[2] E.g. 19 October, 4 November, 18 November, 2 December, 1797.

400 STUDIES IN POLITICAL MORALITY

section of this large mass of literature either stemmed from Catholic sources or influenced the thinking of the Catholic masses. More often than not it represented the cheap reprinting of pirated English publications, for which 18th century Dublin was notorious. The anti-Revolutionary tracts usually represented only the Protestant ascendancy, when they were not actually put out by the government authorities themselves. They had little influence among the Catholic people, who would have been guided rather by the pastorals of their bishops and the exhortations of their priests. As early as 1793, the Archbishop of Dublin, Dr. Troy, had warned his clergy about the dangers in the revolutionary principles. He followed it up in 1797 and 1798. In 1797 too Dr. Hussey, Bishop of Waterford and Lismore, had written to his clergy along similar lines. And in 1798, Dr. Moylan, Bishop of Cork, issued a particularly forthright condemnation of French principles 'to the lower order of Roman Catholic inhabitants' of his diocese.

Catholic support for these principles cannot have been great. The general attitude of Catholics was more likely to have been as Tone described it: 'They saw the brilliant prospect of success which events in France opened to their view, and they determined to avail themselves with promptitude of that opportunity';[1] they would support almost 'any measure which held out to them a chance of bettering their condition'.[2] Their situation was parallel to that of the urban proletariat in England at the time, whom Arthur Young described as both poor and ignorant and ready 'for any revolution' by way of a 'change for the better'.[3] Although the 1792 massacres in France and the

[1] *Autobiography*, vol. I, p 147. Auckland, who in 1792 had believed that there was little danger of Jacobinism spreading to Ireland and had called it a 'ridiculous and insignificant faction', had come by 1798 to speak of the poisons of Jacobinism, republicanism and misunderstanding of England as mixed together in Ireland—Letters of 19 October 1792 and 1 August 1798, cited in Calkin, *loc. cit.* pp 158-159.

[2] *Autobiography*, vol. II, p 379: Memoir to the French Government.

[3] Arthur Young, *An Enquiry into the State of the Public Mind amongst the Lower Classes and of the means of turning it to the welfare of the State*, Dublin 1798, p 15.

confiscation of Church property had served to dampen the enthusiasm of some, the majority of the common people were not affected by them. An English officer, writing in 1796, says that they were unaware of the state of religion in France, and believed implicitly that equality of property and agrarian democracy were the chief fruits of the revolution in that country.[1] Indeed their position was not unlike that of the Russian peasantry in 1847, as described by a writer of their own: 'The people have a desire for potatoes, but none whatsoever for a constitution; the latter is wanted by the educated urban classes'.

If the Catholics were eventually persuaded that true reform did not lie along French lines, the cause must be found in the influence of their religious leaders. It is interesting to note that the remedy for revolution, prescribed by Arthur Young for England at this time, was precisely the revival of religion.[2] The religious instruction of the people, he maintained, was a matter of no small relevance 'and its importance was never so clearly to be recognised as it has been throughout the progress of that

---

[1] *A Letter to the Officers of the Army in Ireland on the subject of an Invasion from France*, Dublin 1796. It was suggested by an anonymous writer at the time that the United Irishmen were inspired by 'levelling notions' which 'tend to subvert all civil government'—*The Rights of Citizens*, Dublin 1793. While it can freely be admitted that 'among the foremost of the grievances complained of is the payment of tithes' (*ibid.* p 17), it cannot be said that the United Irishmen had worked out any systematic radical social thought. Cf R. B. McDowell, Irish Radical Thought at the end of the 18th Century, in *Bulletin of the Irish Committee of Historical Sciences*, nn 6, 8, 9 (1940). 'By liberty we never understood unlimited freedom, nor by equality the levelling of property or the destruction of subordination'—United Irishmen of Dublin to the Volunteers of Ireland, 14 December 1792, cited in T. W. Moody, The Political Ideas of the United Irishmen, in *Ireland Today*, vol. III, no. 1, January 1938.

[2] Young complained bitterly of the lack of care for the poor by the Anglican Church, of the pews 'to which the poor have no admittance', the aisles 'so narrow as to contain very few, compared with the population', and the lack of 'preachers who shall inculcate the vital Christianity of the Church of England', *loc. cit.* pp 19 and 22.

revolution which now threatens the overthrow of everything respectable in Europe: for it ought never to be absent from our minds that it has been reared on the basis of irreligion'.[1] Young hit out at the educated classes who, though they 'rail at Jacobinism on a Saturday', 'pass their Sunday anywhere but at Church . . . A better example must be generally set by the highest classes'.[2] Such counsels were less needed in Ireland, either on the part of the Northern Protestants or on that of the Southern Catholics. Amongst both groups religion was strong, even if some of the leaders of the United Irishmen were lax in its practice. Whatever allegiance these were tempted to give to secularism was, for the most part, superficial and transitory.

Amongst the mass of the people it never really took root. As was the case with the Protestants of the North, there were definite limits beyond which the Southern Catholics would not go. Their loyalty to their priests, from whom Tone admits he could not calculate assistance,[3] was too strong to allow them to give unqualified support to a secularist system. It is erroneous to say that only the higher clergy stood out against the principles of the Revolution. Fr. Synnott of Millima and Fr. Ryan of Arklow are but two of the priests who followed the example of their colleague of Saintfield who, Tone tells us, 'preached against the United Irishmen, and exhorted his people not to join such clubs'.[4] They would have had little difficulty in persuading their flocks to abjure the extreme principles of Rousseau and Paine. It can only have been for this reason that Myles Byrne was able to declare that in the South of Ireland in 1798 'the United Irish system was scarcely known . . . although the people everywhere sighed for that equality of civil and religious liberty so long refused to them'.[5] It is well known that elsewhere, and especially in Wexford, there were many Catholics—including priests—who supported the movement. But it remains to be proved that they did so for any reason other than

---

[1] Young, *loc. cit.* p 19.
[2] *Ibid.*, pp 25 and 26.
[3] *Autobiography*, vol. II, p 75.
[4] *Ibid.* vol. I, p 116.
[5] *Memoirs of Myles Byrne*, Dublin 1907.

the inability to bear longer with oppression'.[1] Despite the exploits of some renegade Irishmen during the Terror in France, the National Convention there made an accurate observation when it declared that 'Republicanism (of the French variety) does not easily enter Irish heads'.[2]

THE INFLUENCE OF AMERICA

A strong case might be made for the idea that the United Irishmen movement was closer in many respects to the spirit of the American than to that of the French Revolution. Unfortunately little has been written on the relations between America and Ireland during the second half of the 18th century. There is one important article, however, by Mr. Homer Calkin, on 'American Influence in Ireland, 1760 to 1800'.[3] Mr. Calkin draws attention to the similarities which at this time existed between the two countries. Both were sources of raw materials for British industry and markets for British manufactured products. Neither possessed any autonomy in the matter of economic development for the Trade and Navigation Acts applied to both. The legislative bodies of both met only at the decision of British governors, while neither had representation in the British parliament, nor any voice in the fixing of the taxation with which they were burdened.

It should cause no surprise then if it were found that the

---

[1] Even anti-Catholic propagandists at the time had to admit, although they made efforts to explain it away, that in Wexford itself the majority of the clergy dissociated themselves from the United Irishmen. Cf Veridicus, *Concise Account of the Present Rebellion*, Dublin 1799, in which a list of these priests can be found, p 37.

[2] Letter to the Committee of Public Safety 1793, cited in Hayes, *op. cit.* p 139. Parentheses mine.

[3] Homer Calkin, American Influence in Ireland, 1760 to 1800, in *The Pennsylvania Magazine of History and Biography*, April 1947. Cf also Reinhard Cassirer, United Irishmen in Democratic America, in *Ireland Today*, vol. III, no. 2, 1938, and Ireland and the American Revolution, in McDowell, *op. cit.*, ch. III.

ideology of the American Revolution had a profound effect on many people in Ireland. There is evidence that this was so from its commencement. As early as 1766, the repeal of the Stamp Act caused great rejoicing, with bells and bonfires, in Dublin. In 1775 the Guild of Dublin Merchants voted thanks to the Earl of Effingham for having refused to join the army for service against 'the lives and liberties of his fellow subjects in America'.[1] During the same year Lord Chatam declared that 'Ireland is with them (the Americans) to a man',[2] while Governor Johnstone said that 'three to one in Ireland are on their side'.[3] Pamphlets relating to the American Revolution were reprinted in Dublin, among them being the first tract by Paine to be published in Ireland,[4] a fact which, by associating him primarily with America, may have had something to do with his later popularity.

Small wonder that the Americans looked on Ireland almost as an ally, preparing plans in 1776 for having a fleet provisioned at Cork and shipping stores at Newry in 1777, saying that 'the Irish are universally in favour of the Americans'.[5] Small wonder too that it was felt that the British army would get but few recruits—not even twenty men in the whole country—for the war in America.[6] Although this fear was not verified, some six hundred and fifty Irish soldiers deserted on arriving in Philadelphia.[7] Franklin was emboldened to visit Ireland twice and prepared an 'Address to the good People of Ireland on behalf

[1] Cited in Calkin, *loc. cit.* p 107.

[2] *Pennsylvania Gazette*, 12 April 1775, cited in Calkin, *loc. cit.* p 115.

[3] *American Archives*, Series 4, VI, 31, in Calkin, *loc. cit.* p 115.

[4] Richard Price, *Observations on the Nature of Civil Liberty, the Principles of Government, and the Justice and Policy of the War with America*; Dublin 1776; John Dickinson, *Letters from a farmer in Pennsylvania*, Dublin 1768 and *Plain Truth: Addressed to the Inhabitants of America;* Thomas Paine, *Letter to the Abbé Raynal on the Affairs of North America*, Dublin 1782.

[5] Cited in Calkin, *loc. cit.* p 109.

[6] Cf Calkin, *loc. cit.*

[7] *Ibid.* p 110.

of America' (1778).[1] So too did the Committee of Correspondence appointed by the Continental Congress.[2]

When the *Northern Star* was founded in 1792, it declared its intention of printing the proceedings of the American Congress regularly.[3] It carried out its promise faithfully in this respect. Periodically its columns carried reports of toasts offered to America at meetings of the United Irishmen. Some of these referred to America as the asylum of liberty.[4] And when it eventually came to the stage of calling for revolt, it did so saying that 'the French and American revolutions were founded upon insurrection'.[5] The truth seems to be, as Calkin has noted,[6] that this period witnessed three distinct, though related, revolutions, the American, the French and the Irish. If the last named attracted little international attention, it is because it was unsuccessful, as well as being on a much smaller scale than others. But it had its own peculiar ideology and *leit motif*. And while it was undeniably influenced profoundly by French principles, it was by no means just a scaled down version of the French programme.

This was particularly so as regards the place of religion in civic life. It cannot be said that the United Irishmen in general were committed to the introduction of a secularist regime in Ireland. In this sphere the movement, on the whole, was more in harmony with American ideas than with French. In fact, a

[1] A pamphlet by Franklin was published in Dublin in 1784: *Two Tracts: Information to those who remove to America and Remarks concerning the Savages of North America.*

[2] Calkin, *loc. cit.* pp 116-117.

[3] No. 1, 1 January 1792.

[4] 'America—the Asylum of Liberty'; 'The Memory of Dr. Franklin'; 'President Washington'; 'Lasting Freedom and Prosperity to the United States of America'. Cf Calkin, *loc. cit.* For an account of similar toasts in Dublin during the American War of Independence see McDowell, *op. cit.*, p 43.

[5] Cf *The Life of Thomas Reynolds*, ii, pp 559-563.

[6] H. Calkin, La propagation en Irlande des idées de la Révolution francaise, in *Annales Historiques de la Révolution Française*, April-June 1955.

pamphlet published in Cork in 1795 contrasts the false 'French' principles of Paine concerning religion with the more acceptable American theory and practice in its regard.[1]

In truth, democracy in Ireland—past and present—can stand up to the criticisms of Mr. Blanshard. If revision is called for it is in his own ideas on democracy. Let him examine his assumption that Liberal Secularism is the purest and highest form of democracy. Let him examine his assumption that Catholic teaching on Church-State relations is essentially a compromise with democracy. In particular, let him examine his assumption that, by reason of its respect for religion, the pattern of democracy of the Irish Republic lacks many of the basic ingredients of freedom. Also his assumption that the people of Northern Ireland stand for a type of democracy—which Mr. Blanshard would dearly though futilely like to call American—that refuses to uphold as extensive a respect for religion in public life as the majority of the citizens expect, care for genuine human liberties allows and the interests of the common good permit.

CHURCH AND STATE IN IRISH DEMOCRACY

It is generally assumed that the Irish democratic tradition stands for the complete separation of Church and State. 'From its early origins', says one writer, 'the (Irish) revolutionary movement had ever been imbued with an intense democratic

[1] Paine, it says, 'saw the exceeding probability that the American revolution in the system of Government would be followed by a revolution in the system of religion. Here his suggestions failed him; the revolution in government has happened, yet Christianity has not been even attempted to be abolished in America, but is settled on a firmer basis than ever. That wise brave people, if they imagined the religion of their oppressors to be inimical to liberty . . . would have soon thrown it off along with the yoke, and with that new form of government have set up a new form of religion. No, though they cast off their obedience to the laws, they still preserved unblemished the unanimous adoration to Christ, knowing his doctrine to be the doctrine of truth, liberty and

radicalism'.[1] We have seen enough, however, to realise that there is a wealth of difference between the Irish and French democratic revolutions. In the case of the former there can be no denying that religion has a part to play that was systematically excluded by the latter. The question to ask is not whether the Irish political tradition is neutral as regards religion, but whether religion, as such, is given any special recognition by the State.

About one thing historians are unanimous. The Irish tradition of democracy is certainly hostile to the establishment of any Church by the State. It is not difficult to find evidence for this. Modern Irish nationalism has never had any room for anything that would drive a wedge between the confessions. Indeed the idea of full civil liberty for all was the main plank on which Protestants and Catholics were united as nationalists. Both the constitutional and revolutionary movements reflect this. It was an important tenet of O'Connell's Repeal Movement and later of the successive Home Rule Bills of Gladstone with their clauses—approved in Ireland—guaranteeing universal religious and civil liberty and undertaking not to establish or endow any religion. It was part and parcel too of the political philosophy of the United Irishmen, of Davis and *The Nation* newspaper, of the Fenians and their successors the Irish Republican Brotherhood, right down to the achievement of self-government. The Declaration of Independence read at the first meeting of Dail Eireann repeated the guarantees of equal rights

equality . . . I believe the world will allow the great Franklin to have at least as much sense as Tom Paine, yet he never attempted in his writings any such doctrine as in the 'Age of Reason,' but lived and dyed (sic) a Christian Philosopher. Though Paine would wish to overturn the religion of America, I am certain his book will not make a single province out of the thirteen proselytes to his doctrine of Deism. That Religion is no enemy to liberty, may be deduced from the present flourishing state of America, where freedom exists in her greatest purity . . . The French, on the contrary, have carried their notion of Freedom beyond the bounds of reason'—Wm. O'Connor, *op. cit.* Cork 1795.

[1] Leo Kohn, *The Constitution of the Irish Free State*, London 1932, p 25.

for all, including the different religions, in the new Ireland that was then being ushered in.

The Church itself in Ireland, it can also be pointed out, has been very desirous to avoid any situation or legal arrangement under which it might become the servant of the State in return for favours received. From 1774 on the Catholic Church in Ireland declared itself to be loyal to the government in power. But it resolutely set its face against accepting any system of recognition that might compromise its spiritual independence. It would not hear of being endowed by the State. Again and again (e.g. in 1795 and 1797) it refused all such offers, by rejecting the condition—a government veto on episcopal appointments—that was appended as a necessary prerequisite. Apart from some hesitancy in 1799, when the offer was extended to include complete emancipation,[1] the Bishops remained firm in their attitude of not accepting any form of Catholic establishment. They continued thus in 1808 and again in 1813, when the Canning Clauses—although accepted by the English Catholic Board—forced them to reject an otherwise acceptable Catholic Relief Bill. So opposed was the Irish Church to such establishment that it reacted violently even to Roman efforts—the Quarantotti Rescript—to secure acceptance of the government scheme. Even after emancipation had been eventually secured without according the veto, the Bishops refused to consider a scheme for the endowment of the Catholic Church at the time of the disestablishment of the Church of Ireland and the discontinuance of the parliamentary grants to Maynooth (1869).

All this and much more can be adduced as proof that neither the Church itself nor the national movement wanted the establishment of the Catholic religion by the State. What is seldom asked is whether this evidence must be regarded as excluding the kind of special recognition of Catholicism that we have shown to constitute the necessary and sufficient civic status of the Church in a State in which the majority of the citizens are

---

[1] Cf Bernard Clinch, *An Inquiry, Legal and Political, into the Consequences of giving His Majesty a Negative upon the Appointment of Irish Catholic Bishops and Priests*, Dublin 1808, p xi.

Catholic. Even a brief look into the relevant documents suggests that it does not. That the Irish tradition of politics is on the side of religious tolerance is beyond question and is not at all at issue here. It was Lecky who pointed out that despite the calamities that followed the Reformation, not a single Protestant suffered for his religion in Ireland during Mary's reign. Again, the Act establishing liberty of conscience passed by the Irish Parliament of 1689, in the full flush of the brief Catholic ascendancy under James II, exhibited very remarkably the tolerant aspect of the Irish character. Indeed one of the first measures of religious tolerance in modern history came from the ecclesiastical Synod that was held in connection with the Confederation of Kilkenny in 1642.[1] The United Irishmen introduced nothing new when they resolved that they look forward 'to a people united in the fellowship of freedom . . . to a prosperity established on civil, political, and religious Liberty'.[2] They demanded nothing more nor less than tolerance for Catholics when, in 1792, they established a special committee to inquire into the scope of the penal laws, that 'black code, worthy of a Turkish divan'.[3] The point to note is that such tolerance in itself is compatible with the kind of special recognition of religion which I have defended in this book as measuring up to the demands of the Catholic Church in the Catholic State.

It can be shown, of course, that the United Irishmen op-

---

[1] 'We ordaine and decree that all and every such as from the beginning of this present warre have invaded the possessions or good, as well moveable as unmoveable, spiritual or temporal, of any Catholic whether Irish or English, or also of any Irish Protestant being not adversaries of this cause, and doe detaine any such goods, shall be excommunicated, as by this present Decree wee doe excommunicate them, if admonished they do not amend'. Cf O'Riordan, Contemporary Ireland and the Religious Question, in J. H. Morgan ed., *The New Irish Constitution*, London 1912.

[2] *Resolution of the Society of United Irishmen,* 30 December 1791. Dublin 1792, p 3.

[3] *Report of Committee of the Society of United Irishmen of Dublin* 1792.

posed establishment. At his examination before the Secret Committee of the House of Lords, Dr. McNeven was asked whether
they 'intended to have a Popish or Roman Catholic establishment'? His answer was that 'the intention was to abolish the
church establishment, and not to have any established religion,
and all persons should exercise their respective religion, and pay
their own clergy: for my own part I would as soon establish the
Mahometan as the Popish religion, though I am myself a Roman
Catholic'. It should be noticed, however, that he seems to connect the idea of establishment with that of the clergy being paid
by the State. It was this that was unacceptable to the United
Irishmen as to the general Catholic population of the country.
It galled the latter to have to pay tithes for the upkeep of the
Protestant clergy; they decided that never should it happen
that the Catholic clergy would be made to subsist on similar
exactions from non-Catholics. It was in this sense that they
decried the establishment of any religion. At his examination
before the same Committee Thomas Addis Emmet also conjoined reference to tithes with established religion: 'I believe
the mass of the people do not care a feather for Catholic Emancipation, neither did they care for Parliamentary Reform, till
it was explained to them as leading to other objects which they
looked to, principally the abolition of tithes . . . My wish was
to destroy the present established church, and to have no
church established'. His insistence that no ecclesiastical establishment was intended by the revolutionary government must
be understood against this background of tithes.[1]

In this he was perfectly in harmony with the official Catholic attitude at the time. On 16th March, 1792, the Catholics
of Ireland issued a declaration of principles after a meeting in
Dublin. The last of these read as follows: 'It has been objected
to us that we wish to subvert the present Church establishment,
for the purpose of substituting a Catholic Establishment in its
stead. Now we do hereby disclaim, disavow and solemnly abjure
any such intention'. They further undertook that, in the event
of their being admitted to the franchise, they would not exercise

---

[1] Cf *Report of the Secret Committee of the House of Lords*, Dublin
1798, pp 45, 55, 56.

it to disturb or weaken the establishment of the Protestant religion in the country.[1] I believe that it is necessary to read between the lines of this declaration. That the Catholics did not want a Catholic establishment on the lines of the Protestant one is something that can be immediately granted. But it does not at all follow that, in the event of their attaining to political power, they would not demand special recognition of their Church in public life. An earlier declaration of 4th February had clearly implied that they thought that this could be effected without interference with the Protestant establishment: 'As to the infringement which our emancipation would make upon the Protestant interest and ascendancy, as to the suggested danger of the Church or of the State . . . we pledge ourselves . . . that a clear, full and satisfactory answer shall be given . . . We have examples of other states and kingdoms, in which established religions are preserved amidst great and numerous diversities of sects'.[2] On 31st October of the same year the matter was discussed at a further meeting of Catholics in Dublin. Mr. Geoghegan posed the problem and its solution: 'With respect to the question, would the admission of Catholics to a share in the Elective Franchise be consistent with the principles of the constitution, and the security of the present establishment'? To which he replied: 'We know that Presbyterianism is the established religion in Scotland, and the Catholic the established religion in Canada, not only without danger, but with important advantage to the British Government'. To which he added the footnote: 'The happy effects which arise from the establishment of a Presbyterian ascendancy in Scotland, and Catholic ascendancy in Canada, unquestionably evince the wise policy of contenting the majority of the people'.[3] And yet the meeting could issue a declaration to the effect that

[1] *Declaration of the General Committee of the Roman Catholics of Ireland*, Dublin 1792.

[2] *An Address from the General Committee of Roman Catholics to their Protestant Fellow Subjects*, Dublin 1792.

[3] *Proceedings at the Catholic Meeting of Dublin*, Dublin 1792, pp 32-33.

'the inclinations of our Body are not to subvert any establishment in this Country'.

But establishments on the lines of the Church of Ireland were on the way out. Non-Catholics themselves gave increasing voice to criticism of the system of tithes on which this rested. During a debate on the Catholic Relief Bill of 1795 a member of the Irish House of Commons summed up the matter: 'I believe, in my soul, that if some very material alteration be not speedily made in our religious establishments, there will be an end very speedily not only to all religion amongst us, but to all moral principle without which religion is a farce. As the legislature of this country have been mistaken in their attempt to promote religion by their system of persecution, so also they have been utterly mistaken in the nature and effects of religious establishments; they have confounded the interest of the clergy with the interests of religion . . . '.[1] By 1823, in the person of J.K.L., the Catholics themselves had begun to say the same thing openly. While insisting that they stood for tolerance, that of religion included, J.K.L. admitted that they were desirous of undoing the legal establishment of the Church of Ireland. 'They object', he explained, 'not to the Church but to the Establishment'—that system of State endowment which once flourished almost universally in Europe but which of late had come to be dropped in the majority of Catholic countries. The sooner the better it was also dropped in Ireland: 'Throughout Europe, with only a few, very few exceptions, . . . bishops are reduced to their primitive rank; their domains have been taken from them; their tythes taxed or abolished, and a new provision, more consonant to the public interests, and the opinions of men, substituted for the old. This current of public mind, and public interest will reach this country, My Lord, sooner or later whatever barriers may be raised against it; and there is no country where it is more necessary; it would be hailed by nineteen twentieths of the inhabitants of Ireland, Protestant and Catholic, as the inundations of the Nile are hailed by the

[1] *Report of Debate in the House of Commons of Ireland,* 4 May 1795, Dublin 1795, p 67.

Egyptians'.[1]

It was in this sense that the democratic political tradition in Ireland became the bitter opponent of 'established' religion. A resolution from an O'Connell meeting of 1835 puts this plainly: 'That we consider the law which compels the Catholics of Ireland to pay tithe to the ministers of the Church of law established, is founded on *injustice* and the spirit of religious *monopoly*, and that we hereby pledge ourselves to co-operate in its extinction'.[2] It was in the same sense that the establishment of Catholicism was opposed. A piece from O'Connell will put the position most forcefully: 'Does any man imagine that the Catholic religion will prosper in Ireland, if our prelates, instead of being what they are at present, shall become the servile tools of the administration? They would then lose all respect for themselves, all respectability in the eyes of others; they would be degraded to the station of excisemen and gaugers . . . The ministerial bishops of Ireland would become like the constitutional bishops of France, one of the means of unCatholicising the land'. And writing in 1850 Dr. Murray of Maynooth said that even if the offer of endowment were unaccompanied by any conditions or limitations, he believed that acceptance of it would mean 'a gradual encroachment on the liberties of the Church'.[3] But there is no evidence to show that the Irish Catholics would have rejected the idea of the State's granting a special recognition to Catholicism that would preserve both the liberty and independence of the Church and respect the rights of Irish non-Catholics. It is true that they frequently protested that they sought no special privileges as Catholics. 'The Catholics', said John Keogh in 1807, 'seek no diminution of taxes . . .; they do not solicit for any peculiar privilege. The extent of our supplication is to be governed, punished or protected by the same

---

[1] J.K.L., *A Vindication of the Religious and Civil Principles of the Irish Catholics addressed to the Marquis Wellesley*, Dublin 1823, pp 29 and 34.

[2] Cited in T. Wallace, *A Letter to Viscount Melbourne*, London 1836, p 24.

[3] P. Murray, State Endowment of the Irish Church, in *Essays Chiefly Theological*, First Series, Dublin 1850, p 54.

laws with every other class of his Majesty's subjects'.[1] It remains to be proved, however, that all special recognition of a Church must necessarily mean such special privilege for its members. The present Constitution of Ireland provides abundant evidence that this conclusion by no means follows. It is an instrument that is at once in accordance both with Catholic theory and with the Irish democratic tradition.

THE CONSTITUTION OF IRELAND

The Preamble begins with an invocation: 'In the name of the Most Holy Trinity, from Whom is all authority and to Whom, as our final end, all actions both of men and States must be referred, We, the people of Eire, humbly acknowledge all our obligations to our Divine Lord, Jesus Christ, Who sustained our fathers through centuries of trial . . . do hereby adopt, enact, and give ourselves this Constitution'. There is here an acknowledgement, not only of the existence of God, but of the Divinity of Christ and the truth of Christianity. It is sometimes suggested that it is not at all clear whether the Preamble forms part of the Constitution as a legal document. If this were so one could not base much on what it states. It is hard to see, however, what evidence there is for such a suggestion. It is true that at one time the preamble of a statute was regarded as forming no part thereof. It is a view that is no longer accepted.[2] The preamble is important for throwing light on the interpretation of the words used in the enacting part of a statute where

[1] *Sketch of a Speech delivered by John Keogh*, 24*th January* 1807, Dublin 1807, p 12.

[2] 'Lord Holt is reported to have said, in Mills v. Wilkins, that 'the preamble of a statute is no part thereof, but contains generally the motives or inducements thereof'; but this *dictum* is not in accordance with the opinion held at the present day. 'The preamble', said Pollock, C. B., in Salkeld v. Johnson, 'is undoubtedly part of the Act'. So also, in Davies v. Kennedy, Christian L. J. said: 'The preamble, which of course is a most important part of the statute, is no less explicit'—*Craies on Statute Law*, fifth edition, by Sir C. Odgers, London 1952, p 187.

these by themselves are incapable of clear and unequivocal application. Where the meaning of the enacting part is clear the preamble can have no effect; otherwise it is of considerable relevance.[1] Preambles were of more importance formerly than they are today. They set out the facts of the situation and the existing state of the law for which it was proposed to legislate by the statutes to which they pertained. The Act of Attainder of Shane O'Neill provides a good example of a preamble which established the entire background for the measure in question. The thirteen foolscap pages which precede the enacting part of the statute contain a bird's eye view of Irish history up to that time.[2] In modern Irish practice we find a preamble to the Prices Act (1958), which serves as a guide to the scope and content of the statute.[3]

There is no reason why the preamble to the Constitution should not have the same force as any other preamble. This view is confirmed by the Supreme Court in the Sinn Fein Funds case. Mr. Justice O'Byrne, delivering judgment, said: 'These most laudable objects (i.e. those reflected in the Preamble) seem to us to inform the various Articles of the Constitution and we are all of the opinion that, as far as possible, the Constitution should be so construed as to give them life and reality'. While it is true that the Constitution is unique as a legal instrument, the general rules of interpretation may apply to it. This is all the more so in that the Irish Constitution has the form of an ordinary Act of Parliament. Hence, if within the enacting part of the Constitution the position of the Catholic Church in Ireland is clearly outlined, recourse to the preamble to prove something different cannot be permitted. If on the other hand the position as set down or described in the enacting part is ambiguous, recourse to the preamble may be legitimate for the purpose of ascertaining what the true position is. The religious sentiments of the preamble are not to be regarded as an act of faith, which, as we have stressed earlier, it is not in the

---

[1] Craies, *op. cit.* p 188. 'The preamble is of value', says Coke, (1 *Inst.*, 79a), 'for the purpose of finding out the meaning of a statute'.

[2] Cf XI Elizabeth, Sess. 3, ch 1 (1569), *Irish Statutes at Large*, 1786.

[3] Cf *Prices Act* 1958. Dublin, Stationery Office.

power of the State to make. Rather do they establish the 'metaphysical' background against which the vast majority of the Irish people forged their Constitution. As such they undoubtedly must be regarded as qualifying the verbs 'adopt, enact and give' which immediately follow them.

Article 44, on the subject of religion, runs as follows:

1. 1 The State acknowledges that the homage of public worship is due to Almighty God. It shall hold His name in reverence, and shall respect and honour religion.

    2 The State recognises the special position of the Holy Catholic Apostolic and Roman Church as the guardian of the Faith professed by the great majority of the citizens.

    3 The State also recognises the Church of Ireland, the Presbyterian Church in Ireland, the Methodist Church in Ireland, the Religious Society of Friends in Ireland, as well as the Jewish Congregations and the other religious denominations existing in Ireland at the date of the coming into operation of this Constitution.

2. 1 Freedom of conscience and the free profession and practice of religion are, subject to public order and morality, guaranteed to every citizen.

    2 The State guarantees not to endow any religion.

    3 The State shall not impose any disabilities or make any discrimination on the ground of religious profession, belief or status.

Further sub-sections of section 2 deal with the educational and property interests of religious denominations; it is not necessary to reproduce them here.

By way of preface to the interpretation of the provisions of Article 44, we should bear in mind that it has been noted that Section 1, sub-section 2, closely resembles the first article of the Concordat between Napoleon and Pius VII, which article was agreed to only reluctantly by the Pope, though it was as much as could be won from France at the time, owing to the strength of anti-clerical opposition.[1] It has been noted too that

---

[1] Cf P. McKevitt, *The Plan of Society*, Dublin 1944, p 150. The formula of the Napoleonic Concordat runs as follows: 'The Government of the Republic recognises that the Catholic, Apostolic and Roman

there were many special considerations which the framers of the Irish Constitution had to bear in mind.[1] Firstly, the Constitution, though passed by a referendum that was confined to the Irish Free State, was intended for the whole of Ireland and so was not geared to the requirements of an almost completely Catholic people. Secondly, the framers had to be careful not to do anything that might stir up the latent religious animosities that the tragic history of Ireland had sown. Thirdly, they had to remember that many Northern Protestants feared that their religious liberties might be interfered with in a united Ireland in which they would be a minority. Finally, it has been noted that the intellectual streams, from which the Constitution in general draws its inspiration, are divergent.[2] As well as the influence of the political teaching of St. Thomas Aquinas and of the Papal Encyclicals, which affects everything in it, there is also the philosophical influence of the tradition of liberal democracy, as well as the impact of the practical turn of mind of the English constitutional lawyers, whose work has so profoundly coloured Irish legal thinking.

For these reasons, it is generally assumed that the Constitution gives no special juridical recognition to the Catholic Church. The Constitution, says Mr. Barrington, 'is not completely Catholic'; it does not effect the ideal union of Church and State for a Catholic people. Instead, it seems to be an 'approximation to the ideal more suited to the needs of modern

---

religion is the religion of the vast majority of French citizens'. There is no evidence, however, that this had any direct influence on the Irish Constitution. Examination of the Dail Debates at the time throws little light on the matter. Cf *Dail Debates*, 4 June 1937 *seq*. (col. 1892 *seq*). In a letter to the Director of Broadcasting, Radio Eireann, 1955, Mr. de Valera denied that Article 44 had been inspired by the Napoleonic formula; it was purely co-incidental. Cf C. Mac an Fhaili, Church and State in a Modern Democracy, in *Aiseiri*, February 1961, p 5.

[1] Cf D. Barrington, *The Church, the State and the Constitution*, Dublin 1959, pp 11-12.

[2] Cf D. Barrington, The Irish Constitution, in *Hibernia*, December 1957.

Ireland'.[1] Mr. Barrington does not say that it places the Catholic Church on the same level as heretical sects. 'It does not. It clearly recognises the "special position" of the Catholic Church'. To this, however, he immediately adds the clause 'although this does not give Catholics any privileged position in law'. It simply recognises 'the position which the Church in actual fact does hold. That is what the Irish Constitution does'.[2] I find this piece of argumentation rather curious, a kind of effort to have things both ways. Either the 'special position' which is accorded the Church is a juridical one, with all its consequences, or else it is simply and solely a factual one, which could not in any case be denied. And if the latter interpretation is the correct one, then, from the juridical point of view, the Church is placed on the same footing as are heretical denominations. If Mr. Barrington holds that what the relevant clause of Article 44 does is to recognise the position which the Church in actual fact does occupy, it would seem that he should have confined himself to saying simply, as does Dr. McKevitt, that, 'this clause merely gives recognition to a fact'.[3]

It is on the basis of the latter interpretation that the Constitution has come in for much criticism from certain quarters. The organisation called *Maria Duce*, now known as *Firinne*, has directed heavy fire on Article 44 for not having given juridical recognition to the Catholic Church as the One True Church. It maintains 'that such indifferentism is quite indefensible in the light of repeated affirmations by the Holy See concerning the wrongness of placing the Church "on the same

---

[1] Barrington, *op. cit.* pp 1 and 9. The view that the Catholic Church receives no special juridical recognition from the Irish Constitution has also been defended by E. McDonagh, The Irish Constitution, in *The Irish Theological Quarterly*, vol. XXVIII (1961), p 131. As against this certain other writers have held that the Church receives 'implicit' juridical recognition from the Constitution. Thus A. Messineo S.J., La nuova constituzione Irlandese, in *Civilità Cattolica*, vol. III (1937), pp 239-250. The latter refers to the position of the Church in Ireland as *un posto di preferenza* (p 242). Dr. McDonagh maintains that this view is 'almost certainly not true'.

[2] Barrington, *op. cit.* pp 4 and 5.

[3] McKevitt, *op. cit.* pp 15-16.

level as heretical sects", that in respect of its attitude to Church-
State relations, the present Irish Constitution is comparable to
the Constitution of 19th century France, to which Cardinal Pie
of Poitiers ascribed his country's failure to meet the challenge
of the revolutionary spirit, and that unless the Constitution is
suitably amended Ireland cannot hope to escape the wrath of
God'.[1] On these grounds an offensive has been launched for the
amendment of Article 44.

It is necessary to deal at once with this criticism—granting
for the moment the contention that the Constitution does not
come up to the Catholic ideal. Such criticism ignores many
practical realities, by reason of which it is not itself true to
Catholic theory. It is centered on respect for the absolute ideal,
the *thesis*, and, in keeping this ideal before us unsullied, it has
served a useful purpose. But it seems to have forgotten that the
hypothesis is also a part of Catholic theory, that concrete circumstances and possibilities have to be taken into account, and that
there can be cases in which a constitutional position which does
not correspond to the ideal can, nevertheless, be acceptable and
should stand. Even if the Twenty Six Counties can be said to
possess the kind of Catholic majority which would demand the
special juridical recognition of Catholicism, it could be argued
that the Constitution was intended for the Thirty Two Counties
and in such a State it could at least be doubted whether Catholics would constitute that absolute majority or quasi-totality of
the population which is required for the implementation of the
ideal: in 1937 something like one million people, out of an all-
Ireland population of four millions, were non-Catholics. In any
circumstances in which its implementation might cause undue
dissention, it should not be demanded of the State. In this connection the Basic Texts, prepared for the Second World Congress
for the Apostolate of the Laity (Rome, 1957), are instructive.
They point out that lay people should be careful not to embarrass
the Church by making demands for a situation that is too difficult to be brought about 'especially where what is better in
itself might prove an obstacle to what is good'. From this point

[1] Hamish Fraser, The Fight for Ireland centres on Article 44, in
Fiat, No. 45. Cf also *The Liberal Ethic*, Dublin 1950.

of view, I cannot but regard the attacks which are levelled against Article 44 as imprudent.

Nor is authority lacking which would endorse this viewpoint. Mr. Barrington has drawn attention to the attitude of Pope Leo XIII to the Belgian Constitution of 1830, which did not establish Catholicism, although the vast majority of the population was Catholic.[1] He cites two high Belgian officials at the Vatican as quoting the Pope to the effect that 'the works of men are not perfect; evil is found beside good, error beside truth. So it is with the Belgian Constitution. It recognises certain principles of which I, as Pope, could not approve, but the position of Catholicism in Belgium shows, after the experience of half a century, that in the present condition of modern society the system of liberty established in that country is the most favourable to the Church. Belgian Catholics, then, should not only refrain from attacking the Constitution but should defend it'. And again: 'People have wrongly concluded that the head of the Church was hostile to the Belgian Constitution. I have never ceased to repeat that your institutions suit the character of the nation. I myself studied the carrying into effect of your Constitution and I know that it safeguards the rights of Catholics. It would be running counter to the views of the Holy See to attack or find fault with your Constitution. Catholics should submit to it without reservation. I hope that this matter is finally settled and that no Catholic will raise it again'.

We might add ourselves another quotation, from the Cardinal Primate of Portugal, concerning the Concordat of 1940 with the Holy See. This Concordat did not establish the Church in Portugal although according to the latest statistics 94.1% of the people are Catholic. Yet of it Cardinal Cerejeira said: 'The Portuguese State recognises the Church as she is, and ensures her freedom; but it does not support or protect her as a State established religion . . . What the Church loses in official protection, she regains in virginal freedom of action. Free from any liability toward the political power, her voice gains greater authority upon consciences. She leaves Caesar a completely clear

---

[1] Barrington, *op. cit.* pp 15-16.

field, in order for herself better to attend to the things that are God's '.

As far as the Irish Constitution is concerned, the words of Cardinal MacRory, at the time of its introduction, are significant: 'The past year will be memorable for the inauguration of the new Constitution of Ireland. The Constitution is a great Christian document, full of faith in God as the Creator, Supreme Law-giver and Ruler, and full also of wise and carefully thought-out provision for the upholding and guidance of a Christian State. Nothing human is perfect, but the new Constitution is a splendid charter, a broad and solid foundation on which to build up a nation that will be at once reverent and dutiful to God and just to all men'.[1]

The most important authoritative statement on the Constitution was made by Pope Pius XII in an address to Mr. de Valera. His Holiness said: 'Your Constitution is intended to be an instrument of "prudence, justice and charity" at the service of a community which has never, through its long Christian history, had any doubt about the eternal, as well as the temporal implications, of that common good which it professes to seek through the conjoined prayer, toil and oftentimes heroic sacrifice of its children. Grounded on the bedrock of the Natural Law, those fundamental human prerogatives which your Constitution undertakes to assure to every citizen, within the limits of order and morality, could find no ampler, no safer guarantee against the godless forces of subversion, the spirit of faction and violence, than mutual trust between the authorities of church and state, independent each in its own sphere, but as it were allied for the common welfare in accordance with the principles of Catholic faith and doctrine'.

The Constitution, in the words of the Pope, is 'intended to

[1] On the same occasion Vatican Radio declared that the new Irish Constitution 'is a Constitution which embodies the Catholic principles of the Irish nation—a Constitution which found its inspiration in the Papal Encyclicals. The Catholic world read the document and admired it tremendously, and congratulated Ireland on a Constitution which opens with a prayer of invocation to the Holy Trinity'.

be' an instrument of prudence, justice and charity. That is the burden of the first part of the statement. The second part goes further. It clearly asserts that the Constitution has chosen the best method of guaranteeing 'those fundamental human pre-rogatives' which it undertakes to assure to every citizen of Ire-land—within the limits of order and morality—so as to safe-guard them against 'the godless forces of subversion, the spirit of faction and violence'. As far as religion goes, this method is said to be one whereby Church and State are 'independent each in its own sphere, but as it were allied for the common welfare'. One might defend the view that the Pope here simply approves of the Constitution according to the principle of the traditional *hypothesis*. One could point to the words in which he seems to regard its provisions for religion as simply being the best that is possible if faction and violence are to be avoided. One could point too to the fact that he clearly states that Church and State are independent and not in a state of union. The main principle which the Pope wished to inculcate was that the best way of securing fundamental human rights in a State is to ensure mutual trust between the authorities of Church and State and an alliance between them for the common welfare. His speech is less a statement of a theoretical position than an exhortation, suitably veiled, addressed to the head of a State predominantly Catholic by the Head of the Universal Church. As such, it could be argued that it is neutral in itself in so far as an opinion as regards the Irish Constitution is to be sought therein.

On the other hand, if one understands the *thesis* as we have explained it in this book, one could make points in favour of the view that the Pope may have been approving of the Irish Constitution as coming up to the ideal in this sense. We have seen that the *thesis* does not necessarily entail the union of Church and State and endowment of the Church by the State that was characteristic of the confessional regimes of the past. The requirements put forward by Cardinal Ottaviani demand much less than this. And, by and large, they are respected in Ireland. Article 44 acknowledges that the homage of public worship is due to Almighty God, that the State shall hold His Name in reverence and shall respect and honour religion.

Dr. McKevitt remarks that the obvious meaning of this is that the State, as such, is bound to give public worship to God, but adds that it is not so clear 'that a judge would be bound to take this interpretation, as "public" could be construed as equivalent to "external" and "public worship" might mean no more than worship carried on in public buildings'.[1] Such an interpretation would surely be a minimising one. There is no question, of course, of the article directly binding the representatives of the State to attend at Mass in a public capacity. But it is probable that it is intended to meet the obligation on men to worship God as members of society. If so, then the State, as the most important natural society, must fulfil this through the participation of its representatives in social worship. But— leaving aside the question of what is legally binding for the moment—the fact is that, since the inauguration of the Constitution, the State (in the sense of the persons of its members, both rulers and citizens) has rendered public homage to God according to the rites of the Catholic Church, on the occasions and in the ways demanded by the first requirement. On the whole too, legislation has been inspired in a way that the second requirement demands. Not only has the Catholic Church full freedom of action, but Catholic social principles (which should be, and frequently are, equally acceptable to non-Catholics) are embodied in the Constitution and the legislation of the State. Nor can there be any doubt that the Catholic religion is adequately protected from the kind of assault that would cause that disturbance to the tranquillity of Catholics which the third requirement seeks to rule out.[2] The fact that one cannot go beyond saying that the second and third requirements have been observed 'on the whole' is not of importance. They would be quite impossible of attainment anywhere if they were such that any transgression of them was inconceivable.[3] Even in the case of

[1] McKevitt, *op. cit.* pp 15-16.

[2] Cf. J. M. Kelly, *Fundamental Rights in the Irish Law and Constitution*, Dublin, 1961, ch III, Freedom of Expression.

[3] The Church of England provides a good example of an established Church whose relations with the State are by no means perfect. In particular, the Divorce Act of 1937 'has made it clear beyond all misunder-

States in which establishment has existed, Concordats between Church and State have sometimes been added, in order to help to make clear the exact sphere of action of each and the rights which each recognises on the part of the other.[1] Even then problems can still arise when there is case of an overlapping of the two spheres.

Cogent points can therefore be made in favour of the view that the practical implementation of the Irish Constitution, and the spirit which allows it to be so implemented, warrant the conclusion that the letter of its provisions concerning religion may be interpreted in a way which would regard them as fulfilling the requirements of Catholic theory.

THE 'SPECIAL' POSITION OF THE CATHOLIC CHURCH

The question remains whether it should properly be so interpreted, which is indeed the crucial point of the matter. Is the special position, which is conceded to the Catholic Church by Article 44, a juridical one, or is the Article merely expressing the factual situation that this Church is certainly that of the great majority of the citizens, even taking the whole of Ireland into account? Should the former alternative be conceded, I take it that the other provision of Article 44, namely that the State

standing that the laws of Church and State are not identical; what is allowed by the State is condemned by the Church'—Dr. C. Garbett, *Church and State in England*, London 1950, pp 108-9. Elsewhere Dr. Garbett writes: 'However satisfactory in practice the position may be between Church and State, is it possible to reconcile with Christian principles a Church whose chief ministers may be nominated by a non-Christian; whose public worship can only be changed by the permission of an assembly which need not be Christian; whose sacred synods can only meet and make rules for its own members by leave of the State; and whose doctrine in the last resort is interpreted by laymen who need be neither Churchmen nor Anglicans? When I ask myself these questions I feel profound disquiet of soul. I find it impossible to regard the present relationship between Church and State without grave heart-searching and discomfort'—*op. cit.* p 140.

[1] E.g. Spain.

acknowledges that the homage of public worship is due to Almighty God, must be understood in a sense that is in harmony with the first of the three requirements which are necessary if the Church is to be regarded as being given special juridical recognition. To recall them to mind again, these requirements, as outlined by Cardinal Ottaviani, demand 1) the social, and not merely the private, profession of the religion of the people; 2) the Christian inspiration of legislation and 3) the defence of the religious patrimony of the people against assault. I have already observed that it is generally assumed that the 'special position' that is accorded to the Church by the Constitution of Ireland is not a juridical one. In my opinion, this is far too readily conceded. Undoubtedly, one sometimes hears an argument to the contrary that is simplistic and easily disposed of. It is to the effect that the special position spoken of by Article 44 must be a juridical one because factual statements have no place in juridical documents. Admittedly they are hard to find, for example, in the Code of Canon Law, yet it is unwarranted to say that they do not and cannot occur in juridical instruments.

On the other hand, the main argument in favour of a 'factual' interpretation of Article 44 is based simply on the fact that the Article also gives recognition to the principal Protestant sects and to the Jewish religious organisation. 'This', says Dr. McKevitt, 'looks suspiciously like the Liberal principle of religious indifference'.[1] But what it may look like and what it may be are different things. It would actually *be* the Liberal principle of religious indifference only if it placed all religions, qua religion, on the same footing. This it certainly does not do. The Constitution recognises the Catholic Church as the guardian of the Faith (with a capital letter) of the majority of the citizens. Apart from this, what it does is simply to recognise 'the Church of Ireland, the Presbyterian Church in Ireland, the Methodist Church in Ireland, the Religious Society of Friends in Ireland, as well as the Jewish Congregations and the other religious denominations existing in Ireland at the date of the coming into operation of this Constitution'. Note well 'and the other religious denominations'. It means that what the State is recog-

---

[1] McKevitt, *op. cit.* p 150.

nising in the case of these denominations is not any religious belief as such, but the rights of the denominations as legitimate societies.

Mr. Barrington has pointed out that 'the word religious "denomination" is used in Art. 44 as meaning not a religious "idea" but a religious "group", "society", or "person". This can be seen from s. 2, ss. 4-6. An idea cannot manage schools or own, acquire or administer property'.[1] This is also true of its use of 'Church', 'Religious Society' and 'Congregation'. In the case of the Catholic Church alone is there mention of a Church as the guardian of the Faith. But let us not read too much into this use of a capital letter. I have already argued that it is quite impossible for a Constitution, as such, to make a profession of faith in the true sense. And, in any case, if what Article 44 does is (merely) to recognise the 'special position' of the Catholic Church as a religious grouping, and the existing position of the other Churches, Society, Congregation and denominations as religious groupings, this is not inconsistent with the possibility that the special position accorded to the Catholic Church is a juridical one. This possibility could certainly be implied in the Pope's reference to the system in Ireland as one in which Church and State are 'as it were allied for the common welfare in accordance with the principles of Catholic faith and doctrine'. Juridical recognition excludes separation of Church and State but can be satisfied with an accord between them that falls short of union.

I believe that close examination of the text of the Constitution itself suggests that it gives juridical recognition to religion. Notice that I say 'to religion'. It is hard to regard Article 44, s. 1, ss. 2 and 3 as merely recognising a statistical fact. On the contrary I submit that the religious denominations that are listed in Article 44 have a juridical position conferred on them by the Article. This indeed is the reason for naming them. It is interesting to note that it also creates a problem as regards those religions that did not exist in Ireland at the date of the coming into operation of the Constitution. They are certainly in a different position from those that are named in Article 44

[1] Barrington, *op. cit.* p 3, n 1.

and the difference is of a juridical nature. It is embodied in the provisions of ss. 4 to 6 of section 2 of the Article, which give certain guarantees to religion as recognised by the Constitution.[1] These guarantees are guarantees to religious bodies, in contrast with the earlier guarantees—for example of Article 43—which were one and all accorded to individuals.[2] In and through them the Constitution gives implicit recognition to the rites and practices of the religious bodies which it recognises. Amongst others, therefore, it recognises the practices of the Church of Ireland, the Presbyterian Church in Ireland etc. This is a juridical result of these bodies being named by the Constitution; their religious practices are accepted *in foro externo*.

Interesting confirmation of this occurred recently during the passage of the Charities Bill (1957), into which a passage was inserted,[3] during the Committee stage, which referred to religious bequests and which is to be 'applied irrespective of the religion concerned'.[4] The operative words were that a valid charitable gift for the advancement of religion should have effect and be construed 'in accordance with the laws, canons, ordinances and tenets of the religion concerned'. There can be no doubt that this holds for all those religions that existed in Ire-

---

[1] Ss 4 says that there shall be no discrimination 'between schools under the management of different religious denominations', while ss 6 says that the property of any religious denomination shall not be diverted except in special circumstances.

[2] Article 43 can be invoked by a Company, but only because of the individuals who comprise it.

[3] The passage reads: 'For the avoidance of the difficulties which arise by giving effect to the intentions of donors of certain gifts for the purpose of the advancement of religion and in order not to frustrate these intentions and notwithstanding that certain gifts for the purpose aforesaid, including gifts for the celebration of Masses, whether in public or in private, are valid charitable gifts, it is hereby enacted that a valid charitable gift for the purpose of the advancement of religion shall have effect and, as respects its having effect, shall be construed in accordance with the laws, canons, ordinances and tenets of the religion concerned' —*Seanad Eireann Debates*, 31 May 1961, vol. 54, n 6.

[4] Mr. Haughey, during the debate of 31 May 1961.

land when the Constitution was enacted and whose ordinances and tenets were implicitly recognised by Article 44. To the extent that it holds of any others which may exist in the country now or in the future depends on whether their practices are acceptable to the State *in foro externo*. It would be unlikely, for example, to hold in the case of Mormonism, since we know that the addition of the restrictive clause 'subject to public order and morality', which is to be found in the Constitution, was originally incorporated into the earlier Constitution of the Irish Free State to preclude the invocation of practices such as those of Mormonism.[1] In other words, juridical recognition is not afforded indiscriminately to all religions. In this connection it is interesting to refer to the 1947 Constitution of Burma, whose articles on religion were modelled on those of the Constitution of Ireland. The Burmese provisions, which were otherwise the same as those of the Irish Article 44, made it quite clear that Buddhism was given a 'special position' in the State while certain other religions were recognised simply as 'some of the religions existing' in the State at the date of the coming into operation of the Constitution.[2] In practice, while tolerance was extended to all, there was little doubt about the reality of the juridical preference enjoyed by Buddhism.

The Irish Constitution gives juridical recognition to a num-

---

[1] Cf *Dail Debates*, vol. 1, col. 695.

[2] Art. 21, concerning religion, runs as follows:

'(1) The State recognises the special position of Buddhism as the faith professed by the great majority of the citizens of the Union.

(2) The State also recognises Islam, Christianity, Hinduism and Animism as some of the religions existing in the Union at the date of the coming into operation of this Constitution'—*The Constitution of Burma*, Rangoon 1947, p 4.

In August 1961, Buddhism was in fact given further legal status by being made the State religion in Burma. An amendment to the Constitution guaranteed the right of non-Buddhists to practise and teach their religion. In practice this has meant little or no change except that the Buddhist Sabbath is now a holiday in all Government offices as well as Sunday.

ber of religious denominations, amongst which the Catholic Church is singled out for special recognition.[1] We are reminded of the ideas of Vattel concerning a graded system of establishment which would make it possible for a State to have more than one official religion. It is important to note the difference between the recognition accorded to the Catholic Church and that which is extended to other denominations by the Constitution of Ireland. In the case of these latter it is a recognition of 'the Church *of Ireland*, the Presbyterian Church *in Ireland*, the Methodist Church *in Ireland*, the Religious Society of Friends *in Ireland*, as well as the Jewish Congregations and the other religious denominations existing *in Ireland* . . . '.[2] In other words, it is a recognition of 'intra-national' bodies. In the case of the Catholic Church there is question of 'the Holy Catholic Apostolic and Roman Church as the guardian of the Faith professed by the great majority of the citizens'. Here there is a recognition not just of an organisation of people within the State but of a universal Church which is accepted as the teaching authority of the majority in matters which concern their religious beliefs. It is far from being a merely factual statement. It gives Catholicism as an ethical system a special position in the State as the norm to which public morality and law ought to conform in so far as they can. Whereas individual Catholics are given no preference in law, their Church as their guardian is—through the recognition of its moral authority to assert the implications of the faith. The immediate consequence of this is that the State must take account of the official teaching of the Catholic Church,

---

[1] Writing of Article 44 in the *Irish Monthly* (vol. 81, n. 381) Mr. D. Barrington declared that it "tolerates the various *Churches* or religious *societies*, but nowhere is there a word which suggests that one *religion* is as good as another". It has been said of this interpretation that it "should satisfy the requirements of Catholic orthodoxy and Catholic tolerance alike"—J. M. Kelly, *Fundamental Rights in the Irish Law and Constitution*, Dublin, 1961, p 185, n 2. It is only proper, however, to point out that, while this is so, there is not a word in the Constitution either which suggests that one religious *denomination* in Ireland is as good as another.

[2] Article 44, s. 1, ss. 3. Italics mine.

irrespective of its proximate origin. The Church as such is entitled to be heard and should be consulted in relation to any legislation that may affect its members prejudically in matters pertaining to their faith or moral code. The other Churches mentioned by Article 44 have similar rights, but since Catholics form the majority in the State, any Act repugnant to the Catholic conscience should not be enforced.[1]

It remains to be seen whether there is any more positive argument for regarding the 'special position' of the Catholic Church as juridical. The attitude of the Courts to the point is our only guide and, so far, it has only come up indirectly, notably in cases judged by Mr. Justice Gavan Duffy. In 1943, in a case concering a charitable bequest, Judge Gavan Duffy gave a decision that was favourable to Catholic interests by drawing on the tradition of the Common Law prior to the Reformation and by refusing to follow certain post-reformation decisions.[2] In doing this he declared that his conclusion was 'in harmony with the Constitution enacted by the Irish people, "In the name of the Most Holy Trinity . . . to whom, as our final end, all actions of both men and States must be referred", thus appearing to attach juridical significance to the Preamble. In 1945, in a case which concerned the extra-confessional pastoral secret of a priest, the same judge not only gave recognition to this secret but sought to give his decision a legal basis that it had not hitherto possessed.[3] 'The common law in force must

---

[1] These views were put forward by C. Mac an Fhaili, *loc. cit.* p 5. This writer raises the question of the possibility of certain of the religious minority Churches objecting to legislation as being opposed to their beliefs, but which it might be impossible to withdraw if it were desired by the majority. He suggests that a remedy for this might be found by exempting from the provisions of the laws in question anyone who objected to it as a matter of conscience. He adds that the Constitution should be clarified by an express provision that all Churches should have *consultative status* vis-a-vis the State regarding matters concerning them or their members.

[2] Cf *The Irish Ecclesiastical Record* (1946), pp 123-133.

[3] *The Irish Ecclesiastical Record* (1945), pp 307-313.

harmonise with our Constitution . . . I have to determine the issue raised in this case on principle and in conformity with the Constitution of Ireland. That Constitution in express terms recognises the special position of the Holy Catholic Apostolic and Roman Church as the guardian of the Faith professed by the great majority of the citizens; and that special recognition is solemn and deliberate. The same Constitution affirms the indefeasible right of the Irish People to develop its life in accordance with its own genius and traditions'.

'In a State where nine out of every ten citizens today are Catholics and in a matter closely touching the religious outlook of the people, it would be intolerable that the common law, as expounded after the Reformation in a Protestant land, should be taken to bind a people which persistently repudiated the Reformation as heresy. When, as a measure of necessary convenience, we allowed the common law to continue in force, we meant to include all the common law in harmony with the national spirit; we never contemplated the maintenance of any construction of the common law affected by the sectarian background. The Oireachtas is free today to determine how far our Courts are to recognise the sacerdotal privilege, but I am not concerned with that aspect of the matter. I am concerned with a juristic system of evidence surviving to us from an alien polity, and it is unthinkable that we should have imposed on ourselves in this matter the regrettable preconceptions of English Judges as having the binding force of law when merely re-echoed by pre-Treaty Judges in Ireland'.

Mr. Justice Gavan Duffy found reasons of equity and public policy for respecting the secret and noted too that this was demanded by true common law. He added, however: 'But, treating the question as one of substantive law, I hold that the emergence of the national Constitution is a complete and conclusive answer to the objection that I have no judicial precedent in favour of the parish priest. I hold that I am free to give judgment, in the light of the Constitution, on principle, and that I am bound to do so'. He here left no doubt that, in his opinion at least, the special position accorded to the Church is a juridical one, which binds judges to give decisions in her favour if there is no question of the rights of others being thereby violated.[1]

The matter came to a head in 1951. Mr. Justice Gavan Duffy had given a decision (1950) in favour of the Catholic party in a case in which a Catholic mother had sought to enforce respect for prenuptial guarantees, given by the Protestant father, that their children would be brought up in the Catholic faith.[2] Mr. Gavan Duffy had to admit that the common law as it had come down to him 'was settled against treating the ante nuptial agreement as an enforceable contract'. The principle on which this was done was probably, though not clearly, a plea of public policy in favour of regarding a father's right in the matter of deciding on how his children should be educated as one that could not be alienated. In face of the provisions of Articles 41 and 42 of the Irish Constitution, which ascribe a cardinal position to the family, and the fact that respect for an antenuptial agreement reinforces the family in one of its vital roles, Mr. Gavan Duffy declared that he 'had the temerity to prefer a principle of public policy that would imperatively require the man to keep faith with the mother whom he has induced to wed him by his categorical engagement . . .' He thought that this was particularly necessary when the engagement concerned the respecting of 'her convictions in the supernatural domain of her childrens' creed' and 'in a State which honours and respects religion'. And if in fact the Constitution 'is found to have superceded the former judge-made law . . . the public policy of other days will have no significance for us'.

Commenting on the Constitution itself, he declared: 'We are a people of deep religious convictions. Accordingly, our fundamental law deliberately establishes a Christian constitution; the indifferentism of our decadent era is utterly rejected by us. The Irish code marks a new departure from time honoured precedents which are not ours and gives us a polity conceived in a spirit and couched in a language unfamiliar to the jurisprudence

[1] It should be noted, of course, that were the question in this case to have related, for example, to the position vis-a-vis a member of his congregation of a minister of the Church of Ireland, Judge Gavan Duffy might have used the same judgment to come to the same conclusion.

[2] Cf *The Irish Ecclesiastical Record* (1951), pp 528-562.

which dominated the United Kingdom of Great Britain and Ireland . . . Possibly the constitutional recognition of the special position of the Catholic Church would authorise our Courts to take judicial notice of Canon Law; but I cannot decide these questions without full debate. Observe that Canon Law is pertinent to the issue as being the key to the antenuptial agreement . . . However, as the evidence stands, I must decide this case without reference to the text of the specific Canons. Quite apart from Canon Law, the doctrine of articles 41, 42 and 44 of the Constitution appears to me to present the antenuptial agreement of the parties . . . in a new setting and . . . to invite the recognition of the argument in our Courts as a compact that serves the social order in Ireland'. He therefore decided that the idea of the father's power to ignore such an agreement 'can find no place in a jurisprudence moulded to fit the Constitution of Ireland', and added in conclusion: 'Sitting under a Christian Constitution in a State publicly pledged to respect and honour religion, this Court is deeply concerned for the spiritual welfare of (the children), which, so far as a Court of Justice can appraise it, must be my first care'.

The interest of this decision is increased by the fact that it was appealed to the Supreme Court. The latter agreed with the verdict but for narrower reasons. It immediately admitted that 'the archaic law of England, rapidly disintegrating under modern conditions need not be a guide for the fundamental principles of a modern State; it is not a proper method of construing a new Constitution in a modern State to make an approach in the light of legal survivals of an earlier law'. In the opinion of the Court, Article 42 of the Constitution (on Education) has given to the mother as one of the partners 'a right greater than she enjoyed before the Constitution', so that an antenuptial agreement which has been put into force holds valid unless rescinded by *both* partners. This being so, it said that there was no need, in coming to the decision, to refer to the Preamble, or to Articles 41 and 44, as had been done by Mr. Justice Gavan Duffy. And lest anyone might think that, in saying this, it was implying that Articles 41 and 44 conferred any juridical privilege on Catholics, it added at once: 'It is right, however, to say that the Court in arriving at its decision

is not now holding that these last mentioned members of the
Roman Catholic Church'.[1]

This was added to avoid misinterpretation of the Court's
decision. But it clearly did not exclude the possibility that the
Articles mentioned could have relevance to the case or that the
Court might have decided that Catholics do indeed have a
privileged position before the law in certain matters. Judgment
was given by Mr. Justice Murnaghan, with the assent of
Justices Maguire, O'Byrne and Lavery. Mr. Justice Black dissented, on the grounds that Article 42 did not constitute a
sufficient basis for arriving at the decision. More significant from
our immediate point of view is the fact that he objected also
to the possible mental reservation contained in the last quotation. In other words, he objected to what he regarded as a possible interpretation of what had been said, an interpretation
which would imply that the Court could decide that the Catho-
olic religion has been juridically privileged by the Constitution.
Only in virtue of such privilege could Articles 41 and 44 confer
any privileged position before the law upon Catholics.[2]

[1] The Supreme Court did not say that an antenuptial agreement
was binding. The effect of its decision was: (a) That parents have a joint
power and duty to determine the religious upbringing of their children;
(b) If they make a joint decision *and put it into practice*, neither can alter
it without the consent of the other; (c) An ante-nuptial agreement is
not itself binding: until put into practice it cannot be enforced.

In the absence of agreement the Court will generally uphold the
father's wishes, even after his death, Cf In re Frost (1947), *Irish Reports* 3.

If two Catholics marry according to the rites of the Church, and the
children—or the elder of them—are baptised according to that rite, and
the family as a unit profess and practice their Faith, an agreement between the parents to bring their children up as Catholics must be implied. It is then not in the power of either parent to depart from the
terms of that agreement. This applies to all children of the marriage.
Cf Cahir Davitt J. In re May, Minors (1959), *I.R.* 74.

[2] In much the same way, Dr. Rowlette, Deputy for Dublin University, had argued against the Draft Constitution: "I suggest, with
considerable reluctance, that the statement here going into the Constitution is unnecessary, and it may give rise to a suggestion in the
future that the Catholic Church, having been specially recognised, is

I have defended the view that the Constitution accords a privileged position to Catholic beliefs, though not to Catholic citizens as individuals. This is the sense in which Article 41, s. 3, which prohibits divorce, must be understood. It is no privilege to Catholics that they should be prevented by law from contracting a second marriage during the lifetime of the first spouse. But it is a privilege to Catholic moral teaching that this prohibition should be incorporated into the law of the land. It marks a recognition of the Catholic interpretation of natural law that flows inevitably from the special position that is accorded to the Catholic Church.

If one were to ask what exactly is the public status of the Catholic Church in Irish law, a variety of answers is possible. One could certainly say that the Church is not juridically established in the sense in which the Church of England, for example, is established in England. If by 'separation' one means the absence of 'establishment' in this sense, there is separation of Church and State in Ireland. On the other hand, if by separation one means that the State ignores religion, the situation in Ireland is certainly not this. The Irish State is not a lay State, in so far as this involves neutrality towards religion of any kind, much less anti-clericalism or anti-religion. Nor is the Irish State a lay State of the kind that would refuse to submit itself to any superior code of morality. The 'lay State' in these senses has been described and condemned in a collective letter of the Bishops of France.[1] In the same letter, however, the Bishops outlined two forms of the 'lay State' which are quite in harmony with Catholic teaching. The first is that which stands for the supreme autonomy of the State in the sphere of merely temporal action. The second is that in which the State permits to all its citizens the free profession and exercise of their religion. One could say with confidence that the Irish State is a lay State in these latter senses and yet comes up to what is expected by

in a position of special privilege as regards giving advice to the State and so on"—*Dail Debates*, vol. 67, col. 1892.

[1] Letter of the French Hierarchy, 13 November 1945. Cf Sotillo, *Compendium Juris Publici Ecclesiastici*, Santander 1958, p 187, n 3.

Catholic teaching when there is question of a State with an absolute Catholic majority.

Perhaps the best description of the Irish situation is that Church and State are related by way of co-ordination.[1] It is the nature of this co-ordination that counts. It is not a system of reciprocal independence that would be tantamount to an unacceptable form of separation. Rather is it a system whereby each society is independent in its own order while preserving in practice the relationship of subordination of Church and State that is required on the one hand by the social implications of theological truth and on the other by the principles of political democracy in a Catholic State.

It is clear then that one must be careful about appending labels to the Irish system of Church-State relations. It is not at all adequate to say that because there is no State Church or established religion, there is a separation of Church and State. There is room for a *tertium quid*, which in fact I have defended —a special juridical recognition of the Catholic Church that is compatible with the lesser juridical recognition of other denominations. The most common mistake that is made in the interpretation of Article 44 is to think that because there is no established Church or no endowment of any religion, there can be no one Church juridically privileged.

PROPORTIONAL EQUALITY

The big question is how such privilege can be enjoyed by the Catholic Church without cutting across the constitutional guarantees against religious discrimination. If there is such privilege it would not conflict, as is sometimes suggested,[2] with the guarantees of the Treaty not to give 'any preference . . . on account of religious belief or religious status'. The privilege would stem rather from the fact that Catholics are members of a religious society (the Church) catering for the great majority of the citizens and whose status *as a society* is accordingly a special one,

---

[1] Cf Sotillo, *op. cit.* p 226.

[2] Barrington, *op. cit.*

demanding special recognition of what it deems important for the safeguarding of the interests of its members. This privilege —inequality if you like—would not interfere with the religious liberty of non-Catholic denominations and religious bodies.

In any case, the relevance of the Treaty is very debatable. It is by no means clear that its provisions cannot be overridden by the Southern Government should it so wish. There can be no doubt that, at the time it was agreed to, it constituted the fundamental law of the Irish Free State—so much so that it has been said that, under the Treaty, there was no need to enact a written Constitution at all.[1] Indeed the provisions of any such Constitution were declared to be void if they were contrary to the Treaty, whereas its implementation was declared to be a legal duty of the Free State.[2] The trouble is that there is a wide difference of opinion regarding the source which gave the Treaty this force of law. According to British interpretation it was the United Kingdom Statute, The Irish Free State Constitution Act, 1922. According to pro-Treaty Irish interpretation at the time, it was the Act of the Third Dail Eireann 'sitting as a Constituent Assembly, the implication of the Preamble to the Constituent Act being that the Constitutent Assembly acted by inherent right as the Assembly on which all lawful legislative authority, coming from God to the people, devolved'. This

[1] Cf V. Grogan, Irish Constitutional Development, in *Studies*, December 1951.

[2] So also the Government of Ireland Act, 1920, section 5 of which reads as follows: 'In the exercise of their power to make laws under this Act neither the Parliament of Southern Ireland nor the Parliament of Northern Ireland shall make a law so as either directly or indirectly to establish or endow any religion, or prohibit or restrain the free exercise thereof, or give a preference, privilege or advantage, or impose any disability or disadvantage, on account of religious belief or religious or ecclesiastical status'—*Public General Acts*, 10 and 11 George V, 1920.

It should be noted too that the Home Rule Bills of 1886 and 1893 contained similar provisions. Clause 4 in these Bills prohibited the Irish legislature from making any laws 'respecting the establishment or endowment of religion, or prohibiting the free exercise thereof; imposing any disability or conferring any privilege on account of religious belief' —Cf *The New Irish Constitution*, J. H. Morgan ed. London 1912.

interpretation was firmly rejected by British constitutional lawyers, who regarded the Free State as subject to the common sovereignty of the United Kingdom and unable, therefore, to deal with matters of international import. It was on this ground that the British Government protested in 1924, when the Irish Free State registered the Treaty with the League of Nations as an international document. Because of this too they regarded the Free State as having no legal power to confirm or repeal the provisions of the Treaty. Of course, from the moral point of view—irrespective of what the legal position might be—a valid Treaty, confirmed by oath, must be unreservedly held to be inviolable as long as it holds."[1]

As far as the Irish Treaty goes, we know that Mr. de Valera's Government, coming into power in 1932, denied the validity of the Treaty altogether and set itself the task of eliminating it from the internal law of the State, beginning with the Constitution (Removal of Oath) Act, 1933. This deprived the Treaty of all force of law and the section requiring amendments to be within the terms of the Treaty was repealed. In reply to a British protest, the Free State Government maintained that, apart altogether from its inherent right to act as it did, it was acting within the powers granted to it by the British Statute of Westminster, which (in 1931) had conferred unlimited legislative power on the Irish Free State, though without formally declaring the sovereignty of the British Parliament at an end.[2] At least the way was open for many further changes. There is no point, therefore, in introducing reference to the Treaty in connection with what the Irish Constitution of 1937 might not do. Nor is it quite accurate to say, as does Mr. Barrington, that the Treaty guarantees of religious liberty and equality (no preference) 'was carried over in substance into the present Constitution'.[3] What the Constitution guarantees is 'freedom of con-

---

[1] The German scholar Dr. Leo Kohn has come to the conclusion that, on the whole, the legal evidence would seem to favour the Irish interpretation—*The Constitution of the Irish Free State*, London 1932, p 71.

[2] Cf Grogan, *loc. cit.* p 394.

[3] Barrington, *op. cit.* p 13.

science and the free practice of religion'. These, 'subject to public order and morality, are guaranteed to every citizen'. It is liberty, rather than equality, that is guaranteed and, as we shall see later, the two are not identical.

The kind of inequality (preference) by reason of religion, which the Treaty guarantees eliminated and which the Free State Constitution also excluded, might be understood as being the kind that principally affected Catholics, in view of the long period of disability which they suffered. At least this seems to be Swift MacNeill's interpretation of the guarantees. His only commentary on Article 8 of the Free State Constitution, which reproduced them verbatim, was to note that they presented a pleasing contrast with the 18th century Irish Penal Code and to give a long quotation from Lecky describing how Irish Catholics were forbidden to sit in Parliament and deprived of the election franchise; were excluded from the corporations, the magistracy, the bar, the bench and the grand juries; were unable to be sheriffs, solicitors, or even gamekeepers or constables; were excluded from the university, forbidden to keep schools, or to send their children abroad for education; were not allowed to buy land or inherit it, to hold life annuities or to have liberty of testament.[1]

It is true that these disabilities of Catholics had long vanished. Yet it would be a serious mistake to think that the Constitution could not have had them in mind. Undoubtedly, as a parliamentary draftsman has pointed out, in modern rigid Constitutions, such as that of the United States and our own, the way in which rights are expressed depends largely on the contemporary history of the country and the apprehensions of danger in the minds of the constitution makers. They tend, he says, to place great stress on political aspirations 'lately realised and oppressions and invasions of liberty recently endured'.[2] But, as he also shows, they can take account equally of remote history. The example which he gives of this is Article 6 of the

[1] Cf J. G. Swift MacNeill, *Studies on the Constitution of the Irish Free State*, Dublin 1925, pp 92-93.

[2] V. Grogan, The Constitution and the Natural Law, in *Christus Rex*, vol. VIII (1954), p 215.

Free State Constitution (and Article 40 of the present Constitution) concerning the right to personal liberty which, he says,
'has its origin in long and bitter experience of the means by
which the guarantees of Magna Carta and the Confirming Charters were rendered nugatory for want of proper machinery of
enforcement, until the passing of the Irish Habeas Corpus Act
of 1781 and the subsequent history of innumerable suspensions
of the operation of that statute'. In like manner, is it not possible that Article 8 of the Free State Constitution was at least
partly designed to undo the kind of injustice—toward Catholics
—that was only too well known in the Ireland of the past? At
all events, Swift MacNeill seems to think so.

I think it a mistake, however, to suggest that they were
primarily or exclusively designed to safeguard Catholics. The
Government of Ireland Act 1920, which also included them, in
addition forbade the State to 'divert from any religious denomination the fabric of cathedral churches'.[1] As far as the Free
State was concerned this was undoubtedly intended to protect
the property of the Church of Ireland that was once in Catholic
hands. Then again the negotiations with the Southern Unionists
that preceded the settlement[2] indicate that the guarantees were
inserted out of fear of the consequences of Catholic domination
rather than out of a desire to assure to the Catholic Church that
freedom and equality with others that she would inevitably be
guaranteed anyway since the majority in the new democratic
State owed allegiance to her. In sum, the intention of the Free
State Constitution was to give the Catholic Church and her
teaching position recognition by way of assurance that the law
would not infringe it, while at the same time protecting individual non-Catholics against discrimination.

All this is effected also by the present Constitution, if in a
somewhat different and more enlightened fashion. There is no
question of egalitarianism. Article 40, s. 1 declares that the
State, in seeking the common good, must take account of
'differences of capacity, physical and moral, and of social func-

[1] Cf *Public General Acts*, 1920, p 398.
[2] Cf Donal O'Sullivan, *The Irish Free State and its Senate*, London
1940, ch III.

tion'. For reasons of social function it affords special recognition to the Catholic Church, by which its beliefs, though not its members, enjoy a special privilege. Non-Catholic denominations and individuals preserve the rights and liberties to which they are entitled in a democratic State. There was no need to incorporate the former guarantees into Article 44, under the heading of religion, as they had already been granted by Articles 40-43 inclusive, which deal with personal rights, the family, education and private property.[1]

It may be objected that in pointing out that the specific guarantee not to 'give any preference . . . on account of religious status' is not included in the present Constitution, and in attaching significance to this, I am adopting a too literal approach. It has been emphasised, though in a different context,[2] that a literal or grammatical mode of interpretation, such as is normally applied to a penal statute, is not appropriate to the construction of broad principles of policy expressed in a constitution and that the application of rules like *eiusdem generis* or the maxim *expressio unius exclusio est alterius*, only lead, in this matter, to unintended and even absurd results. I do not believe that my argument is open to this charge. The fact is that there was no need for Article 44 to spell out any guarantee about 'no preference' on account of religious belief or religious status seeing that the very content and consequences of such preference is excluded *seriatim* by other articles. And this holds for non-Catholics as much as for Catholics.

My contention is that the original guarantee of 'no preference' was designed precisely to exclude these consequences, so that if they are otherwise excluded now an additional formal guarantee would be redundant. There is no denying that the recognition of the 'special position' accorded to the Catholic Church as being a juridical one would involve conferring on the Church a specially privileged status. But the whole point is that this in itself would not necessarily mean that any privilege is granted 'on account of religious status'. Or rather should I say

---

[1] Article 40, section 6, ss 2 declares that there shall be 'no political, religious or class discrimination'.

[2] Cf Grogan, *loc. cit.* pp 213-217.

that the recognition of the status of one Church as specially privileged does not necessarily mean that those of others are underprivileged. What is granted to any one body of citizens is of no concern to the other bodies unless it involves an infringement of their rights and liberties. Within the general framework of respect for fundamental individual and associational rights, guaranteed by the Constitution, there is nothing to prevent a special position being assigned to some—to the extent that it does not conflict with what is universally accorded. Indeed, as we have seen the very texture of democratic government is made up of such differential treatment, of privilege and yet equality before the law. 'To each his due' was recognised by Aristotle as a form of equality. If, as has been said on good authority about the qualification 'in accordance with law' which the Constitution adds to its guarantees of fundamental rights, the form of the draftsmanship 'indicates a reaction against the categorical statement of rights framed during or immediately following periods of revolution,[1] may not something similar be said about the outlook of the Constitution on 'equality'?

The Irish system simply incarnates the demands of a genuine democracy such as I have outlined earlier when dealing with the theory of Church-State relations. It has been well pointed out that the State expresses its political philosophy in its legal code, into which it has the clear duty of absorbing the greatest measure of those moral principles which are commonly accepted by all its citizens, irrespective of whether the State is a multi-confessional one or not.[2] It is easy to secure agreement on the obvious principles of natural ethics, but it becomes increasingly difficult to do so as the list lengthens. This is particularly true of the multi-denominational democratic State. In such circumstances if the majority give their religious beliefs political expression, they must be careful to avoid, in so far as possible, the indirect violation of the civil rights of the minorities that hold different religious faiths. They should refrain

---

[1] *Ibid.*

[2] Cf C. Mac an Fhaili, Church and State in a Modern Democracy, in *Aiseiri*, January 1961, p 4.

from giving legal enforcement to religious beliefs and practices that would cause a conflict of conscience for a substantial number of citizens. This is not only democratic procedure but Catholic theory in that there is no obligation on a predominantly Catholic State to integrate the precepts of Catholicism into its laws if by doing so it would jeopardise the common good by leading to disunity and sectarian strife within the State.

Subject to this, by the very principle of democracy as of Catholic theory, in a predominantly Catholic State the will of the majority should prevail to the extent of colouring the laws of the State with Catholic principles. This is what I have in mind when I say that the recognition of the privileged status of the Church in Ireland does not mean that the status of other Churches is underprivileged. True, if the privilege stemmed not from the social function in Ireland but from the objects of the Catholic Church, the other Churches might reasonably claim the same privilege. I have emphasised, however, that this is not the case.

It is well to remember too that the privilege which the Church enjoys by reason of its special juridical position is not by any means exclusive in every respect. There is no question, for example, of it alone being entitled to call upon the State to restrain those who make public attacks upon it. The other Churches that are recognised juridically by the Constitution are entitled to similar protection of their beliefs against the kind of public assault that it lies within the competence of the State to attend to. What the Catholic Church enjoys, as her exclusive right, concerns the influence of religious and moral ideas on civil legislation. When a choice has to be made between measures that have the support of the religious majority and minority respectively, there is only one way for the government to act. As long as essential rights and liberties of the minority are not infringed, the interests of the majority must be given pride of place. There is here undoubtedly a qualification of the liberty and equality of all but it is inherent in the very texture of democratic life.

In Thomistic philosophy there is no such thing as liberty without limits; unlimited liberty is licence and not liberty at all. 'So seen the apparent limitations expressed in the Constitution are in reality no more than a definition of the right itself'.[1] In the same way, is it not possible that, in the matter of equality, what the Constitution upholds is not an egalitarianism, which would place everyone on the same level, but the Aristotelico-Thomistic conception, which recognises 'proportional' as well as 'arithmetical' equality? There are cases when justice demands the former rather than the latter.

That the Constitution may in fact uphold this idea of equality is not contradicted by Article 44, s. 2, ss. 3, which declares that 'The State shall not impose any disabilities or make any discrimination on the ground of religious profession, belief or status'. None of the rights guaranteed by Articles 40-43 need necessarily be infringed by an interpretation of Article 44 which would regard the 'special position' which it concedes to the Catholic Church as a juridical one. There can be little doubt that it was Mr. Justice Gavan Duffy's personal view that this juridical position might be acknowledged, although, in the absence of full investigation of the subject, he had to base his decisions primarily on other grounds. His appeal to the special position of the Catholic Church was always secondary. But the point to note is that, even if this were the main plank on which they rested, these decisions would not have infringed the rights and liberties of non-Catholics, no more than they were infringed by the application of the common law and the Constitution in the way that he followed. Given a judiciary composed of men like Gavan Duffy, the Catholic Church in Ireland could rest assured of receiving treatment, at least at common law, of a kind that would fully measure up to the requirements that Public Ecclesiastical Law lays down, while non-Catholics, conversely, would be assured that their religious rights and liberties would be respected.

THE RELEVANCE OF PHILOSOPHY

Commenting on the situation, a French jurist has remarked that one cannot be sure that the line of evolution, initiated by

[1] Cf Grogan, loc. cit.

Gavan Duffy, will continue; it was due to the latter's 'person-nalité exceptionnelle'.[1] Already there are examples of depar-tures from it. For it is by no means 'received doctrine' that the special position of the Catholic Church is a juridical one, entail-ing the requirements which are contained in the Catholic *thesis* on Church-State relations. Nevertheless, there seems to be no sufficient reason for excluding the possibility of an inter-pretation of the Constitution which would regard it as such. At present Church and State in Ireland are 'as it were' allied . . . in accordance with the principles of Catholic faith and doctrine' (Pope Pius XII). Very little would be required to make the matter certain—a decision of the Supreme Court would suffice. There would be no absolute need for a Constitutional amend-ment giving formal recognition to the Catholic Church as the One True Church. Certain legal anomalies would still remain— an understandable hangover from the past.[2] But, given due respect for the Constitution in future legislation and judicial decisions, it could be expected that these would pass with time.

No matter how one interprets it, the present Irish Constitu-tion should cause no fears to Northern non-Catholics as regards what might happen to their religious liberties in a United Ire-land in which its writ would run. Even if it juridically privileges the Catholic Church in a way that is conformable with the Catholic ideal, it does not entail any curtailment of the re-ligious beliefs and religious expression of non-Catholics, as such. There is no reason why they should not be eminently con-tent with it. Of course, as Mr. Lemass pointed out in the Oxford Union Debate, it is unlikely that their fears can be removed by such assurances. For this reason, he intimated that 'an arrange-ment which would give them effective power to protect them-selves, very especially in regard to educational and religious matters, must clearly be an essential part of any ultimate agree-ment'. He referred to a proposal for a federal system, whereby the Parliament and Government of the Six Counties would con-tinue to function with their present powers, while an all-Ireland

[1] Jean Blanchard, *Le droit ecclesiastique contemporain d'Irlande*, Paris 1958, p 122, n 53.

[2] Cf McKevitt, *op. cit.* pp 151-153.

Parliament would exercise the powers in relation to that area that are now exercised at Westminster, and added: 'That proposal seems eminently practical and should effectively dispose of the apprehensions of Protestants'. It is hard to see how, from the Constitutional point of view, it would effect any greater guarantee of the religious liberties of non-Catholics than is provided by the present Constitution. About one thing there is certainly no doubt: if that Constitution does not now come up to the theoretical requirements of the Church, the fear one sometimes hears expressed that in a United Ireland it might eventually be amended, with consequential discrimination against non-Catholics, is baseless.

It is undeniable that, in a United Ireland under the present Constitution, just as in the Twenty Six Counties under it, there would at times be difficulties in matters connected with religion and even questionable acts, from the point of view of the Constitution, on the part of the State. No Constitution works of itself; it is operated and interpreted by man. How it operates is largely dependent on the philosophy of law that is held by those who operate it. Even in matters of religion, the guarantee of the present Constitution regarding freedom of conscience and the free practice of religion, being subject to public order and morality, is—through this qualification—dependent in the matter of the kind of implementation it will receive on the philosophy of law of the legislator and the judge.[1]

Mr. Vincent Grogan has provided us with a useful survey of the philosophy of law that has been expressed in Irish Supreme Court decisions.[2] He has shown that different judges can hold opposed legal philosophies, in such a way as can profoundly

[1] In connection with the Free State Constitution it was pointed out that the phrase 'subject to public order and morality' was not free from ambiguity. Its elasticity could allow of restrictive interpretation, for example, the expulsion of a religious order whose teachings were regarded as subversive of public order and morality, as in Switzerland where it was invoked against the Jesuits. Similarly it could be invoked against the Quakers in the event of military service becoming compulsory. Cf. L. Kohn, *op. cit.*

[2] Grogan, *loc. cit. passim.*

influence their interpretation of constitutional provisions. An outstanding example of this occurred in 1935, in a Supreme Court decision under the Constitution of the Irish Free State regarding a matter which concerned the liberty of the citizen.[1] Chief Justice Kennedy based his decision on natural law philosophy, holding that 'every act, whether legislative, executive or judicial, in order to be lawful under the Constitution, must be capable of being justified under the authority thereby declared to be derived from God. From this it seems clear that, if any legislation of the Oireachtas . . . were repugnant to the Natural Law, such legislation would be necessarily unconstitutional and inoperative. I find it very difficult to reconcile with the Natural Law actions and conduct which would appear to be within the legalising of the provisions of the new Article . . .'. The other judges rejected this argument, on grounds expressed by Fitzgibbon J:[2] 'When a written Constitution declares that "the liberty of the person is inviolable", but goes on to provide that "no person shall be deprived of his liberty *except in accordance with law*", then, if a law is passed that a citizen may be imprisoned indefinitely upon a *lettre de cachet* signed by a Minister . . . the citizen *may* be deprived of his "inviolable" liberty, but as the deprivation will have been "in accordance with law", he will be as devoid of redress as he would have been under the regime of a French or Neapolitan Bourbon'.

Mr. Grogan argues convincingly that the present Irish Constitution is not compatible with such parliamentary despotism. Its clear acknowledgement of the existence of inherent rights is such that the subordination of positive law to them is not dependent on its written provisions. And yet, as Mr. Grogan shows, one sometimes comes upon judicial utterances that could easily imply something different. One such is that of Murnaghan J:[3] ' . . . in a Constitution like our own Constitution the object of stating a principle in the Constitution is to limit the exercise

[1] The State (Ryan) v. Lennon (1935). *I.R.*, 170, 183, Cf Grogan, *loc. cit.* pp 204-206.

[2] *I.R.* (1935) at page 230.

[3] National Union of Railwaymen v. Sullivan, (1947), I.R. 77.

by the Legislature of its otherwise unlimited powers of legislation'. Again, even though Article 43, s. 2, ss. 1 of the Constitution declares that the exercise of the rights concerning private property ought to be regulated 'by the principles of social justice', in a decision of 1939 Hanna J said: 'No standard of any kind on this general proposition has been placed before the Court, by the application of which the question could be decided, for the simple reason that there is no such standard. The phrases seem to me to be in the nature of political, economic or sociological tags, used in common language with different meanings by different people and devoid of any legal connotation whatever'.[1] In the same way, referring to the provisions of Article 43 to the effect that the State can limit the exercise of the rights concerning private property with a view to 'reconciling their exercise with the exigencies of the common good', the Justice said: 'I am of the opinion that the Oireachtas must be the judge of whatever limitation is to be enacted . . . and if the law is contrary to the common good, whatever that may mean, it must be clearly proved'.

A similar opinion was given by the Supreme Court in connection with the Offences against the State Act 1940,[2] (which was upheld in 'the State (Lawless) v. O'Sullivan' case in 1957). On the other hand in the Sinn Fein Funds case (1950), the Supreme Court declared that it could not give its assent to the 'far-reaching proposition' that the question of the exigencies of the common good is a matter for the legislature and is not subject to review by the courts.[3] As Mr. Colm Gavan Duffy has pointed out,[4] in 'the State (Burke) v. Lennon' case (1940), the President of the Supreme Court also expressed opposite views, by refusing to regard the determination of the liberty of the individual citizen as an arbitrary matter for the Oireachtas in time of peace. And Mr. Gavan Duffy adds that a similar view was contained in another Supreme Court decision in favour of the

[1] (1939) I.R. 413, at p. 421.
[2] (1940) I.R. 470.
[3] (1950) I.R. at p. 67.
[4] Colm Gavan Duffy, The Irish Constitution and Current Problems, in *Christus Rex*, April, 1958, pp. 111-115.

family.[1] Indeed Mr. Declan Costello has noted that the Supreme Court has tended to interpret the Articles relating to the
family, private property and freedom of association rather
differently than it has the provisions relating to personal freedom.[2]

There is no doubt about it that the same article of a constitution can be interpreted in widely differing ways in accordance
with the philosophy of law that is held by judges. When interpreted in the light of a sound natural law philosophy, by which
its guarantees of rights are regarded as being inspired, a constitution provides reliable protection to the citizen, but not
otherwise. Mr. Declan Costello concludes his aforementioned
study by saying that 'constitutional expression in Ireland for
the past twenty years has shown that where constitutional
guarantees can be traced to philosophical truths and not mere
empty formulas, they are real safeguards of individual liberty'.
He should have added to 'can be traced to philosophical truths'
the equally important phrase 'and are interpreted in a way that
is in accordance with these.'

The main reason for the remarkable impression made by Mr.
Justice Gavan Duffy on Irish Law was his legal philosophy. Unfortunately this is not shared by all. Working within the very
same constitutional and legislative framework and heirs to the
very same tradition of common law as was he, Irish judges can
and sometimes do reach decisions which it would be difficult to
associate with him. There is no guarantee that, even if the
special position of the Catholic Church in Ireland were a juridical one, each and every piece of legislation would be entirely
in harmony with the mind of the Church.[3] It is in order to secure
herself against this, at least in certain important matters, that
certain specific guarantees are required by the Church in the

[1] (1943) I.R. at p. 334.
[2] Cf. Declan Costello, The Natural Law and the Irish Constitution,
in *Studies*, Winter, 1956.
[3] The Catholic Church in Ireland is still under some of the disabilities which were outlined by Dr. M. J. Browne in 1929 in his very
valuable *Legal Disabilities of the Catholic Church in Ireland*, Dublin
1930.

case of Concordats even with States in which Catholicism is definitely established. Without them there can be room for departure from the spirit of the Constitution, which is understood in the light of legal philosophy. Needless to say, if this can happen in the case of the Church which a Constitution establishes, it is also possible in the case of the other religious bodies. But we can say that as far as the Constitution of Ireland itself is concerned it is a model framework of Christian democracy.

INDEX OF NAMES

SUBJECT INDEX

Aggressive war, ethics of, 97-99
Anglo-American democracy:
  258, 344ff
  and religion, 355ff

Bishops:
  extent of teaching authority, 110-113
  Irish bishops on use of force, 69
  Irish bishops on revolt of 1916-21, 163, 170-171, 171 n1.
  letter of Pope Benedict XV to Irish bishops, 170

Church-State relations:
  principles regarding, 211-212
  Fr Courtney Murray's teaching on, 211-212, 215-216, 223-228
  Pope Pius XII on, 228-223
  criticism of Fr Murray's teaching on, 234ff, 241-252
  American attitudes towards, 236-240, 251-252
  relation of dogma to, 240-241
  relation to concrete circumstances, 248-249
  relation to politics, 250-252
  Catholic ideal as regards, 259ff
  according to Maritain, 262-271
  conflict in, 294
  and Irish democratic tradition, 406ff
Community, medieval ideas on, 29-30, 36ff
Conciliar theory, 25-27, 46, 50
Conquest:
  definition of, 118-119

kinds of, 119-120
and acquisition of political authority, 57-59
Vittoria on, 121
Grotius on, 121-122.
conditions for just, 122-124
and Ireland, 125ff
problem of today, 152-154
Conscience:
  right to act according to, 113-118
  and Protestant ethics, 114
  and situation ethics, 117-118
  conscientious objection to war, 76-81
  and liceity of revolt, 169-171
Consent theory:
  and political authority, 53-55
  and feudal contract, 31ff
  and custom, 33-34
  and legitimation of a *de facto* government, 60-61
  and democracy, 24-25, 47-48, 61-62
  causes which suspend consent, 63ff
  when consent is necessary, 66-67
  and Protestant natural law school, 17, n 1.
  as applied to Ireland and America, 33, n 2
  and Germanic monarchy, 34-37
  and Anglo-Saxon monarchy, 37-38
  and Magna Charta, 38
  and origin of parliament, 39-40

455